The Editor

MICHAEL NORTH is Professor of English at the University of California, Los Angeles. He is the author of *The Dialect of Modernism: Race, Language, and Twentieth-Century Literature; The Final Sculpture: Public Monuments and Modern Poets; Reading 1922: A Return to the Scene of the Modern; The Political Aesthetic of Yeats, Eliot, and Pound;* and *Henry Green and the Writing of His Generation,* as well as many articles on various aspects of twentieth-century literature.

W. W. NORTON & COMPANY, INC.
Also Publishes

ENGLISH RENAISSANCE DRAMA: A NORTON ANTHOLOGY
edited by David Bevington et al.

THE NORTON ANTHOLOGY OF AFRICAN AMERICAN LITERATURE
edited by Henry Louis Gates Jr. and Nellie Y. McKay et al.

THE NORTON ANTHOLOGY OF AMERICAN LITERATURE
edited by Nina Baym et al.

THE NORTON ANTHOLOGY OF CHILDREN'S LITERATURE
edited by Jack Zipes et al.

THE NORTON ANTHOLOGY OF ENGLISH LITERATURE
edited by M. H. Abrams and Stephen Greenblatt et al.

THE NORTON ANTHOLOGY OF LITERATURE BY WOMEN
edited by Sandra M. Gilbert and Susan Gubar

THE NORTON ANTHOLOGY OF MODERN AND CONTEMPORARY POETRY
edited by Jahan Ramazani, Richard Ellmann, and Robert O'Clair

THE NORTON ANTHOLOGY OF POETRY
edited by Margaret Ferguson, Mary Jo Salter, and Jon Stallworthy

THE NORTON ANTHOLOGY OF SHORT FICTION
edited by R. V. Cassill and Richard Bausch

THE NORTON ANTHOLOGY OF THEORY AND CRITICISM
edited by Vincent B. Leitch et al.

THE NORTON ANTHOLOGY OF WORLD LITERATURE
edited by Sarah Lawall et al.

THE NORTON FACSIMILE OF THE FIRST FOLIO OF SHAKESPEARE
prepared by Charlton Hinman

THE NORTON INTRODUCTION TO LITERATURE
edited by Alison Booth, J. Paul Hunter, and Kelly J. Mays

THE NORTON INTRODUCTION TO THE SHORT NOVEL
edited by Jerome Beaty

THE NORTON READER
edited by Linda H. Peterson and John C. Brereton

THE NORTON SAMPLER
edited by Thomas Cooley

THE NORTON SHAKESPEARE, BASED ON THE OXFORD EDITION
edited by Stephen Greenblatt et al.

For a complete list of Norton Critical Editions, visit
wwnorton.com/college/English/nce_home.htm

A NORTON CRITICAL EDITION

T. S. Eliot
THE WASTE LAND

AUTHORITATIVE TEXT
CONTEXTS
CRITICISM

Edited by

MICHAEL NORTH

UNIVERSITY OF CALIFORNIA, LOS ANGELES

W • W • NORTON & COMPANY • *New York* • *London*

This title is printed on permanent paper containing 30 percent post-consumer waste recycled fiber.

Copyright © 2001 by W. W. Norton & Company, Inc.

The text of this book is composed in Electra with the display set in Bernhard Modern. Composition by PennSet, Inc. Manufacturing by Maple Vail Book Group. Book design by Antonina Krass.

Library of Congress Cataloging-in-Publication Data

Eliot, T. S. (Thomas Stearns), 1888–1965.
    The waste land : authoritative text, contexts, criticism / T. S. Eliot ; edited by Michael North.
        p. cm.— (A Norton critical edition)
    Includes bibliographical references (p.).

    ISBN 0-393-97499-5 (pbk.)

    1. Eliot, T. S. (Thomas Stearns), 1888–1965. Waste land. I. North, Michael, 1951– II. Title.

PS3509.L43 W3 2000
821'.912 — dc21   00-056643

W. W. Norton & Company, Inc., 500 Fifth Avenue, New York, N.Y. 10110
www.wwnorton.com

W. W. Norton & Company Ltd., Castle House, 75/76 Wells Street,
London W1T 3QT

7 8 9 0

Contents

Criticism

Preface

The Waste Land has surely become one of the most readily identifiable poems in the English language. It was, as Lawrence Rainey's research into the publication of the poem has shown us, famous even before it appeared in 1922, and it has continued to be the most prominent, though not by any means the most popular, poem of the twentieth century. In spite of the tremendous cultural authority that has accrued over the years to this poem, however, and in spite of the fact that it helped to shape a whole new academic discipline devoted to elucidating complex literary works, *The Waste Land* has remained difficult to read. Some of that difficulty is so intrinsic to the poem that it can never be dispelled, and much contemporary criticism has turned from the New Critical effort to explain it away and has attempted instead to account for its ineradicable mystery. But some of the difficulty of reading *The Waste Land* is incidental, and it is the purpose of this edition to provide readers with enough assistance to chip those incidental obscurities away, so as to distinguish the ones that really matter.

The first obstacle facing any such edition was put up by Eliot himself in the form of the notorious notes appended to the first book publication, by Boni and Liveright in the United States. Some of these notes, including the one accounting for the dead sound of the bell of Saint Mary Woolnoth, are so blandly pointless as to suggest a hoax, and others, particularly those citing classical quotations in the original languages, seem determined to establish mysteries rather than dispel them. In any case, the notes themselves need as much annotation as the poem they pretend to explain, and it seems both confusing and textually inappropriate to place them at the foot of the page, where they can become inextricably tangled with the editorial notes. In this edition, therefore, *The Waste Land* is published as it appeared in its first American edition, with Eliot's notes at the end. Reference to these notes, where appropriate and useful, is made in the editorial footnotes, but duplication of material has been avoided wherever possible. Eliot's own notes have been further annotated only where necessary, mainly in the case of material introduced into the notes that is not readily apparent in the text of the poem itself.

Sorting out such a division of labor, however, still does not make the task of annotating *The Waste Land* particularly easy. The sheer breadth of reference within the poem was often overwhelming for its first readers, and it still rather frequently overwhelms attempts to account for it, afflicting even the simplest passages with a kind of annotational elephantiasis. Worse yet, readers are often put at the mercy of interpretive summaries that reduce

Baudelaire or the Upanishads to nuggets scarcely larger than those already in *The Waste Land* itself. No edition can entirely avoid these pitfalls, since it would take a small library to fully represent the materials Eliot drew on for his poem. For this edition, however, I have mobilized as much original material as seemed feasible, so that readers interested in Eliot's debt to Jessie Weston, for example, can at least sample crucial passages as they were originally published. This means that many of the editorial notes direct readers to longer passages contained in the Sources section. In each such case, I have tried to preserve enough context to give some sense of the original and to let the reader imagine how and why Eliot might have committed his literary burglary. Particular difficulties arise in the case of sources outside English, which Eliot tended to read and appropriate in the original languages. In these instances, I have tried to include translations available to Eliot's first readers, though this has not been feasible in every case. My general objective here has been to keep the editorial footnotes as brief and unobtrusive as possible and, whenever possible, to present original material for the reader's judgment rather than providing summaries or interpretations of my own.

Since *The Waste Land* has been at the heart of academic literary criticism virtually from the first moment there was such a thing, it has been especially difficult to select from among the available critical works. I have tended to favor the earliest interpretations of the poem, grouped in this volume as "Reviews and First Reactions," simply because many of these have become well known in their own right, though I have tried to mix with these classic accounts a few less well known, particularly if they register in some striking way the excitement or puzzlement felt by the poem's first readers. In arranging the later criticism, I have marked off as "The New Criticism" several academic accounts of the poem published before 1945. Some of these, particularly John Crowe Ransom's early response, are not as favorable as contemporary readers might have expected, and some, particularly Delmore Schwartz's "T. S. Eliot as the International Hero," seem rather strikingly unlike the stereotypical New Critical account as formulated by Cleanth Brooks. In general, however, the New Critical accounts concentrate on cracking Eliot's code, while the more recent interpretations gathered here as "Reconsiderations and New Readings" tend to speculate as to why there should have been a code in the first place. Even a cursory look at the bibliography at the end of this volume will show that *The Waste Land* has inspired a tremendous amount of critical commentary of all kinds, from biographical speculation to post-structuralist demolition. Fairly representing even the major trends in such criticism would take several volumes, but the selections included here should at least demonstrate this broad shift, whereby New Critical certainty has gradually given way to a renewed sense of the disruptive disorientations of this quintessentially modernist poem.

I would like to thank my research assistant, Erin Templeton, and the staffs of the Clark Library at UCLA and the Beinecke Rare Book and Manuscript Library at Yale University. I would like to acknowledge as well the helpful advice of Joseph C. Baillargeon, who has made an extensive study of the publication history of *The Waste Land*.

A Note on the Text

It is unlikely that there can ever be a definitive text of *The Waste Land*. Though Eliot lived for more than forty years after the first publication of the poem, though he was himself a senior editor at the firm responsible for publishing his work in England, though he inspired through his criticism a scholarly discipline based on the close reading of literary details, there is no single version of his most widely read work that can claim unqualified authority.

The Waste Land was originally published in two versions in the United States and two in England. By agreement among the various parties concerned, the first of these appeared in October 1922 in the inaugural issue of Eliot's own critical monthly, *The Criterion*. Then the poem appeared in the November issue of the venerable American literary magazine *The Dial*. It was first published between hard covers by the New York firm of Boni and Liveright in December, and then in England, where it was hand-printed by Leonard and Virginia Woolf at Hogarth Press in 1923. These editions do not stem from a single source, as Eliot prepared a number of different typescripts of the poem, and they each have oddities and idiosyncrasies. Though it would seem that the two English editions should have been more closely supervised by Eliot himself—he was, after all, the editor of *The Criterion* and he is known to have read proofs of the Hogarth edition[1]—these have more unreliable variants than the American editions, including the inexplicable alteration of Lower Thames Street to Upper Thames Street in l. 260 of the *Criterion* printing, which puts the church of St. Magnus Martyr in distinctly the wrong spot.

Virtually all the differences among these four early versions of the poem are matters of capitalization, punctuation, or spacing, but even the last of these is not trivial in a poem in which spacing is an important indicator of rhythm and organization. It is also the case, of course, that variations of the same kind are likely to accumulate as poems are reprinted, and this has certainly been so in the case of *The Waste Land*. Each new edition, from *Poems 1909–1925* to *Collected Poems 1909–1962*, has introduced subtle alterations of its own, and there are usually minor differences as well between American and English editions.

Eliot himself added considerably to the confusion. In 1960 he prepared a new hand-written copy of the poem and inserted after l. 137 a line ("The ivory men make company between us") that was in early typescripts of the

---

1. Daniel H. Woodward, "Notes on the Publishing History and Text of *The Waste Land*," *Papers of the Bibliographical Society of America* 58 (1964): 262.

poem but not in any of the first printings.[2] But this line was not then inserted in any later publications supervised by Eliot, not even in the limited edition printed in Italy in 1961, which Eliot referred to at least once as "the standard text."[3] Nor were the alterations of punctuation in that edition incorporated into later commercial editions published by the company for which Eliot continued to work as senior editor. Eliot did make a number of corrections in a proof copy of *Collected Poems 1909–1935*, but, for reasons that remain unknown, these were not incorporated into the published text.[4] Thus Eliot's "intentions" for the poem, insofar as they can be perceived in actions such as these, seem as muddled as the texts themselves.

Although the most substantial variant, the line added in 1960, has been universally excluded from printed versions, the remaining variants, though minor, are not entirely trivial. It does make a difference whether the adjective in "hyacinth garden" is capitalized, as it is in the Boni and Liveright edition, or not, as in *The Dial* and then, after a space of forty years, in *Collected Poems 1909–1962*. Line 102 has read in every version and every edition "And still she cried," though Eliot apparently decided for the 1935 *Collected Poems* to change it to the far more sensible "And still she cries." But the fact that the change was not actually incorporated into that or any following published text did not apparently bother Eliot through the three remaining decades of his life, and so it is rather difficult to accept even though it seems to make much better sense of the passage. Even a minor variation of this kind, by altering the sense of a passage, can alter the sense of the entire poem, and there are a considerable number of such minor variations in the different published texts of this poem.

Among the various less-than-ideal solutions to this problem, I have chosen reliance on the Boni and Liveright edition. It is, in fact, the source for most subsequent editions, including the one published by Hogarth. It is the only source for the notes to the poem, which are not included in any surviving typescripts and which did not appear in *The Dial* or *The Criterion*. In the absence of any unambiguous evidence for the authority of later emendations, the Boni and Liveright edition should have priority. This edition also has a certain historical authority as the one most widely read when the poem first became famous.[5] This Norton Critical Edition therefore follows the Boni and Liveright (BL) edition whenever possible, with exceptions as noted and explained below.

dedication: added by Eliot to editions after 1925.
l. 42: BL reads, "Od' und leer das Meer."

---

2. For Eliot's explanation, see Woodward, p. 264.
3. Woodward, p. 264.
4. A. D. Moody, *Thomas Stearns Eliot: Poet* (Cambridge: Cambridge University Press, 1979), p. 303.
5. It should be noted for the especially scrupulous, however, that there are different printings of the Boni and Liveright edition, with various different typographical errors. The particular copy used for this edition is at the Clark Library, UCLA, numbered 827 of the first thousand, and it shares with two numbered copies at the Beinecke Library, Yale University, two obvious typographical errors ("ug" for "jug" on p. 30 and "mount in" for "mountain" on p. 41) that have been silently corrected.

l. 111: BL reads, "My nerves are bad tonight." It is the only edition to omit the hyphen.

l. 112: BL reads, "Why do you never speak." It is the only one of the four first editions to omit the question mark, which seems necessary to the sense as well.

l. 128–31: The spacing of these lines has been utterly confused by the fact that they fall at the bottom of the page in both *The Dial* and BL editions. Later editions have dropped the space that appears after l. 130 in both *The Dial* and *The Criterion*, apparently because it falls at the bottom of p. 21 of BL. It is worth noting, however, that *The Criterion* also has a space after l. 128, which does not appear in any of the other first editions.

l. 131: BL reads, " 'What shall I do now? What shall I do?' " The closing quote is the only one at the end of such a line in BL and is clearly a misprint. It does not appear in the other first editions, but neither do those editions print running quotes down the left-hand margin.

l. 149, 153: BL omits the apostrophe from "don't" in both lines, though other contractions are formed correctly. Apparently a misprint.

l. 161: BL reads, "The chemist said it would be alright." It is the only edition with this nonstandard spelling.

l. 259: BL reads, "O City city." The version adopted appears in *The Criterion* and Hogarth editions and was, according to Moody,[6] inserted by Eliot into proofs of the 1935 *Collected Poems*.

l. 415: BL reads, "aetherial." The *Dial* version also has this spelling, but all other editions adopt the more common spelling.

l. 428: BL reads, "*Quando fiam ceu chelidon.*" All earlier editions have this uncorrected version of the quotation.

notes to ll. 196 and 197: These are reversed in BL.

It should also be noted that adoption of the Boni and Liveright spacing in general has produced a text that differs from most others currently in print in certain subtle ways. This is most evident in the case of ll. 266–311, which were printed flush to the left in all the early editions but came to be indented to represent the song of the Thames-daughters. This indentation was not applied consistently, so that ll. 307–11, which are not part of the song, are also usually indented. In this case, historical and logical consistency seem to favor following the BL spacing. That edition also spaces the conclusion of the poem more generously, so that there is an extra space setting off ll. 426–32 and another setting the last line off by itself, as well as extra spaces between the three iterations of the final "Shantih."

Finally, the line numbers used in BL differ slightly from those in most subsequent editions. What *Collected Poems 1909–1962* and many other editions of the poem now in print count as lines 346 and 347 are counted as one line in BL. This means that the line numbers used in Eliot's own notes, which were, of course, those of the BL edition, must be changed, starting with the note to l. 357. Instead, this edition counts lines as did BL and leaves the line numbers in Eliot's notes intact.

6. Moody, p. 308.

The Text of
THE WASTE LAND

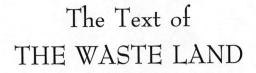

The Waste Land

"NAM Sibyllam quidem Cumis ego ipse oculis meis vidi in ampulla pendere, et cum illi pueri dicerent: Σίβυλλα τί θέλεις; respondebat illa: ἀποθανεῖν θέλω."[1]

For Ezra Pound
il miglior fabbro.[2]

1. "For I once saw with my own eyes the Cumean Sibyl hanging in a jar, and when the boys asked her, 'Sibyl, what do you want?' she answered, 'I want to die' " (Greek). Quoted from the *Satyricon* of Petronius Arbiter, a noted libertine of the first century C.E. It is one of many empty boasts and tall stories delivered at the banquet of Trimalchio, a freedman. The Sibyl, one of a number of prophetic figures so named in ancient times, is confined to a jar because her body threatens to deliquesce. Granted a wish by Apollo, she had asked for as many years of life as there are grains in a handful of sand, but she forgot to ask for eternal youth as well.
2. "The better craftsman" (Italian). Eliot's tribute to friend and fellow poet Ezra Pound (1885–1972), whose poetic craftsmanship was invaluable in editing the *Waste Land* manuscript. The phrase echoes the tribute offered by Dante Alighieri to twelfth-century Provençal poet Arnaut Daniel in Canto 26 of Dante's *Purgatorio*, a section from which Eliot also borrows l. 427.

3

I. The Burial of the Dead[3]

April is the cruellest month, breeding
Lilacs out of the dead land, mixing
Memory and desire, stirring
Dull roots with spring rain.
Winter kept us warm, covering   5
Earth in forgetful snow, feeding
A little life with dried tubers.
Summer surprised us, coming over the Starnbergersee[4]
With a shower of rain; we stopped in the colonnade,
And went on in sunlight, into the Hofgarten,   10
And drank coffee, and talked for an hour.
Bin gar keine Russin, stamm' aus Litauen, echt deutsch.[5]
And when we were children, staying at the arch-duke's,
My cousin's, he took me out on a sled,
And I was frightened. He said, Marie,   15
Marie, hold on tight. And down we went.[6]
In the mountains, there you feel free.
I read, much of the night, and go south in the winter.

What are the roots that clutch, what branches grow
Out of this stony rubbish? Son of man,[7]   20
You cannot say, or guess, for you know only
A heap of broken images, where the sun beats,
And the dead tree gives no shelter, the cricket no relief,[8]
And the dry stone no sound of water. Only
There is shadow under this red rock,   25
(Come in under the shadow of this red rock),
And I will show you something different from either
Your shadow at morning striding behind you

---

3. The title given to the burial service in the Anglican Book of Common Prayer.
4. A lake near Munich, Germany; the Hofgarten (l. 10) is a park in the same city.
5. "I'm not Russian at all; I come from Lithuania, a true German" (German).
6. According to Valerie Eliot's notes to the published manuscript of *The Waste Land*, Eliot based this sledding incident on a conversation he had with the Countess Marie Larisch, who published her reminiscences of the Austrian nobility in *My Past* (1913).
7. In his own note, Eliot cites Ezekiel 2.1: "And he said unto me, Son of man, stand upon thy feet, and I will speak unto thee." Thereafter, God addresses the prophet by this phrase: "Son of man, I have made thee a watchman unto the house of Israel" (3.17).
8. Eliot cites Ecclesiastes 12.5: "Also when they shall be afraid of that which is high, and fears shall be in the way, and the almond tree shall flourish, and the grasshopper shall be a burden, and desire shall fail: because man goeth to his long home, and the mourners go about the streets." The chapter is devoted to the sorrow of old age and decline, when it is discovered that "all is vanity" (12.8).

Or your shadow at evening rising to meet you;[9]
I will show you fear in a handful of dust.   30

> *Frisch weht der Wind*
> *Der Heimat zu*
> *Mein Irisch Kind,*
> *Wo weilest du?*[1]

"You gave me hyacinths first a year ago;   35
"They called me the hyacinth girl."
—Yet when we came back, late, from the Hyacinth[2] garden,
Your arms full, and your hair wet, I could not
Speak, and my eyes failed, I was neither
Living nor dead, and I knew nothing,   40
Looking into the heart of light, the silence.
Oed' und leer das Meer.[3]

Madame Sosostris, famous clairvoyante,[4]
Had a bad cold, nevertheless
Is known to be the wisest woman in Europe,   45
With a wicked pack of cards.[5] Here, said she,
Is your card, the drowned Phoenician Sailor,
(Those are pearls that were his eyes. Look!)[6]
Here is Belladonna, the Lady of the Rocks,[7]

9. Lines 26–29 were salvaged from "The Death of St. Narcissus," which was completed as of 1915 but was never published. Two draft versions of the poem were included with the *Waste Land* manuscript materials.
1. "Fresh blows the wind / To the homeland / My Irish child / Where do you wait?" (German). The first of two quotations from Richard Wagner's *Tristan und Isolde* (first performed in 1865). This one, which occurs at the beginning of the opera, is part of a song overheard by Isolde, who is being taken by Tristan to Ireland, where she is to marry King Mark. The original story, put into German verse in the middle ages by Gottfried von Strassburg (Wagner's source), gradually became part of Arthurian literature and thus came to be associated with the Grail legend Eliot refers to elsewhere in the poem.
2. The flower now referred to by this name is not the one so named by the Greeks, who saw the letters "AI," spelling out a cry of woe, in its petals. The story told about this flower makes it a memorial to a young man loved and accidentally killed by Apollo.
3. "Desolate and empty is the sea" (German). The second quotation from Wagner's *Tristan und Isolde*. This one, taken from the third act of the opera, occurs as the dying Tristan waits for news of Isolde, arriving by sea.
4. The name is taken from Aldous Huxley's novel *Crome Yellow* (1921). See pp. 40–42.
5. As Eliot's own note slyly admits, this passage has only a very loose connection with the Tarot pack used by fortune tellers to probe the past and predict the future. But there is a discussion of the Tarot in Weston's *From Ritual to Romance*, which connects the pack to the Grail legend and fertility rituals. See "[The Tarot Pack]," pp. 37–38.
6. One of a number of borrowings from Shakespeare's *The Tempest*, 1.3. This line is from the song the spirit Ariel sings to Ferdinand of his father's supposed drowning. See also l. 125.
7. The literal meaning of the name is "beautiful lady." She is frequently associated by commentators with Leonardo da Vinci's *Madonna of the Rocks* and with his *Mona Lisa*, who is famously described in Walter Pater's *The Renaissance* (1893) as "older than the rocks among which she sits." There is no such card in the Tarot pack.

The lady of situations.   50
Here is the man with three staves, and here the Wheel,[8]
And here is the one-eyed merchant, and this card,
Which is blank, is something he carries on his back,
Which I am forbidden to see. I do not find
The Hanged Man. Fear death by water.   55
I see crowds of people, walking round in a ring.
Thank you. If you see dear Mrs. Equitone,
Tell her I bring the horoscope myself:
One must be so careful these days.

Unreal City,[9]   60
Under the brown fog of a winter dawn,
A crowd flowed over London Bridge, so many,
I had not thought death had undone so many.[1]
Sighs, short and infrequent, were exhaled,
And each man fixed his eyes before his feet.   65
Flowed up the hill and down King William Street,
To where Saint Mary Woolnoth[2] kept the hours
With a dead sound on the final stroke of nine.
There I saw one I knew, and stopped him, crying, "Stetson!
"You who were with me in the ships at Mylae![3]   70
"That corpse you planted last year in your garden,
"Has it begun to sprout? Will it bloom this year?
"Or has the sudden frost disturbed its bed?
"Oh keep the Dog far hence, that's friend to men,[4]
"Or with his nails he'll dig it up again!   75
"You! hypocrite lecteur!—mon semblable,—mon frère!"[5]

8. The man with the three staves and the wheel are authentic Tarot cards, but the one-eyed merchant is a mystery of Eliot's own devising.
9. As Eliot notes, this is his adaptation of Charles Baudelaire's "Fourmillante cité" from his poem "Le sept vieillards" (in Les Fleurs du Mal, 1857). See "The Seven Old Men," pp. 43–45.
1. In his notes, Eliot refers the reader to two passages from Dante's Inferno. The first is from Canto 3, which takes place just inside the Gates of Hell, in a vestibule to which are consigned those who are equally without blame and without praise. Looking at this great company, Dante delivers the exclamation Eliot translates in l. 63. The next line is taken from Canto 4, in which Dante descends into the first circle of Hell, or Limbo, where those who died without baptism languish, sighing impotently, for there is nothing that can be done about their condition.
2. A church at the corner of Lombard and King William streets in the City (or financial district) of London. The last part of its name refers to Wulfnoth, who may have founded the medieval church that was demolished in the eighteenth century and completely rebuilt by Nicholas Hawksmoor. Bank Station nearby was a frequent stop on Eliot's commute to work.
3. A battle (206 B.C.E.) in the First Punic War between Rome and Carthage.
4. Eliot's adaptation of some lines from a dirge in John Webster's The White Devil (1612), sung by Cornelia as she prepares her son's body for burial. See "[Cornelia's Dirge]," p. 45.
5. "Hypocrite reader!—my likeness,—my brother!" (French). Eliot's version of the final line of Baudelaire's "Au Lecteur," the introductory poem in Les Fleurs du Mal. See "To the Reader," pp. 42–43.

II. A Game of Chess[6]

The Chair she sat in, like a burnished throne,[7]
Glowed on the marble, where the glass
Held up by standards wrought with fruited vines
From which a golden Cupidon peeped out   80
(Another hid his eyes behind his wing)
Doubled the flames of sevenbranched candelabra
Reflecting light upon the table as
The glitter of her jewels rose to meet it,
From satin cases poured in rich profusion;   85
In vials of ivory and coloured glass
Unstoppered, lurked her strange synthetic perfumes,
Unguent, powdered, or liquid—troubled, confused
And drowned the sense in odours; stirred by the air
That freshened from the window, these ascended   90
In fattening the prolonged candle-flames,
Flung their smoke into the laquearia,[8]
Stirring the pattern on the coffered ceiling.
Huge sea-wood fed with copper
Burned green and orange, framed by the coloured stone,   95
In which sad light a carvèd dolphin swam.
Above the antique mantel was displayed
As though a window gave upon the sylvan scene[9]
The change of Philomel, by the barbarous king
So rudely forced;[1] yet there the nightingale   100
Filled all the desert with inviolable voice
And still she cried, and still the world pursues,
"Jug Jug"[2] to dirty ears.
And other withered stumps of time
Were told upon the walls; staring forms   105

6. Eliot takes the title of this section from a satirical play of the same name by Thomas Middleton
   (1570?–1627). First produced in 1625, A *Game of Chess* was suppressed because of the biting
   way in which it allegorized English conflict with Spain as a chess match. The title also alludes
   to Middleton's *Women Beware Women* (published in 1657), in which a young wife is seduced
   while her unwitting mother-in-law plays chess.
7. In his own note, Eliot cites Shakespeare's *Antony and Cleopatra*, 2.2.190. In this passage,
   Enobarbus describes to Agrippa how Cleopatra looked on her first meeting with Mark Antony:
   "The barge she sat in, like a burnished throne, / Burned on the water: the poop was beaten
   gold. . . ."
8. The panels of a coffered ceiling. In his note, Eliot cites a passage from Virgil's *Aeneid*: "Burning torches hang from the gold-panelled ceiling, / And vanquish the night with their flames"
   (Latin).
9. Eliot cites a passage from Milton's *Paradise Lost*, Book 4, in which Satan, approaching Eden,
   sees it as a "delicious Paradise" and a "Sylvan Scene" overgrown with trees and bushes.
1. Eliot refers in his note to the story of Tereus and Philomela as told in Ovid's *Metamorphoses*.
   See "[The Story of Tereus and Philomela]," pp. 46–50.
2. Conventional literary onomatopoeia for the sound a nightingale supposedly makes.

Leaned out, leaning, hushing the room enclosed.
Footsteps shuffled on the stair.
Under the firelight, under the brush, her hair
Spread out in fiery points
Glowed into words, then would be savagely still.   110

"My nerves are bad to-night. Yes, bad. Stay with me.
"Speak to me. Why do you never speak? Speak.
"What are you thinking of? What thinking? What?
"I never know what you are thinking. Think."

I think we are in rats' alley   115
Where the dead men lost their bones.

"What is that noise?"
                    The wind under the door.
"What is that noise now? What is the wind doing?"
                    Nothing again nothing.   120
                              "Do
"You know nothing? Do you see nothing? Do you remember
"Nothing?"
        I remember
Those are pearls that were his eyes.[3]   125
"Are you alive, or not? Is there nothing in your head?"
                              But
O O O O that Shakespeherian Rag[4]—
It's so elegant
So intelligent   130

"What shall I do now? What shall I do?
"I shall rush out as I am, and walk the street
"With my hair down, so. What shall we do tomorrow?
"What shall we ever do?"
                              The hot water at ten.   135
And if it rains, a closed car at four.
And we shall play a game of chess,
Pressing lidless eyes and waiting for a knock upon the door.

When Lil's husband got demobbed,[5] I said—
I didn't mince my words, I said to her myself,   140

3. A reference to the line from Ariel's song in *The Tempest* quoted above, l. 48.
4. Eliot's syncopated version of a popular song, published in 1912, with lyrics by Gene Buck and Herman Ruby and music by Dave Stamper. See "That Shakespearian Rag," pp. 51–54.
5. Demobilized, or released from the armed services after World War I. According to Valerie Eliot's notes to the *Waste Land* manuscript, this final passage was based on gossip recounted to the Eliots by Ellen Kellond, their maid.

HURRY UP PLEASE ITS TIME[6]
Now Albert's coming back, make yourself a bit smart.
He'll want to know what you done with that money he gave you
To get yourself some teeth. He did, I was there.
You have them all out, Lil, and get a nice set,   145
He said, I swear, I can't bear to look at you.
And no more can't I, I said, and think of poor Albert,
He's been in the army four years, he wants a good time,
And if you don't give it him, there's others will, I said.
Oh is there, she said. Something o' that, I said.   150
Then I'll know who to thank, she said, and give me a straight
     look.
HURRY UP PLEASE ITS TIME
If you don't like it you can get on with it, I said.
Others can pick and choose if you can't.
But if Albert makes off, it won't be for lack of telling.   155
You ought to be ashamed, I said, to look so antique.
(And her only thirty-one.)
I can't help it, she said, pulling a long face,
It's them pills I took, to bring it off, she said.
(She's had five already, and nearly died of young George.)   160
The chemist[7] said it would be all right, but I've never been the
     same.
You *are* a proper fool, I said.
Well, if Albert won't leave you alone, there it is, I said,
What you get married for if you don't want children?
HURRY UP PLEASE ITS TIME   165
Well, that Sunday Albert was home, they had a hot gammon,[8]
And they asked me in to dinner, to get the beauty of it hot—
HURRY UP PLEASE ITS TIME
HURRY UP PLEASE ITS TIME
Goonight Bill. Goonight Lou. Goonight May. Goonight.   170
Ta ta. Goonight. Goonight.
Good night, ladies, good night, sweet ladies, good night, good
     night.[9]

6. Closing time, as announced at a pub.
7. Pharmacist.
8. Ham.
9. In *Hamlet*, 4.5.71–72, the mad Ophelia's parting words to Queen Gertrude and King Claudius, before her death.

III. The Fire Sermon[1]

The river's tent is broken: the last fingers of leaf
Clutch and sink into the wet bank. The wind
Crosses the brown land, unheard. The nymphs are departed.   175
Sweet Thames, run softly, till I end my song.[2]
The river bears no empty bottles, sandwich papers,
Silk handkerchiefs, cardboard boxes, cigarette ends
Or other testimony of summer nights. The nymphs are departed.
And their friends, the loitering heirs of city directors;   180
Departed, have left no addresses.
By the waters of Leman I sat down and wept[3] . . .
Sweet Thames, run softly till I end my song,
Sweet Thames, run softly, for I speak not loud or long.
But at my back in a cold blast I hear[4]   185
The rattle of the bones, and chuckle spread from ear to ear.

A rat crept softly through the vegetation
Dragging its slimy belly on the bank
While I was fishing in the dull canal
On a winter evening round behind the gashouse   190
Musing upon the king my brother's wreck
And on the king my father's death before him.[5]
White bodies naked on the low damp ground
And bones cast in a little low dry garret,
Rattled by the rat's foot only, year to year.   195
But at my back from time to time I hear
The sound of horns and motors, which shall bring

1. The title of this section is taken from a sermon preached by Buddha against the things of this world, all figured as consuming fires. See "The Fire-Sermon," pp. 54–55.
2. The refrain from Edmund Spenser's "Prothalamion" (1596). See "From Prothalamion," pp. 55–56.
3. An adaptation of Psalm 137, which begins, "By the rivers of Babylon, there we sat down, yea, we wept, when we remembered Zion." In the original, the people of Israel, in Babylonian exile, remember the city of Jerusalem. Eliot substitutes "Leman," the French name for Lake Geneva, where he spent several weeks in 1921 on a rest-cure, while working on The Waste Land.
4. The first of two references to Andrew Marvell's poem "To His Coy Mistress," first published in 1681, three years after the poet's death. Eliot adapts the lines, "But at my back I always hear / Time's wingèd chariot hurrying near," with which the speaker turns from his leisurely catalog of his lady's physical charms to the urgent carpe diem theme that has made the poem famous. See also l. 196.
5. Another reference to The Tempest, 1.2. Just before hearing Ariel's song (see l. 48), Ferdinand describes himself as "Sitting on a bank, / Weeping again the King my father's wrack."

Sweeney to Mrs. Porter in the spring.[6]
O the moon shone bright on Mrs. Porter
And on her daughter   200
They wash their feet in soda water
Et O ces voix d'enfants, chantant dans la coupole![7]

Twit twit twit
Jug jug jug jug jug jug
So rudely forc'd.   205
Tereu[8]

Unreal City
Under the brown fog of a winter noon
Mr. Eugenides, the Smyrna[9] merchant
Unshaven, with a pocket full of currants   210
C.i.f. London: documents at sight,
Asked me in demotic[1] French
To luncheon at the Cannon Street Hotel[2]
Followed by a weekend at the Metropole.[3]

At the violet hour, when the eyes and back   215
Turn upward from the desk, when the human engine waits
Like a taxi throbbing waiting,

---

6. Eliot apparently had in mind for these lines an elaborate parallel to a story told in, among other places, the allegorical masque *The Parliament of Bees* (1607), by John Day (1574–1640), which is cited in his notes. Sweeney, who seems from his actions in other of Eliot's poems ("Sweeney Erect" and "Sweeney Among the Nightingales") to have been his idea of an urban lout, approaches Mrs. Porter as Actaeon approaches Diana in the story referred to by Day. Actaeon surprises Diana (goddess of chastity as well as the hunt) while she is bathing, is turned into a stag by her, and is subsequently hunted to death by his own hounds.
7. The last line of French poet Paul Verlaine's sonnet "Parsifal," which first appeared in 1886 and was subsequently included in *Amour* (1888). In the original the line reads, "—Et, ô ces voix d'enfants chantant dans la coupole!" It can be translated as "And oh those children's voices singing in the dome!" In Verlaine's poem, Parsifal resists the temptations of female flesh, vanquishes Hell, restores the ailing king, and kneels to adore the Holy Grail, having become its priest. In general, the sonnet paraphrases its source, Richard Wagner's opera *Parsifal* (1877), in which Parsifal resists the wiles of Kundry, seizes the spear that had originally wounded King Amfortas, and heals him with it. The line Eliot quotes refers to the end of the opera, in which the dome of the Grail Castle fills with unearthly voices as Parsifal unwraps and raises the Grail. Many commentators have noticed as well that in the opera (though not in Verlaine's poem) Parsifal receives a ritual footbath before his final approach to the Grail Castle.
8. Noises made by the protagonists in the story of Tereus and Philomela, all of whom were turned into birds. "Tereu" is the vocative form of the name of Tereus, indicating that he is being addressed. In at least one Elizabethan source, *Alexander and Campaspe* (attributed to John Lyly), the ravished Philomela, turned into a nightingale, accuses Tereus in her song: "Jug, jug, jug, jug, tereu!" See "The Story of Tereus and Philomela," pp. 46–50.
9. A city in Anatolia, now the Turkish city of Izmir. After World War I, Smyrna was the focus of a calamitous war between Greece and Turkey, which was much in the news while Eliot composed his poem. Greece's loss of Smyrna resulted in a military coup in that country, while Britain's role became a factor in the fall of the Lloyd George government in 1922.
1. Colloquial (of the people), as opposed to scholarly.
2. A commercial hotel in the City of London.
3. A fashionable hotel in Brighton, a popular resort.

I Tiresias, though blind, throbbing between two lives,[4]
Old man with wrinkled female breasts, can see
At the violet hour, the evening hour that strives   220
Homeward, and brings the sailor home from sea,[5]
The typist home at teatime, clears her breakfast, lights
Her stove, and lays out food in tins.
Out of the window perilously spread
Her drying combinations[6] touched by the sun's last rays,   225
On the divan are piled (at night her bed)
Stockings, slippers, camisoles, and stays.
I Tiresias, old man with wrinkled dugs
Perceived the scene, and foretold the rest—
I too awaited the expected guest.   230
He, the young man carbuncular,[7] arrives,
A small house agent's clerk, with one bold stare,
One of the low on whom assurance sits
As a silk hat on a Bradford millionaire.[8]
The time is now propitious, as he guesses,   235
The meal is ended, she is bored and tired,
Endeavours to engage her in caresses
Which still are unreproved, if undesired.
Flushed and decided, he assaults at once;
Exploring hands encounter no defence;   240
His vanity requires no response,
And makes a welcome of indifference.
(And I Tiresias have foresuffered all
Enacted on this same divan or bed;
I who have sat by Thebes below the wall   245
And walked among the lowest of the dead.)[9]
Bestows one final patronising kiss,
And gropes his way, finding the stairs unlit . . .

She turns and looks a moment in the glass,
Hardly aware of her departed lover;   250
Her brain allows one half-formed thought to pass:
"Well now that's done: and I'm glad it's over."
When lovely woman stoops to folly[1] and

4. Tiresias, who had once been turned into a woman and thus had lived "two lives," was blinded
   in a dispute between Juno and Jove. For the story, see "[The Blinding of Tiresias]," p. 46.
5. In his notes, Eliot refers to a poem by Sappho (Fragment 149), a prayer to the Evening Star.
6. One-piece undergarments.
7. A carbuncle is an infected boil.
8. Bradford is a manufacturing town in the north of England. A millionaire from that town
   would have made his money in trade or manufacturing. Hence, nouveau riche.
9. Ll. 245–46 draw on other classical references to the story of Tiresias, particularly his role (as
   a Theban seer) in *Antigone* and *Oedipus Rex* by Sophocles (496–406 B.C.E.), and in Homer's
   Odyssey, where he appears in the underworld to advise Odysseus.
1. In his notes, Eliot refers to Oliver Goldsmith's novel *The Vicar of Wakefield* (1762). See
   "[Olivia's Song]," p. 57.

Paces about her room again, alone,
She smoothes her hair with automatic hand,   255
And puts a record on the gramophone.

"This music crept by me upon the waters"[2]
And along the Strand, up Queen Victoria Street.[3]
O City, City, I can sometimes hear
Beside a public bar in Lower Thames Street,[4]   260
The pleasant whining of a mandoline
And a clatter and a chatter from within
Where fishmen lounge at noon: where the walls
Of Magnus Martyr[5] hold
Inexplicable splendour of Ionian white and gold.   265

The river sweats
Oil and tar
The barges drift
With the turning tide
Red sails   270
Wide
To leeward, swing on the heavy spar.
The barges wash
Drifting logs
Down Greenwich reach[6]   275
Past the Isle of Dogs.
   Weialala leia
   Wallala leialala[7]
Elizabeth and Leicester[8]
Beating oars   280
The stern was formed
A gilded shell
Red and gold
The brisk swell

2. As Eliot points out in his notes, another reference to Ariel's Song in *The Tempest*. See also
   ll. 48 and 125.
3. Streets in the City of London, running more or less parallel to the Thames.
4. A street in the City of London, running parallel to the Thames near London Bridge. The
   Church of St. Magnus Martyr is on Lower Thames Street.
5. A church on this site, dedicated to the Norse martyr St. Magnus, is mentioned as far back as
   William the Conqueror. Rebuilt after the Great Fire by the English architect Sir Christopher
   Wren (1671–1676), the present church is on Lower Thames Street at the foot of London
   Bridge, in a district traditionally associated with fishmongers. The columns dividing the nave
   from the side aisles are Ionic.
6. The Thames River at Greenwich, downstream from London. The Isle of Dogs is the name
   given to the riverbank opposite Greenwich.
7. The lament of the Rhine-maidens in Richard Wagner's *Die Götterdämmerung*, the last of the
   four operas that comprise *Der Ring des Nibelungen* (first performed as a whole in 1876). In
   Das Rheingold, the first opera in the series, the maidens lose the gold deposited in their river.
   It is this gold, forged into a ring, that sets in motion the events of the four operas.
8. Eliot's note quotes a passage from James Anthony Froude's *History of England*. For the context, see "[Elizabeth and Leicester]," pp. 57–58.

Rippled both shores   285
Southwest wind
Carried down stream
The peal of bells
White towers
        Weialala leia   290
        Wallala leialala
"Trams and dusty trees.
Highbury bore me. Richmond and Kew[9]
Undid me. By Richmond I raised my knees
Supine on the floor of a narrow canoe."   295

"My feet are at Moorgate,[1] and my heart
Under my feet. After the event
He wept. He promised 'a new start.'
I made no comment. What should I resent?"
"On Margate Sands.[2]   300
I can connect
Nothing with nothing.
The broken fingernails of dirty hands.
My people humble people who expect
Nothing."   305
      la la

To Carthage then I came[3]

Burning burning burning burning[4]
O Lord Thou pluckest me out
O Lord Thou pluckest   310

burning

---

9. Eliot's note suggests a parallel between this scene and a passage in Canto 5 of Dante's *Purgatorio*, in which he is addressed in turn by three spirits, the last of whom identifies herself as La Pia, born in Siena and murdered by her husband in Maremma. The formula is common in epitaphs, as, for example, in Virgil's as given by Suetonius: "Mantua me genuit, Calabri rapuere" (Mantua gave me light; Calabria slew me [Latin]). But Eliot adapts it in this case to a seduction; Highbury is the London suburb in which the victim was born, Richmond and Kew two riverside districts west of London where her virtue was "undone."
1. An area in east London.
2. Eliot spent three weeks in October 1921 at the Albemarle Hotel, Cliftonville, Margate, a seaside resort in the Thames estuary. This was the first part of a three-month rest-cure during which he composed the bulk of *The Waste Land*. His hotel bill has survived, attached to the manuscript of "The Fire Sermon."
3. Eliot's notes refer to a passage in Augustine's *Confessions* in which he describes the sensual temptations of his youth. For the context of the passage, see "From *Confessions*," p. 58.
4. Eliot's drastic redaction from Buddha's Fire Sermon. For the text to which he refers in his notes, see "The Fire-Sermon," pp. 54–55.

IV. Death by Water[5]

Phlebas the Phoenician, a fortnight dead,
Forgot the cry of gulls, and the deep sea swell
And the profit and loss.
                    A current under sea   315
Picked his bones in whispers. As he rose and fell
He passed the stages of his age and youth
Entering the whirlpool.
                    Gentile or Jew
O you who turn the wheel and look to windward,   320
Consider Phlebas, who was once handsome and tall as you.

V. What the Thunder Said

After the torchlight red on sweaty faces
After the frosty silence in the gardens
After the agony in stony places
The shouting and the crying   325
Prison and palace and reverberation
Of thunder of spring over distant mountains[6]
He who was living is now dead
We who were living are now dying
With a little patience   330

Here is no water but only rock
Rock and no water and the sandy road
The road winding above among the mountains
Which are mountains of rock without water
If there were water we should stop and drink   335
Amongst the rock one cannot stop or think
Sweat is dry and feet are in the sand
If there were only water amongst the rock
Dead mountain mouth of carious teeth that cannot spit
Here one can neither stand nor lie nor sit   340
There is not even silence in the mountains

---

5. The exact significance of this section, which Pound insisted was "an integral part of the poem," has always been very difficult to determine, especially since it is, as Pound well knew, a close translation of the ending of "Dans le Restaurant," written by Eliot in 1918, before anything existed of the other four parts of *The Waste Land*.
6. Eliot's headnote to this section helps us to see these lines as a description of the betrayal, arrest, interrogation, and crucifixion of Christ, with the earthquake that follows in Matthew 27.

But dry sterile thunder without rain
There is not even solitude in the mountains
But red sullen faces sneer and snarl
From doors of mudcracked houses   345
                              If there were water
    And no rock
    If there were rock
    And also water
    And water
    A spring   350
    A pool among the rock
    If there were the sound of water only
    Not the cicada
    And dry grass singing
    But sound of water over a rock   355
    Where the hermit-thrush sings in the pine trees
    Drip drop drip drop drop drop drop
    But there is no water

Who is the third who walks always beside you?[7]
When I count, there are only you and I together   360
But when I look ahead up the white road
There is always another one walking beside you
Gliding wrapt in a brown mantle, hooded
I do not know whether a man or a woman
—But who is that on the other side of you?   365

What is that sound high in the air[8]
Murmur of maternal lamentation
Who are those hooded hordes swarming
Over endless plains, stumbling in cracked earth
Ringed by the flat horizon only   370
What is the city over the mountains
Cracks and reforms and bursts in the violet air
Falling towers
Jerusalem Athens Alexandria

---

7. According to Eliot's note, he has adapted this passage from an episode in Sir Ernest Shackleton's *South* in which three Antarctic explorers fancy that there is a fourth man with them. The passage also bears a strong resemblance to the story told in Luke 24 of the two men on the road to Emmaus who do not recognize the risen Christ. See "[The Road to Emmaus]," pp. 59–60, and "[The Extra Man]," p. 60.
8. As a source for the next ten lines, Eliot cites in his notes German author Herman Hesse's *Blick ins Chaos* (1922), translated, at Eliot's urging, as *In Sight of Chaos*. For a translation of the excerpt quoted in Eliot's note and the relevant context, see "[The Downfall of Europe]," pp. 60–62.

Vienna London   375
Unreal

A woman drew her long black hair out tight
And fiddled whisper music on those strings
And bats with baby faces in the violet light
Whistled, and beat their wings   380
And crawled head downward down a blackened wall
And upside down in air were towers
Tolling reminiscent bells, that kept the hours
And voices singing out of empty cisterns and exhausted wells.

In this decayed hole among the mountains   385
In the faint moonlight, the grass is singing
Over the tumbled graves, about the chapel
There is the empty chapel, only the wind's home.[9]
It has no windows, and the door swings,
Dry bones can harm no one.   390
Only a cock stood on the rooftree
Co co rico co co rico
In a flash of lightning. Then a damp gust
Bringing rain

Ganga[1] was sunken, and the limp leaves   395
Waited for rain, while the black clouds
Gathered far distant, over Himavant.[2]
The jungle crouched, humped in silence.
Then spoke the thunder
DA   400
Datta: what have we given?[3]
My friend, blood shaking my heart
The awful daring of a moment's surrender
Which an age of prudence can never retract[4]

9. According to the headnote to this section, Eliot has in mind the Chapel Perilous as described in Jessie Weston's *From Ritual to Romance*. See "[The Perilous Chapel]," pp. 38–39.
1. The Ganges, sacred river of India. Ganga is a colloquial version of its name.
2. More commonly Himavat or Himavan. Sanskrit adjective meaning snowy, usually applied to the mountains known as the Himalayas, especially when personified as the father of the Ganges, among other deities.
3. As Eliot reveals in his notes, this part of the poem is based on a section of the *Brihadāranyaka Upanishad* in which God presents three sets of disciples with the enigmatic syllable DA, challenging each group to understand it. Each group is supposed to understand the syllable as the root of a different imperative: "damyata" (control) for the gods, who are naturally unruly; "datta" (give) to men, who are avaricious; "dayadhvam" (compassion) to the demons, who are cruel. For the full passage, see "The Three Great Disciplines," pp. 62–63.
4. Behind this line lies the lament of Francesca da Rimini, whom Dante encounters in the second circle of Hell, where she is being punished eternally for having committed adultery with her brother-in-law Paolo Malatesta. As she tells the story in Canto 5 of the *Inferno*, the two fell in love while reading a romance about Lancelot: "ma solo un punto fu quel che ci vinse" (but one moment alone it was that overcame us [Italian]).

By this, and this only, we have existed   405
Which is not to be found in our obituaries
Or in memories draped by the beneficent spider[5]
Or under seals broken by the lean solicitor
In our empty rooms
DA   410
Dayadhvam: I have heard the key
Turn in the door once and turn once only[6]
We think of the key, each in his prison
Thinking of the key, each confirms a prison
Only at nightfall, aethereal rumours   415
Revive for a moment a broken Coriolanus[7]
DA
Damyata: The boat responded
Gaily, to the hand expert with sail and oar
The sea was calm, your heart would have responded   420
Gaily, when invited, beating obedient
To controlling hands

                    I sat upon the shore[8]
Fishing, with the arid plain behind me
Shall I at least set my lands in order?[9]   425

London Bridge is falling down falling down falling down[1]
Poi s'ascose nel foco che gli affina[2]
Quando fiam uti chelidon[3]—O swallow swallow

5. As Eliot says in his notes, he found the model for this love-denying spider in John Webster's
   The White Devil (1612).
6. According to Eliot's note, these lines combine two references. The first is to the story of Count
   Ugolino, whom Dante encounters in Canto 33 of the *Inferno*. Accused of treason, the count
   was shut up in a tower, where he starved to death. The second reference is to the philosophy
   of F. H. Bradley, on whom Eliot had written his doctoral thesis, which insists on and then
   tries to overcome the radical privacy of all experience.
7. Another image of isolation. Coriolanus was a Roman war hero who defied public opinion
   and ended his life leading a foreign army against Rome. He is the subject of a play by
   Shakespeare (1607–08) and of a poem by Eliot, "Coriolan" (1931).
8. In his notes, Eliot refers the reader to Chapter 9 of Jessie Weston's *From Ritual to Romance*.
   For an excerpt, see "The Fisher King," p. 38.
9. The prophet Isaiah challenges King Hezekiah: "Thus saith the Lord, Set thine house in order;
   for thou shalt die and not live" (Isaiah 38.1).
1. A children's nursery rhyme, made somewhat more pertinent by the fact that most of the
   London place-names in *The Waste Land* are in the vicinity of London Bridge.
2. "Then he hid himself in the fire that refines them" (Italian). This is the last line of Canto
   26 of Dante's *Purgatorio*, in which Dante meets the poet Arnaut Daniel, who warns him in
   his own language, "Sovegna vos a temps de ma dolor" (In due time be heedful of my pain
   [Provençal]). This was a passage of extraordinary importance to Eliot, as evidenced by the
   fact that he borrowed the term applied to Daniel, "miglior fabbro," for his dedicatory line to
   Ezra Pound. *Ara Vos Prec*, a book of poems Eliot published in 1920, takes its title from an
   earlier line in the same passage, to which he returned again in his 1929 essay on Dante.
3. "When shall I be like the swallow?" (Latin). A line from the anonymous poem *Pervigilium
   Veneris*, which ends with a reference to the Philomela story Eliot had already used elsewhere
   in *The Waste Land*. For the context, see pp. 63–64.

Le Prince d'Aquitaine à la tour abolie[4]
These fragments I have shored against my ruins   430
Why then Ile fit you. Hieronymo's mad againe.[5]
Datta. Dayadhvam. Damyata.

Shantih   shantih   shantih

---

4. "The Prince of Aquitaine of the ruined tower" (French). The second line of "El Desdichado" (The Dispossessed) (1854), a sonnet by Gerard de Nerval (1808–1855).
5. Eliot's note refers to Thomas Kyd's *The Spanish Tragedie* (1592), the subtitle of which is *Hieronymo is Mad Againe*. In Act 4 of the play, Hieronymo, driven mad by the murder of his son, stages a play in which he convinces the murderers to act a part. In the course of the play, Heironymo actually kills the murderers and then himself. For the scene in Act 4 in which Hieronymo convinces his adversaries to take part, see "From *The Spanish Tragedie*," pp. 64–66.

Notes[1]

Not only the title, but the plan and a good deal of the incidental symbolism of the poem were suggested by Miss Jessie L. Weston's book on the Grail legend: *From Ritual to Romance* (Cambridge). Indeed, so deeply am I indebted, Miss Weston's book will elucidate the difficulties of the poem much better than my notes can do; and I recommend it (apart from the great interest of the book itself) to any who think such elucidation of the poem worth the trouble.[2] To another work of anthropology I am indebted in general, one which has influenced our generation profoundly; I mean *The Golden Bough*; I have used especially the two volumes *Adonis, Attis, Osiris*.[3] Anyone who is acquainted with these works will immediately recognise in the poem certain references to vegetation ceremonies.

I. THE BURIAL OF THE DEAD

Line 20. Cf. Ezekiel II, i.
23. Cf. Ecclesiastes XII, v.
31. V. Tristan und Isolde, I, verses 5–8.
42. Id. III, verse 24.

1. There are a number of different accounts of the genesis and purpose of these notes, which were first included in the Boni and Liveright edition. Late in his life, Eliot tended to disparage the notes, suggesting in *On Poetry and Poets* (1957) that they were little more than "bogus scholarship" designed to bulk out a poem that was too short to fill a volume by itself (see "[On the *Waste Land* Notes]," pp. 112–13). However, it is clear from the correspondence of Gilbert Seldes and James Sibley Watson of *The Dial* that the notes existed well before the poem was published there, so they cannot have been a mere afterthought. Clive Bell suggested in reminiscences put down in the 1950s that it was the Bloomsbury art critic Roger Fry who first suggested to Eliot that he add notes to the poem, a possibility to which Eliot rather vaguely agreed when asked by Daniel Woodward in the 1960s. The notes are notoriously evasive, and they are the source of some of the most intractable controversies attending the poem. No attempt will be made in the editorial footnotes to adjudicate those controversies, which are well represented in the critical selections. Quotations from original sources in languages other than English will be translated here only if they have not been translated earlier in the notes to the poem or in the Sources section.
2. *From Ritual to Romance* (1920), by Cambridge folklorist Jessie L. Weston, traces medieval stories about the Holy Grail, supposed to be the chalice used at the Last Supper, to much older fertility rituals. The exact extent to which *The Waste Land* depends on Weston's text is one of the central issues addressed by critics, especially those included in this volume under "The New Criticism." At the very least, it can be said that Eliot came to Weston's book after he had already written at least some sections of the poem. Grover Smith, among others who have examined Eliot's copy of *From Ritual to Romance*, notes that a few of the pages are uncut, so that those sections, at the least, must have remained unread. For selections, see pp. 35–40.
3. Sir James George Frazer (1854–1941) was perhaps the best known and most influential anthropologist of his era. He worked exclusively from documents, not from field study, and derived his conclusions from the exhaustive comparison of classical texts and modern practices. His work *The Golden Bough*, first published in 1890, expanded to the twelve-volume edition cited here by Eliot in 1911–15 and then abridged in 1922, affected Eliot primarily by suggesting parallels between ancient and modern beliefs. In particular, Frazer's analysis of ancient rituals having to do with the sacrificial death of an old king and beliefs associating the new king's potency with the fertility of the land left its impression on *The Waste Land*. For selections, see pp. 29–34.

46. I am not familiar with the exact constitution of the Tarot pack of cards, from which I have obviously departed to suit my own convenience. The Hanged Man, a member of the traditional pack, fits my purpose in two ways: because he is associated in my mind with the Hanged God of Frazer, and because I associate him with the hooded figure in the passage of the disciples to Emmaus in Part V. The Phoenician Sailor and the Merchant appear later; also the "crowds of people," and Death by Water is executed in Part IV. The Man with Three Staves (an authentic member of the Tarot pack) I associate, quite arbitrarily, with the Fisher King himself.

60. Cf. Baudelaire:

> "Fourmillante cité, cité pleine de rêves,
> "Où le spectre en plein jour raccroche le passant."[4]

63. Cf. Inferno III, 55–57:

> "si lunga tratta
> di gente, ch'io non avrei mai creduto
> che morte tanta n'avesse disfatta."[5]

64. Cf. Inferno IV, 25–27:

> "Quivi, secondo che per ascoltare,
> "non avea pianto, ma' che di sospiri,
> "che l'aura eterna facevan tremare."[6]

68. A phenomenon which I have often noticed.
74. Cf. the Dirge in Webster's *White Devil*.
76. V. Baudelaire, Preface to *Fleurs du Mal*.

II. A GAME OF CHESS

77. Cf. *Antony and Cleopatra*, II, ii, l. 190.
92. Laquearia. V. *Aeneid*, I, 726:

dependent lychni laquearibus aureis incensi, et noctem flammis funalia vincunt.

98. Sylvan scene. V. Milton, *Paradise Lost*, IV, 140.
99. V. Ovid, *Metamorphoses*, VI, Philomela.
100. Cf. Part III, l. 204.
115. Cf. Part III, l. 195.

---

4. For an English version of the poem from which these lines are taken, see "The Seven Old Men," pp. 43–45.
5. "So long a train / of people, that I should not have believed / that death had undone so many" (Italian).
6. "Here, there was to be heard / no complaint but the sighs, / which caused the eternal air to tremble" (Italian).

118. Cf. Webster: "Is the wind in that door still?"[7]
126. Cf. Part I, l. 37, 48.[8]
138. Cf. The game of chess in Middleton's *Women beware Women*.

III. THE FIRE SERMON

176. V. Spenser, *Prothalamion*.
192. Cf. *The Tempest*, I, ii.
196. Cf. Marvell, *To His Coy Mistress*.
197. Cf. Day, *Parliament of Bees*:

> "When of the sudden, listening, you shall hear,
> "A noise of horns and hunting, which shall bring
> "Actaeon to Diana in the spring,
> "Where all shall see her naked skin . . ."

199. I do not know the origin of the ballad from which these lines are taken: it was reported to me from Sydney, Australia.[9]
202. V. Verlaine, *Parsifal*.
210. The currants were quoted at a price "carriage and insurance free to London"; and the Bill of Lading etc. were to be handed to the buyer upon payment of the sight draft.[1]
218. Tiresias, although a mere spectator and not indeed a "character," is yet the most important personage in the poem, uniting all the rest. Just as the one-eyed merchant, seller of currants, melts into the Phoenician Sailor, and the latter is not wholly distinct from Ferdinand Prince of Naples, so all the women are one woman, and the two sexes meet in Tiresias. What Tiresias *sees*, in fact, is the substance of the poem. The whole passage from Ovid is of great anthropological interest:

> '. . . Cum Iunone iocos et maior vestra profecto est
> Quam, quae contingit maribus,' dixisse, 'voluptas.'
> Illa negat; placuit quae sit sententia docti
> Quaerere Tiresiae: venus huic erat utraque nota.

7. Eliot's reference is to John Webster's play *The Devil's Law-Case* (1623). In Act 3, Scene 2 of the play, two surgeons, caring for Lord Contarino, whose case they assume to be hopeless, are surprised to hear him groan. To the first surgeon's question, "Did he not groane?" the second replies, "Is the wind in that doore still?" The note implies a metaphorical reading of the line, in which the wind would be the dying breath of the patient, and this would give an eery resonance to l. 118 of *The Waste Land*. But according to F. L. Lucas, whose edition of Webster's plays Eliot read and reviewed in 1928, the line is merely idiomatic slang meaning something like "Is that the way the wind blows still?" and the second surgeon is not making any metaphorical reference but merely wondering that Contarino is still alive. Eliot later admitted as much and denied the relationship between this line and *The Devil's Law-Case*.
8. It is not at all clear why Eliot refers the reader back to l. 37, which has nothing to do with this quotation from *The Tempest*.
9. According to Clive Bell, Eliot reported to a dinner party shortly after the poem appeared that Mrs. Porter and her daughter "are known only from an Ayrian camp-fire song of which one other line has been preserved: *And so they oughter.*" Ayr is a town in Queensland, Australia, named after the seaport town in Scotland, and so this may corroborate Eliot's rather vague claim about the origin of these lines.
1. An alternate possibility for the initials "C.i.f." has been suggested: "cost, insurance, freight."

Nam duo magnorum viridi coeuntia silva
Corpora serpentum baculi violaverat ictu
Deque viro factus, mirabile, femina septem
Egerat autumnos; octavo rursus eosdem
Vidit et 'est vestrae si tanta potentia plagae,'
Dixit 'ut auctoris sortem in contraria mutet,
Nunc quoque vos feriam!' percussis anguibus isdem
Forma prior rediit genetivaque venit imago.
Arbiter hic igitur sumptus de lite iocosa
Dicta Iovis firmat; gravius Saturnia iusto
Nec pro materia fertur doluisse suique
Iudicis aeterna damnavit lumina nocte,
At pater omnipotens (neque enim licet inrita cuiquam
Facta dei fecisse deo) pro lumine adempto
Scire futura dedit poenamque levavit honore.[2]

221. This may not appear as exact as Sappho's lines, but I had in mind the "longshore" or "dory" fisherman, who returns at nightfall.

253. V. Goldsmith, the song in *The Vicar of Wakefield*.

257. V. *The Tempest*, as above.

264. The interior of St. Magnus Martyr is to my mind one of the finest among Wren's interiors. See *The Proposed Demolition of Nineteen City Churches*: (P.S. King & Son, Ltd.).[3]

266. The Song of the (three) Thames-daughters begins here. From line 292 to 306 inclusive they speak in turn. V. *Götterdämmerung*, III, i: the Rhine-daughters.

279. V. Froude, *Elizabeth*, Vol. I, ch. iv, letter of De Quadra to Philip of Spain: "In the afternoon we were in a barge, watching the games on the river. (The queen) was alone with Lord Robert and myself on the poop, when they began to talk nonsense, and went so far that Lord Robert at last said, as I was on the spot there was no reason why they should not be married if the queen pleased."

293. Cf. *Purgatorio*, V, 133:

"Ricorditi di me, che son la Pia;
"Siena mi fe', disfecemi Maremma."

---

2. For an English prose version of this passage, see "[The Blinding of Tiresias]," p. 46.
3. In 1920 a commission appointed by the Bishop of London recommended the consolidation of the parishes in the City of London and the "removal" of nineteen churches, some of them dating, in earlier forms, to before the Norman conquest. Both St. Magnus Martyr and St. Mary Woolnoth were slated for demolition, but the plan was voted down by the House of Lords in 1926. Eliot's interest in this question foreshadows the stand he was to take in "Choruses from 'The Rock,' " after his conversion:

I journeyed to London, to the timekept City,
Where the River flows, with foreign flotations.
There I was told: we have too many churches,
And too few chop-houses.

307. V. St. Augustine's *Confessions*: "to Carthage then I came, where a cauldron of unholy loves sang all about mine ears."

308. The complete text of the Buddha's Fire Sermon (which corresponds in importance to the Sermon on the Mount) from which these words are taken, will be found translated in the late Henry Clarke Warren's *Buddhism in Translation* (Harvard Oriental Series). Mr. Warren was one of the great pioneers of Buddhist studies in the Occident.

312. From St. Augustine's *Confessions* again. The collocation of these two representatives of eastern and western asceticism, as the culmination of this part of the poem, is not an accident.

V. WHAT THE THUNDER SAID

In the first part of Part V three themes are employed: the journey to Emmaus, the approach to the Chapel Perilous (see Miss Weston's book) and the present decay of eastern Europe.

357. This is *Turdus aonalaschkae pallasii*, the hermit-thrush which I have heard in Quebec County. Chapman says (*Handbook of Birds of Eastern North America*) "it is most at home in secluded woodland and thickety retreats. . . . Its notes are not remarkable for variety or volume, but in purity and sweetness of tone and exquisite modulation they are unequalled." Its "water-dripping song" is justly celebrated.

360. The following lines were stimulated by the account of one of the Antarctic expeditions (I forget which, but I think one of Shackleton's): it was related that the party of explorers, at the extremity of their strength, had the constant delusion that there *was one more member* than could actually be counted.

366–76. Cf. Hermann Hesse, *Blick ins Chaos*:

> "Schon ist halb Europa, schon ist zumindest der halbe Osten Europas auf dem Wege zum Chaos, fährt betrunken im heiligem Wahn am Abgrund entlang und singt dazu, singt betrunken und hymnisch wie Dmitri Karamasoff sang. Ueber diese Lieder lacht der Bürger beleidigt, der Heilige und Seher hört sie mit Tränen."

401. "Datta, dayadhvam, damyata" (Give, sympathise, control). The fable of the meaning of the Thunder is found in the *Brihadaranyaka —Upanishad*, 5, 1. A translation is found in Deussen's *Sechsig Upanishads des Veda*, p. 489.

407. Cf. Webster, *The White Devil*, V, vi:

> ". . . they'll remarry
> Ere the worm pierce your winding-sheet, ere the spider
> Make a thin curtain for your epitaphs."

411. Cf. *Inferno*, XXXIII, 46:

> "ed io sentii chiavar l'uscio di sotto
> all'orribile torre."[4]

Also F. H. Bradley, *Appearance and Reality*, p. 346.

"My external sensations are no less private to myself than are my thoughts or my feelings. In either case my experience falls within my own circle, a circle closed on the outside; and, with all its elements alike, every sphere is opaque to the others which surround it. . . . In brief, regarded as an existence which appears in a soul, the whole world for each is peculiar and private to that soul."

424. V. Weston: *From Ritual to Romance*; chapter on the Fisher King.

427. V. *Purgatorio*, XXVI, 148.

> " 'Ara vos prec, per aquella valor
> 'que vos guida al som de l'escalina,
> 'sovegna vos a temps de ma dolor.'
> Poi s'ascose nel foco che gli affina."[5]

428. V. *Pervigilium Veneris*. Cf. Philomela in Parts II and III.

429. V. Gerard de Nerval, Sonnet *El Desdichado*.

431. V. Kyd's *Spanish Tragedy*.

433. Shantih. Repeated as here, a formal ending to an Upanishad. "The Peace which passeth understanding" is our equivalent to this word.

---

4. "And below I heard them nailing shut the door / Of the horrible tower" (Italian).
5. " 'Now I pray you, by that power / that guides you to the top of the stair, / be heedful in time of my pain!' / Then he hid himself in the refining fire" (Italian and Provençal).

CONTEXTS

Sources

SIR JAMES G. FRAZER

The King of the Wood†

In antiquity this sylvan landscape was the scene of a strange and recurring tragedy. On the northern shore of the lake, right under the precipitous cliffs on which the modern city of Nemi[1] is perched, stood the sacred grove and sanctuary of Diana Nemorensis, or Diana of the Wood. * * * In this sacred grove there grew a certain tree round which at any time of the day, and probably far into the night, a grim figure might be seen to prowl. In his hand he carried a drawn sword, and he kept peering warily about him as if at every instant he expected to be set upon by an enemy. He was a priest and a murderer; and the man for whom he looked was sooner or later to murder him and hold the priesthood in his stead. Such was the rule of the sanctuary. A candidate for the priesthood could only succeed to office by slaying the priest, and having slain him, he retained office till he was himself slain by a stronger or a craftier.

* * *

The strange rule of this priesthood has no parallel in classical antiquity, and cannot be explained from it. To find an explanation we must go farther afield. No one will probably deny that such a custom savours of a barbarous age, and, surviving into imperial times, stands out in striking isolation from the polished Italian society of the day, like a primaeval rock rising from a smooth-shaven lawn. It is the very rudeness and barbarity of the custom which allow us a hope of explaining it. For recent researches into the early history of man have revealed the essential similarity with which, under many superficial differences, the

---

† Following are selections from Sir James George Frazer, *The Golden Bough: A Study in Magic and Religion*, abr. ed. (London: Macmillan, 1922), pp. 1–2, 135–36, 139–40, 324–25, 345–46.

1. In the Alban Hills of central Italy, Nemi was the site of the principal shrine of the woodland goddess, Diana. Possession of a bough from one of the trees in the sacred grove there was part of the office of the priest-king whose curious role Frazer tries to explain in *The Golden Bough*.

human mind has elaborated its first crude philosophy of life.[2] Accordingly, if we can show that a barbarous custom, like that of the priesthood of Nemi, has existed elsewhere; if we can detect the motives which led to its institution; if we can prove that these motives have operated widely, perhaps universally, in human society, producing in varied circumstances a variety of institutions specifically different but generically alike; if we can show, lastly, that these very motives, with some of their derivative institutions, were actually at work in classical antiquity; then we may fairly infer that at a remoter age the same motives gave birth to the priesthood of Nemi.

The Influence of the Sexes on Vegetation

From the preceding examination of the spring and summer festivals of Europe[3] we may infer that our rude forefathers personified the powers of vegetation as male and female, and attempted, on the principle of homeopathic or imitative magic,[4] to quicken the growth of trees and plants by representing the marriage of the sylvan deities in the persons of a King and Queen of May, a Whitsun Bridegroom and Bride, and so forth. Such representations were accordingly no mere symbolic or allegorical dramas, pastoral plays designed to amuse or instruct a rustic audience. They were charms intended to make the woods to grow green, the fresh grass to sprout, the corn to shoot, and the flowers to blow. And it was natural to suppose that the more closely the mock marriage of the leaf-clad or flower-decked mummers aped the real marriage of the woodland sprites, the more effective would be the charm. Accordingly we may assume with a high degree of probability that the profligacy which notoriously attended these ceremonies was at one time not an accidental excess but an essential part of the rites, and that in the opinion of those who performed them the marriage of trees and plants could not be fertile without the real union of the human sexes. At the present day it might perhaps be vain to look in civilised Europe for customs of this sort observed for the explicit purpose of promoting the growth of vegetation. But ruder races in other parts of the world have consciously employed the intercourse of the sexes as a means to ensure the fruitfulness of the earth; and some rites which are still, or were till lately, kept up in Europe can be reasonably explained only as stunted relics of a similar practice.

2. For Eliot's repetition of this idea, see "[*The Rite of Spring* and *The Golden Bough*]," pp. 131–33.
3. May Day, St. George's Day, St. Brides' Day, and other festivals celebrating the coming of spring, which seem to Frazer to carry ancient nature worship into medieval times.
4. The principle that "like produces like, or that an effect resembles its cause," which was, according to Frazer, at the heart of many ancient rituals and magical practices.

*   *   *

We have seen that according to a widespread belief, which is not without a foundation in fact, plants reproduce their kinds through the sexual union of male and female elements, and that on the principle of homeopathic magic this reproduction is supposed to be stimulated by the real or mock marriage of men and women, who masquerade for the time being as spirits of vegetation. Such magical dramas have played a great part in the popular festivals of Europe, and based as they are on a very crude conception of natural law, it is clear that they must have been handed down from a remote antiquity. We shall hardly, therefore, err in assuming that they date from a time when the forefathers of the civilised nations of Europe were still barbarians, herding their cattle and cultivating patches of corn in the clearings of the vast forests, which then covered the greater part of the continent, from the Mediterranean to the Arctic Ocean. But if these old spells and enchantments for the growth of leaves and blossoms, of grass and flowers and fruit, have lingered down to our own time in the shape of pastoral plays and popular merry-makings, is it not reasonable to suppose that they survived in less attenuated forms some two thousand years ago among the civilised peoples of antiquity? Or, to put it otherwise, is it not likely that in certain festivals of the ancients we may be able to detect the equivalents of our May Day, Whitsuntide, and Midsummer celebrations, with this difference, that in those days the ceremonies had not yet dwindled into mere shows and pageants, but were still religious or magical rites, in which the actors consciously supported the high parts of gods and goddesses? Now in the first chapter of this book we found reason to believe that the priest who bore the title of King of the Wood at Nemi had for his mate the goddess of the grove, Diana herself. May not he and she, as King and Queen of the Wood, have been serious counterparts of the merry mummers who play the King and Queen of May, the Whitsuntide Bridegroom and Bride in modern Europe? and may not their union have been yearly celebrated in a *theogony* or divine marriage? Such dramatic weddings of gods and goddesses, as we shall see presently, were carried out as solemn religious rites in many parts of the ancient world; hence there is no intrinsic improbability in the supposition that the sacred grove at Nemi may have been the scene of an annual ceremony of this sort. Direct evidence that it was so there is none, but analogy pleads in favour of the view. *   *   *

The Killing of the Divine King

If the high gods, who dwell remote from the fret and fever of this earthly life, are yet believed to die at last, it is not to be expected that a god who lodges in a frail tabernacle of flesh should escape the same fate, though we hear of African kings who have imagined themselves immortal by virtue of their sorceries. Now primitive peoples, as we have seen, sometimes believe that their safety and even that of the world is bound up with the life of one of these god-men or human incarnations of the divinity. Naturally, therefore, they take the utmost care of his life, out of a regard for their own. But no amount of care and precaution will prevent the man-god from growing old and feeble and at last dying. His worshippers have to lay their account with this sad necessity and to meet it as best they can. The danger is a formidable one; for if the course of nature is dependent on the man-god's life, what catastrophes may not be expected from the gradual enfeeblement of his powers and their final extinction in death? There is only one way of averting these dangers. The man-god must be killed as soon as he shows symptoms that his powers are beginning to fail, and his soul must be transferred to a vigorous successor before it has been seriously impaired by the threatened decay. The advantages of thus putting the man-god to death instead of allowing him to die of old age and disease are, to the savage, obvious enough. For if the man-god dies what we call a natural death, it means, according to the savage, that his soul has either voluntarily departed from his body and refuses to return, or more commonly, that it has been extracted, or at least detained in its wanderings, by a demon or sorcerer. In any of these cases the soul of the man-god is lost to his worshippers, and with it their prosperity is gone and their very existence endangered. Even if they could arrange to catch the soul of the dying god as it left his lips or his nostrils and so transfer it to a successor, this would not effect their purpose; for dying of disease, his soul would necessarily leave his body in the last stage of weakness and exhaustion, and so enfeebled it would continue to drag out a languid, inert existence in any body to which it might be transferred. Whereas by slaying him his worshipers could, in the first place, make sure of catching his soul as it escaped and transferring it to a suitable successor; and, in the second place, by putting him to death before his natural force was abated, they would secure that the world should not fall into decay with the decay of the man-god. Every purpose, therefore, was answered, and all dangers averted by thus killing the man-god and transferring his soul, while yet at its prime, to a vigorous successor.

[Adonis and Christ]

The spectacle of the great changes which annually pass over the face of the earth has powerfully impressed the minds of men in all ages, and stirred them to meditate on the causes of transformations so vast and wonderful. Their curiosity has not been purely disinterested; for even the savage cannot fail to perceive how intimately his own life is bound up with the life of nature, and how the same processes which freeze the stream and strip the earth of vegetation menace him with extinction. At a certain stage of development men seem to have imagined that the means of averting the threatened calamity were in their own hands, and that they could hasten or retard the flight of the seasons by magic art. Accordingly they performed ceremonies and recited spells to make the rain to fall, the sun to shine, animals to multiply, and the fruits of earth to grow. In course of time, the slow advance of knowledge, which has dispelled so many cherished illusions, convinced at least the more thoughtful portion of mankind that the alternations of summer and winter, of spring and autumn, were not merely the result of their own magical rites, but that some deeper cause, some mightier power, was at work behind the shifting scenes of nature. They now pictured to themselves the growth and decay of vegetation, the birth and death of living creatures, as effects of the waxing and waning strength of divine beings, of gods and goddesses, who were born and died, who married and begot children, on the pattern of human life.

Thus the old magical theory of the seasons was displaced, or rather supplemented, by a religious theory. For although men now attributed the annual cycle of change primarily to corresponding changes in their deities, they still thought that by performing certain magical rites they could aid the god, who was the principle of life, in his struggle with the opposing principle of death. They imagined that they could recruit his failing energies and even raise him from the dead. The ceremonies which they observed for this purpose were in substance a dramatic representation of the natural processes which they wished to facilitate; for it is a familiar tenet of magic that you can produce any desired effect by merely imitating it. And as they now explained the fluctuations of growth and decay, of reproduction and dissolution, by the marriage, the death, and the rebirth or revival of the gods, their religious or rather magical dramas turned in great measure on these themes. They set forth the fruitful union of the powers of fertility, the sad death of one at least of the divine partners, and this joyful resurrection. Thus a religious theory was blended with a magical practice. The combination is familiar in history. Indeed, few religions have ever succeeded in wholly extricating themselves from the old trammels of magic.

*   *   *

Nowhere, apparently, have these rites been more widely and solemnly celebrated than in the lands which border the eastern Mediterranean. Under the names of Osiris, Tammuz, Adonis, and Attis, the peoples of Egypt and Western Asia represented the yearly decay and revival of life, especially of vegetable life, which they personified as a god who annually died and rose again from the dead. In name and detail the rites varied from place to place: in substance they were the same. * * *

* * *

When we reflect how often the Church has skilfully contrived to plant the seeds of the new faith on the old stock of paganism, we may surmise that the Easter celebration of the dead and risen Christ was grafted upon a similar celebration of the dead and risen Adonis,[5] which * * * was celebrated in Syria at the same season. The type, created by Greek artists, of the sorrowful goddess with her dying lover in her arms, resembles and may have been the model of the *Pietà* of Christian art, the Virgin with the dead body of her divine Son in her lap, of which the most celebrated example is the one by Michael Angelo in St. Peter's. That noble group, in which the living sorrow of the mother contrasts so wonderfully with the languor of death in the son, is one of the finest compositions in marble. Ancient Greek art has bequeathed to us few works so beautiful, and none so pathetic.

In this connexion a well-known statement of Jerome[6] may not be without significance. He tells us that Bethlehem, the traditionary birthplace of the Lord, was shaded by a grove of that still older Syrian Lord, Adonis, and that where the infant Jesus had wept, the lover of Venus was bewailed. Though he does not expressly say so, Jerome seems to have thought that the grove of Adonis had been planted by the heathen after the birth of Christ for the purpose of defiling the sacred spot. In this he may have been mistaken. If Adonis was indeed, as I have argued, the spirit of the corn, a more suitable name for his dwelling-place could hardly be found than Bethlehem, "the House of Bread," and he may well have been worshipped there at his House of Bread long ages before the birth of Him who said, "I am the bread of life." Even on the hypothesis that Adonis followed rather than preceded Christ at Bethlehem, the choice of his sad figure to divert the allegiance of Christians from their Lord cannot but strike us as eminently appropriate when we remember the similarity of the rites which commemorated the death and resurrection of the two.

---

5. Adonis, lover of Aphrodite, is killed by a boar. But Frazer is more interested in an earlier part of his story, in which Aphrodite hides the infant Adonis in a chest and entrusts it to Persephone in the underworld. When Persephone refuses to return Adonis to Aphrodite, she must descend to the underworld to ransom him. The dispute is finally settled only when Zeus rules that Adonis will live half the year with Persephone and half with Aphrodite. Adonis is thus a version of the fallen and risen god, of which the Babylonian Tammuz may be the prototype.
6. Pilgrim, scholar, and Christian saint, born in Dalmatia (Slovenia) in 347, died in 419/420 in the monastery he had established in Bethlehem.

JESSIE L. WESTON

[The Grail Legend]†

The main difficulty of our research lies in the fact that the Grail
legend[1] consists of a congeries of widely differing elements—elements
which at first sight appear hopelessly incongruous, if not completely
contradictory, yet at the same time are present to an extent, and in a
form, which no honest critic can afford to ignore.

*   *   *

A prototype, containing the main features of the Grail story—the
Waste Land, the Fisher King, the Hidden Castle with its solemn Feast,
and mysterious Feeding Vessel, the Bleeding Lance and Cup—does
not, so far as we know, exist. None of the great collections of Folk-
tales * * * has preserved specimens of such a type; it is not such a
story as, e.g., *The Three Days Tournament*, examples of which are found
all over the world.

*   *   *

Some years ago, when fresh from the study of Sir J. G. Frazer's
epoch-making work, *The Golden Bough*, I was struck by the resemblance between certain features of the Grail story, and characteristic
details of the Nature Cults described. The more closely I analysed the
tale, the more striking became the resemblance, and I finally asked
myself whether it were not possible that in this mysterious legend—
mysterious alike in its character, its sudden appearance, the importance
apparently assigned to it, followed by as sudden and complete a
disappearance—we might not have the confused record of a ritual, once
popular, later surviving under conditions of strict secrecy? This would
fully account for the atmosphere of awe and reverence which even
under distinctly non-Christian conditions never fails to surround the
Grail * * * ; and also for the presence in the tale of distinctly popular,
and folk-lore, elements.

*   *   *

It has taken me some nine or ten years longer to complete the evidence, but the chain is at last linked up, and we can now prove by

---

† The following selections are from Jessie L. Weston, *From Ritual to Romance* (Cambridge:
   Cambridge University Press, 1920), pp. 2–4, 19, 21, 74–76, 108, 117–19, 165, 176–77.
1. The Holy Grail is the chalice supposed to have been used by Jesus at the Last Supper and
   then by Joseph of Arimathea to catch the blood flowing from Jesus' wounds on the cross. The
   search for this precious relic is the focus of a number of medieval stories, poems, and legends,
   which are, as Weston says, quite miscellaneous.

printed texts the parallels existing between each and every feature of the Grail story and the recorded symbolism of the Mystery cults. Further, we can show that between these Mystery cults and Christianity there existed at one time a close and intimate union, such a union as of itself involved the practical assimilation of the central rite, in each case a 'Eucharistic' Feast, in which the worshippers partook of the Food of Life from the sacred vessels.

[The Grail Quest]

(a) There is a general consensus of evidence to the effect that the main object of the Quest is the restoration to health and vigour of a King suffering from infirmity caused by wounds, sickness, or old age;

(b) and whose infirmity, for some mysterious and unexplained reason, reacts disastrously upon his kingdom, either by depriving it of vegetation, or exposing it to the ravages of war.

(c) In two cases it is definitely stated that the King will be restored to youthful vigour and beauty.

(d) In both cases where we find Gawain[2] as the hero of the story, and in one connected with Perceval, the misfortune which has fallen upon the country is that of a prolonged drought, which has destroyed vegetation, and left the land Waste; the effect of the hero's question is to restore the waters to their channel, and render the land once more fertile.

*   *   *

(e) But this much seems certain, the aim of the grail Quest is twofold; it is to benefit (a) the King, (b) the land. The first of these two is the more important, as it is the infirmity of the King which entails misfortune on his land, the condition of the one reacts, for good or ill, upon the other; how, or why, we are left to discover for ourselves.

*   *   *

(f) To sum up the result of the analysis, I hold that we have solid grounds for the belief that the story postulates a close connection between the vitality of a certain King, and the prosperity of his kingdom; the forces of the ruler being weakened or destroyed, by wound, sickness, old age, or death, the land becomes Waste, and the task of the hero is that of restoration.

---

2. A key figure in Arthurian legend and romance, Gawain is usually represented as the nephew of King Arthur. His character varies a great deal from story to story, so that in some instances he is a model of courtly virtue and in others weak or even cruel. In some versions of the Grail story, particularly that set down by Chrétien de Troyes in the twelfth century, Perceval sees the chalice itself in the castle of a wounded king, and he is challenged to ask the question that will restore the kingdom and heal the king.

[The Tarot Pack]

Students of the Grail texts, whose attention is mainly occupied with Medieval Literature, may not be familiar with the word Tarot, or aware of its meaning. It is the name given to a pack of cards, seventy-eight in number, of which twenty-two are designated as the 'Keys.'

These cards are divided into four suits, which correspond with those of the ordinary cards; they are:

Cup (Chalice, or Goblet)—Hearts.
Lance (Wand, or Sceptre)—Diamonds.
Sword—Spades.
Dish (Circles, or Pentangles, the form varies)—Clubs.

To-day the Tarot has fallen somewhat into disrepute, being principally used for purposes of divination, but its origin, and precise relation to our present playing-cards, are questions of considerable antiquarian interest. Were these cards the direct parents of our modern pack, or are they entirely distinct therefrom?

Some writers are disposed to assign a very high antiquity to the Tarot. Traditionally, it is said to have been brought from Egypt; there is no doubt that parallel designs and combinations are to be found in the surviving decorations of Egyptian temples, notably in the astronomic designs on the ceiling of one of the halls of the palace of Medinet Abou, which is supported on twenty-two columns (a number corresponding to the 'keys' of the Tarot), and also repeated in a calendar sculptured on the southern façade of the same building, under a sovereign of the XXIII dynasty. This calendar is supposed to have been connected with the periodic rise and fall of the waters of the Nile.

The Tarot has also been connected with an ancient Chinese monument, traditionally erected in commemoration of the drying up of the waters of the Deluge by Yao. The face of this monument is divided up into small sections corresponding in size and number with the cards of the Tarot, and bearing characters which have, so far, not been deciphered.

What is certain is that these cards are used to-day by the Gipsies for purposes of divination, and the opinion of those who have studied the subject is that there is some real ground for the popular tradition that they were introduced into Europe by this mysterious people.

* * *

But if the connection with the Egyptian and Chinese monuments, referred to above, is genuine, the original use of the 'Tarot' would seem to have been, not to foretell the future in general, but to predict the rise and fall of the waters which brought fertility to the land.

Such use would bring the 'Suits' into line with the analogous symbols of the Grail castle * * * connected with the embodiment of the reproductive forces of Nature.

The Fisher King

* * * [T]he personality of the King, the nature of the disability under which he is suffering, and the reflex effect exercised upon his folk and his land, correspond, in a most striking manner, to the intimate relation at one time held to exist between the ruler and his land; a relation mainly dependent upon the identification of the King with the Divine principle of Life and Fertility. * * * But what about his title, why should he be called the Fisher King?[3] * * * In my opinion the key to the puzzle is to be found in the rightful understanding of the Fish-Fisher symbolism. Students of the Grail literature have been too prone to treat the question on the Christian basis alone, oblivious of the fact that Christianity did no more than take over, and adapt to its own use, a symbolism already endowed with a deeply rooted prestige and importance. * * * So far as the present state of our knowledge goes we can affirm with certainty that the Fish is a Life symbol of immemorial antiquity, and that the title of Fisher has, from the earliest ages, been associated with Deities who were held to be specially connected with the origin and preservation of life. * * * There is thus little reason to doubt that, if we regard the Fish as a Divine Life symbol, of immemorial antiquity, we shall not go very far astray.

[The Perilous Chapel]

Students of the Grail romances will remember that in many of the versions the hero—sometimes it is a heroine—meets with a strange and terrifying adventure in a mysterious Chapel, an adventure which, we are given to understand, is fraught with extreme peril to life. The details vary: sometimes there is a Dead Body laid on the altar; sometimes a Black Hand extinguishes the tapers; there are strange and threatening

3. In versions of the Grail legend centered on Perceval, the wounded king, whom Perceval is supposed to restore, is usually referred to as the Fisher King. In some versions, those of Chrétien de Troyes and Wolfram von Eschenbach, for example, the king is in fact a fisherman. In one of the versions discussed by Weston, however, a fish is caught as part of a eucharistic ceremony, a reenactment of the Last Supper, in which the fish provides the food and the Grail the wine. The Fisher King is then the hereditary possessor of the Grail and, if not a fisherman himself, a descendant of those who performed the original fishing ritual.

voices, and the general impression is that this is an adventure in which supernatural, and evil, forces are engaged.

Such an adventure befalls Gawain on his way to the Grail Castle. He is overtaken by a terrible storm, and coming to a Chapel, standing at a crossways in the middle of a forest, enters for shelter. The altar is bare, with no cloth, or covering, nothing is thereon but a great golden candlestick with a tall taper burning within it. Behind the altar is a window, and as Gawain looks a Hand, black and hideous, comes through the window, and extinguishes the taper, while a voice makes lamentations loud and dire, beneath which the very building rocks. Gawain's horse shies for terror, and the knight, making the sign of the Cross, rides out of the Chapel, to find the storm abated, and the great wind fallen. Thereafter the night was calm and clear.

[Conclusion]

The Grail romances repose eventually, not upon a poet's imagination, but upon the ruins of an august and ancient ritual, a ritual which once claimed to be the accredited guardian of the deepest secrets of Life. Driven from its high estate by the relentless force of religious evolution—for after all Adonis, Attis,[4] and their congeners, were but the 'half gods' who must needs yield place when 'the Gods' themselves arrive—it yet lingered on; openly, in Folk practice, in Fast and Feast, whereby the well-being of the land might be assured; secretly, in cave or mountain-fastness, or island isolation, where those who craved for a more sensible (not necessarily sensuous) contact with the unseen Spiritual forces of Life than the orthodox development of Christianity afforded, might, and did, find satisfaction.

Were the Templars[5] such? Had they, when in the East, come into touch with a survival of the Naassene, or some kindred sect? It seems exceedingly probable. If it were so we could understand at once the puzzling connection of the Order with the Knights of the Grail, and the doom which fell upon them. That they were held to be Heretics is very generally admitted, but in what their Heresy consisted no one really knows; little credence can be attached to the stories of idol worship often repeated. If their Heresy, however, were such as indicated above, a Creed which struck at the very root and vitals of Christianity, we can understand at once the reason for punishment, and the necessity

4. According to Frazer, Attis was the Phrygian version of Adonis and both were vegetation gods whose death and resurrection were celebrated in the spring. They are thus, by Weston's argument, prototypes of the Fisher King. For the story of Adonis, see p. 34.

5. A religious order of knights, established during the Crusades and quartered in Jerusalem in the area once occupied by the Temple of Solomon, from which they derived their name. After they were displaced from the Holy Land by the Moslem victory of 1291, the Templars fell under suspicion as heretics and were widely persecuted in Europe.

for secrecy. In the same way we can now understand why the Church knows nothing of the Grail; why that Vessel, surrounded as it is with an atmosphere of reverence and awe, equated with the central Sacrament of the Christian Faith,[6] yet appears in no Legendary, is figured in no picture, comes on the scene in no Passion Play. The Church of the eleventh and twelfth centuries knew well what the Grail was, and we, when we realize its genesis and true lineage, need no longer wonder why a theme, for some short space so famous and so fruitful a source of literary inspiration, vanished utterly and completely from the world of literature.

Were Grail romances forbidden? Or were they merely discouraged? Probably we shall never know, but of this one thing we may be sure, the Grail is a living force, it will never die; it may indeed sink out of sight, and, for centuries even, disappear from the field of literature, but it will rise to the surface again, and become once more a theme of vital inspiration even as, after slumbering from the days of Malory, it woke to new life in the nineteenth century, making its fresh appeal through the genius of Tennyson and Wagner.[7]

ALDOUS HUXLEY

[Madame Sosostris]†

Mr. Scogan[1] had been accommodated in a little canvas hut. Dressed in a black skirt and a red bodice, with a yellow-and-red bandanna handkerchief tied round his black wig, he looked—sharp-nosed, brown, and wrinkled—like the Bohemian Hag of Frith's Derby Day.[2] A placard pinned to the curtain of the doorway announced the presence within the tent of "Sesostris,[3] the Sorceress of Ecbatana." Seated at a table, Mr. Scogan received his clients in mysterious silence, indicating with a movement of the finger that they were to sit down opposite him and

6. I.e., Holy Communion.
7. Sir Thomas Malory's *Le Morte Darthur* (1485) is the first English prose version of the Arthurian romances. Tennyson (1809–1892) published his verse treatment of the same material as *Idylls of the King* in 1859, with a revised and extended version in 1885. Richard Wagner (1813–1883) used the stories centered on Perceval for his opera *Parsifal* (1882).
† From *Crome Yellow* (London: Chatto & Windus, 1921), pp. 132–34.
1. A middle-aged academic modeled in part on British philosopher Bertrand Russell (1872–1970), a friend of both Huxley and Eliot's. He is telling fortunes at an annual charity fair.
2. William Powell Frith's *Derby Day* (1858) depicts the crush when the general public is admitted to the racecourse at Epsom on Derby Day, traditionally the first Wednesday in June. It epitomizes a certain kind of busy representational painting very popular in the Victorian period. The Hag referred to is one of a number of Gypsy beggars and fortune-tellers mixing with the crowd.
3. The name of several kings of ancient Egypt, the first of whom ruled almost two thousand years before the birth of Jesus. The name became well known in Europe through the history of Herodotus. Ecbatana was the ancient capital of the Medes, now the city of Hamadan in Iran.

to extend their hands for his inspection. He then examined the palm that was presented him, using a magnifying glass and a pair of horned spectacles. He had a terrifying way of shaking his head, frowning and clicking with his tongue as he looked at the lines. Sometimes he would whisper, as though to himself, "Terrible, terrible!" or "God preserve us!" sketching out the sign of the cross as he uttered the words. The clients who came in laughing grew suddenly grave; they began to take the witch seriously. She was a formidable-looking woman; could it be, was it possible, that there was something in this sort of thing after all? After all, they thought, as the hag shook her head over their hands, after all . . . And they waited, with an uncomfortably beating heart, for the oracle to speak. After a long and silent inspection, Mr. Scogan would suddenly look up and ask, in a hoarse whisper, some horrifying question, such as, "Have you ever been hit on the head with a hammer by a young man with red hair?" When the answer was in the negative, which it could hardly fail to be, Mr. Scogan would nod several times, saying, "I was afraid so. Everything is still to come, still to come, though it can't be very far off now." Sometimes, after a long examination, he would just whisper, "Where ignorance is bliss, 'tis folly to be wise," and refuse to divulge any details of a future too appalling to be envisaged without despair. Sesostris had a success of horror. People stood in a queue outside the witch's booth waiting for the privilege of hearing sentence pronounced upon them.

* * *

"Is there going to be another war?" asked the old lady to whom he had predicted this end.

"Very soon," said Mr. Scogan, with an air of quiet confidence.

The old lady was succeeded by a girl dressed in white muslin, garnished with pink ribbons. She was wearing a broad hat, so that Denis[4] could not see her face; but from her figure and the roundness of her bare arms he judged her young and pleasing. Mr. Scogan looked at her hand, then whispered, "You are still virtuous."

The young lady giggled and exclaimed, "Oh, lor'!"

"But you will not remain so for long," added Mr. Scogan sepulchrally. The young lady giggled again. "Destiny, which interests itself in small things no less than in great, has announced the fact upon your hand." Mr. Scogan took up the magnifying glass and began once more to examine the white palm. "Very interesting," he said, as though to himself—"very interesting. It's as clear as day." He was silent.

"What's clear?" asked the girl.

"I don't think I ought to tell you." Mr. Scogan shook his head; the pendulous brass earrings which he had screwed on to his ears tinkled.

---

4. Denis Stone, a young poet and protagonist of the novel.

"Please, please!" she implored.

The witch seemed to ignore her remark. "Afterwards, it's not at all clear. The fates don't say whether you will settle down to married life and have four children or whether you will try to go on the cinema and have none."

*   *   *

"Is it really true?" asked white muslin.

The witch gave a shrug of the shoulders. "I merely tell you what I read in your hand. Good afternoon. That will be six-pence. Yes, I have change. Thank you. Good afternoon."

CHARLES BAUDELAIRE

To the Reader†

Au Lecteur

Ignorance, error, cupidity, and sin
Possess our souls and exercise our flesh;
Habitually we cultivate remorse
As beggars entertain and nurse their lice.

Our sins are stubborn. Cowards when contrite   5
We overpay confession with our pains,
And when we're back again in human mire
Vile tears, we think, will wash away our stains.

Thrice-potent Satan in our cursèd bed
Lulls us to sleep, our spirit overkissed,   10
Until the precious metal of our will
Is vaporized—that cunning alchemist!

Who but the Devil pulls our waking-strings!
Abominations lure us to their side;
Each day we take another step to hell,   15
Descending through the stench, unhorrified.

Like an exhausted rake who mouths and chews
The martyrized breast of an old withered whore
We steal, in passing, whatever joys we can,
Squeezing the driest orange all the more.   20

† From *The Poems of Stanley Kunitz 1928–1978* by Stanley Kunitz. Copyright 1934, 1944, © 1958, 1971, 1973, 1974, 1976, 1978, 1979 by Stanley Kunitz. Used by permission of W. W. Norton & Company.

Packed in our brains incestuous as worms
Our demons celebrate in drunken gangs,
And when we breathe, that hollow rasp is Death
Sliding invisibly down into our lungs.

If the dull canvas of our wretched life   25
Is unembellished with such pretty ware
As knives or poison, pyromania, rape,
It is because our soul's too weak to dare!

But in this den of jackals, monkeys, curs,
Scorpions, buzzards, snakes . . . this paradise   30
Of filthy beasts that screech, howl, grovel, grunt—
In this menagerie of mankind's vice

There's one supremely hideous and impure!
Soft-spoken, not the type to cause a scene,
He'd willingly make rubble of the earth   35
And swallow up creation in a yawn.

I mean *Ennui!* who in his hookah-dreams
Produces hangmen and real tears together.
How well you know this fastidious monster, reader,
—Hypocrite reader, you!—my double! my brother!   40

TR. STANLEY KUNITZ

The Seven Old Men†

Les Sept vieillards

TO VICTOR HUGO

Teeming city, full of dreams, where in broad
Daylight the specter grips the passer-by!
Mystery flows everywhere like sap
In the ducts of the mighty colossus.

One morning when mist in the gloomy street   5
Made the houses seem taller, like the two
Quays of a swollen river; when—décor
In harmony with the state of my soul—

† From *An Anthology of French Poetry from Nerval to Valery in English Translation*, ed. Angel Flores (New York: Doubleday Anchor 1958). Reproduced by permission of The Estate of Angel Flores, c/o The Permissions Company.

A foul, yellow fog inundated space,
I went, steeling my nerves like a hero,   10
Disputing with my Soul, already weary,
Along the faubourg jarred by heavy carts.

Suddenly I saw an old man, in rags
Of the same yellow as the rainy sky,
Whose aspect would have made alms rain down   15
Except for the wicked gleam in his eye.

You might have thought the pupils of his eyes
Were soaked in bile; his gaze sharpened the sleet,
And his beard of long hairs, stiff as a sword,
Jutted forward like the beard of Judas.   20

He was not bowed, but broken, for his spine
Made a perfect right angle with his leg,
So that his staff, completing his presence,
Gave him the bearing and the clumsy gait

Of a crippled dog or three-legged Jew.   25
He stumbled over the snow and mud as though
He were grinding the dead under his shoes,
Hostile to life, more than indifferent.

His like followed him; beard, eye, back, staff, rags,
Nothing distinguished, come from the same hell,   30
This centenarian twin, and these specters
Walked with the same step towards an unknown goal.

Of what infamous scheme was I the butt
Or what ill chance humiliated me?
Full seven times, from minute to minute,   35
I saw this old man multiply himself!

Let him who laughs at my disquietude
And is not seized by a fraternal chill
Ponder that, for all their decrepitude,
These seven monsters appeared eternal!   40

Would I, and lived, have beheld the eighth
Counterpart, ironical and fatal,
Vile Phoenix, father and son of himself?
—I turned my back on the procession.

Enraged as a drunk man who sees double,   45
I went inside and closed my door, frightened,

Sick and chilled, my mind feverish and turbid,
Offended by the senseless mystery!

In vain my reason tried to take the helm;
The tempest rollicking led it astray,   50
And my soul danced, danced, like an old lighter
Without masts, on a monstrous, shoreless sea!

TR. BARBARA GIBBS

JOHN WEBSTER

[Cornelia's Dirge from *The White Devil*]†

Call for the Robin-Red-brest and the wren,
Since ore shadie groves they hover,
And with leaves and flowres doe cover
The friendlesse bodies of unburied men.[1]
Call unto his funerall Dole   5
The Ante, the field-mouse, and the mole
To reare him hillockes, that shall keepe him warme,
And (when gay tombes are rob'd) sustaine no harme,
But keepe the wolfe far thence, that's foe to men,
For with his nailes hee'l dig them up agen.[2]   10
They would not bury him 'cause hee died in a quarrell
But I have an answere for them.
Let holie church receive him duly
Since hee payd the church tithes truly.
His wealth is sum'd, and this is all his store: 15
This poore men get; and great men get no more.
Now the wares are gone, wee may shut up shop.
Blesse you all good people.

---

† From *The Complete Works of John Webster*, 4 vols., ed. F. L. Lucas (London: Chatto & Windus, 1927), 1:182.
1. Cornelia is preparing the body of her son, Marcello, for burial.
2. In his late-nineteenth-century edition of *The White Devil*, John Addington Symonds quotes this comment from Charles Lamb: "I never saw anything like this dirge, except the ditty which reminds Ferdinand of his drowned father in the Tempest. As that is of the water, watery; so this is of the earth, earthy. Both have that intenseness of feeling, which seems to resolve itself into the elements which it contemplates." Eliot, of course, quotes the "ditty" from *The Tempest* as he does this line from Cornelia's dirge.

OVID

[The Blinding of Tiresias]†

Now while these things were happening on the earth by the decrees of fate, when the cradle of Bacchus, twice born, was safe, it chanced that Jove (as the story goes), while warmed with wine, put care aside and bandied good-humoured jests with Juno in an idle hour. "I maintain," said he, "that your pleasure in love is greater than that which we enjoy." She held the opposite view. And so they decided to ask the judgment of wise Tiresias. He knew both sides of love. For once, with a blow of his staff he had outraged two huge serpents mating in the green forest; and, wonderful to relate, from man he was changed into a woman, and in that form spent seven years. In the eighth year he saw the same serpents again and said: "Since in striking you there is such magic power as to change the nature of the giver of the blow, now will I strike you once again." So saying, he struck the serpents and his former state was restored and he became as he had been born. He therefore, being asked to arbitrate the playful dispute of the gods, took sides with Jove. Saturnia,[1] they say, grieved more deeply than she should and than the issue warranted, and condemned the arbitrator to perpetual blindness. But the Almighty Father (for no god may undo what another god has done) in return for his loss of sight gave Tiresias the power to know the future, lightening the penalty by the honour.

[The Story of Tereus and Philomela]

Now Tereus of Thrace had put these[2] to flight with his relieving troops, and by the victory had a great name. And since he was strong in wealth and in men * * * Pandion, King of Athens, allied him to himself by wedding him to Procne. But neither Juno, bridal goddess, nor Hymen,[3] nor the Graces were present at that wedding. The Furies lighted them with torches stolen from a funeral; the Furies spread the couch; and the uncanny screech-owl brooded and sat on the roof of their chamber. Under this omen were Procne and Tereus wedded;

---

† The following selections are from Ovid, *Metamorphoses*, Volume III, tr. Frank Justus Miller, revised by G. P. Gould. Cambridge, Mass.: Harvard University Press, 1916, revised 1977. The Loeb Classical Library ® is a registered trademark of the President and Fellows of Harvard College.
1. I.e., Juno.
2. Enemies threatening Athens.
3. Hymen is the god of marriage. The Graces were goddesses of fertility, and the Furies were goddesses of vengeance.

under this omen was their child conceived. Thrace, indeed, rejoiced with them, and they themselves gave thanks to the gods; both the day on which Pandion's daughter[4] was married to their illustrious king, and that day on which Itys was born, they made a festival: even so is our true advantage hidden.

Now Titan[5] through five autumnal seasons had brought round the revolving years, when Procne coaxingly to her husband said: "If I have found any favour in your sight, either send me to visit my sister or let my sister come to me. You will promise my father that after a brief stay she shall return. If you give me a chance to see my sister you will confer on me a precious boon." Tereus accordingly bade them launch his ship, and plying oar and sail, he entered the Cecrophian harbour and came to land on the shore of Piraeus.[6] As soon as he came into the presence of his father-in-law they joined right hands, and the talk began with good wishes for their health. He had begun to tell of his wife's request, which was the cause of his coming, and to promise a speedy return should the sister be sent home with him, when lo! Philomela entered, attired in rich apparel, but richer still in beauty; such as we are wont to hear the naiads described, and dryads when they move about in the deep woods, if only one should give to them refinement and apparel like hers. The moment he saw the maiden Tereus was inflamed with love, quick as if one should set fire to ripe grain, or dry leaves, or hay stored away in the mow. Her beauty, indeed, was worth it; but in his case his passionate nature pricked him on, and, besides, the men of his clime are quick to love: his own fire and his nation's burnt in him. His impulse was to corrupt her attendants' care and her nurse's faithfulness, and even by rich gifts to tempt the girl herself, even at the cost of all his kingdom; or else to ravish her and to defend his act by bloody war. There was nothing which he would not do or dare, smitten by this mad passion. His heart could scarce contain the fires that burnt in it. Now, impatient of delay, he eagerly repeated Procne's request, pleading his own cause under her name. * * * Ay, more—Philomela herself has the same wish; winding her arms about her father's neck, she coaxes him to let her visit her sister; by her own welfare (yes, and against it, too) she urges her prayer. Tereus gazes at her, and as he looks feels her already in his arms; as he sees her kisses and her arms about her father's neck, all this goads him on, food and fuel for his passion * * * . The father yields to the prayers of both. The girl is filled with joy; she thanks her father and, poor unhappy wretch, she deems that success for both sisters which is to prove a woeful happening for them both.

4. I.e., Procne.
5. I.e., Cronos, most powerful of the Titans, children of Uranus (Heaven) and Gaia (Earth). He is associated with the harvest.
6. A town that has served since about the fifth century as the seaport of Athens.

*   *   *

And now they were at the end of their journey, now, leaving the
travel-worn ship, they had landed on their own shores; when the king
dragged off Pandion's daughter to a hut deep hidden in the ancient
woods; and there, pale and trembling and all fear, begging with tears
to know where her sister was, he shut her up. Then, openly confessing
his horrid purpose, he violated her, just a weak girl and all alone, vainly
calling, often on her father, often on her sister, but most of all upon
the great gods. *   *   * Soon, when her senses came back, she dragged
at her loosened hair, and like one in mourning, beating and tearing
her arms, with outstretched hands she cried: "Oh, what a horrible thing
you have done, barbarous, cruel wretch! Do you care nothing for my
father's injunctions, his affectionate tears, my sister's love, my own vir-
ginity, the bonds of wedlock? *   *   * If those who dwell on high see
these things, nay, if there are any gods at all, if all things have not
perished with me, sooner or later you shall pay dearly for this deed. I
will myself cast all shame aside and proclaim what you have done. If
I should have the chance, I would go where people throng and tell it;
if I am kept shut up in these woods, I will fill the woods with my story
and move the very rocks to pity." *   *   *

The savage tyrant's wrath was aroused by these words, and his fear
no less. Pricked on by both these spurs, he drew his sword which was
hanging by his side in its sheath, caught her by the hair, and twisting
her arms behind her back, he bound them fast. At sight of the sword,
Philomela gladly offered her throat to the stroke, filled with the eager
hope of death. But he seized her tongue with pincers, as it protested
against the outrage, calling ever on the name of her father and struggling to speak, and cut it off with his merciless blade. *   *   *

With such crimes upon his soul he had the face to return to Procne's
presence. She on seeing him at once asked where her sister was. He
groaned in pretended grief and told a made-up story of death; his tears
gave credence to the tale. Then Procne tore from her shoulders the
robe gleaming with a broad golden border and put on black weeds; she
built also a cenotaph in honour of her sister, brought pious offerings
to her imagined spirit, and mourned her sister's fate, not meet to be so
mourned.

Now through the twelve signs, a whole year's journey, has the sun-
god passed. And what shall Philomela do? A guard prevents her flight;
stout walls of solid stone fence in the hut; speechless lips can give no
token of her wrongs. But grief has sharp wits, and in trouble cunning
comes. She hangs a Thracian web on her loom, and skilfully weaving
purple signs on a white background, she thus tells the story of her
wrongs. This web, when completed, she gives to her one attendant and
begs her with gestures to carry it to the queen. The old woman, as she

was bid, takes the web to Procne, not knowing what she bears in it. The savage tyrant's wife unrolls the cloth, reads the pitiable tale of her misfortune, and (a miracle that she could!) says not a word. Grief chokes the words that rise to her lips, and her questing tongue can find no words strong enough to express her outraged feelings. Here is no room for tears, but she hurries on to confound right and wrong, her whole soul bent on the thought of vengeance.

It was the time when the Thracian matrons were wont to celebrate the biennial festival of Bacchus.[7] * * * [S]o by night the queen goes forth from her house, equips herself for the rites of the god and dons the array of frenzy. * * * She comes to the secluded lodge at last, shrieks aloud and cries "Euhoe!" breaks down the doors, seizes her sister, arrays her in the trappings of a Bacchante, hides her face with ivy-leaves, and, dragging her along in amazement, leads her within her own walls.

When Philomela perceived that she had entered that accursed house the poor girl shook with horror and grew pale as death. Procne found a place, and took off the trappings of the Bacchic rites and, uncovering the shame-blanched face of her wretched sister, folded her in her arms. But Philomela could not lift her eyes to her sister, feeling herself to have wronged her. And, with her face turned to the ground, longing to swear and call all the gods to witness that that shame had been forced upon her, she made her hand serve for voice. But Procne was all on fire, she could not contain her own wrath, and chiding her sister's weeping, she said: "This is no time for tears, but for the sword, for something stronger than the sword, if you have such a thing. I am prepared for any crime, my sister; * * * I am prepared for some great deed; but what it shall be I am still in doubt."

While Procne was thus speaking, Itys came into his mother's presence. His coming suggested what she could do, and regarding him with pitiless eyes, she said: "Ah, how like your father you are!" Saying no more, she began to plan a terrible deed and boiled with inward rage. But when the boy came up to her and greeted his mother, put his little arms around her neck and kissed her in his winsome, boyish way, her mother-heart was touched, her wrath fell away, and her eyes, though all unwilling, were wet with tears that flowed in spite of her. But when she perceived that her purpose was wavering through excess of mother-love, she turned again from her son to her sister; and gazing at both in turn, she said: "Why is one able to make soft, pretty speeches, while her ravished tongue dooms the other to silence? * * * ." Without more words she dragged Itys away, as a tigress drags a suckling fawn through the dark woods on Ganges' banks. And when they reached a

---

7. God of wine. Bacchantes are female participants in his festival, the Bacchanalia, characterized by frenzied dancing. "Euhoe" is a transcription of their traditional cry.

remote part of the great house, while the boy stretched out pleading hands as he saw his fate, and screamed, "Mother! mother!" and sought to throw his arms around her neck, Procne smote him with a knife between breast and side—and with no change of face. This one stroke sufficed to slay the lad; but Philomela cut the throat also, and they cut up the body still warm and quivering with life. * * *

This is the feast to which the wife invites Tereus, little knowing what it is. She pretends that it is a sacred feast after their ancestral fashion, of which only a husband may partake, and removes all attendants and slaves. So Tereus, sitting alone in his high ancestral banquet-chair, begins the feast and gorges himself with flesh of his own flesh. And in the utter blindness of his understanding he cries: "Go, call me Itys hither!" Procne cannot hide her cruel joy, and eager to be the messenger of her bloody news, she says: "You have, within, him whom you want." He looks about and asks where the boy is. And then, as he asks and calls again for his son, just as she was, with streaming hair, and all stained with her mad deed of blood, Philomela springs forward and hurls the gory head of Itys straight into his father's face; nor was there ever any time when she longed more to be able to speak, and to express her joy in fitting words. Then the Thracian king overturns the table with a great cry * * * then with drawn sword he pursues the two daughters of Pandion. As they fly from him you would think that the bodies of the two Athenians were poised on wings: they were poised on wings! One flies to the woods, the other rises to the roof. And even now their breasts have not lost the marks of their murderous deed, their feathers are stained with blood. Tereus, swift in pursuit because of his grief and eager desire for vengeance, is himself changed into a bird. Upon his head a stiff crest appears, and a huge beak stands forth instead of his long sword. His is the hoopoe, with the look of one armed for war.

GENE BUCK AND HERMAN RUBY

That Shakespearian Rag†

Words by
GENE BUCK and HERMAN RUBY

Music by
DAVID STAMPER

on Macduff," Des - de - mon - a was the col - ored pet,

Ro - me - o _____ loved his Ju - li - et ___ And they were some

lov - ers, you can bet, _____ and yet, I know __

___ if they were here to - day, They'd Grizz -

- ly Bear in a diff'-rent way, And you'd hear old

Ham - let say, "To __ be or not to be," That __

Shakespea-ri - an Rag.

GOTAMA BUDDHA

The Fire-Sermon†

All things, O priests, are on fire. And what, O priests, are all these things which are on fire?

The eye, O priests, is on fire; forms are on fire; eye-consciousness is on fire; impressions received by the eye are on fire; and whatever sensation, pleasant, unpleasant, or indifferent, originates in dependence on impressions received by the eye, that also is on fire.

And with what are these on fire?

With the fire of passion, say I, with the fire of hatred, with the fire of infatuation; with birth, old age, death, sorrow, lamentation, misery, grief, and despair are they on fire.

The ear is on fire; sounds are on fire; * * * the nose is on fire; odors are on fire; * * * the tongue is on fire; tastes are on fire; * * * the body is on fire; things tangible are on fire; * * * the mind is on fire; ideas are on fire; * * * mind-consciousness is on fire; impressions received by the mind are on fire; and whatever sensation,

† From Henry Clarke Warren, *Buddhism in Translations* (Cambridge: Harvard University Press, 1922), pp. 350–51.

pleasant, unpleasant, or indifferent, originates in dependence on impressions received by the mind, that also is on fire.

*   *   *

Perceiving this, O priests, the learned and noble disciple conceives an aversion for the eye, conceives an aversion for forms, conceives an aversion for eye-consciousness, conceives an aversion for the impressions received by the eye; and whatever sensation, pleasant, unpleasant, or indifferent, originates in dependence on impressions received by the eye, for that also he conceives an aversion. Conceives an aversion for the ear, conceives an aversion for sounds, * * * conceives an aversion for the nose, conceives an aversion for odors, * * * conceives an aversion for the tongue, conceives an aversion for tastes, * * * conceives an aversion for the body, conceives an aversion for things tangible, * * * conceives an aversion for the mind, conceives an aversion for ideas, conceives an aversion for mind-consciousness, conceives an aversion for the impressions received by the mind; and whatever sensation, unpleasant, or indifferent, originates in dependence on impressions received by the mind, for this also he conceives an aversion. And in conceiving this aversion, he becomes divested of passion, and by the absence of passion he becomes free, and when he is free he becomes aware that he is free; and he knows that re-birth is exhausted, that he has lived the holy life, that he has done what it behooved him to do, and that he is no more for this world.

EDMUND SPENSER

From Prothalamion†

Calme was the day, and through the trembling ayre,
Sweete breathing *Zephyrus* did softly play
A gentle spirit, that lightly did delay
Hot *Titans* beames, which then did glyster¹ fayre:
When I whom sullein care,   5
Through discontent of my long fruitlesse stay
In Princes Court, and expectation vayne

---

† From *The Poetical Works of Edmund Spenser*, ed. J. C. Smith and E. De Selincourt (London: Oxford University Press, 1912), p. 601. The full title of Spenser's poem, first printed in 1596, is "Prothalamion, Or, A Spousall Verse made by Edm. Spenser In Honour of the Double mariage of the two Honorable & vertuous Ladies, the Ladie Elizabeth and the Ladie Katherine Somerset, Daughters to the Right Honourable the Earle of Worcester and espoused to the two worthie Gentlemen M. Henry Gilford, and M. William Peter Esquyers." "Prothalamion" literally means "before the marriage."
1. Glisten.

Of idle hopes, which still doe fly away,
Like empty shaddowes, did aflict my brayne,
Walkt forth to ease my payne   10
Along the shoare of silver streaming *Themmes*,
Whose rutty Bancke, the which his River hemmes,
Was paynted all with variable[2] flowers,
And all the meades[3] adornd with daintie gemmes,
Fit to decke maydens bowres,   15
And crowne their Paramours,
Against the Brydale day, which is not long:[4]
        Sweete *Themmes* runne softly, till I end my Song.

There, in a Meadow, by the Rivers side,
A Flocke of *Nymphes* I chaunced to espy,   20
All lovely Daughters of the Flood thereby,
With goodly greenish locks all loose untyde,
As[5] each had bene a Bryde,
And each one had a little wicker basket,
Made of fine twigs entrayled curiously,[6]   25
In which they gathered flowers to fill their flasket:[7]
And with fine Fingers, cropt full feateously[8]
The tender stalks on hye.
Of every sort, which in that Meadow grew,
They gathered some; the Violet pallid blew,   30
The little Dazie, that at evening closes,
The virgin Lillie, and the Primrose trew,
With store of vermeil[9] Roses,
To decke their Bridegromes posies,
Against the Brydale day, which was not long: 35
        Sweete *Themmes* runne softly, till I end my Song.

                              *   *   *

2. Of various different colors.
3. Meadows.
4. Not far off.
5. As if.
6. Woven carefully.
7. Wicker basket.
8. Picked skillfully.
9. Vermilion.

OLIVER GOLDSMITH

[Olivia's Song from *The Vicar of Wakefield*]†

The next morning the sun rose with peculiar warmth for the season, so that we agreed to breakfast together on the honeysuckle bank; where, while we sat, my youngest daughter, at my request, joined her voice to the concert on the trees about us. It was in this place my poor Olivia first met her seducer, and every object served to recall her sadness.[1] But that melancholy which is excited by objects of pleasure, or inspired by sounds of harmony, soothes the heart instead of corroding it. Her mother, too, upon this occasion, felt a pleasing distress, and wept, and loved her daughter as before. "Do, my pretty Olivia," cried she, "let us have that little melancholy air your pappa was so fond of; your sister Sophy has already obliged us. Do child; it will please your old father." She complied in a manner so exquisitely pathetic as moved me.

> When lovely woman stoops to folly,
>   And finds too late that men betray,
> What charm can sooth her melancholy,
>   What art can wash her guilt away?
>
> The only art her guilt to cover,
>   To hide her shame from every eye,
> To give repentance to her lover,
>   And wring his bosom—is to die.

JAMES ANTHONY FROUDE

[Elizabeth and Leicester]††

The Queen invited me[1] to a party given by Lord Robert[2] on St. John's day.

---

† From *The Collected Works of Oliver Goldsmith*, Volume IV, edited by Arthur Friedman. Copyright © Oxford University Press 1966. Reprinted by permission of Oxford University Press.
1. Olivia, deceived by Mr. Thornhill, entered into a bigamous union with him, and she has just been restored to her family.
†† From James Anthony Froude, *History of England from the Fall of Wolsey to the Death of Elizabeth*, 12 vols. (New York: Scribner, 1865–73), 7:356–57.
1. Alvarez de Quadra, Bishop of Aquila and Spanish ambassador to the court of Queen Elizabeth I, from whose letters to King Philip II of Spain Froude is quoting.
2. Lord Robert Dudley, Earl of Leicester, who is considered by de Quadra and others likely to marry the queen, whose prospects in marriage constitute the main subject of correspondence between de Quadra and King Philip, as well as the main subject of intrigue in the English court.

* * *

In the afternoon we were in a barge, watching the games on the river. She was alone with the Lord Robert and myself on the poop, when they began to talk nonsense, and went so far that Lord Robert at last said, as I was on the spot there was no reason why they should not be married if the Queen pleased. She said that perhaps I did not understand sufficient English. I let them trifle in this way for a time, and then I said gravely to them both, that if they would be guided by me they would shake off the tyranny of those men who were oppressing the realm and them; they would restore religion[3] and good order; and they could then marry when they pleased—and gladly would I be the priest to unite them.

ST. AUGUSTINE

From *Confessions*†

I sank away from Thee, and I wandered, O my God, too much astray from Thee my stay, in these days of my youth, and I became to myself a barren land.

To Carthage I came, where there sang all around me in my ears a cauldron of unholy loves. I loved not yet, yet I loved to love, and out of a deep-seated want, I hated myself for wanting not. I sought what I might love, in love with loving, and safety I hated, and a way without snares. For within me was a famine of that inward food, Thyself, my God; yet, through that famine I was not hungered; but was without all longing for incorruptible sustenance, not because filled therewith, but the more empty, the more I loathed it. For this cause my soul was sickly and full of sores, it miserably cast itself forth, desiring to be scraped by the touch of objects of sense. * * * I defiled, therefore, the spring of friendship with the filth of concupiscence, and I be-clouded its brightness with the hell of lustfulness; and thus foul and unseemly, I would fain, through exceeding vanity, be fine and courtly. I fell headlong into the love, wherein I longed to be ensnared. My God, my Mercy, with how much gall didst thou out of thy great goodness besprinkle for me that sweetness? For I was both beloved, and secretly arrived at the bond of enjoying; and was with joy fettered with sorrow-bringing bonds, that I might be scourged with the iron burning rods of jealousy, and suspicions, and fears, and angers, and quarrels.

3. The Catholic Church.
† From *The Confessions of St. Augustine*, tr. E. B. Pusey (London: Dent, 1907), pp. 31–32.

FROM *THE KING JAMES BIBLE*

[The Road to Emmaus]†

And, behold, two of them went that same day to a village called Emmaus, which was from Jerusalem about three score furlongs.

And they talked together of all these things which had happened.

And it came to pass, that, while they communed together and reasoned, Jesus himself drew near, and went with them.

But their eyes were holden that they should not know him.

And he said unto them, What manner of communication are these that ye have one to another, as ye walk, and are sad?

And the one of them, whose name was Cleopas, answering said unto him, Art thou only a stranger in Jerusalem, and hast not known the things which are come to pass there in these days?

And he said unto them, What things? And they said unto him, Concerning Jesus of Nazareth, which was a prophet mighty in deed and word before God and all the people:

And how the chief priests and our rulers delivered him to be condemned to death, and have crucified him.

But we trusted that it had been he which should have redeemed Israel: and beside all this, to day is the third day since these things were done.

Yea, and certain women also of our company made us astonished, which were early at the sepulchre;

And when they found not his body, they came, saying, that they had also seen a vision of angels, which said that he was alive.

And certain of them which were with us went to the sepulchre, and found it even so as the women had said: but him they saw not.

Then he said unto them, O fools, and slow of heart to believe all that the prophets have spoken:

Ought not Christ to have suffered these things, and to enter into his glory?

And beginning at Moses and all the prophets, he expounded unto them in all the scriptures the things concerning himself.

And they drew nigh unto the village, whither they went; and he made as though he would have gone further.

But they constrained him, saying, Abide with us: for it is toward evening, and the day is far spent. And he went in to tarry with them.

And it came to pass, as he sat at meat with them, he took bread, and blessed it, and brake, and gave to them.

† Luke 24.13–32.

And their eyes were opened, and they knew him; and he vanished out of their sight.

And they said to one another, Did not our heart burn within us, while he talked with us by the way, and while he opened to us the scriptures?

SIR ERNEST SHACKLETON

[The Extra Man]†

Shackleton (1874–1922) led the British Imperial Trans-Antarctic Expedition (1914–16), the aim of which was to cross Antarctica via the South Pole. His ship was trapped in the pack ice and his party survived for five months on ice floes. This episode occurs as Shackleton and two of his crew, having rowed and sailed 800 miles in a whale boat, cross South Georgia island on foot to find help.

When I look back at those days I have no doubt that Providence guided us, not only across those snow-fields, but across the storm-white sea that separated Elephant Island from our landing-place on South Georgia. I know that during that long and racking march of thirty-six hours over the unnamed mountains and glaciers of South Georgia it seemed to me often that we were four, not three. I said nothing to my companions on the point, but afterwards Worsley said to me, "Boss, I had a curious feeling on the march that there was another person with us." Crean confessed to the same idea. One feels "the dearth of human words, the roughness of mortal speech" in trying to describe things intangible, but a record of our journeys would be incomplete without a reference to a subject very near to our hearts.

HERMAN HESSE

[The Downfall of Europe]††

It appears to me that what I call the Downfall of Europe is foretold and explained with extreme clearness in Dostoevsky's works and in the most concentrated form in "The Brothers Karamazoff."

It seems to me that European and especially German youth are destined to find their greatest writer in Dostoevsky—not in Goethe, not

† From Sir Ernest Shackleton, *South: The Story of Shackleton's Last Expedition 1914–1917* (New York: Macmillan, 1920), p. 211.
†† From *In Sight of Chaos*, tr. Stephen Hudson (Zurich: Verlag Seldwyla, 1923), pp. 13–14, 38–39, 44–46.

even in Nietzsche. In the most modern poetry, there is everywhere an approach to Dostoevsky, even though it is sometimes callow and imitative. The ideal of the Karamazoff, primeval, Asiatic and occult, is already beginning to consume the European soul. That is what I mean by the downfall of Europe. This downfall is a returning home to the mother, a turning back to Asia, to the source, to the "Faustischen Müttern"[1] and will necessarily lead, like every death on earth, to a new birth.

We contemporaries see a "downfall" in these events in the same way as the aged who, compelled to leave the home they love, mourn a loss to them irreparable while the young only think of the future, care only for what is new.

What is the Asiatic Ideal that I find in Dostoevsky, the effect of which will be, as I see it, to overwhelm Europe?

Briefly, it is the rejection of every strongly held Ethic and Moral in favor of a comprehensive LAISSEZ-FAIRE. This is the new and dangerous faith. . . .

*   *   *

And do these developments in the souls of imagined characters of fiction really signify the Downfall of Europe? Certainly. They signify it as surely as the mind's eye perceives life and eternity in the grass-blade of spring and death and its inevitability in every falling leaf of autumn. It is possible the whole "Downfall of Europe" will play itself out "only" inwardly, "only" in the souls of a generation, "only" in changing the meaning of worn out symbols, in the dis-valuation of spiritual values. Thus, the ancient world, that first brilliant coming of European culture, did not go down under Nero. Its destruction was not due to Spartacus nor to the Germanic tribes. But "only" to a thought out of Asia, that simple, subtle thought, that had been there very long but which took the form the teacher Christ gave to it.

*   *   *

I said Dostoevsky is not a poet, or he is a poet only in the secondary sense. I called him a prophet. It is difficult to say exactly what a prophet means. It seems to me something like this. A prophet is a sick man, like Dostoevsky, who was an epileptic. A prophet is the sort of sick man who has lost the sound sense of taking care of himself, the sense which is the saving of the efficient citizen. It would not do if there were many such, for the world would go to pieces. This sort of sick man, be he called Dostoevsky or Karamazoff, has that strange occult, godlike fac-

---

1. "Faustian Mothers" (German). A reference to an episode in *Faust* (Part II) by Goethe (1749–1832), in which Faust must enter the underground realm of the Mothers. They are associated by Hesse with a pre-historic, pre-conscious chaos.

ulty, the possibility of which the Asiatic venerates in every maniac. He is a seer and an oracle. A people, a period, a country, a continent has fashioned out of its corpus an organ, a sensory instrument of infinite sensitiveness, a very rare and delicate organ. Other men, thanks to their happiness and health, can never be troubled with this endowment. This sensory instrument, this mantological faculty is not crudely comprehensible like some sort of telepathy or magic, although the gift can also show itself in such confusing forms. Rather is it that the sick man of this sort interprets the movement of his own soul in terms of the universal and of mankind. Every man has visions, every man has fantasies, every man has dreams. And every vision, every dream, every idea and thought of a man on the road from the unconscious to the conscious, can have a thousand different meanings, of which every one can be right. But the appearances and visions of the seer and the prophet are not his own. The nightmare of visions which oppresses him does not warn him of a personal illness, of a personal death but of the illness, the death of that corpus whose sensory organ he is. This corpus can be a family, a clan, a people or it can be all mankind. In the soul of Dostoevsky a certain sickness and sensitiveness to suffering in the bosom of mankind which is otherwise called hysteria, found at once its means of expression and its barometer. Mankind is now on the point of realising this. Already half Europe, at all events half Eastern Europe, is on the road to Chaos. In a state of drunken illusion she is reeling into the abyss and, as she reels, she sings a drunken hymn such as Dmitri Karamazoff sang. The insulted citizen laughs that song to scorn, the saint and seer hear it with tears.[2]

From *BRIHADĀRANYAKA UPANISHAD*†

The Three Great Disciplines

Prajāpati[1] had three kinds of offspring: gods, men, and demons (asuras). They lived with Prajāpati, practising the vows of brahmachārins.[2] After finishing their term, the gods said to him: "Please instruct

2. The last three sentences of the passage are quoted in Eliot's note to ll. 366–76. Eliot was so impressed by this passage, which he had read while convalescing in Switzerland in 1921, that he wrote to Hesse, arranged to meet him in 1922, and commissioned his friend Sidney Schiff (who wrote under the name of Stephen Hudson) to translate the work into English.
† From Swami Nikhilananda, tr., *The Upanishads*, 4 vols. (New York: Harper and Brothers, 1949–59), pp. 321–22. Reprinted by permission of Ramakrishna-Vivekananda Center. Copyright © 1956. The Upanishads are a series of commentaries on the Vedas, ancient Sanskrit texts recorded from the fifteenth to the fifth centuries B.C.E. The religion based on these ancient texts evolved into Hinduism, and the texts became the sacred literature of that religion.
1. The Creator God [from Nikhilananda's glossary].
2. A celibate student who lives with his teacher and devotes himself to the practice of spiritual discipline [from Nikhilananda's glossary].

us, Sir." To them, he uttered the syllable *da* [and asked]: "Have you understood?" They replied: "We have. You said to us, 'Control yourselves (dāmyata).' "³ He said: "Yes, you have understood."

2

Then the men said to him: "Please instruct us, Sir." To them he uttered the same syllable *da* [and asked]: "Have you understood?" They replied: "We have. You said to us, 'Give (datta).' "⁴ He said: "Yes, you have understood."

3

Then the demons said to him: "Please instruct us, Sir." To them he uttered the same syllable *da* [and asked]: "Have you understood?" They replied: "We have. You said to us: "Be compassionate (dayadhvam.)' "⁵ He said: "Yes, you have understood."

That very thing is repeated [even today] by the heavenly voice, in the form of thunder, as "Da," "Da," "Da," which means: "Control yourselves," "Give," and "Have compassion." Therefore one should learn these three: self-control, giving, and mercy.⁶

From *PERVIGILIUM VENERIS*†

XXI

Now hoarse-mouthed swans crash trumpeting over the pools;
the maid of Tereus¹ makes descant under the poplar shade,

3. The gods, in spite of possessing many virtues, are naturally unruly [Nikhilananda's note].
4. The Sanskrit word datta begins with the syllable da. Men are naturally avaricious; so they are asked to distribute their wealth to the best of their power [Nikhilananda's note].
5. Prajāpati asked the demons to show kindness to all; for the demons are naturally cruel and given to injuring others [Nikhilananda's note].
6. Gods and demons * * * may be found among men. Those human beings who are wanting in self-control, but otherwise endowed with many good qualities, are the gods; those who are particularly greedy are men; while those who are cruel and given to injuring others are the demons. So the same species of human beings, according to their lack of self-control, charity, or mercy * * * are distinguished as gods, men, and demons. Hence it is human beings who should be guided by the three instructions mentioned above; for Prajāpati intended his advice for them alone: men are observed to be unrestrained, greedy, and cruel. Though Prajāpati uttered the same syllable *da* in order to teach all his children, yet each one understood the instruction differently, according to his limitations [Nikhilananda's note].
† From *Catullus, Tibullus, and Pervigilium Veneris*, tr. F. W. Cornish, J. P. Postgate, and J. W. Mackail (Cambridge: Harvard University Press, 1913), pp. 361–62. According to Mackail's introduction, the *Pervigilium Veneris* (which he translates as *The Eve of St. Venus*) is "the earliest known poem belonging in spirit to the Middle Ages." The date and authorship of the poem are unknown, and the text is traced back to the *Anthologia Latina*, a collection formed in the fourth century. Mackail regularizes the very disorderly remains of this ancient poem so that they form twenty-two stanzas with a regular refrain. Eliot was apparently attracted by the lament, attributed to Philomela, that ends the poem: "when shall I be as the swallow" ("*quando fiam uti chelidon*," l. 428).
1. I.e., Philomela. For the story of Tereus and Philomela, see pp. 46–50.

that you would think tunes of love issued trilling from her mouth,
and not a sister's complaint of a barbarous lord.

To-morrow shall be love for the loveless, and for the lover
to-morrow shall be love.

XXII

She sings, we are mute: when is my spring coming?
when shall I be as the swallow, that I may cease to be voiceless?
I have lost the Muse in silence, nor does Apollo regard me:
so Amyclae,[2] being mute, perished by silence.

To-morrow shall be love for the loveless, and for the lover
to-morrow shall be love.

THOMAS KYD

From *The Spanish Tragedie*†

BALTHAZAR: It pleasd you, at the entertainement of the Embassadour,
  To grace the King so much as with a shew:
  Now, were your studie so well furnished,
  As for the passing of the first nights sport
  To entertaine my father with the like,
  Or any such like pleasing motion,
  Assure your self, it would content them well.
HIERONIMO: Is this all?
BALTHAZAR: I, this is all.
HIERONIMO: Why then, Ile fit you;[1] say no more.
  When I was yong, I gave my minde
  And plide my self to fruitles Poetrie;
  Which though it profite the professor naught,
  Yet is it passing pleasing to the world.
LORENZO: And how for that?
HIERONIMO: Marrie, my good Lord, thus:
  (And yet me thinks you are too quicke with us):—
  When in Tolledo there I studied
  It was my chance to write a Tragedie,

2. Most probably the Roman city of that name, proverbial for its silence. According to one story,
a law passed there against the spread of false rumors prevented warnings of a real attack from
reaching the authorities.
† From *The Works of Thomas Kyd*, edited from the original texts by Frederick S. Boas (Oxford:
Clarendon Press, 1955), pp. 82–87. Copyright © Oxford University Press 1955. Reprinted by
permission of Oxford University Press. From Act 4, scene 1.
1. I.e., I'll give you something that will suit your wishes. There is a grim irony in the line, since
Hieronimo plans to fool and then to murder Balthazar and Lorenzo.

See heere, my Lords.—   *He shewes them a booke.*
Which, long forgot, I found this other day.
Now would your Lordships favour me so much
As but to grace me with your acting it—
I meane, each one of you to play a part—
Assure you it will proove most passing strange,
And wondrous plausible to that assembly.
BALTHAZAR: What? would you have us plaie a Tragedie?
HIERONIMO: Why, Nero thought it no disparagement,
   And Kings and Emperours have tane delight
   To make experience of their wits in plaies.
LORENZO: Nay, be not angrie, good *Hieronimo;*
   The Prince but asked a question.
BALTHAZAR: In faith, *Hieronimo;* and you be in earnest,
   Ile make one.[2]
LORENZO: And I, another.
HIERONIMO: Now, my good Lord, could you entreat
   Your sister *Bel-imperia* to make one?
   For whats a plaie without a woman in it?
BALTHAZAR: Little intreaty shall serve me, *Hieronimo;*
   For I must needes be imployed in your play.
HIERONIMO: Why this is well; I tell you, Lordings,
   It was determined to have been acted
   By Gentlemen and schollers too,
   Such as could tell what to speak.
BALTHAZAR: And now it shall be plaide by Princes and Courtiers,
   Such as can tell how to speak

                    *   *   *

HIERONIMO: Theres one thing more that rests for us to doe.
BALTHAZAR: Whats that, *Hieronimo?* forget not any thing.
HIERONIMO: Each one of us must act his parte
   In unknowne languages,
   That it may breed the more varietie:
   As you, my Lord, in Latin; I in Greeke;
   You in Italian; and, for because I know
   That *Bel-imperia* hath practised the French,
   In courtly French shall all her phraises be.
BALTHAZAR: You meane to try my cunning then, *Hieronimo?*
   But this will be a meere confusion,
   And hardly shall we all be understood.[3]
HIERONIMO: It must be so; for the conclusion
   Shall prove the intention, and all was good:

---

2. I.e., I'll play a part.
3. This confusion is part of Hieronimo's plot. Eliot copied the effect at the end of *The Waste Land,* where there is a similar confusion of different languages.

And I my selfe in an Oration,
And with a strange and wondrous shew besides,
That I will have there behinde a curtaine,
Assure your selfe, shall make the matter knowne:
And all shalbe concluded in one Scene,
For there's no pleasure tane in tediousness.

BALTHAZAR: How like you this?

LORENZO: Why thus, my Lord, we must resolve
To soothe his humors up.

BALTHAZAR: On, then, *Hieronimo*; farewell till soone.

Composition and Publication

LYNDALL GORDON

[The Composition of *The Waste Land*]†

It is not easy to follow the sequence of *The Waste Land*'s composition
during 1921, but some facts are clear. After resolving to write the poem
at the end of 1919 Eliot did nothing about it during 1920. That year
he busied himself with a volume of criticism, *The Sacred Wood*. The
reviews were disappointing and he went about looking pale and ill.
Then, in the autumn of 1920, Vivienne's[1] father became dangerously
ill and she and Eliot sat up night after night nursing him. The anxiety
was too much for Vivienne, who broke down. Though in March and
April 1921 she was in bed and complaining of pain that made her
scream continuously for several days, Eliot began to see there would
be no end to domestic crises, and that he must keep a part of his mind
intact if he wished to get on with his long-delayed poem.

There were two periods of composition in 1921. New evidence reveals activity at the beginning of the year, for in an unpublished letter
of 6 February, Wyndham Lewis[2] reports to Mrs Schiff that Eliot, whom
he had seen at a production of *Volpone*, 'seems to be engaged in some
obscure & intricate task of late'. Lewis must have pressed him further,
for the very next day Lewis writes again to tell Schiff that Eliot had
shown him 'a new long poem (in 4 parts) which I think will be not
only very good, but a new departure for him'. Between then and May,
there are repeated indications that Eliot was pulling it together: in April
he was revising, and hoped to have it in a final form by June. May,
while Vivienne was away at the seaside, was an opportunity to get more
on paper.

It is not possible to know for sure what he had in hand at this point,
but it was not the poem as we know it. He continued to envisage a

---

† From *T. S. Eliot: An Imperfect Life* (New York: W. W. Norton, 1999), pp. 168–75. Copyright
© 1999 by Lyndall Gordon. Reprinted by permission of W. W. Norton & Company, Inc.
1. Vivien Haigh-Wood, Eliot's first wife [*Editor*].
2. English artist and author (1887–1957), publisher of the avant-garde magazine *Blast*, which
contained some of Eliot's early poetry. Violet Schiff (1876–1962) was a friend of the Eliots'
[*Editor*].

poem in four parts, and it is likely that, by now, he had written the first version of parts I and II, drawing heavily on scenes from his own life. These he rehearsed years later when he drove about London with Mary Trevelyan. He told her that in 1921 he went to dine in Hampstead or Primrose Hill with a woman he had met at the poetry circle of the Lyceum Club, who had showed him her tarot pack, the only time he had seen one. Eliot transformed this into the fortune-teller who introduces the characters of *The Waste Land* through her tarot cards. In 1942, as Eliot and Mary Trevelyan passed the dingy flats of Crawford Mansions on the border of Paddington, he said: 'We lived there—I was very unhappy. There was a pub—I used to watch people coming out at Closing Time. That's the origin of "HURRY UP PLEASE IT'S TIME".' In Trafalgar Square, he said, pointing: 'It was from there that Vivienne threw her nightdress out of the window into the street in the middle of the night.' Her power to shame his sense of propriety was transformed into the frenzied wife in part II who threatens, 'I shall rush out as I am, and walk the street / With my hair down, so.' Vivienne remarked at the time of publication that *The Waste Land* became 'a part of me (or I of it)'.

The second period of composition came in the autumn, from October to December, a more concentrated stretch of writing. For, finally, Eliot himself broke down, and during his recuperation at Margate and Lausanne at the end of 1921 he had, at last, the continuous time he needed to complete his poem.

The event that immediately preceded his breakdown was a long-awaited visit from his mother, accompanied by his sister Marian and brother Henry. He had not seen his mother for six years. He feared that Charlotte, now seventy-seven, would be old and weak, but when they arrived he was taken aback by his mother's formidable energy. Most of the strain was keeping marital problems under wraps and Vivienne at a distance in the country. When she did appear she strove to preserve the even manners an Eliot would take for granted, but Charlotte could tell that her son was afraid of his wife, and at the very last moment Vivienne exploded. She wrote regretfully, and rather touchingly, to Henry Eliot:

> Wigmore Street
> Tuesday 23 [August 1921]
>
> Dear Henry,
>   . . . Now I want you to tell me something truly. You are not to lie. Did your mother and sister show, think, say or intimate that I behaved like 'no lady', and just like a wild animal when [we] saw you off? I was perfectly stunned on that occasion. I had no idea what I was doing. I have been more or less stunned for many months now and when I come to, I suppose it seems deadful, to

an American. I have worried all the time since. Tom said it was perfectly allright, etc, but I am sure he has lived here so long he hardly realises how *very* much less English people mind showing their emotions than Americans—or perhaps he does realise it so perfectly. But I was extremely anxious to show no emotion before your family at any time, and then I ended in a fit!

I found the emotionless condition a great strain, all the time. I used to think I should burst out and scream and dance. That's why I used to think you were so terribly failing me. But I won't talk about that now, except to ask you if ever two people made *such* a fearful mess of their obvious possibilities. I don't understand, and I never shall. . . . Both flats are equally unbearable to us [they had moved to Lucy Thayer's flat, so as to leave Clarence Gate Gardens to their visitors], so we stay here morosely. . . .

Good-bye Henry. And *be personal*, you must be personal, or else it's no good. Nothing's any good.

                                                                          Vivien

Henry took a cool view. 'I have a feeling that subconsciously (or unconsciously) she likes the role of invalid,' he remarked to his mother, 'and that, liking it as she does to be petted, "made a fuss over", condoled and consoled, she . . . encourages her breakdowns, instead of throwing them off by a sort of nervous resistance. It is hard to tell how much is physical and how much mental and controllable by will power; but I think that if she had more of "the Will to Be Well" she would have less suffering. . . . She needs something to take her mind off herself; something to absorb her entire attention.'

After his mother left, Eliot collapsed. 'I really feel very shaky', he wrote to Aldington, 'and seem to have gone down rapidly since my family left.' He felt as though he might lose self-control, but it was 'impossible to describe these feelings even if one wants to'. When overstrained, he said, he used to suffer from a vague but acute sense of horror and apprehension. Clarence Gate Gardens without his family seemed no home, and his brother's departure seemed 'as unreal as death'. Vivienne's lamentations over missing his mother seemed to vie with his own. In late September he went to see a nerve specialist. Though it was Vivienne who proposed the specialist, she was taken aback by the serious view he took of Eliot's case. '. . . Look at *my* position,' she urged Scofield Thayer. 'I have not nearly finished my own nervous breakdown yet.'

When Henry Eliot heard of his brother's condition, he was inclined to blame Vivienne. He put it to their mother: 'I am afraid he finds it impossible to do creative work (other than critical) at home. Vivien demands a good deal of attention, and I imagine is easily offended if she does not get it well buttered with graciousness and sympathy.'

Henry took the view that his brother suffered also from his disguise. 'The strain of going out among people who after all are foreigners to him, and, I believe, always must be to an American—even Henry James never became a complete Englishman—has, I think, been pretty heavy. I remember a year or more ago, in a letter to me, he spoke of always having to be . . . alert to the importance of appearances, always wearing a mask among people. To me he seemed like a man playing a part.'

On 12 October, Eliot was given three months' sick-leave from the bank. It now became clear to him that he was suffering neither from 'nerves' or insanity, but from 'psychological troubles' which, he complained, English doctors at that time simply did not acknowledge. He decided to seek help abroad, and the biologist Julian Huxley and Ottoline Morrell recommended Dr Vittoz in Lausanne. Both had been his patients. Roger Vittoz was an austere Catholic, to some a living saint, who trained his patients in meditation, similar to yoga and Buddhism. His book, *Treatment of Neurasthenia by Means of Brain Control* (1913) appeared in English in 1921. He did not advocate lengthy psychoanalysis, rather mastery, through reason and will, of what he termed *clichés*, the painful thoughts in which a diseased mind had become imprisoned. The method was not to suppress memories and desires, but through a return to moral equilibrium, to free a patient of his pain.

In the meantime, on 22 October, Eliot moved to the Albemarle Hotel, Cliftonville, Margate. Vivienne bought him a mandolin and accompanied him, at his request; after two weeks, she left him to follow the rest-cure his doctor prescribed. He was to be alone, and in the open air, and not think of the future. It is likely that it was during the last of his three weeks there, after Vivienne left, that he did 'a rough draft of part of part III',[3] calling it 'The Fire Sermon'. 'I do not know whether it will do, & must wait for Vivien's opinion as to whether it is printable,' he informed Schiff. 'I have done this while sitting in a shelter on the front[4]—as I am out all day except when taking rest.'

Eliot attached his hotel bill to the manuscript: the work he did at Margate cost him about £16 in all. The first week he indulged himself in the 'white room' and took all his meals. The next two weeks were spent rather more frugally in a modest room *en pension*. Vivienne, reporting to Russell, said that he seemed to like Margate. He was in a precarious state, but the purposeful letters he wrote at this time suggest that he was convalescing rather than declining. Pound, briefly in England in early October, found him enlivened by the prospect of leisure. There was evidently no discussion of Eliot's poem, and I doubt that Eliot showed it to him before he went to Margate.

During the final stages of *The Waste Land*'s composition Eliot put

3. The reference to 'part III' confirms the supposition that parts I and II were already by then in existence.
4. I.e., on the beach [*Editor*].

himself under Pound's direction. On 18 November, on his way to Switzerland, Eliot passed through Paris and left his wife with the Pounds, who were then living there. It seems likely that Eliot now showed Pound what he had done in Margate. Pound called Eliot's Swiss draft 'the 19 page version', which implies that he had previously seen another. He marked certain sheets on two occasions: once in pencil, probably on 18 November; once in ink, on Eliot's return from Lausanne early in January.[5] Pound undoubtedly improved particular passages: his excisions of another anti-Semitic portrait of Bleistein and a misogynist portrait of a woman writer called Fresca[6] curbed Eliot's excessive animus, and his feel for the right word improved odd lines throughout.[7] Pound was proud of his hand in *The Waste Land* and wrote:

> If you must needs enquire
> Know diligent Reader
> That on each Occasion
> Ezra performed the caesarian Operation.

Pound's influence went deeper than this comment during the winter of 1921–2, going back rather to 1918, 1919, and 1920 when he and Eliot were engaged in a common effort to modernise their poetry. Pound's *Hugh Selwyn Mauberley* (1920) is a covert dialogue with Eliot, a composite biography of two great unappreciated poets whose flaws are frankly aired. Pound criticises a Prufrock-like poet too given to hesitation, 'maudlin confession', and the precipitation of 'insubstantial manna' from heaven. As though in answer, Eliot put aside his more confessional fragments, 'Saint Narcissus' and 'Elegy', and in 1921 overlaid them with contemporary characters—the pampered Fresca (like Pound's Lady Valentine), Venus Anadyomene (another *Mauberley* character), Cockneys, a typist in a bedsit, and a 'low' clerk. The Pound colouring in these sketches did not suit Eliot. Where Pound is exuberant in his disgust, Eliot becomes callow or vitriolic—and Pound himself recognised this in his comment on typist and clerk who couple like 'crawling bugs': 'Too easy', he scribbled in the margin. Eliot's characters are not as realistic as Pound's. They are projections of Eliot's

5. 'Exequy' and 'The Fire Sermon' are typed with Eliot's brother's typewriter on yellowish sheets with a 'Verona' watermark. The carbon of 'The Fire Sermon', with Pound's marginalia in pencil, was clearly shown first. Eliot then revised the top copy in accordance with Pound's suggestions before submitting it for further consideration on his return from Lausanne.
6. In an appendix to a biography of Nancy Cunard, Anne Chisholm suggests that she could have been a source for Eliot's Fresca: his 'bitterness may be explained by the contrast between the struggles of Eliot and his wife against illness and poverty, and the affluent, leisured existence of Nancy'; also by 'the ease with which the well-connected amateur, Nancy, found publishers and respectful reviewers for her poems'. TSE had met Nancy several times by 1921, and Vivienne's 1919 diary mentions her presence at an evening the Eliots spent with the Hutchinsons, when Osbert Sitwell and Duncan Grant were also guests.
7. Pound changed 'When Lil's husband was coming out of the Transport Corps' to 'When Lil's husband was demobbed', and suggested that Mr Eugenides should not issue his invitation to lunch in 'abominable' but in 'demotic French'.

consciousness—they could be termed humours.[8] Unlike the satirist, Eliot does not criticise an actual world but creates a 'phantasmal' world of lust, filth, boredom, and malice on which he gazes in fascinated horror. *The Waste Land* is about a psychological hell in which someone is quite alone, 'the other figures in it/Merely projections'.

In 1921 Eliot deliberately played down the loner's voice, and transferred the weight of his poem to the Voices of Society. He had Dickens in mind, the panoramic range of *Our Mutual Friend*, where disconnected fragments of lives on the river and all over London gradually cohere in the horror of the reader.[9] In *The Waste Land* there is no longer a central figure, like Narcissus or Gerontion, hovering between the remote role of religious candidate and a more immediate despair. Yet the medley of voices is put on, even mocking, for the lone voice is never wholly submerged. Stripped of divine love in 'The Death of Saint Narcissus', stripped of marital love in 'The Death of the Duchess', stripped of misplaced fame in 'Exequy', it is the voice of a dissembling ghost, without stable shape. In the guise of St Augustine he repents sexual excess. And in the form of a poet who has misused his gift and buried himself in suburbia, he pleads pity for his pain: 'SOVENHA VOS A TEMPS DE MA DOLOR.'[1]

* * *

HELEN GARDNER

The Waste Land: Paris 1922[†]

Fifty years ago last October *The Waste Land* appeared in the first number of *The Criterion*, and later in the same month Eliot packed up and posted to John Quinn, the wealthy New York banker, as token of his gratitude for Quinn's generous patronage and help, a parcel. It contained what Eliot described as "the MSS of the Waste Land . . . when I say MSS, I mean that it is partly MSS and partly typescript, with Ezra's and my alterations scrawled all over it."[1] This famous collection

8. See Eliot on the comedy of humours, *Sacred Wood*, pp. 112, 116. In the essay on Ben Jonson, Eliot writes of characters that conform to the logic of their creator's emotions. Each character is 'a simplified and somewhat distorted individual with a typical mania'.
9. Eliot used a snatch of *Our Mutual Friend*, 'He do the Police in Different Voices', as his title on typescripts of parts I and II. He refers to the orphan Sloppy, who read the newspaper statements of London policemen 'in different voices'.
1. "In due time be heedful of my pain" (Provençal). Dante, *Purgatorio* 26. See note to l. 427 of the *Waste Land* text [*Editor*].
† From *Eliot in His Time: Essays on the Occasion of the Fiftieth Anniversary of "The Waste Land*," ed. A. Walton Litz (Princeton: Princeton University Press, 1973), pp. 67–94. Copyright © 1973 by Helen Gardner. Reprinted by permission of Princeton University Press.
1. Quotations from Eliot's letters for which no reference is given are taken from Mrs. Eliot's introduction to *The Waste Land: A Facsimile and Transcript* (1971).

of documents was thought to have been lost, since it was not in the Quinn sale, nor was it referred to in his will. In fact it passed to his sister and from her to her daughter, Quinn's niece, to end up in 1958 in the Berg Collection in the New York Public Library. The curator, for reasons that remain obscure, did not announce its presence there until 1968. It was finely edited in facsimile with transcripts, notes, and introduction by Mrs. Valerie Eliot in time for the jubilee of the poem. Everything I have to say is dependent on Mrs. Eliot's work. Her skill in deciphering and identifying hands, her admirably succinct and informative introduction, and her notes, as remarkable for the research they embody as for their splendid economy, make this edition a distinguished feat of scholarship.

We speak, for convenience, of the "manuscript of *The Waste Land*." But we should be careful not to speak of "the first version," as if what we have here is a kind of "*Ur-Waste Land*." Nor should we speak of "the original version." There is only one version of *The Waste Land*, and that is the published text. We are not faced here with anything like the two versions of *The Rape of the Lock* or *The Dunciad*, or the two versions that exist of many of Yeats's early poems, or of the poems of Wordsworth and Auden. In all these cases poems their authors thought of as finished, and had presented to the world as finished, they later decided to alter and revise. The material Eliot sent to Quinn was not a first or original version in any sense. It was working material of very varied kinds: manuscript first drafts, fragments of manuscript drafts, manuscript fair copies, typed drafts, typed copies, carbons; and he included with drafts of the poem drafts of other unpublished poems and unfinished fragments on which he had drawn for lines and passages, three of which he had worked up into fair copies, thinking to publish them as a kind of appendix to *The Waste Land*.

The chronology of the writing of *The Waste Land* is obscure, even with the help of Mrs. Eliot's introduction. It seems likely that it will always remain so. Pound is dead, and it is all fifty years ago. Eliot's own summary statement was made in a tribute to Pound in 1946 where he wrote, "It was in 1922 that I placed before him in Paris the manuscript of a sprawling chaotic poem called *The Waste Land* which left his hands reduced to about half its size, in the form in which it appears in print."[2] Eliot was not here concerned to give a detailed account of the writing of *The Waste Land*; but to pay tribute to Pound. And when, in June 1922, Eliot wrote to Quinn "I have written, mostly when I was at Lausanne for treatment last winter, a long poem of about 450 words [he meant, of course, *lines*]," he was again not concerned to give an accurate account of the poem's gestation but to discuss its publication.

---

2. "Ezra Pound," *Poetry Chicago* (September 1946), reprinted *New English Weekly* (31 October, 7 November 1946).

The first we hear of *The Waste Land* is at the end of 1919. Eliot, who had referred in a letter to Quinn of 5 November to "a poem I have in mind," wrote to his mother in December that his New Year resolution for 1920 was "to write a long poem I have had on my mind for a long time." But through almost all of 1920 he was occupied with preparing *The Sacred Wood* for the press and with checking its proofs. It appeared in November 1920. By May of 1921 he was able to inform Quinn that "a long poem" that he was "wishful to finish" was now "partly on paper." The words "wishful to finish," as well as "partly on paper" suggest that a substantial portion of the poem was extant by May 1921 either in holograph or typed. By September, however, after a gruelling summer, his health was so bad that his wife arranged for him to see a specialist who declared that he must go away for three months alone. His friend Conrad Aiken, who was living in London in the autumn of 1921, tells us that Eliot told him "although every evening he went home to his flat hoping that he could start writing again, and with every confidence that the material was *there* and waiting, night after night, the hope proved illusory: the sharpened pencil lay unused by the untouched sheet of paper."[3] Lloyds gave him three months' sick leave, and he went in mid-October to Margate, and then in November, via Paris, where he left his wife, to a clinic in Lausanne for treatment. Pound had been settled in Paris since June and no doubt Eliot saw him on his way through. It is possible that Eliot showed him the chaotic poem he had been working on at Margate; but Mrs. Eliot tells me that she thinks it unlikely that he lingered in Paris on his way to Lausanne, as he was anxious to begin treatment as soon as possible. After all, he had only three months' leave and one month of it had already been spent at Margate. In early January 1922 Eliot returned to London via Paris, and on this occasion he stopped for some days with Pound. On 21 February Pound wrote to Quinn: "Eliot came back from his Lausanne specialist looking OK; and with a damn good poem (19 pages) in his suitcase; same finished up here."

The description of the poem as being "19 pages" echoes the famous letter of Pound to Eliot dated by Pound "Paris, 24 Saturnus, An I," interpreted by Paige as 24 December 1921. Until I had the privilege of a preview of Professor Kenner's article,[4] I had ignorantly accepted Paige's date and found it very puzzling. I now gratefully acknowledge that his authoritative correction of the date to 24 January 1922 clears up some, though not all, of my difficulties. As he rightly observes, by no feat of juggling can one arrive at 19 pages from the typed drafts. Eliot must have retyped the poem, in accordance with decisions that

3. "An Anatomy of Melancholy," in *T. S. Eliot the Man and His Work,* edited Allen Tate, *Sewanee Review* (January to March 1966), and Chatto and Windus (London, 1967), p. 195.
4. Hugh Kenner, "The Urban Apocalypse," in *Eliot in His Time,* pp. 23–49 [*Editor*].

he and Pound had reached in Paris, when he returned to London and posted this retyping, or a carbon of it, to Pound in Paris for further comment. If this is so, it makes Pound's statement to Quinn that Eliot came back from Lausanne with "a damn good poem (19 pages)" hardly accurate. But what are we to make of Pound's final words: "Same finished up here"? They seem hardly an adequate description of the drastic cutting and rewriting presented by the drafts. The accepted legend of Pound and Eliot sitting down together in one long marathon session in Paris in January 1922 to carve *The Waste Land* out of chaos hardly tallies with Pound's description of what happened there as a "finishing up."

In his letter of "24 Saturnus, An I," enthusiastically acknowledging the revised poem as "MUCH improved," Pound advised that the "remaining superfluities," that is, the shorter poems Eliot had thought of printing with *The Waste Land,* should be abolished; or, if Eliot felt that he must keep them, they should be at the beginning of the volume. For, he declared, "The thing now runs from 'April . . .' to 'shantih' without a break. That is 19 pages, and let us say the longest poem in the English langwidge. Don't try to bust all records by prolonging it three pages further."[5] He concluded with his little self-congratulatory squib on himself as Eliot's man-midwife, the poem headed

SAGE HOMME

These are the poems of Eliot
By the Uranian Muse begot;
A Man their Mother was,
A Muse their Sire.

How did the printed Infancies result
From Nuptials thus doubly difficult?
If you must needs enquire
Know diligent Reader
That on each occasion
Ezra performed the caesarian Operation.

What Pound and Eliot did in their January meeting in Paris when the poem was "finished up," and in correspondence when the revised manuscript seems to have shuffled to and fro between London and Paris may have been only the culmination of a longer process of criticism and discussion than is usually supposed. I suspect that it was a long and difficult pregnancy and birth that Pound assisted at.

I have not seen the original documents, and they have not been subjected to intensive examination. One would like to know what kinds of paper were used and what, if discoverable, were their origins. No

5. *Letters of Ezra Pound,* edited D. D. Paige (1941), pp. 233–34.

doubt the kind of experts who testified in the Hiss case[6] could tell us not only about the different typewriters used but also whether all the typed drafts were typed by the same person. But from the study of the facsimile I should like to make some tentative suggestions. It seems likely to me that when Eliot went to the Albemarle Hotel at Margate in October 1921 he took with him the typed drafts of Parts I and II and the greater part of Part III, which breaks off a few lines after the episode of the typist. (Professor Kenner points out that these were typed on two different typewriters: the unfinished Part III on typewriter A and Parts I and II on typewriter B.) I presume he also had with him a bundle of drafts and fragments of unworked-up poems, mostly in manuscript, but three of them typed, the longest, "The Death of the Duchess," being typed on typewriter B. There exists no typescript of the close of "The Fire Sermon"—the song of the daughters of the Thames, and their speeches—and for Parts IV and V have Eliot's manuscripts, and typed copies of them made on a third machine and typed with a violet ribbon that Mrs. Eliot tells us was used by Pound. Whether Pound himself typed them, or Eliot did so on Pound's typewriter, it is impossible to guess. But it looks as if when Eliot wrote the close of "The Fire Sermon" and Parts IV and V he had not access to a typewriter. The long cancelled section (83 lines) that preceded the lyric on Phlebas the Phoenician is, with the lyric, very carefully and beautifully written out by Eliot in what is plainly a neat fair copy. He would hardly have taken all this trouble to write so neatly and clearly if he had had a typewriter available. The last section, "What the Thunder Said," on the other hand, is an untitled first draft, remarkably free until the close of any alteration or revision. This section we know was written at Lausanne, for Eliot said he was describing his own experience in writing it when he wrote in his essay on Pascal that some forms of illness were extremely favourable to literary composition, and added: "A piece of writing meditated, apparently without progress, for months or years, may suddenly take shape and word; and in this state long passages may be produced which require little or no retouch."[7] The draft strikingly exemplifies poetry that in this way "just came."

The question that teases me is when did Pound make the criticisms, comments, excisions, and queries that abound in the typescripts of the first three parts. Eliot could have posted his poem as far as it had gone from Margate and picked it up in Paris on his way to Lausanne. Or he could have left it with Pound in Paris on his way to Lausanne and Pound could have posted it to him there with comments and markings. But I wonder. Throughout 1920 and 1921 Pound was deeply concerned

6. Celebrated and still controversial prosecution of Alger Hiss, a State Department official, for perjury in 1950 [*Editor*].
7. *Essays Ancient and Modern* (1936), p. 142.

with Eliot's unhappy, even desperate, situation, and he was to and fro between London and the Continent. I cannot believe that if, as Eliot wrote to Quinn in May 1921, his "long poem" was by then "partly on paper" he had not shown what was there to Pound and discussed it with him. Pound's markings and comments may not all have been made at the same time. On some portions he has used both ink and pencil, and the marks themselves are of different kinds. Some are explanatory, making clear what the reader's objection is, as if they were to be communicated by post. Others are marks which suggest that a word or passage needs to be thought over or discussed: queries, boxing in of a word, or a squiggle against a line or word. These are the kind of marks one makes on a piece of work one is going to hand back to the author in person. The long unpublished poem "The Death of the Duchess," which Eliot quarried in for "A Game of Chess," is heavily annotated by Pound in the same kind of way as the typed drafts of *The Waste Land* are. Pound must have worked on this typescript before Eliot decided to use part of this poem for Part II, "A Game of Chess," and not go on with it. But "A Game of Chess" was read and commented on by Vivien Eliot and so must have been typed before Eliot went to Lausanne. I cannot help believing that when Eliot at last had a respite and time to give his mind to his long meditated long poem at Margate, some at least of Pound's criticisms were already there to be digested and absorbed for the rewriting of what had been written and for the completion of the whole at Lausanne. It seems possible that some of Pound's criticisms were made before the period of block that Aiken refers to, when Eliot found himself unable to go on with his poem.

It is impossible to overestimate Eliot's debt to Pound, but it needs defining. Without Pound *The Waste Land* would have been very different from what it is; but we should not therefore assume that it would necessarily have been like the drafts, and that Eliot himself would not have drastically revised it before publication, as he revised his later poems. * * * We should not assume that without Pound Eliot would have published some of the weaker passages in the drafts. But, as soon as one says this, one must add that it is highly doubtful whether, without Pound, *The Waste Land* would have been completed and published at all. The most important thing Pound gave Eliot was the support of a constant affection, encouragement, and belief. And he gave it at a time of deep discouragement verging on despair. It seems almost a miracle when one considers the circumstances in which the poem was written that it was written at all. To Eliot, struggling in ill health and overwork to combine two obligations—his sense of his vocation as a poet, and his duty to the unhappy girl he had married, who was dependent on him—Pound's unwavering belief in his friend's genius was the stimulus without which he might not have found the courage to persevere. But in addition to his selfless promotion of Eliot's interests as man and poet, Pound showed, for all his bluster and boisterousness, his slashings and damnings, an extreme selflessness and sensitivity in the kind of criticism he gave. He concentrated on making the poem as good as Eliot could make it. He gave his whole mind to the problem of "Was this good verse?" "Is this the right word?" "Does this strike a false note?" "Is this becoming monotonous?" He makes no comment on the subject matter of the poem, its religious or philosophic views, its lack of those "life-enhancing" qualities whose absence later critics have deplored. It was Eliot's poem he was working on.[8] He shows his genius as a critic in the applause he gives—"Echt," "OK"—to the most characteristically Eliotian lines and passages. One's heart rises as one sees his "Stet" or "OK." Vivien Eliot, like some of those to whom Eliot showed his later poems, suggested words. She even supplied two lines, and good ones. But Pound, with the exception of the word "demotic," which he supplied on a carbon of "The Fire Sermon," and the word "demobbed" —here Mrs. Eliot tells me she is not absolutely certain it was his suggestion and he has not pencilled over a suggestion of Vivien Eliot's[9]— was content with scoring through or boxing in, or querying words and phrases he thought struck a false note, without proposing improvements. He expressed disquiet, or disapproval, and left it to Eliot to solve his own problems. His little *jeu d'esprit* just quoted was perfectly accurate. He was the midwife: the child that emerged into life was Eliot's. And Eliot found the right words in Dante when he saluted Pound as *il miglior fabbro*, the better craftsman.

Eliot said that when he used this phrase he did not mean to imply that Pound was only a craftsman; but he wanted in dedicating his poem to him to "honour the technical mastery and critical ability manifest in his own work, which had also done so much to turn *The Waste Land* from a jumble of good and bad passages into a poem."[1] This is a very good description of Pound's major surgery. Before the drafts turned up there was a general belief that Pound was responsible for the form of the poem, and that "all the transitions—or lack of them" in the poem "were due to the editor."[2] This is clearly not so. The famous inconsequence or discontinuity was there from the beginning and Pound's reduction did not turn an ordered sequence of action or

8. The publication of the drafts fully confirms Eliot's tribute to Pound as a critic: "He was a marvellous critic because he didn't try to turn you into an imitation of himself. He tried to see what you were trying to do." (*Paris Review Interviews*, reprinted in *Writers at Work*, introduced by Van Wyck Brooks, 2nd series, 1963, pp. 79–84.)
9. Mrs. Eliot tells me she thinks the writing is Vivien's, but that Pound believes that he supplied the word.
1. "On a Recent Piece of Criticism," *Purpose* x, 2 (April to June 1938).
2. See, for instance, Charles Norman, *Ezra Pound* (revised edition, 1969), p. 251. Eliot himself had made the position clear in his *Paris Review* interview in 1959, when, in response to the query, "Did the excisions change the intellectual structure of the poem?" he replied: "No, I think it was just as structureless, only in a more futile way, in the longer poem."

thought into a cryptic puzzle. It was not linking passages that he removed. There never were any links in the poem as Eliot conceived it.
At times, Pound, in his passion for concision, for packing meaning and
omitting connectives that have syntactical or explanatory but not con-
notative functions, has left some phrases or lines obscure; but the major
difficulty, the major originality, of *The Waste Land* was inherent in it
from the beginning. It was, as originally drafted, to be a poem in violently contrasting styles which were to be juxtaposed, a poem of episodes following each other without narrative consequence, of allusions
and quotations that drift across the mind. Its unity was to derive from
its underlying theme of sterility, disordered desire, and impotent longing. Lines from unpublished poems and from fragments of poems jotted
down and never worked up, some written many years before, came
together in Eliot's mind, with memories of incidents, some perhaps
long buried, some recent, and with reminiscences and echoes from
older poets. It was enough that they were all related to a central core
of profound feeling, a feeling summed in the title *The Waste Land.* It
is uncertain when the poem acquired this title—possibly very late. But
the title is its sum.

Eliot himself was responsible for the first big cut. Parts I and II in
the typescript drafts have a general title that links them. They are
headed "He Do the Police in Different Voices, Part I and Part II." I
suppose this is another and unpoetical way of saying "I Tiresias have
foresuffered all." The poem was to be an exercise in ventriloquism.
The poet, like Sloppy reading to Betty Higden in *Our Mutual Friend,*[3]
is behind all the voices of men and women we are to be asked to listen
to. The first part began with a passage of fifty-four lines in loose blank
verse, describing a male night-out in Boston. This would seem a bold
but unsuccessful experiment, inspired by *Ulysses,* to see whether the
kind of material Joyce was engaged in incorporating into the novel
could be made available also for poetry. It is a mild version of a visit
to Night-town.[4] *Ulysses* had been appearing in the *Little Review* and
had made an immense impression on Eliot, and in some ways in *The
Waste Land* he was attempting to do for poetry what Joyce had done
for the novel. This description of the night-out in Boston is the prelude
to the first part as we know it. We pass without transition from this
vulgar male voice to the lamenting, meditative voice of "April is the
cruellest month." Part II, then, reversed this pattern, beginning with
the elaborate poetical passage which is the setting for the Lady of Situations and ending with the vulgar female voice of poor Lil's false

---

3. In Chapter 16 of Charles Dickens's *Our Mutual Friend* (1864–65), Betty Higden, who runs
   a home for foundlings, praises the way that Sloppy, one of her charges, reads the newspaper
   aloud: "He do the Police in different voices" [*Editor*].
4. A reference to James Joyce's *Ulysses,* Chapter 15, which takes place in Dublin's red-light
   district [*Editor*].

friend in the pub. Eliot himself drew a pencil line through the Boston passage. As there are no comments by Pound on it, Eliot had presumably decided to drop it before he showed any of his poem to Pound. It leaves the passage about Lil and Albert as the one example of the low colloquial in the poem, the more effective for its uniqueness. From here on Eliot seems to have abandoned a rather over-schematic plan. The excision of the Boston opening also makes the poem open not with a mere episode but with the announcement of its true subject: "memory and desire."

Two other major cuts we owe to Pound. For his third section, headed "The Fire Sermon," as in the second section, "A Game of Chess," and the original draft of the fourth section, Eliot began with literary parody, opening it with some seventy lines in couplets devoted to Fresca, a fashionable lady with aesthetic and literary pretensions. On the carbon copy of this Pound has scrawled his objections: "Too loose"—"rhyme drags it out to diffuseness"—"trick of Pope etc not to let couple[t] diffuse 'em." On the top copy he has marked only an occasional word with brackets, or by boxing it in, before crossing out, with slashing strokes, as if he quickly saw the passage was beyond help. Eliot said, rather ruefully, in 1928 that Pound had induced him to destroy "what I thought an excellent set of couplets," "for," said he, "Pope has done this so well that you cannot do it better; and if you mean this as a burlesque, you had better suppress it, for you cannot parody Pope unless you can write better verse than Pope—and you can't."[5] Eliot accepted Pound's deletion of the whole passage and substituted the present evocative opening of the third part "The river's tent is broken!" It is written in pencil on the verso of the first leaf of the typescript. It breaks off with "By the waters," leaving us uncertain whether this passage was written at Margate and completed at Lausanne by the extension of the line to "By the waters of Leman I sat down and wept" or wholly at Lausanne. This revives the tone of the opening lines of the poem after our excursion into the world of Lil and Albert. It shows Eliot beginning to draw the poem together and moving away from its original ventriloquial base.

Pound's second major cut was his reduction of Part IV to the brief lyric on Phlebas the Phoenician. Eliot had written out "Part IV" in a beautiful, neat, fair copy, with the title "Death by Water," dividing it by asterisks into three sections. The first section consisted of three quatrains on the sailor:

> The sailor, attentive to the chart or to the sheets,
> A concentrated will against the tempest and the tide,
> Retains, even ashore, in public bars or streets
> Something inhuman, clean and dignified.

5. Introduction to *Selected Poems* of Ezra Pound (1928).

Even the drunken ruffian who descends
Illicit backstreet stairs, to reappear,
For the derision of his sober friends,
Staggering, or limping with a comic gonorrhea,

From his trade with wind and sea and snow, as they
Are, he is, with 'much seen and much endured',
Foolish, impersonal, innocent or gay,
Liking to be shaved, combed, scented, manucured.

Against these quatrains Pound has written "Bad—but cant attack until I get typescript." The second section is a first-person narrative (seventy-one lines) in blank verse, parodying Tennysonian narrative blank verse, telling of a voyage, setting its course from the Dry Salvages, and sailing to the eastern banks to fish cod. It ends with shipwreck. The third section is the Phlebas lyric. On the typescript, typed with his violet ribbon, Pound has made an initial attempt to break up the quatrains and the regularity of the blank verse before deciding, as with the couplets on Fresca, that the passage was beyond salvage. He crossed through, leaving only Phlebas intact. When Eliot was back in London he wrote to Pound with various queries and among them: "Perhaps better omit Phlebas too??" To which Pound replied: "I DO advise keeping Phlebas. In fact I more'n advise. Phlebas is an integral part of the poem; the card pack introduces him, the drowned phoen. sailor. And he is needed ABsolootly where he is. Must stay in."[6] The lines on Phlebas are a free translation of the close of the French poem "Dans le Restaurant" which Eliot had published in his 1920 volume. Reappearing in Madame Sosostris's wicked pack of cards, the Phoenician sailor is gathered up, like so much of Eliot's early poetry and life, into *The Waste Land*, and as Pound rightly saw is needed absolutely where he is. Eliot's intense feeling for the sea, and for sailing and sailors, expressed in the long cancelled passage, found later and more adequate expression at the close of *Ash Wednesday*, in *Marina*, and finally in *The Dry Salvages*. In *The Waste Land* it gave him a beautiful passage, one of the few happy memories in the poem, at the close:

> The boat responded
> Gaily, to the hand expert with sail and oar
> The sea was calm, your heart would have responded
> Gaily, when invited, beating obedient
> To controlling hands.

One shorter passage that Pound struck out, writing a rude word against it in the typescript, was an address to London that gave Eliot

6. *Letters of Ezra Pound*, p. 237.

much trouble. It stands in the typescript between the episode with Mr. Eugenides and the episode of the typist. On a separate sheet there is a pencil draft of two apostrophes to London. At the top is the passage beginning "O City, City, I have heard and hear / The pleasant whining of a mandoline." Then after a line drawn across the paper comes a much-worked-over draft of this second apostrophe. Presumably Eliot composed the two passages at much the same time—they contrast in mood—and put them on one side to await a place for them in the poem. I rather regret that Eliot accepted Pound's advice here and did not instead struggle to improve a potentially impressive vision of London as a city of automata, its people "bound upon the wheel," "Phantasmal gnomes," only alive in "the awareness of the observing eye," which sees them as "pavement toys." It picks up the vision of the crowd flowing over London Bridge at the close of the first part, and makes a break between the two episodes of Mr. Eugenides and the typist, as the "O City, City" passage was to do between the close of the typist episode and the song of the daughters of the Thames.

These were Pound's major cuts. They accord with Eliot's tribute to him for turning "a jumble of good and bad passages into a poem." But in addition to the removing of the couplets on Fresca, with their feeble social satire, the slackly written narrative of the shipwreck, and the over-rhetorical apostrophe to London, Pound worked hard revising, and in one case severely reducing, two passages. The most striking is the famous episode of the typist, a passage that greatly impressed the poem's first readers but that seems less impressive today. This episode originally consisted of seventeen regular quatrains (sixty-eight lines) and was reduced by Eliot, largely in accordance with Pound's criticism, to some forty lines. Pound worked on both a typescript and a carbon, the carbon apparently first, since the typescript has a note "vide other copy." His general comment was "Verse not interesting enough as verse to warrant so much of it." His revision had two ends in view. He worked to destroy the regularity of the quatrains, which after the revision only establish themselves at the climax of the passage, the rhymes at the beginning being irregular, and he worked to reduce what seemed to him irrelevant and sometimes contradictory social detail. Eliot, while accepting the general line of Pound's criticism, did not accept it in all its details. Pound, showing an unexpected modesty, struck out the typist's "stays," which Eliot retained: though he accepted Pound's comment "probably over the mark" and deleted the young man's original exit lines:

> And at the corner where the stable is,
> Delays only to urinate, and spit.

He preserved, in spite of Pound's striking it out, the description of the young man which has set some sensitive critics' teeth on edge:

> One of the low on whom assurance sits
> As a silk hat on a Bradford millionaire.

But Pound's power to recognize the excellent appears again when he comes to the last six stanzas. Apart from the two lines that dismiss the young man, he leaves them, with an "Echt" against the Tiresias quatrain, and only an explosion at the use of "may" in the line "Across her brain one half-formed thought may pass": "Make up yr mind you Tiresias if you know know damn well or else you dont." He had made a similar comment earlier "Perhaps be damned."

The other passage Pound worked hard on is the opening of "A Game of Chess." Here again he disliked the regularity of the metre: "Too tum-pum at a stretch" he wrote against the first three lines, and later on "too penty," presumably meaning too much pentameter. The latter is his comment on the line "Filled all the desert with inviolable voice," where he boxed in the word "inviolable." Luckily Eliot ignored this and did not destroy this beautiful line. Pound was concerned to break up the even movement of the pentameters and in doing so to tighten, condense, and concentrate, by removing connectives and explanatory phrases and clauses. Thus he took out the words "Upon the hearth" in the lines

> Upon the hearth huge sea-wood fed with copper
> Burned green and orange, framed by the coloured stone.

They are unnecessary. One can see the weakness of

> Above the antique mantel was displayed
> In pigment, but so lively, you had thought
> A window gave upon the sylvan scene,
> The change of Philomel. . . .

Pound scored through "but so lively, you had thought" with the comment "had is the weakest point." Eliot retrenched three lines to two, making his second an alexandrine, thus simultaneously condensing and making the rhythm more flexible:

> Above the antique mantel was displayed
> As though a window gave upon the sylvan scene
> The change of Philomel. . . .

Similarly the original lines

> And still she cried (and still the world pursues)
> Jug-Jug, into the dirty ear of [death] lust;

are less impressive than " 'Jug-Jug' to dirty ears."

At times in his passion for loading every rift with ore Pound left lines that are rather cryptic. I was puzzled for years over what was meant by

> And other withered stumps of time
> Were told upon the walls,

though one can see why Pound objected to the lines in the draft:

> And other tales, from the old stumps and bloody ends of time
> Were told upon the walls.

In some of Pound's criticisms and deletions one is aware of a certain lack of response to some strains in Eliot's poetry. His objection to "inviolable" shows a resistance seen elsewhere to the romantic and tender strain in the poem. Thus he also scored out "forgetful" in the lines

> Winter kept us warm, covering
> Earth in forgetful snow.

This may have been an objection to a transferred epithet; but he also placed his squiggles and a query against

> 'You gave me hyacinths first a year ago;
> They called me the hyacinth girl.'

He put against this the cryptic word "Marianne." He deleted the bracketed quotation that follows Madame Sosostris's production of the card of the drowned Phoenician sailor: "(Those are pearls that were his eyes. Look!).'" On these occasions Eliot resisted; but he acquiesced in Pound's removal of another quotation that also comments on Madame Sosostris's visions:

> I see crowds of people walking round in a ring.
> (I John saw these things and heard them).

He also boxed in the word "little" in a line Eliot dropped; an unspoken response of the silent man to the woman's insistent questions in "A Game of Chess":

> 'What is that noise now? What is the wind doing?' Carrying
> Away the little light dead people.

Presumably Pound felt "little" to be a trifle sentimental. The lines are, as Mrs. Eliot says, a reminiscence of Dante's Paolo and Francesca who "go together and seem so light upon the wind." I regret their loss.

Pound seems to have had rather a down on city churches: he scored through

> To where Saint Mary Woolnoth kept the time
> With a dead sound on the final stroke of nine,

which Eliot mercifully kept and also the three lines with which the typescript of "The Fire Sermon" breaks off:

Fading at last, behind the flying feet,
There where the tower was traced against the night
Of Michael Paternoster Royal, red and white.

Eliot gave up St. Michael Paternoster Royal, but gave us St. Magnus
Martyr instead in a passage that we have only in draft on which Pound
has not worked. Again where Pound rightly objected to Madame Sosostris saying "I look in vain," which is an impossible locution for her,
it is odd that he also objected to "there you feel free" in the line "In
the mountains, there you feel free," where the cliché has great pathos.
Here again Eliot resisted the cut.

It is natural to concentrate first on Pound's work on the drafts. There
is, I think, no other example in literature of a poet submitting his work
for criticism to another poet of equal stature and accepting radical
criticism. It was Eliot's habit to submit his work to the criticism of his
friends, or, with his plays, to the criticism of producers and actors. He
was able to accept Pound's surgery gratefully because they shared a
common belief in poetry as an art demanding severe discipline and in
the poem as a thing made with care and skill. So, later on, if a friend
queried a word or line, he accepted with seriousness and humility that
the query suggested there was some fault in his making, that the word
or line lacked exactness, clarity, or force. Apart from Pound, the only
person who worked on *The Waste Land* was his wife, to whom for
obvious reasons he submitted "A Game of Chess." It says much for her
that she applauded as wonderful what Pound queried as a too photographic, that is realistic, presentation of a failed marriage relation. He
took out, at her request, only one line: "The ivory men make company
between us." In the monologue that follows he adopted two lines she
supplied, "If you don't like it you can get on with it" and "What you
get married for if you don't want to have children." Her ear for cockney
was much better than his. But Pound's criticism goes far beyond anything any of Eliot's friends later could attempt, for none of them had
Pound's authority. The drafts he has worked over are a unique record
of the normal interplay between creation and criticism that results in
a poem taking place in two minds instead of in the single mind of the
creator-critic.

But in addition to the drafts Pound worked on we have also some of
Eliot's own first drafts, some going back a long way. Two of these, which
Mrs. Eliot says would seem to have been written in 1914, or even earlier
made their contribution to the fifth part "What the Thunder Said,"
written at Lausanne, and, as the draft shows, written with extraordinary
ease. These early fragments point very clearly to the nature of Eliot's
gift: his power over the phrase or line, for lines of startling beauty and
originality appear in them; and the fleeting and fragmentary nature of
his inspiration, which seems always to have come in jets or spurts,

which would last as long as a certain rhythm lasted. A brief early poem, for instance, supplied the first line of "What the Thunder Said" and set up the tune of its first paragraph. In the early poem it is a monotonous tune:

> After the turning of the inspired days
> After the praying and the silence and the crying
> And the inevitable ending of a thousand ways
> And frosty vigil kept in withered gardens
> After the life and death of lonely places
> After the judges and the advocates and wardens
> And the torchlight red on sweaty faces
> After the turning of inspired nights
> And the shaking spears and flickering lights—
> After the living and the dying—
> After the ending of this inspiration
> And the torches and the faces and the shouting
> The world seemed futile—like a Sunday outing.

This tune is beautifully modulated in the passage built upon it:

> After the torchlight red on sweaty faces
> After the frosty silence in the gardens,
> After the agony in stony places
> The shouting and the crying
> Prison and palace and reverberation
> Of thunder of spring over distant mountains
> He who was living is now dead
> We who were living are now dying
> With a little patience.

This ease and freedom when a tune, as it were, held him in its power can be seen in the almost perfectly clean first draft of the passage that follows, the twenty-nine lines of the passage through the waterless mountains followed by the hermit thrush's "water-dripping song," which Eliot thought the best lines in the poem.[7] It can also be seen in the again almost perfectly clean first draft of the song of the Thames daughters, built on the rhythm of Weiálalá/leiá. This contrasts strikingly with the speeches of the three daughters, which had to be moulded into their final moving form. The leaf containing their speeches is one of the few first drafts on which there are markings by Pound. Mrs. Eliot says they are in pencil and green crayon. I should like to know which are which. The first daughter, the girl from Highbury, was originally allowed a longish speech, giving her exact social position. To read it is

---

7. Eliot to Ford Madox Ford (14 August 1923): "There are I think about 30 *good* lines in *The Waste Land*. Can you find them? The rest is ephemeral." (4 October 1923): "As for the lines I mention you need not scratch your head over them. They are the 29 lines of the water-dripping song in the last part." (Correspondence in Cornell University Library.)

oddly like moving suddenly from *The Waste Land* to *The Confidential Clerk*, as the Fresca couplets anticipate *The Cocktail Party*.

> Highbury bore me. Highbury's children
> Played under green trees and in the dusty Park.
> Mine were humble people and conservative
> As neither the rich nor the working class know.
> My father had a small business, somewhere in the city
> A small business, an anxious business, providing only
> The house in Highbury, and three weeks at [Shanklin] *corrected to* Bognor
> Highbury bore me. Richmond and Kew
> Undid me. At Kew we had tea.
> [At] Near Richmond on the river at last
> [Stretched o] On the floor of a perilous canoe
> I raised my knees.

Eliot crossed this out; but Pound has written against it "Type this out *anyhow*." Beneath it Eliot has written four lines which Pound approved as "OK" and "echt":

> Trams and dusty trees.
> Highbury bore me. Richmond and Kew
> Undid me. [Beyond] By Richmond I raised my knees
> Stretched on the floor of a perilous canoe.

There is no typescript of this so one cannot tell when "Supine" replaced "Stretched on" or when the rather risky word "perilous," which might suggest to the ribald the danger of copulating in a canoe, was replaced by "narrow." The girl who walks the streets at Moorgate then gave little trouble for the form had been found; but on the verso of the sheet Eliot had trouble with the girl on Margate sands: he first wrote two lines "I was to be grateful." / "There were many others." He then crossed these out and replaced them with "On Margate sands / I can connect" and then went on "Nothing with nothing. He had." He then crossed out "He had" and wrote a fourth line "I still feel the pressure of dirty hand." Then the whole was crossed through, and what remained of the first three lines was written out below:

> On Margate Sands.
> I can connect
> Nothing with nothing.

The fourth line was transformed into an image:

> The broken finger nails of dirty hands,

and then a phrase was picked up from the cancelled speech of the girl from Highbury, a phrase that in its final form has lost its purely social connotation, and places the girl not in a social class but in the great class of Dostoevsky's "poor folk," the "insulted and injured":

> My people [are plain] humble people, who expect
> Nothing.

One sees in Eliot's drafts two things, his natural lyricism on the one hand, and a process by which from a rather pedestrian passage words, phrases, lines are rescued to produce brief concise passages pregnant with meaning.

The bad passages that Pound cut out and the weak ones he reduced are passages in which Eliot was attempting to write against the natural bent of his genius, trying to keep to a manner and a style over a longer span than was natural to him, and using a tune or rhythm, whether couplets, quatrains, or blank verse, that was not for him a voice of feeling. Much as I enjoy the brilliance and wit of the early poems in quatrain, they are virtuoso performances. I think those critics are right who see them as a kind of aberration, outside the real line of development of Eliot as a poet. For, as well as needing to find images in which feelings could be expressed, or around which feelings could cluster, the famous "objective correlatives," he had also to find a tune expressive of feeling, a rhythm that was as much an "objective correlative" as the image. In fact which came first, rhythm or image, is difficult to say. Eliot himself said in his lecture on *The Music of Poetry* that he knew that "a poem, or a passage of a poem may tend to realize itself first as a particular rhythm before it reaches expression in words, and that this rhythm may bring to birth the idea and the image." When Eliot made up his mind to write a long poem, perhaps urged on by his wife, who was ambitious for his success, as well as by a natural desire to spread his wings and undertake a longer flight, he invented a form that allowed him to compose in the jets and spurts of inspiration that came naturally to him, and, like a worker in mosaic, to find a place in his pattern for lines and even passages that had been composed at very different times. The discovery that poems written separately were beginning to cohere together and could be brought together as the beginning or nucleus of a long poem was a recurring feature of Eliot's career. *The Hollow Men* began with Doris's Dream Songs, *Ash Wednesday* began as three separate poems, and in the final sequence of six their order was altered. *Burnt Norton* was conceived as an independent poem, and itself developed from a passage cut from *Murder in the Cathedral*. It was only during the writing of *East Coker* as a second poem on the model of *Burnt Norton* that the idea of *Four Quartets* took shape. *The Waste Land* differs from these later examples of poems that were not planned but grew. In this case Eliot had decided to write a long poem, and found that poems written long since, fragments, and lines "belonged" to its theme, and would blend, contrast with, and amplify the poem he conceived. But, and I think one must connect this with exhaustion and the flagging inspiration that preceded or possibly precipitated his breakdown, he attempted to fill out his poem and expand it by parodying the styles of other poets, not merely in lines, but in long passages. It is possible he was influenced here by the example of James Joyce in *Ulysses*, and wished his poem to go through English poetic styles as Joyce had gone through English prose styles in the section called "The Oxen of the Sun." For his parodies occur according to an historic scheme. Jacobean dramatists are parodied at the opening of "A Game of Chess," Pope and eighteenth-century narrative poems in quatrain in "The Fire Sermon," and nineteenth-century blank verse, first person, narrative poetry in "Death by Water." This was a false trail. Although Eliot was much addicted to parody I do not think he was a good parodist—his own idiosyncratic voice is too strong to be disguised. Pound rightly saw that the parodies were weak in themselves and also that the tone of the whole poem was too serious to be able to accept extended passages of parody. I think one must assume from its existence in so carefully and neatly written a fair copy that the shipwreck story was written either at Margate or Lausanne, when Eliot took up his poem again, in order to complete the parodic series; but he found his own true voice again composing the close of "The Fire Sermon." And at Lausanne, in what, by his own evidence and the evidence of the drafts, was a single burst of inspiration, he crowned his poem with a last section that matches the beauty of the first and, as it should, transcends it. He discovered in writing this, in the water-dripping passage, a new style, a style that looks forward from *The Waste Land* to *The Hollow Men* and *Ash Wednesday*.

LAWRENCE RAINEY

The Price of Modernism: Publishing *The Waste Land*†

"History is a nightmare," wrote Joyce. "History has cunning passages, contrived corridors / And issues," murmured T. S. Eliot. It characterizes the epic, declared Pound, in a transparent reference to his own life's

† From Lawrence Rainey, "The Price of Modernism: Publishing *The Waste Land*," in *T. S. Eliot: The Modernist in History*, ed. Ronald Bush (Cambridge: Cambridge University Press, 1991), pp. 91–133. Copyright © 1991 by Lawrence Rainey. Reprinted by permission of Cambridge University Press. The author's notes have been edited.

work, *The Cantos*.[1] The modernists were obsessed with history. They mourned it and damned it, contested it as tenaciously as Jacob wrestling with the image of God: "I will not let thee go, except thou bless me." Yet if the deity of history had ever deigned to reply to them, it might have said: "Behold, I set before you this day a blessing and a curse." Modernism, scholars announced in 1965, had "passed into history." The comment appeared in the preface to a textbook; in part it was a historical description and in part a speech act enacting what it appeared to describe, a key moment in modernism's passage to academic respectability.[2] Today, of course, we confess that we live on the hither side of that moment. We take for granted modernism's place in the canon or even equate its progress among the professors with its trajectory through history. Yet in doing so, we forget that modernism flourished long before 1965, that it had erupted into the public consciousness at least forty years earlier, and that its status as a cultural resource had been secured by an array of institutions quite removed from the tepid confines of the academy. The event that epitomized this

1. References to libraries and their collections are made with the following abbreviations:
   BLUI, *PM.1*   Bloomington, Lilly Library, University of Indiana, Pound Mss. 1
   BLUI, *PM.2*   Bloomington, Lilly Library, University of Indiana, Pound Mss. 2
   BLUI, *PM.3*   Bloomington, Lilly Library, University of Indiana, Pound Mss. 3
   CHH   Cambridge, Houghton Library, Harvard University
   NHBY, *DP*   New Haven, Beinecke Library, Yale University, *Dial* Papers
   NHBY, *BP*   New Haven, Beinecke Library, Yale University, Bird Papers
   NYPL, *JQP*   New York Public Library, John Quinn Papers
   After the reference to the library and collection, further reference is made to (1) the catalogue or archival series, if relevant, (2) the box, if relevant, and (3) folder number or title, if relevant.

   References to names of correspondents are abbreviated as follows:
   TSE   T. S. Eliot, residing in London
   HL   Horace Liveright, residing in New York; in Paris from 29 December 1921 to 4 January 1922, in London 5 to 28 January 1922
   DSP   Dorothy Shakespear Pound, residing in Paris, but visiting in London from 13 July to late October
   EP   Ezra Pound, residing in Paris; traveling in Italy from 27 March to 2 July 1922
   JQ   John Quinn, lawyer in New York
   GS   Gilbert Seldes, managing editor of *The Dial*, in New York
   ST   Scofield Thayer, editor and co-owner of *The Dial*, in Vienna
   JSW   James Sibley Watson, Jr., co-owner of the *The Dial*, resident in New York but traveling in Europe (Paris, Berlin, Paris) in July–August, 1922

   The abbreviation *LOTSE 1* is used to cite: T. S. Eliot, *Letters of T. S. Eliot*, vol. 1, *1898–1922*, edited by Valerie Eliot (New York: Harcourt, Brace, Jovanovich, 1988). I wish to thank Patricia Willis, Curator for American Literature at the Beinecke Rare Book and Manuscript Library, for her assistance in facilitating consultation of the *Dial Papers*, and especially Diane Ducharmes for her help in locating specific materials.
   The following conventions are used for the transcription of letters and documents. All editorial interventions are placed between square brackets, [thus]. An illegible word is represented by a series of *x*'s approximating the number of letters in the word, and is placed between square brackets, [xxxx]. Authorial additions to a document are presented in angled brackets, with the additional words placed in italics, ⟨*thus*⟩.
   The quotations are from Joyce's *Ulysses*, Eliot's "Gerontion," and Pound's *Guide to Kulchur*.
2. Richard Ellmann and Charles Feidelson, Jr., eds., *The Modern Tradition: Backgrounds of Modern Literature* (New York: Oxford, 1965), vi. For helpful comments and suggestions about an earlier version of this paper, I wish to thank Ronald Bush, A. Walton Litz, Michael North, James Longenbach, Lyndall Gordon, and Jerome J. McGann.

process was the publication of *The Waste Land* in late 1922, which announced modernism's unprecedented triumph. It generated an avalanche of publicity that marked a crucial moment in its critical fortunes, establishing the poem as a reference point for the assessment of modernism by a wider public. Long before textbooks about it were written, popular and critical understanding of modernism had already been configured by a specific dynamics of transmission that characterized modernism's productive processes and grounded its extraordinary success. The complex events that culminated in the 1922 publication of *The Waste Land* articulated both its essential features and its contradictions. It behooves us to reconsider that earlier, more fractured moment, to reconnoiter the problematic terrain suggested by the preposition *into* in the phrase *into history*. For *into* evokes transition, a liminal moment attended by the possibility of failure, a risk that modernism's passage through the "contrived corridors" might have miscarried.

A core of basic facts about the publication of *The Waste Land* has long been known. In October 1922 it received quasi-simultaneous publication in two journals: *The Criterion* in England, on 16 October, and *The Dial* in the United States, on around 20 October (though in the November issue). In December it appeared in a third form as an independent volume including Eliot's explanatory notes, published by the American firm of Boni and Liveright.[3] Together these constituted an event that has become a staple in the legend of modernism's emergence and triumph. Yet a reconsideration of this event might begin by exploring not where the poem was ultimately published, but where it was *not* published: the witty, sophisticated pages of *Vanity Fair* or the intransigent leaves of *The Little Review*. Though neither has been discussed in connection with the release of *The Waste Land*, both were

---

3. For the English publication, see TSE to Henry Ware Eliot, 11 October 1922: "The *Criterion* is due to appear next Monday," or 16 October, in *LOTSE 1*, 580. See also TSE to Richard Cobden-Sanderson, 16 October 1922, in *LOTSE 1*, 582. The exact date of the American publication in *The Dial* is less clear. "We are to publish the text of the poem, without the notes, in the November Dial, which will be published about October 20th": copy of GS to HL, 7 September 1922. With a delay of perhaps one or two days, *The Dial* apparently met its schedule: Burton Rascoe reported that he received his copy of the November issue on Thursday, 26 October 1922. (See Burton Rascoe, "A Bookman's Day Book," *The New York Tribune*, 5 November 1922, section V, 8.) More mystery surrounds the exact date of the Liveright release. In a letter to Seldes of 12 September, Liveright confirmed that his firm was "not to publish The Waste Land prior to its appearance in The Dial," and speculated, "I don't think that we'll publish it before January." (Both in NHBY, *DP*, series 4, box 40, 1922.) However, it is clear that the book had already been typeset in August, for Eliot had received and corrected the proofs by 15 September (see *LOTSE 1*, 570), and by late October the volume must have needed only binding. Apparently Liveright hastened to release it on 15 December in order to capitalize on the publicity generated by the announcement of the Dial Award in its December issue (presumably released around 20 November). For the date, see Donald Gallup, *T. S. Eliot. A Bibliography* (London: Faber and Faber, 1969), A6, 29–32. For an earlier study on *The Waste Land*'s publication, see Daniel Woodward, "Notes on the Publishing History and Text of *The Waste Land*," *Papers of the Bibliographical Society of America* 58 (1964): 252–69.

considered as potential publishers at various points in 1922 as negotiations for the poem pursued a fragile, unpredictable course. And together these possibilities, with the untold stories that lie behind them,
serve to register a spectrum of the possibilities of modernist
publishing—a spectrum of how modernism negotiated its way among
the "contrived corridors" of its own production.

One might begin by examining an unnoticed occasion in early August 1922, when John Peale Bishop visited the Paris studio of Ezra
Pound. Two weeks earlier Bishop had resigned his post as managing
editor of *Vanity Fair*, and ostensibly he was traveling on an extended
honeymoon after his recent marriage. Unofficially, however, Bishop
had come to visit the savage god of modern experimentalism—and to
talk business.[4] The topic was the publication of *The Waste Land*, a
work that Bishop had never read, but whose vicissitudes he had been
following for five months. In early March, while still in New York and
laboring for *Vanity Fair*, he had received an article from Aldous Huxley
that reported the poem's composition and announced—mistakenly, it
would subsequently turn out—its imminent publication in *The Dial*.
An astute and conscientious editor, Bishop had phoned to confirm the
report with his colleague and counterpart at *The Dial*, Gilbert Seldes.
Seldes was puzzled, having heard nothing about the poem; on 6 March
he cabled *The Dial* co-owner and chief editor, Scofield Thayer, who
was then residing in Vienna:

Cable whether Eliot poetry coming Seldes

Three days later Thayer replied in French:

ELIOT REFUSA THAYER

Seldes immediately contacted Bishop and urged him to alter Huxley's
article, which was to indicate that the poem's appearance in *The Dial*
was, as Seldes expressed it, "problematical but probable."[5] More important, Bishop had now glimpsed the growing rift between Eliot and
The Dial.

By late April 1922, in fact, relations between Eliot and Thayer had
completely broken down; and in the wake of their collapse Pound had
begun to intervene actively in the search for a publisher. On 6 May
1922 he wrote to Jeanne Foster, beloved companion of New York lawyer and patron John Quinn, a contributor to *Vanity Fair* and friend of
Bishop.[6] Pound was soliciting an offer of publication for the poem in
the bluntest possible terms:

4. On Bishop, see Elizabeth Carroll Spindler, *John Peale Bishop* (Morganton: West Virginia
University Library, 1980), chs. 5–7. However, it should be noted that the work often errs on
points of detail, especially in transcribing letters. See below, n. 7, for examples.
5. GS to ST, cable 6 March 1922, ST to GS, cable 9 March 1922; GS to ST, letter 11 March
1922. All are NHBY, *DP*, series 4, box 40, 1922.
6. EP to Jeanne Foster, 6 May 1922; CHH, bMS Am 1635. * * *

What wd. Vanity Fair pay Eliot for "Waste Land".
Cd. yr. friend there [i.e., Bishop] get in touch with T.S.E., address 12 Wigmore St., London W.I.

By August, when he visited Pound, Bishop was clearly apprised of the situation—indeed, was responding to a suggestion advanced by Pound himself. The two met on 3 August, and two days later Bishop reported their conversation to Edmund Wilson, his closest friend and his successor as managing editor at *Vanity Fair*:

> Pound I met the other afternoon. I found him extended on a bright green couch, swathed in a hieratic bathrobe made of a maiden-aunt-shit-brown blanket. His head is quite fine, but his voice is offensively soft, almost effeminate and [xxxx], and his body is rather disagreeably soft. However, he was quite gracious, and the twinkle of his eyes whenever he makes a point is worth something. He held forth for two hours on the intellectual moribundity of England—the old stuff. Here's the thing however—Eliot is starting a quarterly review: he is to run 'Waste Land,' the new series of lyrics in the first number: he and Thayer have split and *The Dial* will not publish it. Perhaps you might want to arrange for the American publication. Pound says they are as fine as anything written in English since 1900. I'm lunching with EP tomorrow [6 August] and will report further.

Whether Bishop wrote again to Wilson as he promised is unknown. On 7 August he left for Vienna, and by the time his letter could have reached Wilson in New York (around 16 August) and Wilson could have replied, his proposal had already been overtaken by events previously set in motion.[7] Yet the seriousness with which it was advanced by both Bishop and Pound should indicate that *Vanity Fair* was considered a serious contender to publish the poem. How serious, indeed, we shall see later.

Bishop's meeting in August also indicates the centrality of Pound's role in prompting and facilitating this abortive plan, recapitulating a story that grows increasingly familiar: Pound was the cultural impressario and entrepeneur who, precisely by virtue of these roles, occupied a critical position at the heart of modernism.[8] It is this position, in fact,

7. John Peale Bishop to Edmund Wilson, 5 August 1922; NHBY, Edmund Wilson Papers, series 2. The letter is reported by Spindler, *John Peale Bishop*, 68–9, though with numerous errors. * * * It is important to note that Bishop was apparently acting in collaboration with Edmund Wilson in his effort to purchase *The Waste Land*, a point elaborated below.

8. Pound himself was conscious of the dilemma presented by his role as impresario and its effects on his literary reputation. Consider his remarks to Margaret Anderson in 1921: "Point I never can seem to get you to take is that I have done more log rolling and attending to other people's affairs, Joyce, Lewis, Gaudier, etc. (don't regret it). But I am in my own small way, a writer myself, and as before stated I shd. like (and won't in any case get) the chance of being considered as the author of my own poems rather than as literary politician and a very active stage manager of rising talent." See EP to Margaret Anderson, [June 1921]; Milwaukee, University of Wisconsin at Milwaukee.

that informs the rhetoric in which he articulated his advocacy of *The Waste Land*'s publication: "Pound says they are as fine as anything written in English since 1900," wrote Bishop, evidently quoting him verbatim. A month earlier Pound had written to Felix Schelling, his former professor at the University of Pennsylvania: "Eliot's *Waste Land* is I think the justification of the 'movement,' of our modern experiment, since 1900."[9] Bishop had clearly been subjected to a variant of the same argument: The poem was important precisely for its representative quality, and publishing it was not necessarily a matter of appreciating its quality or sympathizing with its substantive components—whatever those were—but of one's eagerness to position oneself as the spokesperson of a field of cultural production, the voice for an array of institutions ("the justification of the 'movement,' of our modern experiment, since 1900"). Indeed, how much this animated Bishop's interest in the poem is underscored by a curious anomaly in the nature of his enthusiasm, for Bishop was praising a poem that he had as yet not read, indeed, whose exact title was still a bit obscure to him (" 'Waste Land,' the new series of lyrics").[1]

Bishop's imperfect knowledge was not unique. Indeed, insofar as he knew the title of the poem at all, he knew more than Horace Liveright had known when he first advanced his own offer of publication for the poem. The date was 3 January 1922, notable because it took place before the poem was completed, before it had even acquired its present title. Liveright's interest, like Bishop's, was not the consequence of an aesthetic encounter with a work he had read and admired, but an eagerness to buy a product that promised to meet a series of minimum conditions. But what were these conditions?

Liveright's access to Eliot's poem, like Bishop's, had been mediated by Pound. It was he who assumed the function of stage director cueing the characters in their parts: the shy reserved poet played by T. S. Eliot, the brash young publisher acted by Horace Liveright. Eliot had arrived in Paris on 2 January 1922 and would stay for two weeks, until 16 January. He had come from Lausanne, bearing the disorderly sheaf of manuscripts that he and Pound began to edit and revise, producing a

9. EP to Felix Schelling, 8–9 July 1922; in Ezra Pound, *Selected Letters 1907–1941*, edited by D. D. Paige (New York: New Directions, 1971), 180.
1. It should be stressed that Pound did not at this time have a copy of the manuscript and so could not lend it to Bishop. One week before their meeting of 3 August, on 27 July, Pound had written to Eliot requesting a copy of the manuscript precisely because he had none available to show Watson, who was then visiting Pound and wished to read it. This can be inferred from Eliot's reply of 28 July, when he stated that he had only one copy to hand but would make another and send it as soon as he could (see *LOTSE 1*, 552). Equally important, the typescript did not arrive until 14 August, or seven days after Bishop's departure, as reported by Watson to Thayer when he sends it on to him in Vienna (JSW to ST, 16 August 1922, NHBY, *DP*, series 4, box 44, Watson 1922).

quasi-final version of *The Waste Land*.[2] His arrival coincided with the visit of Liveright, the partner who was guiding editorial policy at Boni and Liveright. Liveright was touring Europe to acquire new works of literature, and his visit to Pound was designed to set their relations on firmer grounds. In 1919 he had published his *Instigations*, in 1920 he had undertaken *Poems 1918–1921*, a volume released only three weeks before his arrival in Paris, and in the summer of 1921 he had paid Pound for a translation of Remy de Gourmont's *Physique de l'amour*, an engagement that had helped Pound avert financial disaster. Now Liveright hoped to establish more stable relations; he trusted Pound's capacity to recognize new talent, saw him as a valuable link to other authors whose work interested him, and even entertained the idea that Pound's work might prove commercially viable at some point in the future.[3] In turn, Pound thought that he might turn Liveright into the principal publisher of modernism and hoped to secure a long-term agreement guaranteeing financial security and time for work.

Poet and publisher courted one another actively. During the six days of Liveright's stay in Paris (30 December 1921–4 January 1922), they saw each other daily.[4] Pound treated Liveright to visits with Paul Morand and Constantin Brancusi, and the young publisher left "a good impression" on Pound, who felt that he was "going toward the light[,] not from it." He was "much more of a man than publishers usually are" and, indeed, "perhaps the only man in the business."[5] He was "a

2. The dates of Eliot's arrival and departure are inferred from Vivienne Eliot to Mary Hutchinson, 12 January 1922; in *LOTSE 1*, 501. Vivienne reports that "Tom has been here ten days," implying that he arrived on 2 January, and states that "he will be back [in London] on Monday," or 17 January 1922, suggesting that he would leave the day before, or 16 January. The new dates also make clear that all of Pound's editorial interventions occurred between 2 and 16 January 1922. Further, as scholars have previously suspected, these consisted principally of two editorial sessions. This hypothesis is confirmed by Eliot's letter of 20 January 1922 to Scofield Thayer, in which he reports that his poem "will have been three times through the sieve by Pound as well as myself" (*LOTSE 1*, 503). In other words, in addition to the two times that Pound had already gone over the poem while the two men were in Paris, Eliot was planning to send it to him yet again, for a third time. Eliot probably sent the poem to Pound on 19 or 20 January, at roughly the same time as he was writing to Thayer, and in response to this Pound wrote his letter dated "24 Saturnus" or 24 January 1922 (mistakenly assigned to 24 December 1921 by Valerie Eliot and printed in *LOTSE 1*, 497–8).
3. On *Instigations*, see Donald Gallup, *Ezra Pound: A Bibliography* (Charlottesville: University of Virginia, 1985), A18. For Liveright's acceptance of *Poems 1918–1921*, see HL to EP, 13 September 1920; BLUI, PM.2, Liveright. For his helpful role in Pound's personal finances in 1921, see Lawrence S. Rainey, *Ezra Pound and the Monument of Culture* (Chicago: University of Chicago, 1991).
4. Copy of HL to JQ, 24 March 1922; BLUI, PM.1, Quinn:

  I am attaching to this letter a card which James Joyce gave me in Paris one evening when I had dinner with him. [. . .] Ezra Pound and T. S. Eliot had dinner with us that night and as I am publishing Ezra Pound, and I'm about to publish Eliot, providing that Knopf has no legal claim on his next book, I think Joyce belongs in the Boni and Liveright fold.
  I saw Pound each day during the six days I was in Paris, and I made a little arrangement with him that will take care of his rent over there for the next two years anyhow.
5. EP to Jeanne Foster, 5 April 1922.

pearl among publishers."[6] The masculine publisher had arrived at an opportune moment. Joyce was looking for an American publisher of *Ulysses*, and Eliot would need a publisher for his unfinished poem. On 3 January 1922, Liveright had an extraordinary dinner with Joyce, Eliot, and Pound to discuss a milestone publishing program. The encounter was productive. With Joyce he agreed to publish *Ulysses* and to advance $1,000 against royalties. To Pound he offered a contract guaranteeing $500 annually for two years in addition to translator's fees for any work from French agreed upon by both parties. To Eliot he offered a $150 advance against 15 percent royalties and promised publication in the fall list. Liveright was nervous only about its length; in a brief note dated 11 January, a week before Eliot had left Paris, he expressed his concern that the poem might not be long enough. "I'm disappointed that Eliot's material is as short. Can't he add anything?" he pleaded with Pound.[7]

Pound, it is clear, was eager to gather under one roof the principal works and authors of modernism, including Yeats, whom he encouraged to abandon a longstanding contract with Macmillan in favor of Liveright.[8] At stake in these efforts was an effort to present modernist writings as the articulation of an idiom, a serviceable language that was shared (and in this sense collective in character) yet amenable to a high degree of individuation: the voice of the " 'movement,' of our modern experiment since 1900." In short, his activity was characterized by programmatic ambitions and a coherent sense of their interaction with market conditions.

These traits also appear in every stage of his dealings with Thayer, the editor of *The Dial* who was eventually to purchase *The Waste Land*. Pound lobbied forcefully for the poem's publication from the outset, invoking a rhetoric by now familiar. On 18 February 1922, when

6. EP to JQ, 20 June 1920; NYPL, *JQP*, box 34, folder 4.
7. HL to EP, 11 January 1922; NHBY, *BP*, folder 23. It is Liveright's concern with the length of the poem that explains Eliot's repeated proposals designed to make the book longer: (1) that he retain three minor pieces as prefatory matter for the poem, a suggestion that Pound rejected on 24 January, (2) that he reprint "Gerontion" as a preface to *The Waste Land*, advanced to Pound in his letter of around 26 January (assigned to [24? January] by Valerie Eliot), and (3) that he use one or two poems by Pound as prefatory matter to the poem, also advanced in the same letter of around 26 January to Pound. In addition, however, Liveright was nervous about its publication in periodical form and whether it would be printed in a single issue: "And does it *all* appear in *one* issue of the Dial—please let me know." This concern prompted Eliot to worry about the same question, as emerges in his letter offering the poem to *The Dial* (20 January 1922): "It could easily go into 4 issues if you like, but not more." Liveright may have communicated his concerns directly to Eliot after he arrived in London on 17 January, for Liveright did not depart for the United States until 28 January and could easily have met or contacted the poet until then. Surely this explains Eliot's anxiety in his letters to Thayer (20 January) and Pound (around 26 January) on precisely those matters raised earlier in Liveright's note of 11 January to Pound.
8. See HL to EP, 12 October 1922; NHBY, *BP*, folder 23: "It doesn't seem that we've found the right thing yet, does it? [. . .] And if Yeats insists on sticking to Macmillan, and I firmly believe that Yeats has more to do with it than Watt [his agent] because I did have a long talk with Watt and he seemed inclined to let me have a look-in,—well, all the worse for Yeats."

Thayer and Eliot were still at a preliminary stage of discussion, Pound wrote to Thayer: "Eliot's poem is very important, almost enough to make everyone else shut up shop." When Thayer replied (5 March) that he could not comment on the poem's merits, since Eliot had not yet sent him the text, Pound persisted:

> His poem is as good in its way as Ulysses in its way, and there is so DAMN little genius, so DAMN little work that one can take hold of and say, "This at any rate stands, makes a definite part of literature".

The Waste Land was represented as a verse equivalent of *Ulysses*, a work that epitomized not just the experiences of an individual, whether author or protagonist, but the modernist claim to a hegemonic position in the institution of "literature," an ambiguous entity that was distinct yet inseparable from the commercial production of reading matter and discourse. Its merits did not reside in a specific set of words or text, but in its capacity to articulate this collective aspiration of an elite.

Pound's letter of 9–10 March also outlined practical suggestions that would prove pivotal both for *The Waste Land* and for subsequent literature: "I wish to Christ he had had the December award," he hinted. But other solutions were also available. Eliot might be granted "a professorship," as Frost had recently been. Or he might be given a job on *The Century* or *The Atlantic*, since "he is not an alarming revolutionary, and he don't, as I at moments, get mistaken for a labour-leader or bolshy bomb-thrower."[9] Yet it was the hint of "the December award," the Dial Award for services in the cause of letters (granted for the first time four months earlier), that would bear fruit both for Eliot and for modernism.

Pound's suggestions were advanced precisely when communications between Eliot and Thayer were breaking down. On 8 March Eliot had telegraphed Thayer that he could not accept less than £50 (or $250). Unfortunately, the message was distorted in transmission, and Thayer had received a shocking request for an unprecedented sum:

cannot accept under !8!56 pounds = eliot + [*sic*]

In reply, on 12 March Thayer reiterated his offer of $150 for the poem, a figure that was advanced without sight of the manuscript and was 25 percent higher than the $110 to $120 he would normally have paid.[1] (One should recall that the national income per capita in the United

---

9. EP to ST, 18 February 1922; ST to EP, 5 March 1922; EP to ST, 9–10 March 1922; NHBY, DP, series 4, box 38, 1922.

1. Thayer's marginalia on Eliot's letter of 20 January 1922 record his diligent calculations of the poem's price at normal rates: If typeset at thirty-five lines per page, the poem would come to slightly under twelve pages, yielding a price of $120; if typeset at forty lines per page, it would come to 11.25 pages, yielding a price of slightly over $110. Summarizing his results, Thayer firmly concludes; "12 pp. $120." His offer of $150, then, was already 25 percent higher than normal rates.

States at this time was about $750 per annum. By contrast, the 1986 national income per capita was $14,166. Viewed as a percentage of national income per capita, Thayer's offer is the equivalent of roughly $2,850 in 1986 dollars.) Not unreasonably, Thayer also asked to receive a copy of the manuscript. In addition, he pointed out the staggering deficits *The Dial* was incurring and argued that it could not alter its policy of "pay[ing] all contributors famous and unknown at the same rates." In a reply on 16 March Eliot was curt and frankly insulting, and he proceeded to withdraw the poem entirely:

> Please excuse my not replying sooner to your letter, except by my wire; but I have had a good deal of trouble over letting my flat furnished and moving here, where I shall be till the 20th June. In addition, there have been engrossing personal affairs, and I have been prevented from dealing with any correspondence.
>
> I also took some days to think about your offer, during which time I happened to hear on good authority that you paid £.100 [*sic*] to George Moore for a short story, and I must confess that this influenced me in declining $150 for a poem which has taken me a year to write and which is my biggest work. To have it published in a journal was not in any case the way I should choose for bringing it out; and certainly if I am to be offered only 30 to 35 pounds for such a publication it is out of the question.
>
> I have written to Ezra Pound to explain my reasons for refusing to dispose of the poem to the Dial at that price and he concurs with me.
>
> [Paragraph omitted.]
>
> You have asked me several times to give you the right of first refusal of any new work of mine, and I gave you the first refusal of this poem.

Opposite Eliot's charge about George Moore, Thayer noted in pencil: "novellette length / serially." At the bottom of the letter he also commented:

> Seen Moore work
> exception for him
> and because review had
> offended
> Moore had already sacrificed several hundred
> dollars

True, *The Dial* had paid Moore a higher than usual fee, but in part this was because of the work's length, in part because *The Dial* had been remiss in fulfilling earlier obligations to Moore ("had offended"), thereby forcing him to sacrifice "several hundred dollars," for which the larger payment had been a form of compensation. But more important was Thayer's remark opposite Eliot's last sentence, withdrawing the offer to publish. Thayer vented his tart indignation: "Not submitted."[2]

Eliot's allegations about Moore appeared to invoke a principle of equal pay for all contributors. In fact, it was precisely the opposite principle that interested him, as he had explained a few days earlier to Pound:

> I think these people should learn to recognize Merit instead of Senility, and I think it is an outrage that we should be paid less merely because Thayer thinks we will take less and be thankful for it, and I thought that somebody ought to take steps to point this out.

At first sight Eliot's argument may strike us as sympathetic, if only because it seems so familiar.[3] But the issues were rather more complicated: In an important sense the question of aesthetic value is inseparable from commercial success in a market economy, a difficulty that has beset every argument for the intrinsic merit of literary modernism. By 1922 literary modernism desperately required a financial-critical success that would seem comparable to the stunning achievement of modernist painting, yet every step in this direction was hampered by market constraints less amenable to the kinds of pressures from elite patronage and investment that had secured the fortunes of Cubism and modern painting. The legal definition of intellectual property—which continued to belong to the author after its purchase by the consumer, in contrast to a painting or statue, which became the property of the purchaser—posed a series of intractable dilemmas. Patronage could nurture literary modernism only to the threshold of its confrontation with a wider public; beyond that point it would require commercial success to ratify its viability as a significant idiom. That was the question that permeated discussion about publication of *The Waste Land*: Assuming that the poem epitomized the investment of twenty years in the creation of a collective idiom—"our modern experiment, since 1900"—the protagonists were obliged to find a return on their investment in modernity.

Thayer was shocked and insulted by Eliot's letter of 16 March, and refused to engage in further communications with him. Instead he turned to Pound, who was more vulnerable to the threat of losing his job with *The Dial* and might be reproached for having encouraged Eliot's intransigence. On 10 April Thayer demanded that he explain himself: "Perhaps you will be able to enlighten me as to why you concur with Eliot in his refusal to let The Dial have his poem. . . ."[4] In reply, Pound rehearsed the same charge (which Eliot had commu-

2. TSE to ST, 16 March 1922; in NHBY, *DP*, series 4, box 31, 1922.
3. TSE to EP, 12 March 1922; in *LOTSE 1*, 507.
4. Thayer visited Pound for the first time on 12 July 1921. * * *

nicated to him), that George Moore was "getting special rates from The Dial (also Sherwood Anderson)," and he concluded:

> That being the case I can hardly reprove Eliot—if you have put the thin on a commercial basis, for holding out for as high a price as he can get. [Added in autograph in margin:] (*i.e. if The Dial is a business house, it gets business treatment. If The Dial is a patron of literature T. contends it should not pay extra rates for "mere senility", all of which is extreme theory-ism, perhaps, on his part.*)

But in passing, Pound added another point. He could hardly attest to the veracity of Eliot's or Thayer's claims, but in general he preferred that the poem be published in *The Dial*:

> I shd. perhaps prefer one good review to several less good ones. I have, as I think you know, always wanted to see a concentration of the authors I believe in, in one review. The Dial perhaps looks better to me than it does to Eliot. (Life in general does.)

As always, Pound displayed a keen understanding of the nexus between cultural ambitions and their institutional actualization.[5] Implicit in his remarks to Thayer was his view that literary modernism could best present itself as a shared language through a centralization suggesting the coherence of its ambitions—the same project that animated his endeavor to unite the works of Joyce, Eliot, Yeats, and himself under the umbrella of a single publisher. Such a project would facilitate the perception of modernism as an idiom both collective and capable of individuation: an identifiable, distinctive, and serviceable language. Yet with equal acuteness Pound also articulated a central dilemma that characterized *The Dial* and the role it might play in any such project. Was *The Dial* a form of patronage, or was it a commercial venture? Unlike the traditional journals that were organs of publishing houses, *The Dial* could shun the increasing diversity and heterogeneity that typified the ordinary journals, presenting itself as a benign and disinterested patron. Its owners, on the other hand, were actively engaged in purchasing works of modern painting and sculpture and in this sense were investors in a market commodity whose value was rapidly rising, in part through the efforts of the publicity apparatus that they themselves owned and controlled. Literary modernism, by analogy, was now courting the risk of becoming "smart art," an investment that would pay and pay big if successful in an expanding market. But pay whom?

The contradictions were irreconcilable. Driven by conflicting imperatives, the participants muddled through the summer of 1922. On 30 April Thayer summarized the state of his relations with Eliot: "We now correspond only through Pound with whom my relations are also

5. EP to ST, 23 April 1922; NHBY, *DP*, series 4, box 38, 1922.

strained, but who seems to desire to keep his job." Pound himself was more cavalier. On 6 May, while traveling through Italy, he paused to send Thayer a postcard:

My present impression of the case is "Oh you two Bostonians."

The surface gaiety, however, was a pose.[6] The same day he also posted his letter inquiring about the price that might be offered by *Vanity Fair*.

Discussions remained stalled throughout the rest of May and June as the participants reconsidered their strategies. On 2 June Pound and Eliot met in Verona, a meeting recorded a few weeks later by Pound in a series of drafts and draft fragments suggesting the substance of their conversations. One of these (later incorporated into *The Cantos*) makes clear that they considered the editorial program of Eliot's new review (still untitled, but soon to be named *The Criterion*), a topic that probably led to another: where to publish *The Waste Land*.[7] From the outset of his undertaking *The Criterion*, Eliot had entertained the idea that it might collaborate with American reviews in simultaneous publication; his first letter announcing the new journal to Pound, written on 12 March, had proposed exactly this:

I also see no reason why some things should not appear in this and in the Little Review concurrently.

The timing of this suggestion should be noted: it was four days after Eliot had sent his provocative telegram to Thayer and four days before he withdrew his offer of publication to *The Dial*.[8] It was a curious proposal; Eliot had not published in *The Little Review* since 1918 and had never evinced particular interest in its fortunes. Yet if Eliot was already assuming that *The Waste Land* would be published by his own journal in England, then his 12 March reference to *The Little Review* —addressed to Pound, a primary force behind its editorial activity—was probably an effort to suggest a replacement for *The Dial*. The same idea, we may suppose, arose in their discussions at Verona. And quite naturally so, since the editors of *The Little Review* were now in Paris and often in touch with Pound, who had recently assembled a special Brancusi number for them. Like *Vanity Fair*, *The Little Review* was also a possible candidate for what had now become a project of simultaneous publication.

In the wake of the Verona meeting, the decisive episodes in the story occurred. Pound returned to Paris on 2 July 1922 and two weeks later

6. EP to ST, 6 May 1922; NHBY, *DP*, series 4, box 38, 1922.
7. The visit is mentioned in TSE to Sidney Schiff, attributed to "[Early June 1922]" by Valerie Eliot in *LOTSE*, 528: "I also went to Verona and saw Pound." * * *
8. TSE to EP, 12 March 1922; in *LOTSE* 1, 508. Eliot mentions *The Little Review* only twice in his correspondence for 1922, and both times in letters to Pound. Clearly he considered the journal to be largely Pound's.

received a personal visit from James Sibley Watson, Jr., the co-owner and co-editor of *The Dial*, and the partner of Thayer. Two days later Pound reported the meeting to his wife Dorothy:

> Usual flood [of people visiting]: Lunch with Watson of Dial, on Wed. [19 July], amiable [. . .] wants T's poem for Dial, etc.

The report leaves no doubt about the purpose of Watson's visit: he had come to purchase *The Waste Land*.[9] Influenced by the assumption that the poem vindicated the project of modern experimentalism since 1900, Watson was seized with anxiety that *The Dial* would suffer an ignominious defeat in its effort to position itself as *the* representative of advanced cultural life. What if the poem were published in *The Little Review* or even *Vanity Fair*? The day after his meeting with Pound, Watson flew to Berlin and met with Thayer.[1] Among other matters, they discussed *The Waste Land* and *The Dial*'s prospects for publishing it. Now, increasingly fearful and excited, the two editors reached an unprecedented decision: They would offer Eliot the second annual Dial Award in confidence as the price for the poem, whereas officially they would pay only the $150 that had been their original offer.[2] Literary history records few spectacles so curious or so touching, i.e., two editors of a major review offering a figure nearly three times the national income per capita—in 1986 terms, the same ratio yields over $40,000—for a poem that neither had seen or read. What they had decided to purchase was less a specific poem, more a bid for discursive hegemony. Moreover, their strategy for reaching their goal was exquisitely self-fulfilling: Since news of the Dial Award would attract media attention, it would augment the sales of the work and further redound to the credit of *The Dial*.

Seven days after his encounter with Thayer, Watson returned to Paris and met with Pound a second time. Two accounts of the meeting survive, one by Pound addressed to his wife Dorothy:

> Watson in Thursday [27 July] with Cummings [. . .] Wat. troubled at not having T.S.'s poem for Dial.[3]

More revealing is Watson's account, addressed to Thayer:

> Pound has written a ⟨very⟩ veiled hint to Eliot. He took me to see Brancusi, who [xxxx] appears very anxious not to be reproduced

---

9. EP to DSP, 21 July 1922; BLUI, *PM*.3, 1922.
1. ST to GS, 20 July 1922; NHBY, *DP*, series 4, box 40, 1922. Thayer reports that Watson "is present as I dictate," leaving no doubt that Watson departed within hours of his meeting with Pound on 19 July (date of meeting from EP to DSP, 21 July 1922).
2. ST to TSE, 5 October 1922; NHBY, *DP*, series 4, box 31, 1922: "I have been very glad to learn from New York that *the suggestion I made to Mr. Watson while he was with me in Berlin last July* has borne fruit and that we are despite your asperity to have the pleasure of recognizing publicly your contribution to contemporary letters." (Italics added.)
3. EP to DSP, 29 July 1922; BLUI, *PM*.3.

anymore. I gather this is mostly a pose. Such chittering and apol-
ogizing and kowtowing as Pound indulged in I have never before
seen. It was disgusting. I pointed out several things I thought you
would like, but no, I must take what the master will give. "You
win the victory," says Brancusi, as though I had been beseeching
him for a week. A dam' Pyrrhic victory, by me! [. . .] He will, of
course, be furious if we don't take any; and Pound will say that
we have destroyed his only remaining Parisian friendship. I hope
you will write Brancusi rather than have me to go see him again;
if I go, I shan't take Pound, that's sure, [. . .] Pound looks pretty
unhealthy. He handed me two lemons which he recommends very
highly and which I send to you on the [canceled: hope] chance
you may like one of them.[4]

Pound's letter to Eliot, which has not survived, was written immediately
after Watson's visit on 27 July. And while his "hint" had been "⟨very⟩
veiled" when issued from Paris, a certain rending evidently took place
as it crossed the channel. Eliot understood fully the implications of his
request for a typescript:

> I will let you have a copy of the Waste Land for confidential use
> as soon as I can make one. [. . .] I infer from your remarks that
> Watson is at present in Paris. I have no objection to either his or
> Thayer's seeing the manuscript.[5]

Evidently it took Eliot some two weeks to arrange (or type himself) a
copy of the typescript, and it was not until 12 or 13 August that he sent
it to Watson in Paris. When it arrived, Watson hastily read it and reported the news to Thayer in Vienna:

> In response to Pound's letter Eliot has assumed a more conciliatory
> attitude and has sent on a copy of Wasteland for our perusal. I am
> forwarding it to you. . . . Anyway I wrote him more plainly about
> the prize and await his answer. I found the poem disappointing
> on first reading but after a third shot I think it up to his usual—
> all the styles are there, somewhat toned down in language [auto-
> graph addition:] ⟨adjectives!⟩ and theatricalized in sentiment at
> least I thought.[6]

Here, too, one is struck by the discrepancy between Watson's initial
assessment of the poem and views of it later enshrined in criticism.
"On first reading" Watson found the poem "disappointing," and after
perusing it three times he considered it merely "up to [Eliot's] usual."
Indeed, in some respects it was below his usual: The diction seemed
flat ("somewhat toned down"), and the tone was "theatricalized." Yet

4. JSW to ST, 29 July 1922; NHBY, *DP*, series 4, box 44, 1922.
5. TSE to EP, 28 July 1922, in *LOTSE*, 552.
6. JSW to ST, 16 August 1922; NHBY, *DP*, series 4, box 44, 1922.

all this makes only more remarkable his decision to advance a publication proposal that entailed an unprecedented scale of payment, presented in his letter of 13 or 14 August to Eliot.

Eliot responded on 15 August:

> Subject to Mr. Liveright's consent I would let the *Dial* publish the poem for $150, not before November 1st. In this event I would forego the $150 advance from Mr. Liveright, and he would delay publication as a book until the new year. Possibly he would be glad to do this, on the possibility of the book's getting the prize, which might increase the sales.

His proposal reached Watson late in the afternoon of 16 August.[7] The next day, however, he was seized with panic at the audacity of his own proposal, and sent a telegram reporting that he could not make up his mind. On 19 August Watson reported both events to Thayer:

> Got a letter from Eliot [received 16 August] regretting his haste in thinking we were trying to rob him, and offering us the right of publishing his poem simultaneously in Dial with its pub. in the Criterion. I find from Pound that Bel Esprit hasn't enough yet for one year, that it goes to Eliot only when he leaves his bank and engages in writing exclusively. He gets only a nominal salary from Lady Rothermere. In other words I don't see why we shouldn't be doing something moderately popular in giving him the award. But the next day [17 August] I got a [canceled: cable] telegram saying ["]don't act till you receive a second letter." Haven't received it yet, though it may come on board tonight when we touch at Plymouth. So the matter is still in the air. Please don't do anything definitive without letting me know first. I reach New York probably August 26, and there is also the telegraphie sans fil.[8]

Pound had clearly informed him about the difficult state of Eliot's personal finances. Watson, in turn, hoped that this might be exploited to the advantage of *The Dial*, that it might be viewed as "doing something moderately popular in giving him the award." Eliot's actual services to letters (the ostensible justification for the award) and the merits of *The Waste Land* were issues that never appeared in his discussion of the Dial Award. Instead, Watson cheerily admitted his view that the proposal was a device intended to garner goodwill for *The Dial* or a tactic in its struggle to consolidate its position as the dominant journal of advanced culture.

Meanwhile, on 21 August Eliot sent his own letter to Quinn, apprising him of the recent developments and leaving open the possibility for action:

7. TSE to JSW, 15 August 1922; in *LOTSE*, 560.
8. JSW to ST, 19 August 1922; NHBY, *DP*, series 4, box 44, 1922.

A few days ago I had an attractive proposal from Mr. Watson of the *Dial* who are very anxious to publish the poem. [. . .] They suggest getting Liveright to postpone the date of publication as a book, but I have written to them to say that it seemed to me too late to be proper to make any change now and that I should not care to trouble either Mr. Liveright or yourself with any questions of alterations in the contract.[9]

Nine days later Eliot wrote to Pound and reported his letters to Watson and to Quinn:

I received a letter from your friend Watson most amiable in tone [. . .] offering $150 for the "Waste Land" (not "Waste Land", please, but "*The* Waste Land"), and (in the strictest confidence) the award for virtue also. Unfortunately, it seemed considerably too late, as I had the preceding day [14 August] got contract, signed by Liveright and Quinn, [(]book to be out by Nov. 1st, etc.) I can't bother Quinn any more about it, I don't see why Liveright should find it to his advantage to postpone publication in order to let the Dial kill the sale by printing it first, and there has been so much fluster and business about this contract that I don't want to start the whole thing up again, so I see nothing but to hope that the Dial will be more businesslike with other people. Watson's manner was charming, if Thayer had behaved in the same way the Dial might have published it long ago, instead of pretending that I had given him the lie as if he was *ehrenfähig* anyhow. Anyway, it's my loss, I suppose; if Watson wants to try to fix it up with Liveright I suppose he can, that's his affair. I suppose the move was entirely due to your beneficent and pacific efforts, which are appreciated. Dam but [why] don't they give the prize to you? More presently.[1]

Notwithstanding the disingenuous demur by Eliot, the issue was already all but settled. The suggestion which he had advanced—that *The Dial* undertake to arrange terms with Liveright—was rapidly realized through the agency of Watson. On 29 August his ship arrived in New York; the next day he received Eliot's letter of 21 August, broaching the new arrangement. He set to work immediately, as Seldes duly reported to Thayer: "Watson has just come back and the Eliot affair is taking up much of our time."[2] A week later he and Seldes met with Liveright in the office of the New York lawyer John Quinn, and there the deal was concluded. Liveright required that *The Dial* purchase 350 copies of the volume at standard discounts, assuring himself an advance sale and adding $315 to *The Dial*'s costs for procuring the poem. But

9. TSE to JQ, 21 August 1922, in *LOTSE 1*, 564. Also cited in Valerie Eliot, ed., *T. S. Eliot, The Waste Land. A Facsimile* (New York: Harcourt, Brace, 1971), xxiv.
1. TSE to EP, 30 August 1922, in *LOTSE 1*, 567; punctuation here reproduces the original.
2. TSE to JSW, 21 August 1922, in *LOTSE 1*, 564–5. GS to ST, 31 August 1922; NHBY, *DP*, series 4, box 40, 1922.

The Dial had achieved its victory, and the outcome was a remarkable success.

Liveright reported on the later events in a letter to Pound written on 5 February 1923, eleven weeks after the poem's publication in *The Dial*, seven weeks after his own release of the book-cum-notes:

> God bless you and Cantos IX to XII. If we can get as much publicity from them as The Waste Land has received, you will be a millionaire. The Waste Land has sold 1000 copies to date and who knows, it may go up to 2000 or 3000 copies. Just think, Eliot may make almost $500 on the book rights of this poem. And Gene Stratton Porter makes $40,000.000 to $60,000 a year out of her books. Well, it's all in a life time, so who cares.[3]

Liveright's sales estimate was remarkably accurate. Yet more important was the tenor of his comments, insofar as it tended to echo Watson's rationale in urging Thayer to take on the poem, his argument that *The Dial* would "be doing something moderately popular in giving him the award." Liveright's stress on how much publicity the award-and-publication package received is telling. For by now it is clear that the publication of *The Waste Land* marked the crucial moment in the transition of modernism from a minority culture to one supported by an important institutional and financial apparatus.

*   *   *

The Waste Land, as is well known, was not published in book form solely by Horace Liveright; nearly ten months later (12 September 1923) it also appeared a second time, issued by Virginia Woolf's Hogarth Press in a limited edition of about 460 copies. The date suggests a tardy afterthought, as if Eliot were seeking to retrace a missed step in the normal process of avant-garde publishing. Yet the idea of a limited edition was anything but tardy. Eliot had begun to worry about the precarious implications of his agreement with Liveright almost immediately after their encounter in January 1922. It was a precipitous move that bypassed the normal rhythms of avant-garde production, in which a work was transmitted from a small elite to an ever wider yet presumably less discriminating audience, and therefore a move that threatened the status of his work. Like anyone who works within a specific institution, Eliot had internalized an array of unwritten procedures and practices considered normal and appropriate. No sooner had he completed the poem in its final version (probably in the first week of February 1922) than he began to seek a publisher who would issue a limited edition. On 14 February he lunched with Conrad Aiken and discussed his dilemma. Aiken, the next day, reported their conversation

3. HL to EP, 5 February 1922; BLUI, *PM.1*, Liveright.

to Maurice Firuski, who was issuing Aiken's own book of poetry, *The Pool of Priapus:*

> Brief is this note, and chiefly occasioned by a talk with Tom Eliot at lunch yesterday. He has a poem, 450 lines long, wh. I haven't seen. He seeks a publisher who will produce it nicely, and in America, and in a small edition. Firuski! cried I, and there you are. When I elucidated, mentioning [Bruce] Rogers and 450 copies and two years exclusive right and a possible hundred dollars and a beautifully produced book, his eyes glowed with a tawny golden light like fierce doubloons, his hands took on singularly the aspect of claws, his nails tore the table-cloth, and he took your address. . . . . . . As I say, I have not seen the poem. It may or may not be good, or intelligible. But, reflect: Eliot has a real reputation; a poem of that length by him will be a real curiosity, even perhaps an event; and he assumes that you will have, of course, the English as well as the American market. He may have to get Knopf's permission, as I did, to make the arrangement: he doesn't remember how his contract stands. But that, I fancy, will present no difficulty, for the book is too small for Knopf, and besides Knopf doesn't regard Eliot as a golconda. . . . . . Address: 9 Clarence Gate Gardens, London, W. W. 1.[4]

Eleven days later, on 26 February, Eliot himself also wrote to Firuski, pursuing the same question more fully in a letter that has not previously been published:

> Dear Sir,
>
> Your name has been given me by Mr. Conrad Aiken, who has also shown me a volume of poems by Mr. John Freeman, recently published by you, with the appearance of which I was very much pleased.
>
> I have now ready a poem for which that form of publication seems to me the most suitable. I understand that you issue these books in limited editions, and that for the volumes you take for this series you give a sum in advance royalty.
>
> My poem is of 435 lines; with certain spacings essential to the sense, 475 book lines; furthermore, it consists of five parts, which would increase the space necessary; and with title pages, some notes that I propose to add, etc., I guess that it would run to from 28 to 32 pages.
>
> I have had a good offer for the publication of it in a periodical. But it is, I think, much the best poem I have ever written, and I

---

4. Conrad Aiken to Maurice Firuski, 15 February 1922, Chapin Library, Williams College, T. S. Eliot Collection. I wish to thank Robert L. Volz, Rare Book Custodian, for his kindness in drawing this letter to my attention.

think it would make a much more distinct impression and attract much more attention if published as a book.

If you are interested in this, I should be glad to hear from you what terms you would be prepared to offer for it, at your earliest convenience, as the other offers for it cannot be held in suspence very long.

                                             I am,
                                        yours faithfully,
                                          [Signature]

Eliot's letter, of course, is fascinating.[5] Among other things, it affects the long-standing debate about the poem's notes, suggesting that they were not merely a late and arbitrary addition imposed by the publishing exigencies of Horace Liveright, as often argued, but an integral part of the work as Eliot himself wished to have it published—a nod, perhaps, to the eighteenth-century tradition of poetry (e.g., Pope's notes to *The Dunciad*) that had so informed some of the poem's earliest drafts. But more important for our purpose, the letter demonstrates how fully Eliot understood the normative rhythms of avant-garde publishing, as well as how easily those procedures could be assimilated to features already long established in a genteel tradition of private and limited editions. The book of poems by John Freeman (1880–1929) that Eliot had seen and admired was *The Red Path, a narrative, and the Wounded Bird*, a slender volume of poems issued in 425 copies that was printed for Firuski's Dunster House at the Press of William Edwin Rudge, its design executed by Bruce Rogers. The volume was handsome and, like all of Rogers' work, inspired by rather classical models of typography and design; it suggested a tone of genteel decorum, a distinctly Harvardian note, and yet sounded that tone with even greater subtlety, as if to hint at an elite within the elite, or select and more reflective minority with discriminating taste, a minority lodged within the wider elite that unreflectively assumed its privileges solely on the basis of class, money, and inherited status.

Despite the fact that Eliot had already received "a good offer" of $150 for the poem from Thayer and *The Dial* and despite his preliminary agreement with Liveright in Paris, Eliot preferred to see the work issued in a limited edition: "I think it would make a much more distinct impression and attract much more attention if published as a book." To be sure, Liveright had also offered to publish the poem as a book, but as a different kind of book: a public and more commercial edition that would directly address a wider audience, not preceded by the lim-

5. T. S. Eliot to Maurice Firuski, 26 February 1922, Chapin Library, Williams College, T. S. Eliot Collection. Mention of this letter is made by Valerie Eliot in *LOTSE 1*, 515, n. 1. I am grateful to Mrs. Eliot for permission to quote from this letter in its entirety and to her kindness in responding to my inquiries. The letter from T. S. Eliot to Edmund Wilson quoted below is also printed by permission of Mrs. Eliot, and both are copyrighted by her.

ited edition typical of the avant-garde. That proposal violated the institutional logic of avant-garde production, so much so that Eliot instinctively sought a form of publication that would set matters right. Firuski, however, was slow to respond. Moreover, by 12 March (only two weeks after his letter to Firuski), Eliot had received another note from Liveright reaffirming his interest in publishing the poem. As Eliot promptly informed Pound: "Liveright wrote to say he wanted it, and I have written asking what he wants to give and telling him the exact length," adding cryptically, "and I have other plans also if Thayer doesn't cough out."[6] The other plans, of course, were those with Firuski, presented as an acceptable alternative to publication in *The Dial.* * * *

Eliot, it is clear, wanted his poem to be successful, yet not too successful. For the prospect of immediate publication by a commercial firm raised prospects that were largely unimaginable within the logic of modernism. And similar considerations must also have influenced the discussions concerning *Vanity Fair* as a possible venue for the poem. Pound, after raising the issue on 6 May 1922, presumably reported his action to Eliot during their meeting in Verona a month later, though how the two men viewed this prospect cannot be stated with any degree of certainty. Still, it is clear enough not only that Pound and Eliot considered *Vanity Fair* a potential publisher, but also that *Vanity Fair* considered itself a serious candidate. The journal not only sent John Peale Bishop to discuss the project with Pound in Paris, but even advanced an explicit offer of publication. The proposal appeared in a letter written by Edmund Wilson to Eliot on 1 August 1922. Eliot, in a letter that has also not been previously published, replied on 14 August:

> Thank you for your letter of the 1st inst., I should be very glad to do for you such an article as you suggest. For the next two months I shall be far too busy to attempt such a thing, but I think that I should be able to provide one during October or November if that is satisfactory to you. As for a poem, I am afraid that is quite impossible at present as I have only one for which I have already contracted.[7]

Eliot, plainly, was not being straightforward; as yet he had not "contracted" for *The Waste Land* in a journal at all. Only a day or two prior to his letter to Wilson, in fact, Eliot had sent off the typescript of *The Waste Land* to Pound and James Sibley Watson, Jr., in Paris, and only the day *after* his letter to Wilson did he write to Watson announcing his terms for the poem: the Dial Award plus $150, providing the poem

---

6. T. S. Eliot to Ezra Pound, 12 March 1922, in *LOTSE 1*, 507.
7. T. S. Eliot to Edmund Wilson, 14 August 1922; NHBYU, Edmund Wilson Papers.

were published not much before the book issued by Liveright. Eliot, it is clear, did not reject the offer from *Vanity Fair* solely because he had "already contracted" for its serial publication, but because *Vanity Fair* represented a degree of commercial success and popular acceptance that would have undermined the very status of the work that he was trying to establish. That status, however, was not simply intrinsic or implanted in the poem's text, but a function of the institutional structures that had informed its production at every step in the poem's life.

In retrospect, we can see that the proposal for a limited edition by Firuski not only looked back to the Cambridge and Harvard environment of Eliot's college days, but also looked to modernism's future, to the moment when Eliot would make his triumphant return to Harvard in 1932 and seal the fateful association between modernism and the academy. Yet that association, which has been so much commented on, did not occur naturally or without relations to other changes in the wider culture. By the early 1930s, in fact, all the magazines that Eliot had once considered for *The Waste Land* were dead or dying. *The Little Review* and *The Dial* had both closed in 1929, and *Vanity Fair* would expire in 1936. The Great Depression, it is clear, effectively eliminated the structures of private patronage that had sustained modernism's growth and its emergence as a significant idiom within the languages of the twentieth century. Thereafter, modernism would be slowly but inexorably absorbed into the university, as it had also been appropriated by the marketing and publicity apparatus of *Vanity Fair*.

The price of modernism, in this sense, was a double one. In part, it was a specific and concrete figure epitomized in the sums paid to Eliot for publication of *The Waste Land*: $150 as the price of the poem proper, $2,000 for The Dial Award, a subsequent $580.28 in royalties on the sales of the Liveright edition, and perhaps another £20 from the Hogarth Press edition—altogether about $2,800, a figure that in modern terms would surely be somewhere between $45,000 and $55,000. (It was 2.5 times the $1,150 per annum earned by the executive secretary to the editor of *Vanity Fair*.)[8] But hidden among such figures was another price that was more important; an obscuring of a determinate productive space, the elision of boundaries between specific institutions and wider zones of cultural activity, the illusion that "art" or "the poem" or "the text" had been the central concern of participants whose decisions were consistently made when as yet they had not read a word of the work in question. And not without reason, for the text was largely irrelevant. When *The Waste Land* was published, it did not enter a conduit of transmission that received and reproduced a neutral image

---

8. For the wages of Jeanne Ballot, executive secretary to Frank Crowninshield, who earned $22 per week, or $1,144 per year, see Cohn Cooper, 48. Needless to say, the $2,000 paid to Eliot in the form of the Dial Award was a remarkable figure: The highest sum that *Vanity Fair* ever paid was given in 1925 to F. Scott Fitzgerald for a short story, and it was $100.

of its original, but a multiplicity of social structures driven by conflicting imperatives: It became part of a social event in a discontinuous yet coherent process, an unprecedented effort to affirm the output of a specific marketing-publicity apparatus through the enactment of a triumphal and triumphant occasion. It was not simply the institutions that were the vehicle of the poem, but the poem that was the vehicle of the institutions. The poem, like any cultural work, was more than a sum of meanings implanted or intended by its author; it was inseparable, finally, from the contradictory network of utilizations that constituted it historically.

If nothing else, reconsidering the publication history of *The Waste Land* might prompt us to question the dominant methodology of modern literary studies since roughly the end of World War II. Generations of students have been exhorted to look closely at the poem, to examine only the text, to indulge in a scholastic scrutiny of linguistic minutiae. Yet if we were to consider more fully the experience of the figures who actually engaged in modern textual production, assuming the case of *The Waste Land* tells us anything, we might elect a rather different procedure. Indeed, if we named it in their honor, we could call it the modernist principle of reading and formulate it thus: The best reading of a work is often one that does not read it at all. Such an extreme formulation would, no doubt, be misleading. Yet it might at least remind us that close reading is itself a historical form of activity that appears at a precise moment in the development of professional literary studies and that other kinds of reading are and have been practiced, not least among them, the not-reading that was practiced by the editors of *The Dial*, itself a trenchant "reading" of *The Waste Land*'s place in the structural logic and development of literary modernism. We might learn from them. For reading as we do, instead of as they did, we leave the ambiguous heritage of modernism in history just as desocialized, unexplored, and unexplorable as it was before. History may be a nightmare, as the modernists often claimed, but when they entered the "contrived corridors" of its making, at least they remembered to "protract the profit of their chilled delirium."

Eliot on *The Waste Land*

[The Disillusionment of a Generation]†

* * * I dislike the word "generation", which has been a talisman for the last ten years; when I wrote a poem called *The Waste Land* some of the more approving critics[1] said that I had expressed the 'disillusionment of a generation', which is nonsense. I may have expressed for them their own illusion of being disillusioned, but that did not form part of my intention. * * *

[A Piece of Rhythmical Grumbling]††

'Various critics have done me the honour to interpret the poem in terms of criticism of the contemporary world, have considered it, indeed, as an important bit of social criticism. To me it was only the relief of a personal and wholly insignificant grouse against life; it is just a piece of rhythmical grumbling.'—*Quoted by the late Professor Theodore Spencer during a lecture at Harvard University, and recorded by the late Henry Ware Eliot, Jr., the poet's brother.*

[On the *Waste Land* Notes]†††

Here I must admit that I am, on one conspicuous occasion, not guiltless of having led critics into temptation. The notes to *The Waste*

---

† From T. S. Eliot, *Thoughts after Lambeth* (London: Faber, 1931), p. 10.
1. A reference to the following footnote in I. A. Richards's *Science and Poetry* (New York: Norton, 1926): "He seems to me by this poem to have performed two considerable services for this generation. He has given a perfect emotive description of a state of mind which is probably inevitable for a while to all meditative people. Secondly, by effecting a complete severance between his poetry and *all* beliefs, and this without any weakening of the poetry, he has realised what might otherwise have remained largely a speculative possibility, and has shown the way to the only solution of these difficulties" (p. 76). Richards repeats the same argument in slightly different words at the end of "The Poetry of T. S. Eliot." See p. 173.
†† From T. S. Eliot, *"The Waste Land": A Facsimile and Transcript of the Original Drafts Including the Annotations of Ezra Pound,* ed. Valerie Eliot (New York: Harcourt Brace Jovanovich, 1971), p. 1, epigraph.
††† From T. S. Eliot, "The Frontiers of Criticism," in *On Poetry and Poets* (London: Faber, 1957), pp. 109–10.

Land! I had at first intended only to put down all the references for my quotations, with a view to spiking the guns of critics of my earlier poems who had accused me of plagiarism. Then, when it came to print *The Waste Land* as a little book—for the poem on its first appearance in *The Dial* and in *The Criterion* had no notes whatever—it was discovered that the poem was inconveniently short, so I set to work to expand the notes, in order to provide a few more pages of printed matter, with the result that they became the remarkable exposition of bogus scholarship that is still on view to-day. I have sometimes thought of getting rid of these notes; but now they can never be unstuck. They have had almost greater popularity than the poem itself—anyone who bought my book of poems, and found that the notes to *The Waste Land* were not in it, would demand his money back. But I don't think that these notes did any harm to other poets: certainly I cannot think of any good contemporary poet who has abused this same practice. (As for Miss Marianne Moore, *her* notes to poems are always pertinent, curious, conclusive, delightful and give no encouragement whatever to the researcher of origins.) No, it is not because of my bad example to other poets that I am penitent; it is because my notes stimulated the wrong kind of interest among the seekers of sources. It was just, no doubt, that I should pay my tribute to the work of Miss Jessie Weston; but I regret having sent so many enquirers off on a wild goose chase after Tarot cards and the Holy Grail.

[Allusions to Dante]†

Certainly I have borrowed lines from [Dante], in the attempt to reproduce, or rather to arouse in the reader's mind the memory, of some Dantesque scene, and thus establish a relationship between the medieval inferno and modern life. Readers of my *Waste Land* will perhaps remember that the vision of my city clerks trooping over London Bridge from the railway station to their offices evoked the reflection "I had not thought death had undone so many": and that in another place I deliberately modified a line of Dante by altering it—"sighs, short and infrequent, were exhaled." And I gave the references in my notes, in order to make the reader who recognized the allusion, know that I meant him to recognize it, and know that he would have missed the point if he did not recognize it.

† From T. S. Eliot, "What Dante Means to Me," in *To Criticize the Critic* (New York: Farrar, Straus, Giroux, 1965), p. 128.

Eliot: Essays and London Letters

From Tradition and the Individual Talent[†]

In English writing we seldom speak of tradition, though we occasionally apply its name in deploring its absence. We cannot refer to "the tradition" or to "a tradition"; at most, we employ the adjective in saying that the poetry of So-and-so is "traditional" or even "too traditional." Seldom, perhaps, does the word appear except in a phrase of censure. If otherwise, it is vaguely approbative, with the implication, as to the work approved, of some pleasing archaeological reconstruction. You can hardly make the word agreeable to English ears without this comfortable reference to the reassuring science of archaeology.

* * * One of the facts that might come to light in this process is our tendency to insist, when we praise a poet, upon those aspects of his work in which he least resembles any one else. In these aspects or parts of his work we pretend to find what is individual, what is the peculiar essence of the man. We dwell with satisfaction upon the poet's difference from his predecessors, especially his immediate predecessors; we endeavour to find something that can be isolated in order to be enjoyed. Whereas if we approach a poet without this prejudice we shall often find that not only the best, but the most individual parts of his work may be those in which the dead poets, his ancestors, assert their immortality most vigorously. And I do not mean the impressionable period of adolescence, but the period of full maturity.

Yet if the only form of tradition, of handing down, consisted in following the ways of the immediate generation before us in a blind or timid adherence to its successes, "tradition" should positively be discouraged. We have seen many such simple currents soon lost in the sand; and novelty is better than repetition. Tradition is a matter of much wider significance. It cannot be inherited, and if you want it you must obtain it by great labour. It involves, in the first place, the historical sense, which we may call nearly indispensable to any one who would

† The following selections are from T. S. Eliot, *Selected Essays 1917–1932* (New York: Harcourt, Brace and Company, 1932), pp. 3–11, 121–26, 241–50. All notes are by the editor of this Norton Critical Edition.

continue to be a poet beyond his twenty-fifth year; and the historical sense involves a perception, not only of the pastness of the past, but of its presence; the historical sense compels a man to write not merely with his own generation in his bones, but with a feeling that the whole of the literature of Europe from Homer and within it the whole of the literature of his own country has a simultaneous existence and composes a simultaneous order. This historical sense, which is a sense of the timeless as well as of the temporal and of the timeless and of the temporal together, is what makes a writer traditional. And it is at the same time what makes a writer most acutely conscious of his place in time, of his own contemporaneity.

No poet, no artist of any art, has his complete meaning alone. His significance, his appreciation is the appreciation of his relation to the dead poets and artists. You cannot value him alone; you must set him, for contrast and comparison, among the dead. I mean this as a principle of aesthetic, not merely historical, criticism. The necessity that he shall conform, that he shall cohere, is not onesided; what happens when a new work of art is created is something that happens simultaneously to all the works of art which preceded it. The existing monuments form an ideal order among themselves, which is modified by the introduction of the new (the really new) work of art among them. The existing order is complete before the new work arrives; for order to persist after the supervention of novelty, the *whole* existing order must be, if ever so slightly, altered; and so the relations, proportions, values of each work of art toward the whole are readjusted; and this is conformity between the old and the new. Whoever has approved this idea of order, of the form of European, of English literature will not find it preposterous that the past should be altered by the present as much as the present is directed by the past. And the poet who is aware of this will be aware of great difficulties and responsibilities.

In a peculiar sense he will be aware also that he must inevitably be judged by the standards of the past. I say judged, not amputated, by them; not judged to be as good as, or worse or better than, the dead; and certainly not judged by the canons of dead critics. It is a judgment, a comparison, in which two things are measured by each other. To conform merely would be for the new work not really to conform at all; it would not be new, and would therefore not be a work of art. And we do not quite say that the new is more valuable because it fits in; but its fitting in is a test of its value—a test, it is true, which can only be slowly and cautiously applied, for we are none of us infallible judges of conformity. We say: it appears to conform, and is perhaps individual, or it appears individual, and may conform; but we are hardly likely to find that it is one and not the other.

To proceed to a more intelligible exposition of the relation of the poet to the past: he can neither take the past as a lump, an indiscriminate bolus, nor can he form himself wholly on one or two private admirations, nor can he form himself wholly upon one preferred period. The first course is inadmissible, the second is an important experience of youth, and the third is a pleasant and highly desirable supplement. The poet must be very conscious of the main current, which does not at all flow invariably through the most distinguished reputations. He must be quite aware of the obvious fact that art never improves, but that the material of art is never quite the same. He must be aware that the mind of Europe—the mind of his own country—a mind which he learns in time to be much more important than his own private mind—is a mind which changes, and that this change is a development which abandons nothing *en route*, which does not superannuate either Shakespeare, or Homer, or the rock drawing of the Magdalenian draughtsmen.[1] That this development, refinement perhaps, complication certainly, is not, from the point of view of the artist, any improvement. Perhaps not even an improvement from the point of view of the psychologist or not to the extent which we imagine; perhaps only in the end based upon a complication in economics and machinery. But the difference between the present and the past is that the conscious present is an awareness of the past in a way and to an extent which the past's awareness of itself cannot show.

Some one said: "The dead writers are remote from us because we *know* so much more than they did." Precisely, and they are that which we know.

I am alive to a usual objection to what is clearly part of my programme for the *métier* of poetry. The objection is that the doctrine requires a ridiculous amount of erudition (pedantry), a claim which can be rejected by appeal to the lives of poets in any pantheon. It will even be affirmed that much learning deadens or perverts poetic sensibility. While, however, we persist in believing that a poet ought to know as much as will not encroach upon his necessary receptivity and necessary laziness, it is not desirable to confine knowledge to whatever can be put into a useful shape for examinations, drawing-rooms, or the still more pretentious modes of publicity. Some can absorb knowledge, the more tardy must sweat for it. Shakespeare acquired more essential history from Plutarch[2] than most men could from the whole British Museum. What is to be insisted upon is that the poet must develop or procure the consciousness of the past and that he should continue to develop this consciousness throughout his career.

What happens is a continual surrender of himself as he is at the

---

1. Anonymous artists responsible for the cave paintings at Altamira, Spain, and La Madeleine, France.
2. Greek biographer and historian (first century C.E.) whose most famous work, the *Lives*, provided biographical information for a number of Shakespeare's history plays.

moment to something which is more valuable. The progress of an artist is a continual self-sacrifice, a continual extinction of personality.

There remains to define this process of depersonalization and its relation to the sense of tradition. It is in this depersonalization that art may be said to approach the condition of science. I, therefore, invite you to consider, as a suggestive analogy, the action which takes place when a bit of finely filiated platinum is introduced into a chamber containing oxygen and sulphur dioxide.

II

* * * I have tried to point out the importance of the relation of the poem to other poems by other authors, and suggested the conception of poetry as a living whole of all the poetry that has ever been written. The other aspect of this Impersonal theory of poetry is the relation of the poem to its author. And I hinted, by an analogy, that the mind of the mature poet differs from that of the immature one not precisely in any valuation of "personality," not being necessarily more interesting, or having "more to say," but rather by being a more finely perfected medium in which special, or very varied, feelings are at liberty to enter into new combinations.

The analogy was that of the catalyst. When the two gases previously mentioned are mixed in the presence of a filament of platinum, they form sulphurous acid. This combination takes place only if the platinum is present; nevertheless the newly formed acid contains no trace of platinum, and the platinum itself is apparently unaffected; has remained inert, neutral, and unchanged. The mind of the poet is the shred of platinum. It may partly or exclusively operate upon the experience of the man himself; but, the more perfect the artist, the more completely separate in him will be the man who suffers and the mind which creates; the more perfectly will the mind digest and transmute the passions which are its material.

The experience, you will notice, the elements which enter the presence of the transforming catalyst, are of two kinds: emotions and feelings. The effect of a work of art upon the person who enjoys it is an experience different in kind from any experience not of art. It may be formed out of one emotion, or may be a combination of several; and various feelings, inhering for the writer in particular words or phrases or images, may be added to compose the final result. Or great poetry may be made without the direct use of any emotion whatever: composed out of feelings solely. * * * The poet's mind is in fact a receptacle for seizing and storing up numberless feelings, phrases, images, which remain there until all the particles which can unite to form a new compound are present together.

If you compare several representative passages of the greatest poetry you see how great is the variety of types of combination, and also how completely any semi-ethical criterion of "sublimity" misses the mark. For it is not the "greatness," the intensity, of the emotions, the components, but the intensity of the artistic process, the pressure, so to speak, under which the fusion takes place, that counts. The episode of Paolo and Francesca[3] employs a definite emotion, but the intensity of the poetry is something quite different from whatever intensity in the supposed experience it may give the impression of. It is no more intense, furthermore, than Canto XXVI, the voyage of Ulysses, which has not the direct dependence upon an emotion. Great variety is possible in the process of transmutation of emotion: the murder of Agamemnon[4] or the agony of Othello, gives an artistic effect apparently closer to a possible original than the scenes from Dante. In the *Agamemnon*, the artistic emotion approximates to the emotion of an actual spectator; in *Othello* to the emotion of the protagonist himself. But the difference between art and the event is always absolute; the combination which is the murder of Agamemnon is probably as complex as that which is the voyage of Ulysses. In either case there has been a fusion of elements. The ode of Keats contains a number of feelings which have nothing particular to do with the nightingale, but which the nightingale, partly, perhaps, because of its attractive name, and partly because of its reputation, served to bring together.

The point of view which I am struggling to attack is perhaps related to the metaphysical theory of the substantial unity of the soul: for my meaning is, that the poet has, not a "personality" to express, but a particular medium, which is only a medium and not a personality, in which impressions and experiences combine in peculiar and unexpected ways. Impressions and experiences which are important for the man may take no place in the poetry, and those which become important in the poetry may play quite a negligible part in the man, the personality.

*   *   *

It is not in his personal emotions, the emotions provoked by particular events in his life, that the poet is in any way remarkable or interesting. His particular emotions may be simple, or crude, or flat. The emotion in his poetry will be a very complex thing, but not with the complexity of the emotions of people who have very complex or unusual emotions in life. One error, in fact, of eccentricity in poetry is to

---

3. Paolo Malatesta and his sister-in-law Francesca da Rimini, illicit lovers whom Dante meets in Canto 5 of the *Inferno*. Line 404 of *The Waste Land* bears a trace of their story. In Canto 26, Dante meets Ulysses.
4. Murdered by his wife, Clytemnestra, on his return from the Trojan War. Eliot loaned his copy of Aeschylus' *Agamemnon* to Pound while they were editing *The Waste Land*.

seek for new human emotions to express; and in this search for novelty in the wrong place it discovers the perverse. The business of the poet is not to find new emotions, but to use the ordinary ones and, in working them up into poetry, to express feelings which are not in actual emotions at all. And emotions which he has never experienced will serve his turn as well as those familiar to him. Consequently, we must believe that "emotion recollected in tranquillity" is an inexact formula. For it is neither emotion, nor recollection, nor, without distortion of meaning, tranquility. It is a concentration, and a new thing resulting from the concentration, of a very great number of experiences which to the practical and active person would not seem to be experiences at all; it is a concentration which does not happen consciously or of deliberation. These experiences are not "recollected," and they finally unite in an atmosphere which is "tranquil" only in that it is a passive attending upon the event. Of course this is not quite the whole story. There is a great deal, in the writing of poetry, which must be conscious and deliberate. In fact, the bad poet is usually unconscious where he ought to be conscious, and conscious where he ought to be unconscious. Both errors tend to make him "personal." Poetry is not a turning loose of emotion, but an escape from emotion; it is not the expression of personality, but an escape from personality. But, of course, only those who have personality and emotions know what it means to want to escape from these things.

III

ὁ δὲ νοῦς ἴσως θειότερόν τι χαὶ ἀπαθές ἐστιν.[5]

This essay proposes to halt at the frontier of metaphysics or mysticism, and confine itself to such practical conclusions as can be applied by the responsible person interested in poetry. To divert interest from the poet to the poetry is a laudable aim: for it would conduce to a juster estimation of actual poetry, good and bad. There are many people who appreciate the expression of sincere emotion in verse, and there is a smaller number of people who can appreciate technical excellence. But very few know when there is an expression of *significant* emotion, emotion which has its life in the poem and not in the history of the poet. The emotion of art is impersonal. And the poet cannot reach this impersonality without surrendering himself wholly to the work to be done. And he is not likely to know what is to be done unless he lives in what is not merely the present, but the present moment of the past, unless he is conscious, not of what is dead, but of what is already living.

---

5. "The mind is doubtless more divine and less subject to passion" (Greek). From Aristotle's *De Anima* ("On the Soul") 1.4.

From Hamlet

* * *

The only way of expressing emotion in the form of art is by finding an "objective correlative"; in other words, a set of objects, a situation, a chain of events which shall be the formula of that *particular* emotion; such that when the external facts, which must terminate in sensory experience, are given, the emotion is immediately evoked. If you examine any of Shakespeare's more successful tragedies, you will find this exact equivalence; you will find that the state of mind of Lady Macbeth walking in her sleep has been communicated to you by a skilful accumulation of imagined sensory impressions; the words of Macbeth on hearing of his wife's death strike us as if, given the sequence of events, these words were automatically released by the last event in the series. The artistic "inevitability" lies in this complete adequacy of the external to the emotion; and this is precisely what is deficient in *Hamlet*. Hamlet (the man) is dominated by an emotion which is inexpressible, because it is in *excess* of the facts as they appear. And the supposed identity of Hamlet with his author is genuine to this point: that Hamlet's bafflement at the absence of objective equivalent to his feelings is a prolongation of the bafflement of his creator in the face of his artistic problem. Hamlet is up against the difficulty that his disgust is occasioned by his mother, but that his mother is not an adequate equivalent for it; his disgust envelops and exceeds her. It is thus a feeling which he cannot understand; he cannot objectify it, and it therefore remains to poison life and obstruct action. None of the possible actions can satisfy it; and nothing that Shakespeare can do with the plot can express Hamlet for him. And it must be noticed that the very nature of the *données* of the problem precludes objective equivalence. To have heightened the criminality of Gertrude would have been to provide the formula for a totally different emotion in Hamlet; it is just *because* her character is so negative and insignificant that she arouses in Hamlet the feeling which she is incapable of representing.

The "madness" of Hamlet lay to Shakespeare's hand; in the earlier play a simple ruse, and to the end, we may presume, understood as a ruse by the audience. For Shakespeare it is less than madness and more than feigned. The levity of Hamlet, his repetition of phrase, his puns, are not part of a deliberate plan of dissimulation, but a form of emotional relief. In the character Hamlet it is the buffoonery of an emotion which can find no outlet in action; in the dramatist it is the buffoonery of an emotion which he cannot express in art. The intense feeling, ecstatic or terrible, without an object or exceeding its object, is something which every person of sensibility has known; it is doubtless a subject of study for pathologists. It often occurs in adolescence: the ordinary person puts these feelings to sleep, or trims down his feelings to fit the business world; the artist keeps them alive by his ability to intensify the world to his emotions. The Hamlet of Laforgue[1] is an adolescent; the Hamlet of Shakespeare is not, he has not that explanation and excuse. We must simply admit that here Shakespeare tackled a problem which proved too much for him. Why he attempted it at all is an insoluble puzzle; under compulsion of what experience he attempted to express the inexpressibly horrible, we cannot ever know. We need a great many facts in his biography; and we should like to know whether, and when, and after or at the same time as what personal experience, he read Montaigne, II. xii, *Apologie de Raimond Sebond.*[2] We should have, finally, to know something which is by hypothesis unknowable, for we assume it to be an experience which, in the manner indicated, exceeded the facts. We should have to understand things which Shakespeare did not understand himself.

From The Metaphysical Poets†

*   *   *

Not only is it extremely difficult to define metaphysical poetry, but difficult to decide what poets practise it and in which of their verses. * * * It is difficult to find any precise use of metaphor, simile, or other conceit, which is common to all the poets and at the same time important enough as an element of style to isolate these poets as a group. Donne, and often Cowley,[1] employ a device which is sometimes considered characteristically "metaphysical"; the elaboration (contrasted with the condensation) of a figure of speech to the farthest stage to which ingenuity can carry it. Thus Cowley develops the commonplace comparison of the world to a chess-board through long stanzas (*To Destiny*), and Donne, with more grace, in A *Valediction,*[2] the comparison of two lovers to a pair of compasses. But elsewhere we find, instead of the mere explication of the content of a comparison, a de-

---

1. Jules Laforgue (1860–1887), French symbolist poet, "to whom," Eliot says in "To Criticize the Critic" (1965), "I owe more than to any one poet in any language." One of Laforgue's *Moral Tales*, a set of experimental prose works, is entitled "Hamlet, or the Consequences of Filial Piety."
2. Michel de Montaigne (1533–1592), whose *Essais* established the essay as a literary form, wrote the *Apology for Raymond Sebond* (1580) as an oblique defense of his own skepticism.
† From *Selected Essays* by T. S. Eliot, Copyright © 1950 by Harcourt, Inc., and renewed 1978 by Esme Valerie Eliot, reprinted by permission of the publisher.
1. John Donne (1572–1631) and Abraham Cowley (1618–1667).
2. "A Valediction: Forbidding Mourning." The lines quoted below are from Donne's "A Valediction: Of Weeping."

122   T. S. Eliot

velopment by rapid association of thought which requires considerable agility on the part of the reader.

> On a round ball
> A workman that hath copies by, can lay
> An Europe, Afrique, and an Asia,
> And quickly make that, which was nothing, All,
> > So doth each teare,
> > Which thee doth weare,
> A globe, yea, world by that impression grow,
> Till thy tears mixt with mine doe overflow
> This world, by waters sent from thee, my heaven dissolved so.

Here we find at least two connexions which are not implicit in the first figure, but are forced upon it by the poet: from the geographer's globe to the tear, and the tear to the deluge. On the other hand, some of Donne's most successful and characteristic effects are secured by brief words and sudden contrasts:

> A bracelet of bright hair about the bone,[3]

where the most powerful effect is produced by the sudden contrast of associations of "bright hair" and of "bone." This telescoping of images and multiplied associations is characteristic of the phrase of some of the dramatists of the period which Donne knew: not to mention Shakespeare, it is frequent in Middleton, Webster, and Tourneur[4] and is one of the sources of the vitality of their language.

Johnson, who employed the term "metaphysical poets," apparently having Donne, Cleveland, and Cowley chiefly in mind, remarks of them that "the most heterogeneous ideas are yoked by violence together."[5] The force of this impeachment lies in the failure of the conjunction, the fact that often the ideas are yoked but not united; and if we are to judge of styles of poetry by their abuse, enough examples may be found in Cleveland to justify Johnson's condemnation. But a degree of heterogeneity of material compelled into unity by the operation of the poet's mind is omnipresent in poetry. We need not select for illustration such a line as:

> Notre âme est un trois-mâts cherchant son Icarie;[6]

3. From "The Relic."
4. Middleton and Webster are alluded to in *The Waste Land* and are identified in the notes to the poem. Cyril Tourneur (1575–1626) was an Irish dramatist known as a practitioner of revenge tragedy.
5. From Samuel Johnson's life of Cowley, one of his famous *Lives of the English Poets*, which influentially voiced the neoclassical disapproval of the wit of the metaphysicals. John Cleveland (1613–1658) has always been considered the most extreme of the metaphysical poets.
6. "Our soul is a three-master seeking her Icarie" (French). From Charles Baudelaire's "Le Voyage," the final poem in *Les Fleurs du Mal* (2nd ed., 1861). Icarie is an imaginary utopia, the subject of Étienne Cabet's *Voyage en Icarie* (1840) and an experimental community established by Cabet in Illinois in 1849.

we may find it in some of the best lines of Johnson himself (*The Vanity of Human Wishes*):

> His fate was destined to a barren strand,
> A petty fortress, and a dubious hand;
> He left a name at which the world grew pale,
> To point a moral, or adorn a tale.

where the effect is due to a contrast of ideas, different in degree but the same in principle, as that which Johnson mildly reprehended. * * * Again, we may justly take these quatrains from Lord Herbert's Ode;[7] stanzas which would, we think, be immediately pronounced to be of the metaphysical school:

> So when from hence we shall be gone,
>   And be no more, nor you, nor I,
>   As one another's mystery,
> Each shall be both, yet both but one.

> This said, in her up-lifted face,
>   Her eyes, which did that beauty crown,
>   Were like two starrs, that having faln down,
> Look up again to find their place:

> While such a moveless silent peace
>   Did seize on their becalmed sense,
>   One would have thought some influence
> Their ravished spirits did possess.

There is nothing in these lines (with the possible exception of the stars, a simile not at once grasped, but lovely and justified) which fits Johnson's general observations on the metaphysical poets in his essay on Cowley. A good deal resides in the richness of association which is at the same time borrowed from and given to the word "becalmed"; but the meaning is clear, the language simple and elegant. It is to be observed that the language of these poets is as a rule simple and pure; in the verse of George Herbert this simplicity is carried as far as it can go—a simplicity emulated without success by numerous modern poets. The *structure* of the sentences, on the other hand, is sometimes far from simple, but this is not a vice; it is a fidelity to thought and feeling. The effect, at its best, is far less artificial than that of an ode by Gray. And as this fidelity induces variety of thought and feeling, so it induces variety of music. We doubt whether, in the eighteenth century, could be found two poems in nominally the same metre, so dissimilar as Marvell's *Coy Mistress* and Crashaw's *Saint Teresa*;[8] the one producing

---

7. Lord Herbert of Cherbury's "Ode upon a Question Moved, Whether Love Should Continue Forever?"
8. Richard Crashaw (1613–1649), poet and convert to Catholicism, who modeled his work on the devotional writings of St. Teresa of Avila.

an effect of great speed by the use of short syllables, and the other an ecclesiastical solemnity by the use of long ones:

> Love, thou art absolute sole lord
> Of life and death.

If so shrewd and sensitive (though so limited) a critic as Johnson failed to define metaphysical poetry by its faults, it is worth while to inquire whether we may not have more success by adopting the opposite method: by assuming that the poets of the seventeenth century (up to the Revolution)[9] were the direct and normal development of the precedent age; and, without prejudicing their case by the adjective "metaphysical," consider whether their virtue was not something permanently valuable, which subsequently disappeared, but ought not to have disappeared. Johnson has hit, perhaps by accident, on one of their peculiarities, when he observes that "their attempts were always analytic"; he would not agree that, after the dissociation, they put the material together again in a new unity.

It is certain that the dramatic verse of the later Elizabethan and early Jacobean poets expresses a degree of development of sensibility which is not found in any of the prose, good as it often is. If we except Marlowe, a man of prodigious intelligence, these dramatists were directly or indirectly (it is at least a tenable theory) affected by Montaigne. Even if we except also Johnson and Chapman, these two were notably erudite, and were notably men who incorporated their erudition into their sensibility: their mode of feeling was directly and freshly altered by their reading and thought. In Chapman especially there is a direct sensuous apprehension of thought, or a recreation of thought into feeling, which is exactly what we find in Donne:

> in this one thing, all the discipline
> Of manners and of manhood is contained;
> A man to join himself with th' Universe
> In his main sway, and make in all things fit
> One with that All, and go on, round as it;
> Not plucking from the whole his wretched part,
> And into straits, or into nought revert,
> Wishing the complete Universe might be
> Subject to such a rag of it as he;
> But to consider great Necessity.[1]

We compare this with some modern passage:

> No, when the fight begins within himself,
> A man's worth something. God stoops o'er his head,

9. The Revolution of 1688, in which William of Orange was invited by Protestant forces to invade England and replace James II.
1. From The Revenge of Bussy d'Ambois (1610–1611), by George Chapman (1559–1634).

> Satan looks up between his feet—both tug—
> He's left, himself, i' the middle; the soul wakes
> And grows. Prolong that battle through his life![2]

It is perhaps somewhat less fair, though very tempting (as both poets are concerned with the perpetuation of love by offspring), to compare with the stanzas already quoted from Lord Herbert's Ode the following from Tennyson:

> One walked between his wife and child,
> With measured footfall firm and mild,
> And now and then he gravely smiled.
>   The prudent partner of his blood
>   Leaned on him, faithful, gentle, good,
>   Wearing the rose of womanhood.
> And in their double love secure,
> The little maiden walked demure,
> Pacing with downward eyelids pure.
> These three made unity so sweet,
> My frozen heart began to beat,
> Remembering its ancient heat.[3]

The difference is not a simple difference of degree between poets. It is something which had happened to the mind of England between the time of Donne or Lord Herbert of Cherbury and the time of Tennyson and Browning; it is the difference between the intellectual poet and the reflective poet. Tennyson and Browning are poets, and they think; but they do not feel their thought as immediately as the odour of a rose. A thought to Donne was an experience; it modified his sensibility. When a poet's mind is perfectly equipped for its work, it is constantly amalgamating disparate experience; the ordinary man's experience is chaotic, irregular, fragmentary. The latter falls in love, or reads Spinoza, and these two experiences have nothing to do with each other, or with the noise of the typewriter or the smell of cooking; in the mind of the poet these experiences are always forming new wholes.

We may express the difference by the following theory: The poets of the seventeenth century, the successors of the dramatists of the sixteenth, possessed a mechanism of sensibility which could devour any kind of experience. They are simple, artificial, difficult, or fantastic, as their predecessors were; no less nor more than Dante, Guido Cavalcanti, Guinizelli, or Cino.[4] In the seventeenth century a dissociation of sensibility set in, from which we have never recovered; and this disso-

2. From "Bishop Blougram's Apology" (1855), by Robert Browning (1812–1889).
3. From "The Two Voices," begun by Tennyson in 1833 somewhat in anticipation of *In Memoriam*.
4. Italian poets of the thirteenth century. The four had been credited by Ezra Pound (in *The Spirit of Romance* [1910]) with reviving in their *canzoni*, or love songs, the pure poetic beauty of the troubadours.

ciation, as is natural, was aggravated by the influence of the two most powerful poets of the century, Milton and Dryden. Each of these men performed certain poetic functions so magnificently well that the magnitude of the effect concealed the absence of others. The language went on and in some respects improved; the best verse of Collins, Gray, Johnson, and even Goldsmith[5] satisfies some of our fastidious demands better than that of Donne or Marvell or King. But while the language became more refined, the feeling became more crude. The feeling, the sensibility, expressed in the *Country Churchyard* (to say nothing of Tennyson and Browning) is cruder than that in the *Coy Mistress*.

The second effect of the influence of Milton and Dryden followed from the first, and was therefore slow in manifestation. The sentimental age began early in the eighteenth century, and continued. The poets revolted against the ratiocinative, the descriptive; they thought and felt by fits, unbalanced; they reflected. In one or two passages of Shelley's *Triumph of Life*, in the second *Hyperion*, there are traces of a struggle toward unification of sensibility. But Keats and Shelley died, and Tennyson and Browning ruminated.

After this brief exposition of a theory—too brief, perhaps, to carry conviction—we may ask, what would have been the fate of the "metaphysical" had the current of poetry descended in a direct line from them, as it descended in a direct line to them? They would not, certainly, be classified as metaphysical. The possible interests of a poet are unlimited; the more intelligent he is the better; the more intelligent he is the more likely that he will have interests: our only condition is that he turn them into poetry, and not merely meditate on them poetically. A philosophical theory which has entered into poetry is established, for its truth or falsity in one sense ceases to matter, and its truth in another sense is proved. The poets in question have, like other poets, various faults. But they were, at best, engaged in the task of trying to find the verbal equivalent for states of mind and feeling. And this means both that they are more mature, and that they wear better, than later poets of certainly not less literary ability.

It is not a permanent necessity that poets should be interested in philosophy, or in any other subject. We can only say that it appears likely that poets in our civilization, as it exists at present, must be *difficult*. Our civilization comprehends great variety and complexity, and this variety and complexity, playing upon a refined sensibility, must produce various and complex results. The poet must become more and more comprehensive, more allusive, more indirect, in order to force, to dislocate if necessary, language into his meaning. (A brilliant and

---

5. Poets associated with the neoclassical reaction against the excesses of metaphysical poetry. Thomas Gray is best known for his "Elegy Written in a Country Churchyard" (1750), disparaged by Eliot below. Oliver Goldsmith, interestingly, provides as many lines for *The Waste Land* as Marvell.

extreme statement of this view, with which it is not requisite to associate oneself, is that of M. Jean Epstein, *La Poésie d' aujourd-hui.*)[6] Hence we get something which looks very much like the conceit—we get, in fact, a method curiously similar to that of the "metaphysical poets," similar also in its use of obscure words and of simple phrasing. * * * It is interesting to speculate whether it is not a misfortune that two of the greatest masters of diction in our language, Milton and Dryden, triumph with a dazzling disregard of the soul. If we continued to produce Miltons and Drydens it might not so much matter, but as things are it is a pity that English poetry has remained so incomplete. Those who object to the "artificiality" of Milton or Dryden sometimes tell us to "look into our hearts and write." But that is not looking deep enough; Racine or Donne looked into a good deal more than the heart. One must look into the cerebral cortex, the nervous system, and the digestive tracts.

May we not conclude, then, that Donne, Crashaw, Vaughan, Herbert and Lord Herbert, Marvell, King, Cowley at his best, are in the direct current of English poetry, and that their faults should be reprimanded by this standard rather than coddled by antiquarian affection? They have been enough praised in terms which are implicit limitations because they are "metaphysical" or "witty," "quaint" or "obscure," though at their best they have not these attributes more than other serious poets. On the other hand, we must not reject the criticism of Johnson (a dangerous person to disagree with) without having mastered it, without having assimilated the Johnsonian canons of taste. In reading the celebrated passage in his essay on Cowley we must remember that by wit he clearly means something more serious than we usually mean today; in his criticism of their versification we must remember in what a narrow discipline he was trained, but also how well trained; we must remember that Johnson tortures chiefly the chief offenders, Cowley and Cleveland. It would be a fruitful work, and one requiring a substantial book, to break up the classification of Johnson (for there has been none since) and exhibit these poets in all their difference of kind and degree, from the massive music of Donne to the faint, pleasing tinkle of Aurelian Townshend—whose *Dialogue between a Pilgrim and Time* is one of the few regrettable omissions from the excellent anthology of Professor Grierson.[7]

6. "Poetry of Today" (French), published as a letter to Blaise Cendrars in Paris in 1921.
7. This essay was originally a review of *Metaphysical Lyrics and Poems of the Seventeenth Century: Donne to Butler,* an anthology edited by Herbert J. C. Grierson, which did include two other poems by Aurelian Townshend, a little-known follower of Donne whose few works survived only in manuscript collections.

Ulysses, Order, and Myth†

Mr Joyce's book has been out long enough for no more general expression of praise, or expostulation with its detractors, to be necessary;
and it has not been out long enough for any attempt at a complete
measurement of its place and significance to be possible. All that one
can usefully do at this time, and it is a great deal to do, for such a
book, is to elucidate any aspect of the book—and the number of aspects
is indefinite—which has not yet been fixed. I hold this book to be the
most important expression which the present age has found; it is a book
to which we are all indebted, and from which none of us can escape.
These are postulates for anything that I have to say about it, and I have
no wish to waste the reader's time by elaborating my eulogies; it has
given me all the surprise, delight, and terror that I can require, and I
will leave it at that.

Amongst all the criticisms I have seen of the book, I have seen
nothing—unless we except, in its way, M Valery Larbaud's[1] valuable
paper which is rather an Introduction than a criticism—which seemed
to me to appreciate the significance of the method employed—the parallel to the Odyssey, and the use of appropriate styles and symbols to
each division. Yet one might expect this to be the first peculiarity to
attract attention; but it has been treated as an amusing dodge, or scaffolding erected by the author for the purpose of disposing his realistic
tale, of no interest in the completed structure. The criticism which Mr
Aldington directed upon Ulysses several years ago seems to me to fail
by this oversight—but, as Mr Aldington wrote before the complete work
had appeared, fails more honourably than the attempts of those who
had the whole book before them. Mr Aldington treated Mr Joyce as a
prophet of chaos; and wailed at the flood of Dadaism which his pre-
scient eye saw bursting forth at the tap of the magician's rod. Of course,
the influence which Mr Joyce's book may have is from my point of
view an irrelevance. A very great book may have a very bad influence
indeed; and a mediocre book may be in the event most salutary. The
next generation is responsible for its own soul; a man of genius is responsible to his peers, not to a studio-full of uneducated and undisciplined coxcombs. Still, Mr Aldington's pathetic solicitude for the
half-witted seems to me to carry certain implications about the nature
of the book itself to which I cannot assent; and this is the important
issue. He finds the book, if I understand him, to be an invitation to

† From Selected Prose of T. S. Eliot, edited and with an introduction by Frank Kermode (London: Faber and Faber, 1975). Reprinted by permission of Faber and Faber Ltd.
1. Valery Larbaud (1881–1957), French novelist whose early lecture on Ulysses was useful in
building an audience for the book. It was published in Nouvelle Revue Française in 1921 and
then in Eliot's journal, The Criterion [Editor].

chaos, and an expression of feelings which are perverse, partial, and a distortion of reality. But unless I quote Mr Aldington's words I am likely to falsify. "I say, moreover," he says,[2] "that when Mr Joyce, with his marvellous gifts, uses them to disgust us with mankind, he is doing something which is false and a libel on humanity." It is somewhat similar to the opinion of the urbane Thackeray upon Swift. "As for the moral, I think it horrible, shameful, unmanly, blasphemous: and giant and great as this Dean is, I say we should hoot him." (This, of the conclusion of the Voyage to the Houyhnhnms—which seems to me one of the greatest triumphs that the human soul has ever achieved.— It is true that Thackeray later pays Swift one of the finest tributes that a man has ever given or received: "So great a man he seems to me that thinking of him is like thinking of an empire falling." And Mr Aldington, in his time, is almost equally generous.)

Whether it is possible to libel humanity (in distinction to libel in the usual sense, which is libelling an individual or a group in contrast with the rest of humanity) is a question for philosophical societies to discuss; but of course if Ulysses were a "libel" it would simply be a forged document, a powerless fraud, which would never have extracted from Mr Aldington a moment's attention. I do not wish to linger over this point: the interesting question is that begged by Mr Aldington when he refers to Mr Joyce's "great *undisciplined* talent."

I think that Mr Aldington and I are more or less agreed as to what we want in principle, and agreed to call it classicism. It is because of this agreement that I have chosen Mr Aldington to attack on the present issue. We are agreed as to what we want, but not as to how to get it, or as to what contemporary writing exhibits a tendency in that direction. We agree, I hope, that "classicism" is not an alternative to "romanticism," as of political parties, Conservative and Liberal, Republican and Democrat, on a "turn-the-rascals-out" platform. It is a goal toward which all good literature strives, so far as it is good, according to the possibilities of its place and time. One can be "classical," in a sense, by turning away from nine-tenths of the material which lies at hand, and selecting only mummified stuff from a museum—like some contemporary writers, about whom one could say some nasty things in this connexion, if it were worth while (Mr Aldington is not one of them). Or one can be classical in tendency by doing the best one can with the material at hand. The confusion springs from the fact that the term is applied to literature and to the whole complex of interests and modes of behaviour and society of which literature is a part; and it has not the same bearing in both applications. It is much easier to be a classicist in literary criticism than in creative art—because in criticism you are responsible only for what you want, and in creation you are responsible

2. *English Review*, April 1921.

for what you can do with material which you must simply accept. And in this material I include the emotions and feelings of the writer himself, which, for that writer, are simply material which he must accept —not virtues to be enlarged or vices to be diminished. The question, then, about Mr Joyce, is: how much living material does he deal with, and how does he deal with it: deal with, not as a legislator or exhorter, but as an artist?

It is here that Mr Joyce's parallel use of the Odyssey has a great importance. It has the importance of a scientific discovery. No one else has built a novel upon such a foundation before: it has never before been necessary. I am not begging the question in calling Ulysses a "novel"; and if you call it an epic it will not matter. If it is not a novel, that is simply because the novel is a form which will no longer serve; it is because the novel, instead of being a form, was simply the expression of an age which had not sufficiently lost all form to feel the need of something stricter. Mr Joyce has written one novel—the Portrait; Mr Wyndham Lewis has written one novel—Tarr. I do not suppose that either of them will ever write another "novel." The novel ended with Flaubert and with James. It is, I think, because Mr Joyce and Mr Lewis, being "in advance" of their time, felt a conscious or probably unconscious dissatisfaction with the form, that their novels are more formless than those of a dozen clever writers who are unaware of its obsolescence.

In using the myth, in manipulating a continuous parallel between contemporaneity and antiquity, Mr Joyce is pursuing a method which others must pursue after him. They will not be imitators, any more than the scientist who uses the discoveries of an Einstein in pursuing his own, independent, further investigations. It is simply a way of controlling, of ordering, of giving a shape and a significance to the immense panorama of futility and anarchy which is contemporary history. It is a method already adumbrated by Mr Yeats, and of the need for which I believe Mr Yeats to have been the first contemporary to be conscious. It is a method for which the horoscope is auspicious. Psychology (such as it is, and whether our reaction to it be comic or serious) ethnology, and The Golden Bough[3] have concurred to make possible what was impossible even a few years ago. Instead of narrative method, we may now use the mythical method. It is, I seriously believe, a step toward making the modern world possible for art, toward that order and form which Mr Aldington so earnestly desires. And only those who have won their own discipline in secret and without aid, in a world which offers very little assistance to that end, can be of any use in furthering this advance.

3. Major work of Sir James George Frazer (1854–1941), which Eliot credited with significant influence on The Waste Land. For selections, see pp. 29–34 [Editor].

The True Church and the Nineteen Churches†

While the poetry lovers have been subscribing to purchase for the nation the Keats house in Hampstead as a museum, the Church of England has apparently persisted in its design to sell for demolition nineteen religious edifices in the City of London.[1] Probably few American visitors, and certainly few natives, ever inspect these disconsolate fanes; but they give to the business quarter of London a beauty which its hideous banks and commercial houses have not quite defaced. Some are by Christopher Wren[2] himself, others by his school; the least precious redeems some vulgar street, like the plain little church of All Hallows at the end of London Wall. Some, like St Michael Paternoster Royal, are of great beauty. As the prosperity of London has increased, the City Churches have fallen into desuetude; for their destruction the lack of congregation is the ecclesiastical excuse, and the need of money the ecclesiastical reason. The fact that the erection of these churches was apparently paid for out of a public coal tax and their decoration probably by the parishioners, does not seem to invalidate the right of the True Church to bring them to the ground. To one who, like the present writer, passes his days in this City of London (*quand'io sentii chiavar l'uscio di sotto*)[3] the loss of these towers, to meet the eye down a grimy lane, and of these empty naves, to receive the solitary visitor at noon from the dust and tumult of Lombard Street, will be irreparable and unforgotten. A small pamphlet issued for the London County Council (*Proposed Demolition of Nineteen City Churches*: P. S. King & Son, Ltd., 2-4 Gt. Smith Street, Westminster, S.W.1, 3s.6d. net) should be enough to persuade of what I have said.

[*The Rite of Spring* and *The Golden Bough*]††

Looking back upon the past season in London—for no new season has yet begun—it remains certain that Strawinsky[1] was our two months'

---

† From "London Letter," *The Dial* 70 (June 1921): 690–91. All notes are by the editor of this Norton Critical Edition.
1. See both Eliot's note and the editorial note to *The Waste Land*, l. 264.
2. English architect and scientist (1632–1723). Probably the most widely known of all English architects, he designed St. Paul's Cathedral and fifty-two other London churches, which were rebuilt after the Great Fire of 1666.
3. "When I heard them nailing up the door" (Italian). A reference to Canto 33 of Dante's *Inferno*, in which the Count Ugolino is imprisoned in a tower for treason. See Eliot's note to l. 411 of *The Waste Land*, in which he quotes the same passage.
†† From "London Letter," *The Dial* 71 (October 1921): 452–53. All notes are by the editor of this Norton Critical Edition.
1. Igor Stravinsky, Russian composer (1882–1971), whose ballet *Le Sacre du Printemps* (The Rite of Spring) premiered in Paris in 1913. Eliot uses the transliteration of his name common at the time.

lion. He has been the greatest success since Picasso. In London all the stars obey their seasons, though these seasons no more conform to the almanac than those which concern the weather. A mysterious law of appearance and disappearance governs everybody—or at least everybody who is wise enough to obey it. * * * Why this should have happened this year rather than last year, perhaps rather than next year, I for one cannot tell. Even very insignificant people feel the occult influence; one knows, oneself, that there are times when it is desirable to be seen and times when it is felicitous to vanish.

But Strawinsky, Lucifer of the season, brightest in the firmament[2] took the call many times, small and correctly neat in pince-nez. His advent was well prepared by Mr Eugene Goossens[3]—also rather conspicuous this year—who conducted two Sacre du Printemps concerts, and other Strawinsky concerts were given before his arrival. The music was certainly too new and strange to please very many people; it is true that on the first night it was received with wild applause, and it is to be regretted that only three performances were given. If the ballet was not perfect, the fault does not lie either in the music, or in the choreography—which was admirable, or in the dancing—where Madame Sokolova[4] distinguished herself. To me the music seemed very remarkable—but at all events struck me as possessing a quality of modernity which I missed from the ballet which accompanied it. The effect was like Ulysses with illustrations by the best contemporary illustrator.

Strawinsky, that is to say, had done his job in the music. But music that is to be taken like operatic music, music accompanying and explained by an action, must have a drama which has been put through the same process of development as the music itself. The spirit of the music was modern, and the spirit of the ballet was primitive ceremony. The Vegetation Rite upon which the ballet is founded remained, in spite of the music, a pageant of primitive culture. It was interesting to any one who had read The Golden Bough and similar works, but hardly more than interesting. In art there should be interpenetration and metamorphosis. Even The Golden Bough can be read in two ways: as a collection of entertaining myths, or as a revelation of that vanished mind of which our mind is a continuation. In everything in the Sacre du Printemps, except in the music, one missed the sense of the present. Whether Strawinsky's music be permanent or ephemeral I do not know;

2. Lucifer, literally "lightbearer," is traditionally the name given to Satan before his fall from heaven. In classical times, and in Isaiah 14.12, he is associated with the morning star or Venus.
3. English conductor and composer (1893–1962).
4. Lydia Sokolova (1896–1974), English ballerina, born Hilda Munnings.

but it did seem to transform the rhythm of the steppes into the scream of the motor horn, the rattle of machinery, the grind of wheels, the beating of iron and steel, the roar of the underground railway, and the other barbaric cries of modern life; and to transform these despairing noises into music.

CRITICISM

Reviews and First Reactions

VIRGINIA WOOLF

[Eliot Chants *The Waste Land*]†

* * * Eliot dined last Sunday & read his poem. He sang it & chanted it rhythmed it. It has great beauty & force of phrase: symmetry; & tensity. What connects it together, I'm not so sure. But he read till he had to rush—letters to write about the London Magazine—& discussion thus was curtailed. One was left, however, with some strong emotion. The Waste Land, it is called; & Mary Hutch,[1] who has heard it more quietly, interprets it to be Tom's autobiography—a melancholy one.

TIMES LITERARY SUPPLEMENT

[Mr. Eliot's Poem]††

Mr. Eliot's poem is also a collection of flashes, but there is no effect of heterogeneity, since all these flashes are relevant to the same thing and together give what seems to be a complete expression of this poet's vision of modern life. We have here range, depth, and beautiful expression. What more is necessary to a great poem? This vision is singularly complex and in all its labyrinths utterly sincere. It is the mystery of life that it shows two faces, and we know of no other modern poet who can more adequately and movingly reveal to us the inextricable tangle of the sordid and the beautiful that make up life. Life is neither hellish nor heavenly; it has a purgatorial quality. And since it is purgatory, deliverance is possible. Students of Mr. Eliot's work will find a new note, and a profoundly interesting one, in the latter part of this poem.

---

† From *The Diary of Virginia Woolf* (New York: Harcourt Brace, 1978), 2:178. Copyright © 1978.

1. Mary Hutchinson (1889–1977), friend of Vivien Eliot's, mistress of Clive Bell's (Woolf's brother-in-law), and Eliot's confidant in the early twenties [*Editor*].

†† From an anonymous review of *The Criterion* 1.1, October 26, 1922, p. 690.

GILBERT SELDES

T. S. Eliot†

*   *   *

In essence 'The Waste Land' says something which is not new: that
life has become barren and sterile, that man is withering, impotent,
and without assurance that the waters which made the land fruitful will
ever rise again. (I need not say that 'thoughtful' as the poem is, it does
not 'express an idea'; it deals with emotions, and ends precisely in that
significant emotion, inherent in the poem, which Mr. Eliot has described.) The title, the plan, and much of the symbolism of the poem,
the author tells us in his 'Notes,' were suggested by Miss Weston's
remarkable book on the Grail legend, 'From Ritual to Romance'; it is
only indispensable to know that there exists the legend of a king rendered impotent, and his country sterile, both awaiting deliverance by a
knight on his way to seek the Grail; it is interesting to know further
that this is part of the Life or Fertility mysteries; but the poem is self-
contained. It seems at first sight remarkably disconnected, confused,
the emotion seems to disengage itself in spite of the objects and events
chosen by the poet as their vehicle. The poem begins with a memory
of summer showers, gaiety, joyful and perilous escapades; a moment
later someone else is saying 'I will show you fear in a handful of dust,'
and this is followed by the first lines of 'Tristan und Isolde,' and then
again by a fleeting recollection of loveliness. The symbolism of the
poem is introduced by means of the Tarot pack of cards; quotations,
precise or dislocated, occur; gradually one discovers a rhythm of alter-
nation between the visionary (so to name the memories of the past)
and the actual, between the spoken and the unspoken thought. There
are scraps, fragments; then sustained episodes; the poem culminates
with the juxtaposition of the highest types of Eastern and Western asceticism, by means of allusions to St. Augustine and Buddha; and ends
with a sour commentary on the injunctions 'Give, sympathize, control'
of the Upanishads, a commentary which reaches its conclusion in a
pastiche recalling all that is despairing and disinherited in the memory
of man.

A closer view of the poem does more than illuminate the difficulties;
it reveals the hidden form of the work, indicates how each thing falls
into place, and to the reader's surprise shows that the emotion which
at first seemed to come in spite of the framework and the detail could
not otherwise have been communicated. For the theme is not a distaste

† *Nation*, December 6, 1922, pp. 614–16.

for life, nor is it a disillusion, a romantic pessimism of any kind. It is specifically concerned with the idea of the Waste Land—that the land *was* fruitful and now is not, that life had been rich, beautiful, assured, organized, lofty, and now is dragging itself out in a poverty-stricken, and disrupted and ugly tedium, without health, and with no consolation in morality; there may remain for the poet the labor of poetry, but in the poem there remain only 'these fragments I have shored against my ruins'—the broken glimpses of what was. The poem is not an argument and I can only add, to be fair, that it contains no romantic idealization of the past; one feels simply that even in the cruelty and madness which have left their record in history and in art, there was an intensity of life, a germination and fruitfulness, which are now gone, and that even the creative imagination, even hallucination and vision have atrophied, so that water shall never again be struck from a rock in the desert. Mr. Bertrand Russell has recently said that since the Renaissance the clock of Europe has been running down; without the feeling that it was once wound up, without the contrasting emotions as one looks at the past and at the present, 'The Waste Land' would be a different poem, and the problem of the poem would have been solved in another way.

The present solution is in part by juxtaposition of opposites. We have a passage seemingly spoken by a slut, ending

> Goonight Bill. Goonight Lou. Goonight May. Goonight.
> Ta ta. Goonight. Goonight.

and then the ineffable

> Good night, ladies, good night, sweet ladies, goodnight, good night.

Conversely the turn is accomplished from nobility or beauty of utterance to

> The sounds of horns and motors, which shall bring
> Sweeney to Mrs. Porter in the spring.

And in the long passage where Tiresias, the central character of the poem, appears the method is at its height, for here is the coldest and unhappiest revelation of the assault of lust made in the terms of beauty * * *.

It will be interesting for those who have knowledge of another great work of our time, Mr Joyce's 'Ulysses,' to think of the two together. That 'The Waste Land' is, in a sense, the inversion and the complement of 'Ulysses' is at least tenable. We have in 'Ulysses' the poet defeated, turning outward, savoring the ugliness which is no longer transmutable into beauty, and, in the end, homeless. We have in 'The Waste Land' some indication of the inner life of such a poet. The contrast between the forms of these two works is not expressed in the recognition that one is among the longest and one among the shortest of works in its

genre; the important thing is that in each the theme, once it is comprehended, is seen to have dictated the form. More important still, I
fancy, is that each has expressed something of supreme relevance to
our present life in the everlasting terms of art.

EDMUND WILSON

The Poetry of Drouth†

Mr T. S. Eliot's first meagre volume of twenty-four poems was dropped
into the waters of contemporary verse without stirring more than a few
ripples. But when two or three years had passed, it was found to stain
the whole sea. Or, to change the metaphor a little, it became evident
that Mr Eliot had fished a murex¹ up. His productions, which had
originally been received as a sort of glorified *vers de société*, turned out
to be unforgettable poems, which everyone was trying to rewrite. There
might not be very much of him, but what there was had come somehow
to seem precious and now the publication of his long poem, The Waste
Land, confirms the opinion which we had begun gradually to cherish,
that Mr Eliot, with all his limitations, is one of our only authentic poets.
For this new poem—which presents itself as so far his most considerable
claim to eminence—not only recapitulates all his earlier and already
familiar motifs, but it sounds for the first time in all their intensity,
untempered by irony or disguise, the hunger for beauty and the anguish
at living which lie at the bottom of all his work.

Perhaps the best point of departure for a discussion of The Waste
Land is an explanation of its title. Mr Eliot asserts that he derived this
title, as well as the plan of the poem "and much of the incidental
symbolism," from a book by Miss Jessie L. Weston called From Ritual
to Romance. The Waste Land, it appears, is one of the many mysterious
elements which have made of the Holy Grail legend a perennial puzzle
of folk-lore; it is a desolate and sterile country, ruled over by an impotent king, in which not only have the crops ceased to grow and the
animals to reproduce their kind, but the very human inhabitants have
become unable to bear children. The renewal of the Waste Land and
the healing of the "Fisher King's" wound depend somehow upon the
success of the Knight who has come to find the Holy Grail.

Miss Weston, who has spent her whole life in the study of the Arthurian legends, has at last propounded a new solution for the problems

---

† From *The Dial* 73 (December 1922): 611–16. All notes are by the editor of this Norton
Critical Edition.
1. A sea snail (*Murex brandaris*) sought after in ancient times as the source of Tyrian purple
dye.

presented by this strange tale. Stimulated by Frazer's Golden Bough—
of which this extraordinarily interesting book is a sort of offshoot—she
has attempted to explain the Fisher King as a primitive vegetable god
—one of those creatures who, like Attis and Adonis, is identified with
Nature herself and in the temporary loss of whose virility the drouth or
inclemency of the season is symbolized; and whose mock burial is a
sort of earnest of his coming to life again. Such a cult, Miss Weston
contends, became attached to the popular Persian religion of Mithraism
and was brought north to Gaul and Britain by the Roman legionaries.
When Christianity finally prevailed, Attis was driven underground and
survived only as a secret cult, like the Venus of the Venusberg.[2] The
Grail legend, according to Miss Weston, had its origin in such a cult;
the Lance and Grail are the sexual symbols appropriate to a fertility
rite and the eerie adventure of the Chapel Perilous is the description
of an initiation.

Now Mr Eliot uses the Waste Land as the concrete image of a spiritual drouth. His poem takes place half in the real world—the world of
contemporary London, and half in a haunted wilderness—the Waste
Land of the mediaeval legend; but the Waste Land is only the hero's
arid soul and the intolerable world about him. The water which he
longs for in the twilit desert is to quench the thirst which torments him
in the London dusk.—And he exists not only upon these two planes,
but as if throughout the whole of human history. Miss Weston's interpretation of the Grail legend lent itself with peculiar aptness to Mr
Eliot's extraordinarily complex mind (which always finds itself looking
out upon the present with the prouder eyes of the past and which loves
to make its oracles as deep as the experience of the race itself by piling
up stratum upon stratum of reference, as the Italian painters used to
paint over one another); because she took pains to trace the Buried
God not only to Attis and Adonis, but further back to the recently
revealed Tammuz of the Sumerian-Babylonian civilization and to the
god invited to loosen the waters in the abysmally ancient Vedic
Hymns.[3] So Mr Eliot hears in his own parched cry the voices of all the
thirsty men of the past—of the author of Ecclesiastes in majestic bitterness at life's futility, of the Children of Israel weeping for Zion by
the unrefreshing rivers of Babylon, of the disciples after the Crucifixion
meeting the phantom of Christ on their journey; of Buddha's renunciation of life and Dante's astonishment at the weary hordes of Hell,
and of the sinister dirge with which Webster blessed the "friendless
bodies of unburied men." In the centre of his poem he places the weary
figure of the blind immortal prophet Tiresias, who, having been woman

---

2. The secret mountain cavern sacred to Venus, discovered in Richard Wagner's opera *Tann-
   häuser* (1845).
3. Ancient Sanskrit poems, on which the Upanishads (including the *Brihadāranyaka Upanishad*
   from which Eliot quotes in "What the Thunder Said") are elaborations and commentaries.

as well as man, has exhausted all human experience and, having "sat by Thebes below the wall and walked among the lowest of the dead," knows exactly what will happen in the London flat between the typist and the house-agent's clerk; and at its beginning the almost identical figure of the Cumaean Sibyl mentioned in Petronius, who—gifted also with extreme longevity and preserved as a sort of living mummy—when asked by little boys what she wanted, replied only "I want to die." Not only is life sterile and futile, but men have tasted its sterility and futility a thousand times before. T. S. Eliot, walking the desert of London, feels profoundly that the desert has always been there. Like Tiresias, he has sat below the wall of Thebes; like Buddha, he has seen the world as an arid conflagration; like the Sibyl, he has known everything and known everything vain.

Yet something else, too, reaches him from the past: as he wanders among the vulgarities which surround him, his soul is haunted by heroic strains of an unfading music. Sometimes it turns suddenly and shockingly into the jazz of the music-halls, sometimes it breaks in the middle of a bar and leaves its hearer with dry ears again, but still it sounds like the divine rumour of some high destiny from which he has fallen, like indestructible pride in the citizenship of some world which he never can reach. In a London boudoir, where the air is stifling with a dust of futility, he hears, as he approaches his hostess, an echo of Anthony and Cleopatra and of Aeneas coming to the house of Dido— and a painted panel above the mantel gives his mind a moment's swift release by reminding him of Milton's Paradise and of the nightingale that sang there.—Yet though it is most often things from books which refresh him, he has also a slight spring of memory. He remembers someone who came to him with wet hair and with hyacinths in her arms, and before her he was stricken senseless and dumb—"looking into the heart of light, the silence." There were rain and flowers growing then. Nothing ever grows during the action of the poem and no rain ever falls. The thunder of the final vision is "dry sterile thunder without rain." But as Gerontion in his dry rented house thinks wistfully of the young men who fought in the rain, as Prufrock longs to ride green waves and linger in the chambers of the sea, as Mr Apollinax is imagined drawing strength from the deep sea-caves of coral islands, so in this new poem Mr Eliot identifies water with all freedom and illumination of the soul. He drinks the rain that once fell on his youth as—to use an analogy in Mr Eliot's own manner—Dante drank at the river of Eunoë that the old joys he had known might be remembered. But—to note also the tragic discrepancy, as Mr Eliot always does—the draught, so far from renewing his soul and leaving him pure to rise to the stars, is only a drop absorbed in the desert; to think of it is to register its death. The memory is the dead god whom—as Hyacinth—he buries at the beginning of the poem and which—unlike his ancient prototype—is never to come to life again. Hereafter, fertility will fail; we shall see women deliberately making themselves sterile; we shall find that love has lost its life-giving power and can bring nothing but an asceticism of disgust. He is travelling in a country cracked by drouth in which he can only dream feverishly of drowning or of hearing the song of the hermit-thrush which has at least the music of water. The only reappearance of the god is as a phantom which walks beside him, the delirious hallucination of a man who is dying of thirst. In the end the dry-rotted world is crumbling about him—his own soul is falling apart. There is nothing left to prop it up but some dry stoic Sanskrit maxims and the broken sighs from the past, of singers exiled or oppressed. Like de Nerval, he is disinherited; like the poet of the Pervigilium Veneris, he is dumb; like Arnaut Daniel in Purgatory, he begs the world to raise a prayer for his torment, as he disappears in the fire.

It will be seen from this brief description that the poem is complicated; and it is actually even more complicated than I have made it appear. It is sure to be objected that Mr Eliot has written a puzzle rather than a poem and that his work can possess no higher interest than a full-rigged ship built in a bottle. It will be said that he depends too much upon books and borrows too much from other men and that there can be no room for original quality in a poem of little more than four hundred lines which contains allusions to, parodies of, or quotations from, the Vedic Hymns, Buddha, the Psalms, Ezekiel, Ecclesiastes, Luke, Sappho, Virgil, Ovid, Petronius, the Pervigilium Veneris, St Augustine, Dante, the Grail Legends, early English poetry, Kyd, Spenser, Shakespeare, John Day, Webster, Middleton, Milton, Goldsmith, Gérard de Nerval. Froude, Baudelaire, Verlaine, Swinburne, Wagner, The Golden Bough, Miss Weston's book, various popular ballads, and the author's own earlier poems. It has already been charged against Mr Eliot that he does not feel enough to be a poet and that the emotions of longing and disgust which he does have belong essentially to a delayed adolescence. It has already been suggested that his distate for the celebrated Sweeney shows a superficial mind and that if he only looked more closely into poor Sweeney he would find Eugene O'Neill's Hairy Ape;[4] and I suppose it will be felt in connexion with this new poem that if his vulgar London girls had only been studied by Sherwood Anderson they would have presented a very different appearance. At bottom, it is sure to be said, Mr Eliot is timid and prosaic like Mr Prufrock; he has no capacity for life, and nothing which happens to Mr Prufrock can be important.

Well: all these objections are founded on realities, but they are out-

---

4. *The Hairy Ape* (1922), by Eugene O'Neill (1888–1953), is about a coal stoker on a steamship. Sherwood Anderson (1876–1941) was thought at this time to be a rather daring writer, especially on sexual themes.

weighed by one major fact—the fact that Mr Eliot is a poet. It is true his poems seem the products of a constricted emotional experience and that he appears to have drawn rather heavily on books for the heat he could not derive from life. There is a certain grudging margin, to be sure, about all that Mr Eliot writes—as if he were compensating himself for his limitations by a peevish assumption of superiority. But it is the very acuteness of his suffering from this starvation which gives such poignancy to his art. And, as I say, Mr Eliot is a poet—that is, he feels intensely and with distinction and speaks naturally in beautiful verse— so that, no matter within what walls he lives, he belongs to the divine company. His verse is sometimes much too scrappy—he does not dwell long enough upon one idea to give it its proportionate value before passing on to the next—but these drops, though they be wrung from flint, are none the less authentic crystals. They are broken and some- times infinitely tiny, but they are worth all the rhinestones on the mar- ket. I doubt whether there is a single other poem of equal length by a contemporary American which displays so high and so varied a mastery of English verse. The poem is—in spite of its lack of structural unity— simply one triumph after another—from the white April light of the opening and the sweet wistfulness of the nightingale passage—one of the only successful pieces of contemporary blank verse—to the shabby sadness of the Thames Maidens, the cruel irony of Tiresias' vision, and the dry grim stony style of the descriptions of the Waste Land itself.

That is why Mr Eliot's trivialities are more valuable than other peo- ple's epics—why Mr Eliot's detestation of Sweeney is more precious than Mr Sandburg's sympathy for him, and Mr Prufrock's tea-table tragedy more important than all the passions of the New Adam[5]—sin- cere and carefully expressed as these latter emotions indubitably are. That is also why, for all its complicated correspondences and its re- condite references and quotations, The Waste Land is intelligible at first reading. It is not necessary to know anything about the Grail Legend or any but the most obvious of Mr Eliot's allusions to feel the force of the intense emotion which the poem is intended to convey—as one cannot do, for example, with the extremely ill-focussed Eight Cantos of his imitator Mr Ezra Pound, who presents only a bewildering mosaic with no central emotion to provide a key. In Eliot the very images and the sound of the words—even when we do not know precisely why he has chosen them—are charged with a strange poignancy which seems to bring us into the heart of the singer. And sometimes we feel that he is speaking not only for a personal distress, but for the starvation of a whole civilization—for people grinding at barren office-routine in the cells of gigantic cities, drying up their souls in eternal toil whose prod- ucts never bring them profit, where their pleasures are so vulgar and

5. *The New Adam* (1920), by Louis Untermeyer (1885–1977).

so feeble that they are almost sadder than their pains. It is our whole world of strained nerves and shattered institutions, in which "some infinitely gentle, infinitely suffering thing" is somehow being done to death—in which the maiden Philomel "by the barbarous king so rudely forced" can no longer even fill the desert "with inviolable voice." It is the world in which the pursuit of grace and beauty is something which is felt to be obsolete—the reflections which reach us from the past cannot illumine so dingy a scene; that heroic prelude has ironic echoes among the streets and the drawing-rooms where we live. Yet the race of the poets—though grown rarer—is not yet quite dead: there is at least one who, as Mr Pound says, has brought a new personal rhythm into the language and who has lent even to the words of his great predecessors a new music and a new meaning.

ELINOR WYLIE

Mr. Eliot's Slug-Horn†

The reviewer who must essay, within the limits of a few hundred temperate and well-chosen words, to lead even a willing reader into the ensorcelled[1] mazes of Mr. T. S. Eliot's 'Waste Land' perceives, as the public prints have it, no easy task before him. He will appear to the mental traveller as dubious a guide as Childe Roland's hoary cripple with malicious eye;[2] he lies in every word, unless by some stroke of luck, some lightning flash of revelation, he succeeds in showing forth the tragic sincerity and true power of that mysterious and moving spectacle, 'The Waste Land,' the mind of Mr. Eliot, the reflected and refracted mind of a good—or rather a bad—quarter of the present generation.

Amazing comparisons have been drawn between Mr. Eliot and certain celebrated poets; his admirers do not couple him with Pound nor his detractors with Dante, and both are justified in any annoyance which they may feel when others do so. His detractors say that he is obscure; his friends reply that he is no more cryptic than Donne and Yeats; his detractors shift their ground and point out with perfect truth that he has not the one's incomparable wit nor the other's incomparable magic; his friends, if they are wise, acquiesce. It is stated that he is not so universal a genius as Joyce; the proposition appears self-evident to any one who believes with the present reviewer, that Joyce is the sea

---

† From *New York Evening Post Literary Review*, January 20, 1923, p. 396. All notes are by the editor of this Norton Critical Edition.
1. Bewitched.
2. From Robert Browning's poem "Childe Roland to the Dark Tower Came" (1855), in which the protagonist confronts such a cripple at the beginning of his quest.

from whose profundity Eliot has fished up that very Tyrian murex with which Mr. Wilson rightly credits him.[3] Some comparisons, indeed, suggest the lunatic asylums where gentlemen imagine themselves to be the authors of Caesar's Commentaries and the Code Napoléon.

But when we begin to inquire what Mr. Eliot is, instead of what he is not—then if we fail to respond to his accusing cry of '*Mon semblable—mon frère!*' I am inclined to think that we are really either hypocrite readers or stubborn ones closing deliberate eyes against beauty and passion still pitifully alive in the midst of horror. I confess that once upon a time I believed Mr. Eliot to be a brutal person: this was when I first read the 'Portrait of a Lady.' I now recognize my error, but my sense of the hopeless sadness and humiliation of the poor lady was perfectly sound. I felt that Mr. Eliot had torn the shrinking creature's clothes from her back and pulled the drawing-room curtains aside with a click to admit a flood of shameful sunlight, and I hated him for his cruelty. Only now that I know he is Tiresias have I lost my desire to strike him blind as Peeping Tom.

This power of suggesting intolerable tragedy at the heart of the trivial or the sordid is used with a skill little less than miraculous in 'The Waste Land,' and the power is the more moving because of the attendant conviction, that this terrible resembling contrast between nobility and baseness is an agony in the mind of Mr. Eliot of which only a portion is transferred to that of the reader. He is a cadaver, dissecting himself in our sight; he is the god Atthis who was buried in Stetson's garden and who now arises to give us the benefit of an anatomy lesson. Of course it hurts him more than it does us, and yet it hurts some of us a great deal at that. If this is a trick, it is an inspired one. I do not believe that it is a trick; I think that Mr. Eliot conceived 'The Waste Land' out of an extremity of tragic emotion and expressed it in his own voice and in the voices of other unhappy men not carefully and elaborately trained in close harmony, but coming as a confused and frightening and beautiful murmur out of the bowels of the earth. 'I did not know death had undone so many.' If it were merely a piece of virtuosity it would remain astonishing; it would be a work of art like a fine choir of various singers or a rose window executed in bright fragments of glass. But it is far more than this; it is infused with spirit and passion and despair, and it shoots up into stars of brilliance or flows down dying falls of music which nothing can obscure or silence. These things, rather than other men's outcries, are shored against any ruin which may overtake Mr. Eliot at the hands of Fate or the critics. As for the frequently reiterated statement that Mr. Eliot is a dry intellectual, without depth or sincerity of feeling, it is difficult for me to refute an idea which I am totally at a loss to understand; to me he seems almost

---

3. See Wilson's essay "The Poetry of Drouth," p. 140.

inexcusably sensitive and sympathetic and quite inexcusably poignant, since he forces me to employ this horrid word to describe certain qualities which perhaps deserve a nobler tag in mingling pity with terror. That he expresses the emotion of an intellectual is perfectly true, but of the intensity of that emotion there is, to my mind, no question, nor do I recognize any reason for such a question. A very simple mind expresses emotion by action: a kiss or a murder will not make a song until they have passed through the mind of a poet, and a subtile mind may make a simple song about a murder because the murder was a simple one. But the simplicity of the song will be most apparent to the subtlest minds; it will be like a queer masquerading as a dairy maid. But as for Mr. Eliot, he has discarded all disguises; nothing could be more personal and direct than his method of presenting his weariness and despair by means of a stream of memories and images the like of which, a little dulled and narrowed, runs through the brain of any educated and imaginative man whose thoughts are sharpened by suffering. I should perhaps have doubted the suitability of such a stream as material for poetry, just as I do now very much doubt the suitability of Sanskrit amens and abracadabras, but these dubieties are matters of personal taste and comparatively unimportant beside the fact that, though Mr. Eliot may speak with the seven tongues of men and of angels, he has not become as sounding brass and tinkling cymbal. His gifts, whatever they are, profit him much; his charity, like Tiresias, has suffered and foresuffered all. If he is intellectually arrogant and detached—and I cannot for the life of me believe that he is—he is not spiritually either the one or the other; I could sooner accuse him of being sentimental. Indeed, in his tortured pity for ugly and ignoble things he sometimes comes near to losing his hardness of outline along with his hardness of heart; his is not a kindly tolerance for weakness and misery, but an obsessed and agonized sense of kinship with it which occasionally leads him into excesses of speech, ejaculations whose flippancy is the expression of profound despair.

Were I unable to feel this passion shaking the dry bones of 'The Waste Land' like a great wind I would not give a penny for all the thoughts and riddles of the poem; the fact that Mr. Eliot has failed to convince many readers that he has a soul must be laid as a black mark against him. Either you see him as a parlor prestidigitator, a character in which I am personally unable to visualize him, or else you see him as a disenchanted wizard, a disinherited prince. When he says *Shantih* three times as he emerges from 'The Waste Land' you may not think he means it: my own impulse to write *Amen* at the end of a poem has been too often and too hardly curbed to leave any doubt in my mind as to Mr. Eliot's absorbed seriousness; he is fanatically in earnest. His 'Waste Land' is Childe Roland's evil ground, the names of all the lost adventurers his peers toll in his mind increasing like a bell. He has set the slug-horn to his lips and blown it once and twice: the squat, round tower, blind as the fool's heart, is watching him, but he will blow the horn again.[4]

CONRAD AIKEN

An Anatomy of Melancholy†

Mr. T. S. Eliot is one of the most individual of contemporary poets, and at the same time, anomalously, one of the most 'traditional.' By individual I mean that he can be, and often is (distressingly, to some) aware in his own way; as when he observes of a woman (in 'Rhapsody on a Windy Night') that the door 'opens on her like a grin' and that the corner of her eye 'Twists like a crooked pin.' Everywhere, in the very small body of his work, is similar evidence of a delicate sensibility, somewhat shrinking, somewhat injured, and always sharply itself. But also, with this capacity or necessity for being aware in his own way, Mr. Eliot has a haunting, a tyrannous awareness that there have been many other awarenesses before; and that the extent of his own awareness, and perhaps even the nature of it, is a consequence of these. He is, more than most poets, conscious of his roots. If this consciousness had not become acute in 'Prufrock' or the 'Portrait of a Lady,' it was nevertheless probably there: and the roots were quite conspicuously French, and dated, say, 1870–1900. A little later, as if his sense of the past had become more pressing, it seemed that he was positively redirecting his roots—urging them to draw a morbid dramatic sharpness from Webster and Donne, a faded dry gilt of cynicism and formality from the Restoration. This search of the tomb produced 'Sweeney' and 'Whispers of Immortality.' And finally, in 'The Waste Land,' Mr. Eliot's sense of the literary past has become so overmastering as almost to constitute the motive of the work. It is as if, in conjunction with the Mr. Pound of the 'Cantos,'[1] he wanted to make a 'literature of literature'—a poetry not more actuated by life itself than by poetry; as if he had concluded that the characteristic awareness of a poet of the 20th century must inevitably, or ideally, be a very complex and very literary awareness able to speak only, or best, in terms of the literary past, the terms which had moulded its tongue. This involves a kind of idolatry of literature with

4. At the end of Browning's poem, Roland blows his "slug-horn." The word is in fact an early form of the word "slogan," but Browning uses it as if it means trumpet. In any case, the blowing of it is supposed to be a doomed, romantic gesture.
† From *New Republic*, February 7, 1923, pp. 294–95. Reprinted by permission. All notes are by the editor of this Norton Critical Edition.
1. Ezra Pound published his modernist literary epic in separate "Cantos" between 1917 and 1969.

which it is a little difficult to sympathize. In positing, as it seems to, that there is nothing left for literature to do but become a kind of parasitic growth on literature, a sort of mistletoe, it involves, I think, a definite astigmatism—a distortion. But the theory is interesting if only because it has colored an important and brilliant piece of work.

'The Waste Land' is unquestionably important, unquestionably brilliant. It is important partly because its 433 lines summarize Mr. Eliot, for the moment, and demonstrate that he is an even better poet than most had thought; and partly because it embodies the theory just touched upon, the theory of the 'allusive' method in poetry. 'The Waste Land' is, indeed, a poem of allusion all compact. It purports to be symbolical; most of its symbols are drawn from literature or legend; and Mr. Eliot has thought it necessary to supply, in notes, a list of the many quotations, references, and translations with which it bristles. He observes candidly that the poem presents 'difficulties,' and requires 'elucidation.' This serves to raise at once, the question whether these difficulties, in which perhaps Mr. Eliot takes a little pride, are so much the result of complexity, a fine elaborateness, as of confusion. The poem has been compared, by one reviewer, to a 'full-rigged ship built in a bottle,' the suggestion being that it is a perfect piece of construction. But *is* it a perfect piece of construction? Is the complex material mastered, and made coherent? Or, if the poem is not successful in that way, in what way *is* it successful? Has it the formal and intellectual complex unity of a microscopic 'Divine Comedy'; or is its unity—supposing it to have one—of another sort?

If we leave aside for the moment all other considerations, and read the poem solely with the intention of understanding, with the aid of the notes, the symbolism, of making out what it is that is symbolized, and how these symbolized feelings are brought into relation with each other and with the other matters in the poem; I think we must, with reservations, and with no invidiousness, conclude that the poem is not, in any formal sense, coherent. We cannot feel that all the symbolisms belong quite inevitably where they have been put; that the order of the parts is an inevitable order; that there is anything more than a rudimentary progress from one theme to another; nor that the relation between the more symbolic parts and the less is always as definite as it should be. What we feel is that Mr. Eliot has not wholly annealed the allusive matter, has left it unabsorbed, lodged in gleaming fragments amid material alien to it. Again, there is a distinct weakness consequent on the use of allusions which may have both intellectual and emotional value for Mr. Eliot, but (even with the notes) none for us. The 'Waste Land,' of the Grail Legend, might be a good symbol, if it were something with which we were sufficiently familiar. But it can never, even when explained, be a good symbol, simply because it has no immediate associations for us. It might, of course, be a good *theme*. In that case it would be given us. But Mr. Eliot uses it for purposes of overtone; he refers to it; and as overtone it quite clearly fails. He gives us, superbly, a waste land—not *the* Waste Land. Why, then, refer to the latter at all—if he is not, in the poem, really going to use it? Hyacinth fails in the same way. So does the Fisher King. So does the Hanged Man, which Mr. Eliot tells us he associates with Frazer's Hanged God—we take his word for it. But if the precise association is worth anything, it is worth *putting into the poem*; otherwise there can be no purpose in mentioning it. Why, again, Datta, Dayadhvam, Damyata? Or Shantih. Do they not say a good deal less for us than 'Give: sympathize: control' or 'Peace'? Of course; but Mr. Eliot replies that he wants them not merely to mean those particular things, but also to mean them in a particular way—that is, to be remembered in connection with a Upanishad. Unfortunately, we have none of us this memory, nor can he give it to us; and in the upshot he gives us only a series of agreeable sounds which might as well have been nonsense. What we get at, and I think it is important, is that in none of these particular cases does the reference, the allusion, justify itself intrinsically, make itself felt. When we are aware of these references at all (sometimes they are unidentifiable) we are aware of them simply as something unintelligible but suggestive. When they have been explained, we are aware of the material referred to, the fact, (for instance, a vegetation ceremony,) as something useless for our enjoyment or understanding of the poem, something distinctly 'dragged in,' and only, perhaps, of interest as having suggested a pleasantly ambiguous line. For unless an allusion is made to live identifiably, to flower, where transplanted, it is otiose. We admit the beauty of the implicational or allusive method; but the key to an implication should be in the implication itself, not outside of it. We admit the value of esoteric pattern: but the pattern should itself disclose its secret, should not be dependent on a cypher. Mr. Eliot assumes for his allusions, and for the fact that they actually allude to something, an importance which the allusions themselves do not, as expressed, aesthetically command, nor, as explained, logically command; which is pretentious. He is a little pretentious, too, in his 'plan,'—'qui pourtant n'existe pas.'[2] If it is a plan, then its principle is oddly akin to planlessness. Here and there, in the wilderness, a broken finger-post.

I enumerate these objections not, I must emphasize, in derogation of the poem, but to dispel, if possible, an illusion as to its nature. It is perhaps important to note that Mr. Eliot, with his comment on the 'plan,' and several critics, with their admiration of the poem's woven complexity, minister to the idea that 'The Waste Land' is, precisely, a kind of epic in a walnut shell: elaborate, ordered, unfolded with a logic at every joint discernible; but it is also important to note that this idea

---

2. "Which, nonetheless, does not exist" (French).

is false. With or without the notes the poem belongs rather to that symbolical order in which one may justly say that the 'meaning' is not explicitly, or exactly, worked out. Mr. Eliot's net is wide, its meshes are small; and he catches a good deal more—thank heaven—than he pretends to. If space permitted one could pick out many lines and passages and parodies and quotations which do not demonstrably, in any 'logical' sense, carry forward the theme, passages which unjustifiably, but happily, 'expand' beyond its purpose. Thus the poem has an emotional value far clearer and richer than its arbitrary and rather unworkable logical value. One might assume that it originally consisted of a number of separate poems which have been telescoped — given a kind of forced unity. The Waste Land conception offered itself as a generous net which would, if not unify, at any rate contain these varied elements. We are aware of a superficial 'binding'—we observe the anticipation and repetition of themes, motifs; 'Fear death by water' anticipates the episode of Phlebas, the cry of the nightingale is repeated, but these are pretty flimsy links, and do not genuinely bind because they do not reappear naturally, but arbitrarily. This suggests, indeed, that Mr. Eliot is perhaps attempting a kind of program music in words, endeavoring to rule out 'emotional accidents' by supplying his readers, in notes, with only those associations which are correct. He himself hints at the musical analogy when he observes that 'In the first part of Part V three themes are employed.'

I think, therefore, that the poem must be taken,—most invitingly offers itself,—as a brilliant and kaleidoscopic confusion; as a series of sharp, discrete, slightly related perceptions and feelings, dramatically and lyrically presented, and violently juxtaposed, (for effect of dissonance) so as to give us an impression of an intensely modern, intensely literary consciousness which perceives itself to be not a unit but a chance correlation or conglomerate of mutually discolorative fragments. We are invited into a mind, a world, which is a 'broken bundle of mirrors'; a 'heap of broken images,' Isn't it that Mr. Eliot, finding it 'impossible to say just what he means,'[3]—to recapitulate, to enumerate all the events and discoveries and memories that make a consciousness,—has emulated the 'magic lantern' that throws 'the nerves in patterns on a screen'? If we perceive the poem in this light, as a series of brilliant, brief, unrelated or dimly related pictures by which a consciousness empties itself of its characteristic contents, then we also perceive that, anomalously, though the dropping out of any one picture would not in the least affect the logic or 'meaning' of the whole, it would seriously detract from the value of the portrait. The 'plan' of the poem would not greatly suffer, one makes bold to assert, by the elimination of 'April is the cruellest month,' or Phlebas, or the Thames

3. A reference to l. 104 of "The Love Song of J. Alfred Prufrock."

daughters, or Sosostris or 'You gave me hyacinths' or 'A woman drew her long black hair out tight'; nor would it matter if it did. These things are not important parts of an important or careful intellectual pattern, but they are important parts of an important emotional ensemble. The relations between Tiresias (who is said to unify the poem, in a sense, as spectator) and the Waste Land, or Mr. Eugenides, or Hyacinth, or any other fragment, is a dim and tonal one, not exact. It will not bear analysis, it is not always operating, nor can one with assurance, at any given point, say how much it is operating. In this sense 'The Waste Land' is a series of separate poems or passages, not perhaps all written at one time or with one aim, to which a spurious but happy sequence has been given. This spurious sequence has a value—it creates the necessary superficial formal unity; but it need not be stressed, as the Notes stress it. Could one not wholly rely for one's unity,—as Mr. Eliot *has* largely relied—simply on the dim unity of 'personality' which would underlie the retailed contents of a single consciousness? Unless one is going to carry unification very far, weave and interweave very closely, it would perhaps be as well not to unify at all; to dispense, for example, with arbitrary repetitions.

We reach thus the conclusion that the poem succeeds—as it brilliantly does—by virtue of its incoherence, not of its plan; by virtue of its ambiguities, not of its explanations. Its incoherence is a virtue because its 'donnée' is incoherence. Its rich, vivid, crowded use of implication is a virtue, as implication is *always* a virtue;—it shimmers, it suggests, it gives the desired strangeness. But when, as often, Mr. Eliot uses an implication beautifully—conveys by means of a picture-symbol or action-symbol a feeling—we do not require to be told that he had in mind a passage in the Encyclopedia, or the color of his nursery wall; the information is disquieting, has a sour air of pedantry. We 'accept' the poem as we would accept a powerful, melancholy tone-poem. We do not want to be told what occurs; nor is it more than mildly amusing to know what passages are, in the Straussian manner, echoes or parodies. We cannot believe that every syllable has an algebraic inevitability, nor would we wish it so. We could dispense with the French, Italian, Latin and Hindu phrases—they are irritating. But when our reservations have all been made, we accept 'The Waste Land' as one of the most moving and original poems of our time. It captures us. And we sigh, with a dubious eye on the 'notes' and 'plan,' our bewilderment that after so fine a performance Mr. Eliot should have thought it an occasion for calling 'Tullia's ape a marmosyte.' Tullia's ape is good enough.[4]

---

4. "He tickles this age that can / Call Tullia's ape a marmosite / And Leda's goose a swan." From an anonymous seventeenth-century song.

TIME

Shantih, Shantih, Shantih: Has the Reader Any Rights Before the Bar of Literature?†

There is a new kind of literature abroad in the land, whose only obvious fault is that no one can understand it. Last year there appeared a gigantic volume entitled *Ulysses*, by James Joyce. To the uninitiated it appeared that Mr. Joyce had taken some half million assorted words—many such as are not ordinarily heard in reputable circles—shaken them up in a colossal hat, laid them end to end. To those in on the secret the result represented the greatest achievement of modern letters—a new idea in novels.

The Dial has awarded its $2,000 prize for the best poem of 1922 to an opus entitled *The Waste Land*, by T. S. Eliot. Burton Rascoe, of *The New York Tribune*, hails it as incomparably great. Edmund Wilson, Jr., of *Vanity Fair*, is no less enthusiastic in praise of it. So is J. Middleton Murry, British critic.

*   *   *

The case for the defense, as presented by the admirers of Messrs. Eliot, Joyce, et al., runs something like this:

Literature is self-expression. It is up to the reader to extract the meaning, not up to the writer to offer it. If the author writes everything that pops into his head—or that is supposed to pop into the head of a given character—that is all that should be asked. Lucidity is no part of the auctorial task.

It is rumoured that *The Waste Land* was written as a hoax. Several of its supporters explain that that is immaterial, literature being concerned not with intentions but results.

TIMES LITERARY SUPPLEMENT

[A Zig-Zag of Allusion]††

Between the emotion from which a poem rises and the reader there is always a cultural layer of more or less density from which the images or characters in which it is expressed may be drawn. In the ballad 'I wish I were where Helen lies' this middle ground is but faintly indi-

† From *Time*, March 3, 1923, p. 12. Copyright © 1923 Time Inc.
†† From the *Times Literary Supplement*, September 20, 1923, p. 616. Reprinted by permission of the *Times Literary Supplement*. All notes are by the editor of this Norton Critical Edition.

cated.[1] The ballad, we say, is *simpler* than the 'Ode to the Nightingale'; it evokes very directly an emotional response. In the ode the emotion gains resonance from the atmosphere of legendary association through which it passes before reaching us. It cannot be called better art, but it is certainly more sophisticated and to some minds less poignant. From time to time there appear poets and a poetic audience to whom this refractory haze of allusion must be very dense; without it the meanings of the words strike them so rapidly as to be inappreciable, just as, without the air, we could not detect the vibration of light. We may remember with what elaboration Addison, among others, was obliged to undertake the defence of the old ballads before it was recognized that their bare style might be admired by gentlemen familiar with the classics.[2]

The poetic personality of Mr Eliot is extremely sophisticated. His emotions hardly ever reach us without traversing a zig-zag of allusion. In the course of his four hundred lines he quotes from a score of authors and in three foreign languages, though his artistry has reached that point at which it knows the wisdom of sometimes concealing itself. There is in general in his work a disinclination to awake in us a direct emotional response. It is only, the reader feels; out of regard for someone else that he has been induced to mount the platform at all. From there he conducts a magic-lantern show; but being too reserved to expose in public the impressions stamped on his own soul by the journey through the Waste Land, he employs the slides made by others, indicating with a touch the difference between his reaction and theirs. So the familiar stanza of Goldsmith becomes

> When lovely woman stoops to folly and
> Paces about her room again, alone,
> She smoothes her hair with automatic hand,
> And puts a record on the gramophone.

To help us to elucidate the poem Mr Eliot has provided some notes which will be of more interest to the pedantic than the poetic critic. Certainly they warn us to be prepared to recognize some references to vegetation ceremonies. This is the cultural or middle layer, which, whilst it helps us to perceive the underlying emotion, is of no poetic value in itself. We desire to touch the inspiration itself, and if the apparatus of reserve is too strongly constructed, it will defeat the poet's end. The theme is announced frankly enough in the title, *The Waste Land*; and in the concluding confession,

> These fragments I have shored against my ruins,

1. An anonymous seventeenth- or eighteenth-century Scottish ballad, sometimes called "Fair Helen" or "Helen of Kirconnell."
2. For example, Joseph Addison's essay in *The Spectator* (May 21, 1711) on the ballad of Chevy Chase.

we receive a direct communication which throws light on much which had preceded it. From the opening part, 'The Burial of the Dead', to the final one we seem to see a world, or a mind, in disaster and mocking its despair. We are aware of the toppling of aspirations, the swift disintegration of accepted stability, the crash of an ideal. Set at a distance by a poetic method which is reticence itself, we can only judge of the strength of the emotion by the visible violence of the reaction. Here is Mr Eliot, a dandy of the choicest phrase, permitting himself blatancies like 'the young man carbuncular'. Here is a poet capable of a style more refined than that of any of his generation parodying without taste or skill—and of this the example from Goldsmith is not the most astonishing. Here is a writer to whom originality is almost an inspiration borrowing the greater number of his best lines, creating hardly any himself. It seems to us as if the *The Waste Land* exists in the greater part in the state of notes. This quotation is a particularly obvious instance:

> London Bridge is falling down falling down falling down
> *Poi s' ascose nel foco che gli affina*
> *Quando fiam uti chelidon*—O swallow swallow
> *Le Prince d'Aquitaine à la tour abolie.*

The method has a number of theoretical justifications. Mr Eliot has himself employed it discreetly with delicious effect. It suits well the disillusioned smile which he had in common with Laforgue;[3] but we do sometimes wish to hear the poet's full voice. Perhaps if the reader were sufficiently sophisticated he would find these echoes suggestive hints, as rich in significance as the sonorous amplifications of the romantic poets. None the less, we do not derive from this poem as a whole the satisfaction we ask from poetry. Numerous passages are finely written; there is an amusing monologue in the vernacular, and the fifth part is nearly wholly admirable. The section beginning

> What is that sound high in the air . . .

has a nervous strength which perfectly suits the theme; but he declines to a mere notation, the result of an indolence of the imagination.

Mr Eliot, always evasive of the grand manner, has reached a stage at which he can no longer refuse to recognize the limitations of his medium; he is sometimes walking very near the limits of coherency. But it is the finest horses which have the most tender mouths, and some unsympathetic tug has sent Mr Eliot's gift awry. When he recovers control we shall expect his poetry to have gained in variety and strength from this ambitious experiment.

---

3. Jules Laforgue (1860–1887), French Symbolist poet. For Eliot's tribute to him, see *"From Hamlet,"* p. 121.

CHARLES POWELL

[So Much Waste Paper]†

This poem of 433 lines, with a page of notes to every three pages of text, is not for the ordinary reader. He will make nothing of it. Its five sections, called successively "The Burial of the Dead", "A Game of Chess", and so on, for all they will signify to him, might as well be called "Tom Thumb at the Giant's Causeway" or "The Devil among the Bailiffs", and so on. The thing is a mad medley. It has a plan, because its author says so: and presumably it has some meaning, because he speaks of its symbolism; but meaning, plan, and intention alike are massed behind a smoke-screen of anthropological and literary erudition, and only the pundit, the pedant, or the clairvoyant will be in the least aware of them. Dr Frazer and Miss J. L. Weston are freely and admittedly his creditors, and the bulk of the poem is under an enormously composite and cosmopolitan mortgage: to Spenser, Shakespeare, Webster, Kyd, Middleton, Milton, Marvell, Goldsmith, Ezekiel, Buddha, Virgil, Ovid, Dante, St Augustine, Baudelaire, Verlaine, and others. Lines of German, French and Italian are thrown in at will or whim; so, too, are solos from nightingales, cocks, hermit-thrushes, and Ophelia. * * * For the rest one can only say that if Mr Eliot had been pleased to write in demotic English *The Waste Land* might not have been, as it just is to all but anthropologists and *literati*, so much waste paper.

GORHAM MUNSON

The Esotericism of T. S. Eliot††

Some expert—my choice would be Mr. Ezra Pound—should write a moderately long brochure on the versification of T. S. Eliot. Mr. Eliot wrote such a brochure on the metric of Pound and it sharpened considerably our insight into the construction and finesse of his poetry. We need much more of this precise service. Mr. Pound, for example, could show us very exactly the crossing of Mr. Eliot's style by French influences, he could discuss at length what he has already mentioned; 'Mr. Eliot's two sorts of metaphor: his wholly unrealizable, always apt, half

---

† From *Manchester Guardian*, October 31, 1923, p. 7. Copyright © *The Guardian*. Reprinted by permission of *The Guardian*.
†† From *1924*, July 1, 1924, 3–10. Copyright © 1924 by Gorham Munson. Permission granted by McIntosh and Otis, Inc., literary agents for the Estate of Elizabeth Munson. All notes are by the editor of this Norton Critical Edition.

ironic suggestion, and his precise realizable picture,'[1] he could elaborate on Mr. Eliot's thematic invention.

Surely in reading the 'Poems' and 'The Waste Land' all serious students of poetry feel what Mr. Pound calls the sense of an unusual intelligence working behind the words. I shall make a trial at placing this intelligence in relation to the complicated and confused literary and cultural currents of our era. We can make a start toward such placement if we examine closely the peculiar esotericism of 'The Waste Land.' It is permissible to concentrate only on 'The Waste Land' because that poem is a summation of Mr. Eliot's intellectual and emotional attitudes: it recapitulates almost all the themes which were given shape in the collected 'Poems.'

The full purport of esoteric writing is concealed from the 'average reader.' It requires for comprehension a more or less stringent initiation in certain ways of feeling, thinking and expressing, which are not common. To the uninitiated such writing is simply obscure. But esotericism is not properly a term of reproach, for it may be inescapable.

One type, that arising from the nature of the subject-matter, Mr. Pound has admirably explained. 'Obscurities inherent in the thing occur when the author is piercing, or trying to pierce into, uncharted regions; when he is trying to express things not yet current, not yet worn into phrase; when he is ahead of the emotional, or philosophic sense (as a painter might be ahead of the color-sense) of his contemporaries.' I think this is true of certain modern writers, whom I call the higher Romantics. If they have an intense desire to communicate experience, they suffer peculiarly, for their desire is constantly frustrated by the undeveloped emotional or philosophical sense of their readers.

Another type arises from obscurities inherent in the treatment. The author is an experimenter and tries to pierce into uncharted regions of technic and form. He tries to arrange the non-representative properties of literature *in vacuo*, to devise what Mr. Eliot in his essay on Jonson calls a 'creative fiction.'[2] The subject-matter perhaps has little logic of its own, and the author's structural logic is ahead of the contemporary aesthetic sense.

Either type of esotericism is highly commendable. Each represents an advance and each if well done is complete in itself. The demand upon the reader is legitimate, for he has only to find the proper key in his own sensibility or in his own experience, and then turn it with his own intellect. If the reader fails, it is he who is deficient, not the work.

But the esotericism of 'The Waste Land' is different: it is deliberate mystification. For in structure the poem is loose: it is full of interstices. Episode does not inevitably follow episode: transitions do not carry us,

1. From Pound's 1917 review of *Prufrock and Other Observations*.
2. "Ben Jonson," in *The Sacred Wood* (1920).

willy-nilly, from theme to theme, from movement to movement. Its
unity depends upon Mr. Eliot's personality, not upon the poem's functions and their adjustments and relations. The structural effect is very
much like that given by a revolving light: a sequence of flashes and
blanks without significance until referred to the purpose of the light-
house and the controlling hand of the keeper. I say this in spite of
certain formal achievements within the poem: the firm Virgilian outline
of the seduction scene witnessed by Tiresias, the triumphant progression through most utterly banal chatter, speeded up by the bartender's
cries, 'HURRY UP PLEASE IT'S TIME,' to the cool and lovely line from
'Hamlet,' 'Good night, ladies, good night, sweet ladies, good night, good
night.' Themes are stated, caught up later, recur. There is a general
cumulative movement, the poem has a half-visible crescendo. It dies
nicely with 'shantih shantih shantih.' But the two planes on which 'The
Waste Land' moves—the plane of myth and the plane of present day
London—are not strictly related. Passages of fine poetry may be deleted
without spoiling one's aesthetic pleasure of the whole, though dimin-
ishing the sum total derived from the detail. Symbols, characters, and
associations appear quite arbitrarily.

I am compelled to reject the poem as a sustained harmoniously func-
tioning structural unit.

On the other hand, it is amazing how simple is the state of mind
which these broken forms convey. The poet is hurt, wistful, melancholy, frail: modern civilization is a waste land, a sterile desert, in which
he wanders forlornly: there is no water to slake his spiritual drouth. Yet
there was water once, there was beauty, and the poem shifts to the
plane of the past, to the plane of great mythology.

> When lovely woman stoops to folly and
> Paces about her room again, alone,
> She smoothes her hair with automatic hand,
> And puts a record on the gramophone.

The stanza is a minute simulacrum of the central process of the poem
which is to take ancient beauty by the neck and twist it into modern
ugliness. Mr. Eliot is very fatigued. There can be no question that he
suffers, at moments his cry is as sharp as that of a man mangled by the
speeding wheels of a subway express, it is bitter as a confession extorted
by wheel and rack. We respect that cry.

But about the nature of this state of mind there is nothing occult. It
is in fact a very familiar mood. We have had a great deal of the poetry
of melancholy and drouth in the last half century, most of it inferior
to Mr. Eliot's, but nevertheless it has worn into common currency its
emotions.

Assuming that Mr. Eliot wished to convey such emotions to the
reader, to make them still more deeply a part of our general experience,

it should not have been difficult for him to escape opacity. Classical lucidity was entirely possible. How shall we account then for the obstacles he has placed to the reader's ready comprehension?

To win a complete understanding of 'The Waste Land,' the reader must scan eleven pages of notes, he must have a considerable learning in letters or be willing to look up references in Milton, Ovid, Middleton, Webster, Spenser, Verlaine, St. Augustine, etc., etc., in order to associate them with their first context, he must read Latin, Greek, French and German, he must know Frazer's 'Golden Bough' and steep himself in the legend of the Holy Grail, studying in particular Miss Weston's 'From Ritual to Romance.' The texture of 'The Waste Land' is excessively heavy with literary allusions which the reader of good will, knowing that it is not unjust to make severe requisitions upon his knowledge, will diligently track down. But our reader of good will is entitled, I think, to turn sour when he discovers that after all his research he has not penetrated into some strange uncharted region of experience but has only fathomed the cipher of a quite ordinary and easily understandable state of mind.

I know that more whole-hearted admirers of the poem than I are exclaiming at this point: 'But you are missing the point! Mr. Eliot wished to give a cumulative effect to his cries of hurt and barrenness. He wished to give a sense of one long cry of protest throughout history, a sense of dryness running through the ages, a yearning passed on from one individual to another until it reaches him in twentieth-century London.' To that my answer is that the sense of outcry reinforced by outcry is simply not created in the text. It is added to the text by deliberate processes of memory and learning by Mr. Eliot. It is added to the text by equally deliberate processes on the part of the reader. It is dependent on something too removed from the actual lines, and so I cannot feel it as integral.

The conclusion must be that the esotericism of 'The Waste Land' derives neither from abstruseness of subject nor from abstruseness of technic. It is artificially concocted by omissions, incompletions and unnecessary specialization in the assembling of those circumstances which ought to evoke in the reader the whole effect of the given emotion. Again the question rises, why does Mr. Eliot tamper with these circumstances so as to make them not explicable in themselves?

It is a reasonable conjecture to say that Mr. Eliot does not want to communicate his suffering to the general reader. To such he desires to be incomprehensible. His obfuscation of the circumstances which react together as a formula for his emotion is an example of dandyism. In his desire to make his suffering inscrutable to all but a chosen coterie of his similars, he is affecting what is commonly called a romantic mannerism, a mannerism that cannot be credited, however, to the great romantics. He constructs a mask for himself.

Our ideas of aristocracy have become sentimentalized. In its healthy state, the idea of aristocracy is a union of some idea of what is best in human nature with the idea of rule or control. For our purpose I suppose we can agree that the highest value is intelligence, so I can be more precise and say that the union of the ideas of intelligence and control constitutes the idea of aristocracy. In certain epochs the vortices of intelligence and social power have coincided, and the idea of aristocracy has been healthy. But in our epoch it is a truism that social power is vested in men of an inventive acquisitive narrow nature whose general intelligence is relatively low, whose care for humane values is slight, whose cunning is abnormally developed. The men of creative intelligence are thus forced to work against the grain of a society ruled by the acquisitive impulse. Many of them have become depressed at the odds against them and have pinned the insignia of an aloof defeat upon their work. Depression and even collapse in this state of affairs are certainly marks of a sensitive spirit. But it is a sentimentality of which I suspect Mr. Eliot guilty to believe that depression is a symptom of aristocracy. For the aristocrat cannot take pride in a dandyism of defeat, he cannot relinquish the effort to control. With the whole force of his being he seeks to understand; to understand the forces in himself, the forces of his age. With the whole force of his being he seeks to externalize his knowledge of these so lucidly and powerfully that it wins a place as leaven in the general cultural experience. He does not accept the crucifixion of his sensibility as a proof of superiority. He finds his proof in the transcendance of his crucifixions. Joy, serenity, the tokens of victory are his distinguishing marks. In the surrender to despair of its creative will the European mind loses its aristocracy.

Mr. Eliot, we know, has taken great pains to blend with the European mind. Who will dispute his thorough naturalization? But the mind into which he has been assimilated is in wretched case. Founded upon classicism, it has been shaken by the tremendous challenges issued to classical authorities from revolutionary science. It lacks the vitality to surrender the old and to make adjustment to the new. The upheavals of war and politics have agonized it to the last point. It has no hope, no vision. In 'Der Untergang des Abendlandes'[3] Oswald Spengler crystallizes its resignation into an attitude. Herr Spengler is a fatalist. Cultures, he believes, obey definite biological laws. They are rigidly deterministic. They live out a birth, growth, brilliant maturity, decay, death, and these processes cannot be halted. Decay he calls 'civilization': it is the stage of huge cities and their nomadic life, of great wars and dictators, of the advent of formless traditionless masses. We are in it: 'We must will the inevitable or nothing': the inevitable is fellahdom.[4]

3. *The Decline of the West*, published in English translation in 1926.
4. The rule of the masses.

It is easy to see that in part 'The Waste Land' is a poetic equivalent to 'Der Untergang des Abendlandes.' Mr. Eliot recalls the brilliant apogee of culture, he portrays in contrast the sterile decay of contemporary 'civilization,' he makes his own positive assertion in the detestable apeneck guffawing Sweeney, symbol of the formless and the traditionless. Before the age, which he has characterized elsewhere as singularly dull, the poet is weary.

The reader has observed that I have been shifting the interest in 'The Waste Land' from the aesthetic to the moral and cultural, and that we are now wholly involved in the poem as a summary of the modern cultural situation. The possibility not allowed for by the mind of Mr. Eliot is this: the entrance into consciousness of some new factor. We can only say, the future will be so and thus, provided no indeterminable elements of human consciousness, now dormant, commence to function. The fallacy of rationalism of the determinist type is that it is not rational enough. It does not question its assumptions. Trace back far enough and its fundamental entities turn out to be matter and motion, both as a matter of fact unknowns, and defined in terms of each other. This type of rationalism is not a coordinating part of the complex vision of the whole human being: it is really uncontrolled and amok.

* * *

Let us not take too seriously the 'scientific' pretensions nor grant too much authority to those who tell us that in view of our future the arts are twaddle, for the future belongs to mechanics, technology, economics and especially politics.

How far the American mind reproduces the vision or rather the supine attitude of the European mind is a speculation. I say speculation, because in spite of the best will to discover it I cannot say that there exists, in the sense that the European mind exists, an American mind. There are in my estimation several American writers who contain the nucleus for a striking and vastly important American mind, but America is not yet an intelligent community. Europe is: it has a concensus of intelligent opinion which I have called its mind: I can find no such concensus in America to compare with it. But although we cannot make distinctions in thought, we can in those things that nourish thought. America has a fresh boundless energy which Europe has lost. Most of it is quantitative, but the possibility always exists of converting some of it to qualitative. Energy is the first requisite to meet the elastic situation of today. America has hope, whereas Europe moves toward hopelessness and resignation. Hope is the spur of energy. America has laxer traditions than Europe. Ordinarily, this is deplorable. But if we are called upon to put away old traditions and to formulate new, it is an advantage. There is less inertia to overcome. And from the laxness of traditions in America, it follows that we are by temperament probably romantics. In chaos, it is generally agreed, the romantic is better able to find footing than the less flexible classicist.

Consequently, it is not surprising that such a viewpoint as that published by Mr. Eliot does not initiate any movement in America, does not even secure a general passive acceptance, does not least of all awake anything in our experience which impulsively corroborates it. Nay, we are scarcely enough affected to make a serious contradiction. A decade ago, smarting with a sense of inferiority, blaspheming our environment on which we transferred our weaknesses, we looked to Europe as the determinator of values. It was the heyday of the exile and the cosmopolitan mind. Today, our painters, writers and intellectuals know that they are deeply implicated in the unformed and unpredictable American destiny. They hibernate in Europe and rush back as from a feast which has unexpectedly turned out to be a famine. They are conscious of a great though unarticulated difference between the activity of the American scene and that of Europe. They have even met Europeans who have calmly declared that Europe is dead and the future belongs to America. They realize that the power of initiative has crossed the Atlantic.

America has energy and hope. It has weak traditions and a romantic temperament. It is becoming conscious of a fundamental difference between it and Europe. In the words of the Cumaean Sibyl, inscribed at the top of 'The Waste Land,' Europe 'wants only to die.' America wants to live.

But America has not realized its responsibility in the present crisis. It has not realized that its national destiny is more than a matter of national self-respect. It has not recognized clearly that the leadership of the human spirit has been resigned and that it, if anyone, must assume it. It has the primary qualifications: untapped energetics and spiritual naivete. It has lately acquired self-reliance. It seems not fanciful to predict that it will next acquire a sense of international responsibility.

And then perhaps it will at last be ready to receive Whitman. It will be expectant and humble, waiting for the Word that will release it, for the Word that will spell a new slope of human consciousness. Whitman is not the Word, but he formed syllables of it, immense generative syllables. America will wait while these do their deep hidden work, arousing latent power. On the threshold of creative vision one must wait.

Mr. Eliot lacks those deeper dimensions that the new slope will utilize. He is almost purely a sensibility and an intellect: he seems a unified man: at least one gets no sense of a disastrous internecine conflict in him. He loves beauty, he is wounded by ugliness: the age is severe on 'beauty-lovers' who cannot go below the surface. It lacerates unmercifully those whose intellects work only at the tips of their sense, who make an ideal of the senses thinking, of sensuous thought. This formula

Mr. Eliot believes accounts for much of the excellence of Elizabethan literature.

The formula for literary masterwork in our age will be more complex, more inclusive, much more difficult than that. It will involve the correlated functions of the whole human consciousness and it will demand the utmost purification of that consciousness. On a tremendous scale our age duplicates some of the features which introduced so much zest into Elizabethan life. Our vital source in antiquity will be, perhaps, the religious and philosophical cultures of the East instead of Graeco-Roman culture. Our New World will be Higher Space, and our explorers, our Columbuses and Magellans, will be such scientists as Einstein and Bohr. Our artists will have a wealth of new materials: our intellectual world expands and fills with possibilities; it is a time for curiosity and daring. 'The Waste Land' is a funeral keen for the nineteenth century. In the twentieth it is a subjective aberration from the facts.

MALCOLM COWLEY

[The Dilemma of *The Waste Land*]†

* * * No other American poet had so many disciples as Eliot, in so many stages of his career. Until 1925 his influence seemed omnipresent, and it continued to be important in the years that followed. But in 1922, at the moment when he was least known to the general public and most fervently worshiped by young poets, there was a sudden crisis. More than half of his disciples began slowly to drop away.

When *The Waste Land* first appeared, we were confronted with a dilemma. Here was a poem that agreed with all our recipes and prescriptions of what a great modern poem should be. Its form was not only perfect but was far richer musically and architecturally than that of Eliot's earlier verse. Its diction was superb. It employed in a magisterial fashion the technical discoveries made by the French writers who followed Baudelaire. Strangeness, abstractness, simplification, respect for literature as an art with traditions—it had all the qualities demanded in our slogans. We were prepared fervently to defend it against the attacks of the people who didn't understand what Eliot was trying to do—but we made private reservations. The poem had forced us into a false position, had brought our consciously adopted principles into conflict with our instincts. At heart—not intellectually, but in a purely

† From *Exile's Return: A Literary Odyssey of the 1920's* (New York: Viking, 1951), pp. 112–15. Copyright © 1934, 1935, 1941, 1951 by Malcolm Cowley. Used by permission of Viking Penguin, a division of Penguin Putnam Inc.

emotional fashion—we didn't like it. We didn't agree with what we regarded as the principal idea that the poem set forth.

The idea was a simple one. Beneath the rich symbolism of *The Waste Land*, the wide learning expressed in seven languages, the actions conducted on three planes, the musical episodes, the geometrical structure—beneath and by means of all this, we felt the poet was saying that the present is inferior to the past. The past was dignified; the present is barren of emotion. The past was a landscape nourished by living fountains; now the fountains of spiritual grace are dry. . . . Often in his earlier poems Eliot had suggested this idea; he had used such symbols of dead glory as the Roman eagles and trumpets or the Lion of St. Mark's to emphasize the vulgarities of the present. In those early poems, however, the present was his real subject. Even though he seemed to abhor it, even though he thought "of all the hands that are raising dingy shades in a thousand furnished rooms"[1] and was continually "aware of the damp souls of housemaids sprouting despondently at area gates," still he was writing about the life that all of us knew—and more than that, he was endowing our daily life with distinction by means of the same distinguished metaphors in which he decried and belittled it. *The Waste Land* marked a real change. This time he not only expressed the idea with all his mature resources but carried it to a new extreme. He not only abused the present but robbed it of vitality. It was as if he were saying, this time, that our age was prematurely senile and could not even find words of its own in which to bewail its impotence; that it was forever condemned to borrow and patch together the songs of dead poets.

The seven-page appendix to *The Waste Land*, in which Eliot paraded his scholarship and explained the Elizabethan or Italian sources of what had seemed to be his most personal phrases, was a painful dose for us to swallow. But the truth was that the poet had not changed so much as his younger readers. We were becoming less preoccupied with technique and were looking for poems that portrayed our own picture of the world. As for the question proposed to us by Eliot, whether the values of past ages were superior or inferior to present values, we could bring no objective evidence to bear on it. Values are created by living men. If they believe—if their manner of life induces them to believe —that greatness died with Virgil or Dante or Napoleon, who can change their opinion or teach them new values? It happened that we were excited by the adventure of living in the present. The famous "postwar mood of aristocratic disillusionment" was a mood we had never really shared. It happened that Eliot's subjective truth was not our own.

---

1. "Preludes." The next line quoted comes from "Morning at the Window." Both poems appeared originally in *Prufrock and Other Observations* (1917) [*Editor*].

I say "it happened" although, as a matter of fact, our beliefs grew out of the lives we had led. I say "we" although I can refer only to a majority, perhaps two-thirds, of those already influenced by Eliot's poems. When *The Waste Land* was published it revealed a social division among writers that was not a division between rich and poor or—in the Marxian terms that would later be popular—between capitalist and proletarian.[2] Not many of the younger writers belonged to either the top or the bottom layer of society. Some of them, it is true, were the children of factory workers or tenant farmers, but even those few had received the education of the middle class and had for the most part adopted its standards. The middle class had come to dominate the world of letters; the dominant educational background was that of the public high school and the big Midwestern university. And the writers of this class—roughly corresponding to Marx's petty bourgeoisie—were those who began to ask where Eliot was leading and whether they should follow.

But there were also many young writers who had been sent to good preparatory schools, usually Episcopalian, before they went on to Yale, Harvard, Princeton, Williams or Dartmouth. Whether rich or poor, they had received the training and acquired the standards of the small but powerful class in American society that might be described as the bourgeoisie proper. These, in general, were the "young poets old before their time" who not only admired *The Waste Land* but insisted on dwelling there in spirit; as Edmund Wilson said, they "took to inhabiting exclusively barren beaches, cactus-grown deserts and dusty attics overrun with rats."[3] Their special education, their social environment and also, I think, their feeling of mingled privilege and insecurity had prepared them to follow Eliot in his desert pilgrimage toward the shrines of tradition and authority.

There were exceptions in both groups, and Eliot continued to be recited and praised behind the dingy shades of a thousand furnished rooms, but most of the struggling middle-class writers were beginning to look for other patterns of literary conduct. We were new men, without inherited traditions, and we were entering a new world of art that did not impress us as being a spiritual desert. Although we did not see

2. It seems to me now that the division was more a matter of temperament, and less a result of social background, than I believed in 1934. The division was real, however, and it reflected attitudes toward life in our own time. When *The Waste Land* appeared, complete with notes, E. E. Cummings asked me why Eliot couldn't write his own lines instead of borrowing from dead poets. In his remarks I sensed a feeling almost of betrayal. Hemingway said in the *Transatlantic Review*, "If I knew that by grinding Mr. Eliot into a fine dry powder and sprinkling that powder over Mr. Conrad's grave Mr. Conrad would shortly appear, looking very annoyed at the forced return, and commence writing, I would leave for London early tomorrow with a sausage grinder." On the other hand John Peale Bishop, of Princeton, who was also in Paris at the time, told me that he was studying Italian so that he could get the full force of the quotations from Dante identified in Eliot's notes.
3. From Wilson's essay on Eliot in *Axel's Castle* (New York: Charles Scribner's Sons, 1931), p. 114 [*Editor*].

our own path, we instinctively rejected Eliot's. In the future we should still honor his poems and the clearness and integrity of his prose, but the Eliot picture had ceased to be our guide.

RALPH ELLISON

[*The Waste Land* and Jazz]†

Mrs. L. C. McFarland had taught us much of Negro history in grade school and from her I'd learned of the New Negro Movement of the twenties, of Langston Hughes, Countee Cullen, Claude McKay, James Weldon Johnson and the others. They had inspired pride and had given me a closer identification with poetry * * * but with music so much on my mind it never occurred to me to try to imitate them. Still I read their work and was excited by the glamour of the Harlem which emerged from their poems and it was good to know that there were Negro writers.—Then came *The Waste Land*.

I was much more under the spell of literature than I realized at the time. *Wuthering Heights* had caused me an agony of unexpressible emotion and the same was true of *Jude the Obscure*, but *The Waste Land* seized my mind. I was intrigued by its power to move me while eluding my understanding. Somehow its rhythms were often closer to those of jazz than were those of the Negro poets, and even though I could not understand then, its range of allusion was as mixed and as varied as that of Louis Armstrong. Yet there were its discontinuities, its changes of pace and its hidden system of organization which escaped me.

There was nothing to do but look up the references in the footnotes to the poem, and thus began my conscious education in literature.

† From *Shadow and Act* (New York: Random House, 1964), pp. 159–60.

The New Criticism

JOHN CROWE RANSOM

Waste Lands†

* * *

But what a congenial exercise is furnished the critic by that strange poem, 'The Waste Land.' In the first place, everybody agrees beforehand that its author is possessed of uncommon literary powers, and it is certain that, whatever credit the critic may try to take from him, a flattering residue will remain. And then his poem has won a spectacular triumph over a certain public and is entitled to an extra quantity of review. Best of all, Mr. Eliot's performance is the apotheosis of modernity, and seems to bring to a head all the specifically modern errors, and to cry for critic's ink of a volume quite disproportionate to its merits as a poem.

The most notable surface fact about 'The Waste Land' is of course its extreme disconnection. I do not know just how many parts the poem is supposed to have, but to me there are something like fifty parts which offer no bridges the one to the other and which are quite distinct in time, place, action, persons, tone, and nearly all the unities to which art is accustomed. This discreteness reaches also to the inside of the parts, where it is indicated by a frequent want of grammatical joints and marks of punctuation; as if it were the function of art to break down the usual singleness of the artistic image, and then to attack the integrity of the individual fragments. I presume that poetry has rarely gone further in this direction. It is a species of the same error which modern writers of fiction practice when they laboriously disconnect the stream of consciousness and present items which do not enter into wholes. Evidently they think with Hume[1] that reality is facts and pluralism, not compounds and systems. But Mr. Eliot is more enterprising than they, because almost in so many words he assails the philosophical

---

† From the *New York Evening Post Literary Review*, July 14, 1923, pp. 825–26. Reproduced by permission of the Estate of John Crowe Ransom.
1. David Hume (1711–1776), British empiricist philosopher [*Editor*].

or cosmical principles under which we form the usual images of reality, naming the whole phantasmagoria Waste Land almost as plainly as if he were naming cosmos Chaos. His intention is evidently to present a wilderness in which both he and the reader may be bewildered, in which one is never to see the wood for the trees.

Against this philosophy—or negation of philosophy—the critic must stand fast. It is good for some purposes, but not for art. The mind of the artist is an integer, and the imaginative vision is a single act which fuses its elements. It is to be suspected that the author who holds his elements apart is not using his imagination, but using a formula, like a scientist anxious to make out a 'case'; at any rate, for art such a procedure suggests far too much strain and tension. For imagination things cohere; pluralism cannot exist when we relax our obsessions and allow such testimony as is in us to come out. Even the most refractory elements in experience, like the powerful opposing wills in a tragedy, arrive automatically at their 'higher synthesis' if the imagination is allowed to treat them.

There is a reason besides philosophical bias which makes the disconnection in the poem. The fragments could not be joined on any principle and remain what they are. And that is because they are at different stages of fertilization; they are not the children of a single act of birth. Among their disparities one notes that scraps from many tongues are juxtaposed; and yet one knows well that we are in different 'ages of intelligence' when we take the different languages on our lips; we do not quote Greek tragedy and modern cockney with the same breath or with the same kinds of mind. We cannot pass, in 'The Waste Land,' without a convulsion of the mind from 'O O O O that Shakespeherian Rag,' to 'Shantih shantih shantih.' And likewise, the fragments are in many metres, from the comparatively formal metre which we know as the medium of romantic experiences in the English thesaurus to an extremely free verse which we know as the medium of a half-hearted and disillusioned art. But, above all, some fragments are emotions recollected in tranquillity and others are emotions kept raw and bleeding, like sores we continue to pick. In other words, the fragments vary through almost every stage, from pure realism to some point just short of complete fertilization by the romantic imagination, and this is a material which is incapable of synthesis.

A consequence of this inequality of material is a certain novelty of Mr. Eliot's which is not fundamentally different from parody. To parody is to borrow a phrase whose meaning lies on one plane of intelligence and to insert it into the context of a lower plane; an attempt to compound two incommensurable imaginative creations. Mr. Eliot inserts beautiful quotations into ugly contexts. For example:

> When lovely woman stoops to folly, and
> Paces about her room again, alone,
> She smoothes her hair with automatic hand,
> And puts a record on the gramophone.

A considerable affront against aesthetic sensibilities. Using these lovely borrowed lines for his own peculiar purposes, Mr. Eliot debases them every time; there is not, I believe, a single occasion where his context is as mature as the quotation which he inserts into it; he does not invent such phrases for himself, nor, evidently, does his understanding quite appreciate them, for they require an organization of experience which is yet beyond him. The difficulty in which he finds himself is typically an American one. Our native poets are after novelty; they believe, as does Mr. Eliot in one of his prose chapters, that each age must have its own 'form.' The form in which our traditionary poetry is cast is that of another generation and therefore No-thoroughfare. What the new form is to be they have not yet determined. Each of the new poets must experiment with a few usually, it appears, conceiving forms rather naively, as something which will give quick effects without the pains and delays of complete fertilization. Mr. Eliot has here tried out such a form and thereby reverted to the frailties of his nativity. The English poets, so far as they may be generalized, are still content to work under the old forms and, it must be said in their favor, it is purely an empirical question whether these are unfit for further use; the poets need not denounce them on principle. But it may be put to the credit of Mr. Eliot that he is a man of better parts generally than most of the new poets, as in the fact that he certainly bears no animus against the old poetry except as it is taken for a model by the new poets; he is sufficiently sensitive to its beauties at least to have held on with his memory to some of its ripest texts and to have introduced them rather wistfully into the forbidding context of his own poems, where they are thoroughly ill at ease.

The criticism does not complete itself till it has compared 'The Waste Land' with the earlier work of its author. The volume of 'Poems' which appeared a year previously hardly presaged the disordered work that was to follow. The discrepancy is astonishing. Sweeney and Prufrock, those heroes who bid so gayly for immortality in their own right, seem to come out of a fairly mature and at any rate an equal art. They are elegant and precious creations rather than substantial, with a very reduced emotional background, like the art of a man of the world rather than of a man of frankly poetic susceptibilities; but the putative author is at least responsible. He has 'arrived'; he has by self-discipline and the unconscious lessons of experience integrated his mind. The poem which comes a year later takes a number of years out of this author's history, restores him intellectually to his minority. I presume that 'The

Waste Land,' with its burden of unregenerate fury, was disheartening
to such critics as Mr. Aldington, who had found in the 'Poems' the
voice of a completely articulate soul; I presume that for these critics
the 'Poems' are automatically voided and recalled by the later testament; they were diabolically specious, and the true heart of the author
was to be revealed by a very different gesture. But I prefer to think that
they were merely precocious. They pretended to an intellectual synthesis of which the author was only intellectually aware, but which proved
quite too fragile to contain the ferment of experience. One prefers 'The
Waste Land' after all, for of the two kinds it bears the better witness to
its own sincerity.

'The Waste Land' is one of the most insubordinate poems in the
language, and perhaps it is the most unequal. But I do not mean in
saying this to indicate that it is permanently a part of the language; I
do not entertain that as a probability. The genius of our language is
notoriously given to feats of hospitality: but it seems to me it will be
hard pressed to find accommodations at the same time for two such
incompatibles as Mr. Wordsworth and the present Mr. Eliot; and any
realist must admit that what happens to be the prior tenure of the
mansion in this case is likely to be stubbornly defended.

I. A. RICHARDS

The Poetry of T. S. Eliot†

* * *

Mr. Eliot's poetry has occasioned an unusual amount of irritated or
enthusiastic bewilderment. The bewilderment has several sources. The
most formidable is the unobtrusiveness, in some cases the absence, of
any coherent intellectual thread upon which the items of the poem are
strung. A reader of 'Gerontion,' of 'Preludes,' or of 'The Waste Land,'
may, if he will, after repeated readings, introduce such a thread. Another reader after much effort may fail to contrive one. But in either
case energy will have been misapplied. For the items are united by the
accord, contrast, and interaction of their emotional effects, not by an
intellectual scheme that analysis must work out. The value lies in the
unified response which this interaction creates in the right reader. The
only intellectual activity required takes place in the realisation of the
separate items. We can, of course, make a 'rationalisation' of the whole
experience, as we can of any experience. If we do, we are adding something which does not belong to the poem. Such a logical scheme is,

† From *Principles of Literary Criticism* (1926; rpt. New York: Harcourt Brace, 1949), pp. 289–95.

at best, a scaffolding that vanishes when the poem is constructed. But
we have so built into our nervous systems a demand for intellectual
coherence, even in poetry, that we find a difficulty in doing without it.

This point may be misunderstood, for the charge most usually
brought against Mr. Eliot's poetry is that it is overintellectualised. One
reason for this is his use of allusion. A reader who in one short poem
picks up allusions to *The Aspern Papers*, *Othello*, 'A Toccata of Ga-
luppi's,' Marston, *The Phœnix and the Turtle*, *Antony and Cleopatra*
(twice), 'The Extasie,' *Macbeth*, *The Merchant of Venice*, and Ruskin,
feels that his wits are being unusually well exercised. He may easily
leap to the conclusion that the basis of the poem is in wit also. But
this would be a mistake. These things come in, not that the reader may
be ingenious or admire the writer's erudition (this last accusation has
tempted several critics to disgrace themselves), but for the sake of the
emotional aura which they bring and the attitudes they incite. Allusion
in Mr. Eliot's hands is a technical device for compression. 'The Waste
Land' is the equivalent in content to an epic. Without this device twelve
books would have been needed. But these allusions and the notes in
which some of them are elucidated have made many a petulant reader
turn down his thumb at once. Such a reader has not begun to understand what it is all about.

This objection is connected with another, that of obscurity. To quote
a recent pronouncement upon 'The Waste Land' from Mr. Middleton
Murry: 'The reader is compelled, in the mere effort to understand, to
adopt an attitude of intellectual suspicion, which makes impossible the
communication of feeling. The work offends against the most elemen-
tary canon of good writing: that the immediate effect should be unambiguous.'[1] Consider first this 'canon.' What would happen, if we
pressed it, to Shakespeare's greatest sonnets or to *Hamlet*? The truth is
that very much of the best poetry is necessarily ambiguous in its immediate effect. Even the most careful and responsive reader must reread
and do hard work before the poem forms itself clearly and unambigu-
ously in his mind. An original poem, as much as a new branch of
mathematics, compels the mind which receives it to grow, and this
takes time. Anyone who upon reflection asserts the contrary for his own
case must be either a demigod or dishonest; probably Mr. Murray was
in haste. His remarks show that he has failed in his attempt to read the
poem, and they reveal, in part, the reason for his failure—namely, his
own overintellectual approach. To read it successfully he would have
to discontinue his present self-mystifications.

The critical question in all cases is whether the poem is worth the
trouble it entails. For 'The Waste Land' this is considerable. There is

1. J. Middleton Murry, "The 'Classical' Revival," *Adelphi* 3 (February 1926): 585–95; and
(March 1926): 648–53 [*Editor*].

Miss Weston's *From Ritual to Romance* to read, and its 'astral' trim-
mings to be discarded—they have nothing to do with Mr. Eliot's poem.
There is Canto xxvi of the *Purgatorio* to be studied—the relevance of
the close of that canto to the whole of Mr. Eliot's work must be insisted
upon. It illuminates his persistent concern with sex, the problem of our
generation, as religion was the problem of the last. There is the central
position of Tiresias in the poem to be puzzled out—the cryptic form
of the note which Mr. Eliot writes on this point is just a little tiresome.
It is a way of underlining the fact that the poem is concerned with
many aspects of the one fact of sex, a hint that is perhaps neither
indispensable nor entirely successful.

When all this has been done by the reader, when the materials with
which the words are to clothe themselves have been collected, the
poem still remains to be read. And it is easy to fail in this undertaking.
An 'attitude of intellectual suspicion' must certainly be abandoned. But
this is not difficult to those who still know how to give their feelings
precedence to their thoughts, who can accept and unify an experience
without trying to catch it in an intellectual net or to squeeze out a
doctrine. One form of this attempt must be mentioned. Some, misled
no doubt by its origin in a Mystery, have endeavoured to give the poem
a symbolical reading. But its symbols are not mystical, but emotional.
They stand, that is, not for ineffable objects, but for normal human
experience. The poem, in fact, is radically naturalistic; only its compression makes it appear otherwise. And in this it probably comes nearer
to the original Mystery which it perpetuates than transcendentalism
does.

If it were desired to label in three words the most characteristic feature of Mr. Eliot's technique, this might be done by calling his poetry
a 'music of ideas.' The ideas are of all kinds, abstract and concrete,
general and particular, and, like the musician's phrases, they are arranged, not that they may tell us something, but that their effects in us
may combine into a coherent whole of feeling and attitude and produce
a peculiar liberation of the will. They are there to be responded to, not
to be pondered or worked out. * * *

How this technique lends itself to misunderstandings we have seen.
But many readers who have failed in the end to escape bewilderment
have begun by finding on almost every line that Mr. Eliot has written
—if we except certain youthful poems on American topics—that personal stamp which is the hardest thing for the craftsman to imitate and
perhaps the most certain sign that the experience, good or bad, rendered in the poem is authentic. Only those unfortunate persons who
are incapable of reading poetry can resist Mr. Eliot's rhythms. The
poem as a whole may elude us while every fragment, as a fragment,
comes victoriously home. It is difficult to believe that this is Mr. Eliot's
fault rather than his reader's, because a parallel case of a poet who so

constantly achieves the hardest part of his task and yet fails in the easier is not to be found. It is much more likely that we have been trying to put the fragments together on a wrong principle.

Another doubt has been expressed. Mr. Eliot repeats himself in two ways. The nightingale, Cleopatra's barge, the rats, and the smoky candle-end, recur and recur. Is this a sign of a poverty of inspiration? A more plausible explanation is that this repetition is in part a consequence of the technique above described, and in part something which many writers who are not accused of poverty also show. Shelley, with his rivers, towers, and stars, Conrad, Hardy, Walt Whitman, and Dostoevski spring to mind. When a writer has found a theme or image which fixes a point of relative stability in the drift of experience, it is not to be expected that he will avoid it. Such themes are a means of orientation. And it is quite true that the central process in all Mr. Eliot's best poems is the same; the conjunction of feelings which, though superficially opposed,—as squalor, for example, is opposed to grandeur,—yet tend as they develop to change places and even to unite. If they do not develop far enough the intention of the poet is missed. Mr. Eliot is neither sighing after vanished glories nor holding contemporary experience up to scorn.

Both bitterness and desolation are superficial aspects of his poetry. There are those who think that he merely takes his readers into the Waste Land and leaves them there, that in his last poem he confesses his impotence to release the healing waters. The reply is that some readers find in his poetry not only a clearer, fuller realisation of their plight, the plight of a whole generation, than they find elsewhere, but also through the very energies set free in that realisation a return of the saving passion.

F. R. LEAVIS

[The Significance of the Modern Waste Land]†

* * *

[*The Waste Land*] appeared first in the opening numbers of *The Criterion* (October 1922 and January 1923). The title, we know, comes from Miss J. L. Weston's book, *From Ritual to Romance*, the theme of which is anthropological: the Waste Land there has a significance in terms of Fertility Ritual. What is the significance of the modern Waste Land? The answer may be read in what appears as the rich disorganization of the poem. The seeming disjointedness is intimately related to

† From *New Bearings in English Poetry* (London: Chatto and Windus, 1932), pp. 90–113. With thanks for permission from the Leavis Literary Estate.

the erudition that has annoyed so many readers and to the wealth of literary borrowings and allusions. These characteristics reflect the present state of civilization. The traditions and cultures have mingled, and the historical imagination makes the past contemporary; no one tradition can digest so great a variety of materials, and the result is a breakdown of forms and the irrevocable loss of that sense of absoluteness which seems necessary to a robust culture. * * *

In considering our present plight we have also to take account of the incessant rapid change that characterizes the Machine Age. The result is breach of continuity and the uprooting of life. This last metaphor has a peculiar aptness, for what we are witnessing to-day is the final uprooting of the immemorial ways of life, of life rooted in the soil. * * *

The remoteness of the civilization celebrated in *The Waste Land* from the natural rhythms is brought out, in ironical contrast, by the anthropological theme. Vegetation cults, fertility ritual, with their sympathetic magic, represent a harmony of human culture with the natural environment, and express an extreme sense of the unity of life. In the modern Waste Land

> April is the cruellest month, breeding
> Lilacs out of the dead land,

but bringing no quickening to the human spirit. Sex here is sterile, breeding not life and fulfilment but disgust, accidia and unanswerable questions. It is not easy to-day to accept the perpetuation and multiplication of life as ultimate ends.

But the anthropological background has positive functions. It plays an obvious part in evoking that particular sense of the unity of life which is essential to the poem. It helps to establish the level of experience at which the poem works, the mode of consciousness to which it belongs. In *The Waste Land* the development of impersonality that *Gerontion* shows in comparison with *Prufrock* reaches an extreme limit: it would be difficult to imagine a completer transcendence of the individual self, a completer projection of awareness. We have, in the introductory chapter, considered the poet as being at the conscious point of his age.[1] There are ways in which it is possible to be too conscious; and to be so is, as a result of the break-up of forms and the loss of axioms noted above, one of the troubles of the present age (if the abstraction may be permitted, consciousness being in any case a minority affair). We recognize in modern literature the accompanying sense of futility.

The part that science in general has played in the process of disin-

---

1. "Poetry matters because of the kind of poet who is more alive than other people, more alive in his own age. He is, as it were, at the most conscious point of his race in his time" (Leavis, *New Bearings*, p. 13) [*Editor*].

tegration is matter of commonplace: anthropology is, in the present context, a peculiarly significant expression of the scientific spirit. To the anthropological eye beliefs, religions and moralities are human habits—in their odd variety too human. Where the anthropological out-look prevails, sanctions wither. In a contemporary consciousness there is inevitably a great deal of the anthropological, and the background of *The Waste Land* is thus seen to have a further significance.

To be, then, too much conscious and conscious of too much—that is the plight:

> After such knowledge, what forgiveness?

At this point Mr. Eliot's note on Tiresias deserves attention:

> Tiresias, although a mere spectator and not indeed a 'character,' is yet the most important personage in the poem, uniting all the rest. Just as the one-eyed merchant, seller of currants, melts into the Phoenician Sailor, and the latter is not wholly distinct from Ferdinand Prince of Naples, so all the women are one woman, and the two sexes meet in Tiresias. What Tiresias *sees*, in fact, is the substance of the poem.

If Mr Eliot's readers have a right to a grievance, is it that he has not given this note more salience; for it provides the clue to *The Waste Land*. It indicates plainly enough what the poem is: an effort to focus an inclusive human consciousness. The effort, in ways suggested above, is characteristic of the age; and in an age of psycho-analysis, an age that has produced the last section of *Ulysses*, Tiresias—'venus huic erat ut-raque nota'[2]—presents himself as the appropriate impersonation. A cul-tivated modern is (or feels himself to be) intimately aware of the experience of the opposite sex.

Such an undertaking offers a difficult problem of organization, a distinguishing character of the mode of consciousness that promotes it being a lack of organizing principle, the absence of any inherent di-rection. A poem that is to contain all myths cannot construct itself upon one. It is here that *From Ritual to Romance* comes in. It provides a background of reference that makes possible something in the nature of a musical[3] organization. Let us start by considering the use of the Tarot pack. Introduced in the first section, suggesting, as it does, des-tiny, chance and the eternal mysteries, it at once intimates the scope of the poem, the mode of its contemplation of life. It informs us as to the nature of the characters: we know that they are such as could not have relations with one another in any narrative scheme, and could not

---

2. "For he knew both sides of love" (Latin). From the account of Tiresias in Ovid's *Metamor-phoses*. For the context, see Sources "[The Blinding of Tiresias]," p. 46 [*Editor*].
3. Mr I. A. Richards uses the analogy from music in some valuable notes on Mr Eliot that are printed in an appendix to the later editions of *The Principles of Literary Criticism*.

be brought together on any stage, no matter what liberties were taken with the Unities. The immediate function of the passage introducing the pack, moreover, is to evoke, in contrast with what has preceded, cosmopolitan 'high life,' and the charlatanism that battens upon it:

> Madame Sosostris, famous clairvoyante,
> Had a bad cold, nevertheless
> Is known to be the wisest woman in Europe,
> With a wicked pack of cards.

Mr Eliot can achieve the banality appropriate here, and achieve at the same time, when he wants it, a deep undertone, a resonance, as it were, of fate:

>   . . . and this card,
> Which is blank, is something he carries on his back,
> Which I am forbidden to see. I do not find
> The Hanged Man. Fear death by water.
> I see crowds of people, walking round in a ring.

The peculiar menacing undertone of this associates it with a passage in the fifth section:

> Who is the third who walks always beside you?
> When I count, there are only you and I together
> But when I look ahead up the white road
> There is always another one walking beside you
> Gliding wrapt in a brown mantle, hooded
> I do not know whether a man or a woman
> —But who is that on the other side of you?

The association establishes itself without any help from Mr Eliot's note; it is there in any case, as any fit reader of poetry can report; but the note helps us to recognize its significance:

> The Hanged Man, a member of the traditional pack, fits my purpose in two ways: because he is associated in my mind with the Hanged God of Frazer, and because I associate him with the hooded figure in the passage of the disciples to Emmaus in Part V.

The Tarot pack, Miss Weston has established, has affiliations with fertility ritual, and so lends itself peculiarly to Mr Eliot's purpose: the instance before us illustrates admirably how he has used its possibilities. The hooded figure in the passage just quoted is Jesus. Perhaps our being able to say so depends rather too much upon Mr Eliot's note; but the effect of the passage does not depend so much upon the note as might appear. For Christ has figured already in the opening of the section (see *What the Thunder Said*):

> After the torchlight red on sweaty faces
> After the frosty silence in the gardens
> After the agony in stony places
> The shouting and the crying
> Prison and palace and reverberation
> Of thunder of spring over distant mountains
> He who was living is now dead
> We who were living are now dying
> With a little patience

The reference is unmistakable. Yet it is not only Christ; it is also the Hanged God and all the sacrificed gods: with the 'thunder of spring' 'Adonis, Attis, Osiris' and all the others of *The Golden Bough* come in. And the 'agony in stony places' is not merely the Agony in the Garden; it is also the agony of the Waste Land, introduced in the first section: (*The Burial of the Dead*, ll. 19 ff.).

> What are the roots that clutch, what branches grow
> Out of this stony rubbish? Son of man,
> You cannot say, or guess, for you know only
> A heap of broken images, where the sun beats,
> And the dead tree gives no shelter, the cricket no relief,
> And the dry stone no sound of water.

In *What the Thunder Said* the drouth becomes (among other things) a thirst for the waters of faith and healing, and the specifically religious enters into the orchestration of the poem. But the thunder is 'dry sterile thunder without rain'; there is no resurrection or renewal; and after the opening passage the verse loses all buoyancy, and takes on a dragging, persistent movement as of hopeless exhaustion—

> Here is no water but only rock
> Rock and no water and the sandy road
> The road winding above among the mountains
> Which are mountains of rock without water

—the imagined sound of water coming in as a torment. There is a suggestion of fever here, a sultry ominousness—

> There is not even solitude in the mountains

—and it is this which provides the transition to the passage about the hooded figure quoted above. The ominous tone of this last passage associates it, as we have seen, with the reference (ll. 55–56) to the Hanged Man in the Tarot passage of *The Burial of the Dead*. So Christ becomes the Hanged Man, the Vegetation God; and at the same time the journey through the Waste Land along 'the sandy road' becomes the Journey to Emmaus. Mr Eliot gives us a note on the 'third who walks always beside you':

The following lines were stimulated by the account of one of the Antarctic expeditions (I forget which, but I think one of Shackleton's): it was related that the party of explorers, at the extremity of their strength, had the constant delusion that there was *one more member* than could actually be counted.

This might be taken to be, from our point of view, merely an interesting irrelevance, and it certainly is not necessary. But it nevertheless serves to intimate the degree of generality that Mr Eliot intends to accompany his concrete precision: he is both definite and vague at once. 'Just as the one-eyed merchant, seller of currants, melts into the Phoenician Sailor, and the latter is not wholly distinct from Ferdinand Prince of Naples'—so one experience is not wholly distinct from another experience of the same general order; and just as all experiences 'meet in Tiresias,' so a multitude of experiences meet in each passage of the poem. Thus the passage immediately in question has still further associations. That same hallucinatory quality which relates it to what goes before recalls also the neurasthenic episode (ll. 111 ff.) in *A Game of Chess* (the second section):

> 'What is that noise?'
>   The wind under the door.
> 'What is that noise now? . . .'

All this illustrates the method of the poem, and the concentration, the depth of orchestration that Mr Eliot achieves; the way in which the themes move in and out of one another and the predominance shifts from level to level. The transition from this passage is again by way of the general ominousness, which passes into hallucinated vision and then into nightmare:

> —But who is that on the other side of you?
>
> What is that sound high in the air
> Murmur of maternal lamentation
> Who are those hooded hordes swarming
> Over endless plains, stumbling in cracked earth
> Ringed by the flat horizon only
> What is the city over the mountains
> Cracks and reforms and bursts in the violet air
> Falling towers
> Jerusalem Athens Alexandria
> Vienna London
> Unreal.

The focus of attention shifts here to the outer disintegration in its large, obvious aspects, and the references to Russia and to post-war Europe in general are plain. The link between the hooded figure of the road to Emmaus and the 'hooded hordes swarming' is not much more than verbal (though appropriate to a fevered consciousness), but this phrase has an essential association with a line (56) in the passage that introduces the Tarot pack:

> I see crowds of people, walking round in a ring.

These 'hooded hordes,' 'ringed by the flat horizon only,' are not merely Russians, suggestively related to the barbarian invaders of civilization; they are also humanity walking endlessly round in a ring, a further illustration of the eternal futility. 'Unreal' picks up the 'Unreal city' of *The Burial of the Dead* (1. 60), where 'Saint Mary Woolnoth kept the hours,' and the unreality gets further development in the nightmare passage that follows:

> And upside down in air were towers
> Tolling reminiscent bells, that kept the hours
> And voices singing out of empty cisterns and exhausted wells.

Then, with a transitional reference (which will be commented on later) to the theme of the Chapel Perilous, the focus shifts inwards again. 'Datta,' 'dayadhvam,' and 'damyata,' the admonitions of the thunder, are explained in a note, and in this case, at any rate, the reliance upon the note justifies itself. We need only be told once that they mean 'give, sympathize, control,' and the context preserves the meaning. The Sanscrit lends an appropriate portentousness, intimating that this is the sum of wisdom according to a great tradition, and that what we have here is a radical scrutiny into the profit of life. The irony, too, is radical:

> *Datta:* what have we given?
> My friend, blood shaking my heart
> The awful daring of a moment's surrender
> Which an age of prudence can never retract
> By this, and this only, we have existed

—it is an equivocal comment. And for comment on 'sympathize' we have a reminder of the irremediable isolation of the individual. After all the agony of sympathetic transcendence, it is to the individual, the focus of consciousness, that we return:

> Shall I at least set my lands in order?

The answer comes in the bundle of fragments that ends the poem, and, in a sense, sums it up.

Not that the *poem* lacks organization and unity. The frequent judgments that it does betray a wrong approach. * * * The unity the poem aims at is that of an inclusive consciousness: the organization it achieves as a work of art is of the kind that has been illustrated, an organization that may, by analogy, be called musical. It exhibits no progression:

> I sat upon the shore
> Fishing, with the arid plain behind me

—the thunder brings no rain to revive the Waste Land, and the poem ends where it began.

At this point the criticism has to be met that, while all this may be so, the poem in any case exists, and can exist, only for an extremely limited public equipped with special knowledge. The criticism must be admitted. But that the public for it is limited is one of the symptoms of the state of culture that produced the poem. Works expressing the finest consciousness of the age in which the word 'high-brow' has become current are almost inevitably such as to appeal only to a tiny minority. It is still more serious that this minority should be more and more cut off from the world around it—should, indeed, be aware of a hostile and overwhelming environment. This amounts to an admission that there must be something limited about the kind of artistic achievement possible in our time: even Shakespeare in such conditions could hardly have been the 'universal' genius. And *The Waste Land*, clearly, is not of the order of *The Divine Comedy* or of *Lear*. The important admission, then, is not that *The Waste Land* can be appreciated only by a very small minority (how large in any age has the minority been that has really comprehended the masterpieces?), but that this limitation carries with it limitations in self-sufficiency.

These limitations, however, are easily overstressed. Most of the 'special knowledge,' dependence upon which is urged against *The Waste Land*, can fairly be held to be common to the public that would in any case read modern poetry. The poem does, indeed, to some extent lean frankly upon *From Ritual to Romance*. And sometimes it depends upon external support in ways that can hardly be justified. Let us take, for instance, the end of the third section, *The Fire Sermon*:

> la la
>
> To Carthage then I came
>
> Burning, burning, burning, burning
> O Lord Thou pluckest me out
> O Lord Thou pluckest
>
> burning

It is plain from Mr Eliot's note on this passage—'The collocation of these two representatives of eastern and western asceticism, as the culmination of this part of the poem, is not an accident'—that he intends St Augustine and the Buddha to be actively present here. But whereas one cursory reading of *From Ritual to Romance* does all (practically) that is assigned as function to that book, no amount of reading of the *Confessions* or *Buddhism in Translation* will give these few words power to evoke the kind of presence of 'eastern and western asceticism' that seems necessary to the poem: they remain, these words, mere pointers to something outside. We can only conclude that Mr Eliot here has not done as much as he supposes. And so with the passage (ll. 385 ff.) in *What the Thunder Said* bringing in the theme of the Chapel Perilous: it leaves too much to Miss Weston; repeated recourse to *From Ritual to Romance* will not invest it with the virtue it would assume. The irony, too, of the

Shantih   shantih   shantih

that ends the poem is largely ineffective, for Mr Eliot's note that ' "The Peace which passeth understanding" is a feeble translation of the content of this word' can impart to the word only a feeble ghost of that content for the Western reader.

Yet the weaknesses of this kind are not nearly as frequent or as damaging as critics of *The Waste Land* seem commonly to suppose. It is a self-subsistent poem, and should be obviously such. The allusions, references and quotations usually carry their own power with them as well as being justified in the appeal they make to special knowledge. 'Unreal City' (l. 60), to take an extreme instance from one end of the scale, owes nothing to Baudelaire (whatever Mr Eliot may have owed); the note is merely interesting—though, of course, it is probable that a reader unacquainted with Baudelaire will be otherwise unqualified. The reference to Dante that follows—

A crowd flowed over London Bridge, so many,
I had not thought death had undone so many

—has an independent force, but much is lost to the reader who does not catch the implied comparison between London and Dante's Hell. Yet the requisite knowledge of Dante is a fair demand. The knowledge of *Antony and Cleopatra* assumed in the opening of *A Game of Chess*, or of *The Tempest* in various places elsewhere, no one will boggle at. The main references in *The Waste Land* come within the classes represented by these to Dante and Shakespeare; while of the many others most of the essential carry enough of their power with them. By means of such references and quotations Mr Eliot attains a compression, otherwise unattainable, that is essential to his aim; a compression approaching simultaneity—the co-presence in the mind of a number of different orientations, fundamental attitudes, orders of experience.

This compression and the methods it entails do make the poem difficult reading at first, and a full response comes only with familiarity. Yet the complete rout so often reported, or inadvertently revealed * * * can be accounted for only by a wrong approach, an approach with inappropriate expectations. For the general nature and method of the poem should be obvious at first reading. Yet so com-

monly does the obvious seem to be missed that perhaps a little more
elucidation (this time of the opening section) will not be found offen-
sively superfluous. What follows is a brief analysis of *The Burial of the
Dead*, the avowed intention being to point out the obvious themes and
transitions: anything like a full analysis would occupy many times the
space.

The first seven lines introduce the vegetation theme, associating it
with the stirring of 'memory and desire.' The transition is simple: 'April,'
'spring,' 'winter,'—then

> Summer surprised us, coming over the Starnbergersee
> With a shower of rain . . .

We seem to be going straight forward, but (as the change of movement
intimates) we have modulated into another plane. We are now given a
particular 'memory,' and a representative one. It introduces the cosmopolitan note, a note of empty sophistication:

> In the mountains, there you feel free.
> I read, much of the night, and go south in the winter.
>   [Cf. 'Winter kept us warm']

The next transition is a contrast and a comment, bringing this last
passage into relation with the first. April may stir dull roots with spring
rain, but

> What are the roots that clutch, what branches grow
> Out of this stony rubbish?

And there follows an evocation of the Waste Land, with references to
Ezekiel and *Ecclesiastes*, confirming the tone that intimates that this is
an agony of the soul ('Son of man' relates with the Hanged Man and
the Hanged God: with him 'who was living' and 'is now dead' at the
opening of *What the Thunder Said*). The 'fear'—

> I will show you fear in a handful of dust

—recurs, in different modes, in the neurasthenic passage (ll. 111 ff.) of
A Game of Chess, and in the episode of the hooded figure in *What the
Thunder Said*. The fear is partly the fear of death, but still more a
nameless, ultimate fear, a horror of the completely negative.

Then comes the verse from *Tristan und Isolde*, offering a positive in
contrast—the romantic absolute, love. The 'hyacinth girl,' we may say,
represents 'memory and desire' (the hyacinth, directly evocative like the
lilacs bred out of the Waste Land, was also one of the flowers associated
with the slain vegetation god), and the 'nothing' of the Waste Land
changes into the ecstasy of passion—a contrast, and something more:

—Yet when we came back, late, from the Hyacinth garden,
Your arms full, and your hair wet, I could not
Speak, and my eyes failed, I was neither
Living nor dead, and I knew nothing,
Looking into the heart of light, the silence.

In the Waste Land one is neither living nor dead. Moreover, the neurasthenic passage referred to above recalls these lines unmistakably,
giving them a sinister modulation:

'Speak to me. Why do you never speak. Speak.
'What are you thinking of? What thinking? What?
'I never know what you are thinking. Think.'

.   .   .   .

                         'Do
'You know nothing? Do you see nothing? Do you remember
'Nothing?'

The further line from *Tristan und Isolde* ends the passage of romantic
love with romantic desolation. Madame Sosostris, famous clairvoyante,
follows; she brings in the demi-monde, so offering a further contrast—

Here is Belladonna, the Lady of the Rocks,
The lady of situations

—and introduces the Tarot pack. This passage has already received
some comment, and it invites a great deal more. The 'lady of situations,'
to make an obvious point, appears in the *Game of Chess*. The admo-
nition, 'Fear death by water,' gets its response in the fourth section,
Death by Water: death is inevitable, and the life-giving water thirsted
for (and the water out of which all life comes) cannot save. But enough
has been said to indicate the function of the Tarot pack, the way in
which it serves in the organization of the poem.

With the 'Unreal City' the background of urban—of 'megalopol-
itan'—civilization becomes explicit. The allusion to Dante has already
been remarked upon, and so has the way in which Saint Mary Woolnoth is echoed by the 'reminiscent bells' of *What the Thunder Said*.
The portentousness of the 'dead sound on the final stroke of nine' serves
as a transition, and the unreality of the City turns into the intense but
meaningless horror, the absurd inconsequence, of a nightmare:

There I saw one I knew, and stopped him, crying: 'Stetson!
'You who were with me in the ships at Mylae!
'That corpse you planted last year in your garden,
'Has it begun to sprout? Will it bloom this year? . . .'

These last two lines pick up again the opening theme. The corpse
acquires a kind of nightmare association with the slain god of *The
Golden Bough*, and is at the same time a buried memory. Then, after

a reference to Webster (Webster's sepulchral horrors are robust), *The Burial of the Dead* ends with the line in which Baudelaire, having developed the themes of

La sottise, l'erreur, le péché, la lésine[4]

and finally *L'Ennui*, suddenly turns upon the reader to remind him that he is something more.

The way in which *The Waste Land* is organized, then, should be obvious even without the aid of notes. And the poet's mastery should be as apparent in the organization as in the parts (where it has been freely acclaimed). The touch with which he manages his difficult transitions, his delicate collocations, is exquisitely sure. His tone, in all its subtle variations, exhibits a perfect control. If there is any instance where this last judgment must be qualified, it is perhaps here (from the first passage of *The Fire Sermon*):

> Sweet Thames, run softly till I end my song,
> Sweet Thames, run softly, for I speak not loud or long.
> But at my back in a cold blast I hear
> The rattle of the bones, and chuckle spread from ear to ear.

These last two lines seem to have too much of the caricature quality of *Prufrock* to be in keeping—for a certain keeping is necessary (and Mr Eliot commonly maintains it) even in contrasts. But even if the comment is just, the occasion for it is a very rare exception.

The Waste Land, then, whatever its difficulty, is, or should be, obviously a poem.[5] It is a self-subsistent poem. Indeed, though it would lose if the notes could be suppressed and forgotten, yet the more important criticism might be said to be, not that it depends upon them too much, but rather that without them, and without the support of *From Ritual to Romance*, it would not lose more. It has, that is, certain limitations in any case; limitations inherent in the conditions that produced it. Comprehensiveness, in the very nature of the undertaking, must be in some sense at the cost of structure: absence of direction, of organizing principle, in life could hardly be made to subserve the highest kind of organization in art.

But when all qualifications have been urged, *The Waste Land* remains a great positive achievement, and one of the first importance for English poetry. In it a mind fully alive in the age compels a poetic triumph out of the peculiar difficulties facing a poet in the age. And in solving his own problem as a poet Mr Eliot did more than solve the problem for himself. Even if *The Waste Land* had been, as used to be

---

4. The first line of Baudelaire's "Au Lecteur." For an English translation of the whole poem, see "To the Reader," p. 42 [*Editor*].

5. It is a test (a positive test, I do not assert that it is always valid negatively), that genuine poetry can communicate before it is understood.'—T. S. Eliot, *Dante*, p. 16.

said, a 'dead end' for him, it would still have been a new start for English poetry.

CLEANTH BROOKS, JR.

The Waste Land: An Analysis†

To venture to write anything further on *The Waste Land*, particularly after the work of F. R. Leavis and F. O. Matthiessen, may call for some explanation and even apology. I am obviously indebted to both critics. The justification for such a commentary as this must be made primarily in terms of a difference of intention. Leavis is interested predominantly in Eliot's method of organization. One or two passages in the poem are treated in detail and are highly valuable for a knowledge of the "meaning" of the poem, but the bulk of the poem does not receive this kind of examination. Moreover, I believe, Leavis makes some positive errors. Matthiessen examines more of the poem in detail, and, as far as it goes, his account is excellent. But the plan of his *Achievement of T. S. Eliot* does not allow for a consecutive examination either. He puts his finger on the basic theme, death-in-life, but I do not think that he has given it all the salience which it deserves.

I prefer not to raise here the question of how important it is for the reader of the poem to have an explicit intellectual account of the various symbols, and a logical account of their relationships. It may well be that such rationalization is no more than a scaffolding to be got out of the way before we contemplate the poem itself as a poem. But many readers (including myself) find the erection of such a scaffolding valuable—if not absolutely necessary—and if some readers will be tempted to lay more stress on the scaffolding than they properly should, there are perhaps still more readers who will be prevented from getting at the poem at all without the help of such a scaffolding. Furthermore, an interest attaches to Mr. Eliot's own mental processes, and whereas Mr. Matthiessen has quite properly warned us that Eliot's poetry cannot be read as autobiography, many of the symbols and ideas which occur in *The Waste Land* are ideas which are definitely central to Eliot's general intellectual position.

The basic symbol used, that of the waste land, is taken, of course, from Miss Jessie Weston's *From Ritual to Romance*. In the legends which she treats there, the land has been blighted by a curse. The crops do not grow, and the animals cannot reproduce. The plight of the land is summed up by, and connected with, the plight of the lord of the

† From *Southern Review* 3 (Summer 1937): 106–36. By permission of the Estate of Cleanth Brooks. All notes are by the editor of this Norton Critical Edition.

land, the Fisher King, who has been rendered impotent by maiming or sickness. The curse can only be removed by the appearance of a knight who will ask the meanings of the various symbols which are displayed to him in the castle. The shift in meaning from physical to spiritual sterility is easily made, and was, as a matter of fact, made in certain of the legends. A knowledge of this symbolism is, as Eliot has already pointed out, essential for an understanding of the poem.

Of hardly less importance to the reader, however, is a knowledge of Eliot's basic method. *The Waste Land* is built on a major contrast—a device which is a favorite of Eliot's and to be found in many of his poems, particularly his later poems. The contrast is between two kinds of life and two kinds of death. Life devoid of meaning is death; sacrifice, even the sacrificial death, may be life-giving, an awaking to life. The poem occupies itself to a great extent with this paradox, and with a number of variations on it.

Eliot has stated the matter quite explicitly himself in one of his essays. In his "Baudelaire" he says: "One aphorism which has been especially noticed is the following: *la volupté unique et suprême de l'amour gît dans la certitude de faire le mal.*[1] This means, I think, that Baudelaire has perceived that what distinguishes the relations of man and woman from the copulation of beasts is the knowledge of Good and Evil (of *moral* Good and Evil which are not natural Good and Bad or puritan Right and Wrong). Having an imperfect, vague romantic conception of Good, he was at least able to understand that the sexual act as evil is more dignified, less boring, than as the natural, 'life-giving,' cheery automatism of the modern world . . . So far as we are human, what we do must be either evil or good; so far as we do evil or good, we are human; and it is better, in a paradoxical way, to do evil than to do nothing: at least, *we exist* [*italics mine*]." The last statement is highly important for an understanding of *The Waste Land*. The fact that men have lost the knowledge of good and evil, keeps them from being alive, and is the justification for viewing the modern waste land as a realm in which people do not even exist.

This theme is stated in the quotation which prefaces the poem. The Sybil says: "I wish to die." Her statement has several possible interpretations. For one thing, she is saying what the people who inhabit the waste land are saying. But she also may be saying what the speaker says in "The Journey of the Magi," . . . "this Birth was / Hard and bitter agony for us, like Death, our death / . . . I should be glad of another death."

---

1. "The most singular and the highest delight of love lies in the certainty of doing evil" (French). A line from Baudelaire's *Intimate Journals*, quoted by Eliot in "Baudelaire" (1930).

I

The first section of "The Burial of the Dead" develops the theme of the attractiveness of death, or of the difficulty in rousing oneself from the death in life in which the people of the waste land live. Men are afraid to live in reality. April, the month of rebirth, is not the most joyful season but the cruelest. Winter at least kept us warm in forgetful snow. The idea is one which Eliot has stressed elsewhere. Earlier in "Gerontion" he had written

> In the juvescence of the year
> Came Christ the tiger
> . . . .
> The tiger springs in the new year. Us he devours.

More lately, in *Murder in the Cathedral*, he has the chorus say

> We do not wish anything to happen.
> Seven years we have lived quietly,
> Succeeded in avoiding notice,
> Living and partly living.

And in another passage: "Now I fear disturbance of the quiet seasons." Men dislike to be aroused from their death-in-life.

The first part of "The Burial of the Dead" introduces this theme through a sort of reverie on the part of the protagonist—a reverie in which speculation on life glides off into memory of an actual conversation in the Hofgarten and back into speculation again. The function of the conversation is to establish to some extent the class and character of the protagonist. The reverie is resumed with line 19.

> What are the roots that clutch, what branches grow
> Out of this stony rubbish?

The protagonist answers for himself:

>   Son of man,
> You cannot say, or guess, for you know only
> A heap of broken images, where the sun beats,
> And the dead tree gives no shelter, the cricket no relief,
> And the dry stone no sound of water.

In this passage there are references to *Ezekiel* and to *Ecclesiastes*, and these references indicate what it is that men no longer know: the passage referred to in *Ezekiel*, II, pictures a world thoroughly secularized:

> 1. And he said unto me, Son of man, stand upon thy feet, and I will speak unto thee. 2. And the spirit entered into me when he spake unto me, and set me upon my feet, that I heard him that

spake unto me. 3. And he said unto me, Son of man, I send thee to the children of Israel, to a rebellious nation that hath rebelled against me: they and their fathers have transgressed against me, even unto this very day.

The following passage from *Ecclesiastes*, XII, is not only referred to in this passage; a reference to it also is evidently made in the nightmare vision of Section V of the poem:

> 1. Remember now thy Creator in the days of thy youth, while the evil days come not, nor the years draw nigh, when thou shalt say, I have no pleasure in them; 2. While the sun, or the light, or the moon, or the stars, be not darkened, nor the clouds return after the rain: 3. In the day when the keepers of the house shall tremble, and the strong men shall bow themselves, and the grinders cease because they are few, and those that look out of the windows be darkened, 4. And the doors shall be shut in the streets, when the sound of the grinding is low, and he shall rise up at the voice of the bird, and all the daughters of music shall be brought low; 5. Also when they shall be afraid of that which is high, and fears shall be in the way, and the almond tree shall flourish, and the grasshopper shall be a burden, *and desire shall fail* [*italics mine*]: because man goeth to his long home, and the mourners go about the streets; 6. Or ever the silver cord be loosed, or the golden bowl be broken, or the pitcher be broken at the fountain, or the wheel broken at the cistern. 7. Then shall the dust return to the earth as it was: and the spirit shall return unto God who gave it. 8. Vanity of vanities, saith the preacher; all is vanity.

The next section which begins with the scrap of song quoted from Wagner (perhaps another item in the reverie of the protagonist), states the opposite half of the paradox which underlies the poem: namely, that life at its highest moments of meaning and intensity resembles death. The song from Act I of Wagner's *Tristan und Isolde,* "*Frisch weht der Wind,*" is sung in the opera by a young sailor aboard the ship which is bringing Isolde to Cornwall. The "*Irisch kind*" of the song does not properly apply to Isolde at all. The song is merely one of happy and naïve love. It brings to the mind of the protagonist an experience of love—the vision of the hyacinth girl as she came back from the hyacinth garden. The poet says

> . . . . my eyes failed, I was neither
> Living nor dead, and I knew nothing,
> Looking into the heart of light, the silence.

The line which immediately follows this passage, "*Oed' und leer das Meer,*" seems at first to be simply an extension of the last figure: that is, "Empty and wide the sea [of silence]." The line, however, as a matter of fact, makes an ironic contrast; for the line, as it occurs in Act III of the opera, is the reply of the watcher who reports to the wounded Tristan that Isolde's ship is nowhere in sight; the sea is empty. And, though the *"Irisch kind"* of the first quotation is not Isolde, the reader familiar with the opera will apply it to Isolde when he comes to the line *"Oed' und leer das Meer."* For the question in the song is in essence Tristan's question in Act III: My Irish child, where dwellest thou? The two quotations from the opera which frame the ecstasy-of-love passage thus take on a new meaning in the altered context. In the first, love is happy; the boat rushes on with a fair wind behind it. In the second, love is absent; the sea is wide and empty. And the last quotation reminds us that even love cannot exist in the waste land.

The next passage, that in which Madame Sosostris figures, calls for further reference to Miss Weston's book. As Miss Weston has shown, the Tarot cards were originally used to determine the event of the highest importance to the people, the rising of the waters. Madame Sosostris has fallen a long way from the high function of her predecessors. She is engaged merely in vulgar fortune-telling—is merely one item in a generally vulgar civilization. But the symbols of the Tarot pack are still unchanged. The various characters are still inscribed on the cards, and she is reading in reality, though she does not know it, the fortune of the protagonist. She finds that his card is that of the drowned Phoenician Sailor, and so she warns him against death by water, not realizing any more than do the other inhabitants of the modern waste land that the way into life may be by death itself. The drowned Phoenician Sailor is a type of the fertility god whose image was thrown into the sea annually as a symbol of the death of summer. As for the other figures in the pack: Belladonna, the Lady of the Rocks, is woman in the waste land. The man with three staves, Eliot says he associates rather arbitrarily with the Fisher King. The term *arbitrarily* indicates that we are not to attempt to find a logical connection here. (It may be interesting to point out, however, that Eliot seems to have given in a later poem his reason for making the association. In "The Hollow Men" he writes, speaking as one of the Hollow Men:

> Let me also wear
> Such deliberate disguises
> Rat's coat, crowskin, crossed staves
> In a field
> Behaving as the wind behaves.

The figure is that of a scarecrow, fit symbol of the man who possesses no reality, and fit type of the Fisher King, the maimed, impotent king who ruled over the waste land of the legend. The man with three staves in the deck of cards may thus have appealed to the poet as an appropriate figure to which to assign the function of the Fisher King, although the process of identification was too difficult to expect the reader to follow and although knowledge of the process was not necessary to an understanding of the poem.)

The Hanged Man, who represents the hanged god of Frazer (including the Christ), Eliot states in a note, is associated with the hooded figure who appears in "What the Thunder Said." That he is hooded accounts for Madame Sosostris' inability to see him; or rather, here again the palaver of the modern fortune-teller is turned to new and important account by the poet's shifting the matter into a new and serious context. The Wheel and the one-eyed merchant will be discussed later.

After the Madame Sosostris passage, Eliot proceeds to complicate his symbols for the sterility and unreality of the modern waste land by associating it with Baudelaire's *"fourmillante cité"* and with Dante's Limbo. The passages already quoted from Eliot's essay on Baudelaire will indicate one of the reasons why Baudelaire's lines are evoked here. In Baudelaire's city, dream and reality seem to mix, and it is interesting that Eliot in "The Hollow Men" refers to this same realm of death-in-life as "death's dream kingdom" in contradistinction to "death's other kingdom."

The references to Dante are most important. The line, "I had not thought death had undone so many," is taken from the Third Canto of the *Inferno*; the line, "Sighs, short and infrequent, were exhaled," from the Fourth Canto. Mr. Matthiessen has already pointed out that the Third Canto deals with Dante's Limbo which is occupied by those who on earth had "lived without praise or blame." They share this abode with the angels, "Who were not rebels, nor were faithful to God, but were for themselves." They exemplify almost perfectly the secular attitude which dominates the modern world. Their grief, according to Dante, arises from the fact that they "have no hope of death; and their blind life is so debased, that they are envious of every other lot." But though they may not hope for death, Dante calls them "these wretches who never were alive." The people who are treated in the Fourth Canto are those who lived virtuously but who died before the proclamation of the Gospel—they are the unbaptized. This completes the categories of people who inhabit the modern waste land: those who are secularized and those who have no knowledge of the faith. Without a faith their life is in reality a death. To repeat the sentence from Eliot previously quoted: "So far as we do evil or good, we are human; and it is better, in a paradoxical way, to do evil than to do nothing: at least we exist."

The Dante and Baudelaire references, then, come to the same thing as the allusion to the waste land of the medieval legends; and these various allusions drawn from widely differing sources enrich the comment on the modern city so that it becomes "unreal" on a number of levels: as seen through "the brown fog of a winter dawn"; as the medieval waste land and Dante's Limbo and Baudelaire's Paris are unreal.

The reference to Stetson stresses again the connection between the modern London of the poem and Dante's hell. After the statement, "I could never have believed death had undone so many," follow the words "After I had distinguished some among them, I saw and knew the shade of him who made, through cowardice, the great refusal." The protagonist, like Dante, sees among the inhabitants of the contemporary waste land one whom he recognizes. (The name "Stetson" I take to have no ulterior significance. It is merely an ordinary name such as might be borne by the friend one might see in a crowd in a great city.) Mylae, as Mr. Matthiessen has pointed out to us, is the name of a battle between the Romans and the Carthaginians in the Punic War. The Punic War was a trade war—might be considered a rather close parallel to our late war. At any rate, it is plain that Eliot in having the protagonist address the friend in a London street as one who was with him in the Punic War rather than as one who was with him in the World War is making the point that all the wars are one war; all experience, one experience. As Eliot put the idea in *Murder in the Cathedral*:

> We do not know very much of the future
> Except that from generation to generation
> The same things happen again and again.

I am not sure that Leavis and Matthiessen are correct in inferring that the line, "That corpse you planted last year in your garden," refers to the attempt to bury a memory. But whether or not this is true, the line certainly refers also to the buried god of the old fertility rites. It also is to be linked with the earlier passage—"What are the roots that clutch, what branches grow," etc. This allusion to the buried god will account for the ironical, almost taunting tone of the passage. The burial of the dead is now a sterile planting—without hope. But the advice to "keep the Dog far hence," in spite of the tone, is, I believe, well taken and serious. The passage in Webster goes as follows

> O keep the wolf far hence, that's foe to men,
> Or with his nails he'll dig it up again.

Why does Eliot turn the wolf into a dog? And why does he reverse the point of importance from the animal's normal hostility to men to its friendliness? If, as some critics have suggested, he is merely interested in making a reference to Webster's darkest play, why alter the line? I am inclined to take the Dog (the capital letter is Eliot's) as Humanitarianism and the related philosophies which in their concern for man extirpate the supernatural—dig up the corpse of the buried god and thus prevent the rebirth of life. For the general idea, see Eliot's essay, "The Humanism of Irving Babbitt."[2]

The last line of "The Burial of the Dead"—"You! *hypocrite lecteur!* —*mon semblable,—mon frère!*"—the quotation from Baudelaire, completes the universalization of Stetson begun by the reference to Mylae. Stetson is every man including the reader and Mr. Eliot himself.

II

If "The Burial of the Dead" gives the general abstract statement of the situation, the second part of *The Waste Land*, "A Game of Chess," gives a more concrete illustration. The easiest contrast in this section —and one which may easily blind the casual reader to a continued emphasis on the contrast between the two kinds of life, or the two kinds of death, already commented on—is the contrast between life in a rich and magnificent setting, and life in the low and vulgar setting of a London pub. But both scenes, however antithetical they may appear superficially, are scenes taken from the contemporary waste land. In both of them life has lost its meaning.

I am particularly indebted to Mr. Allen Tate's brilliant comment on the first part of this section. To quote from him, "the woman . . . is, I believe, the symbol of man at the present time. He is surrounded by the grandeurs of the past, but he does not participate in them; they don't sustain him." And to quote from another section of his commentary: "The rich experience of the great tradition depicted in the room receives a violent shock in contrast with a game that symbolizes the inhuman abstraction of the modern mind." Life has no meaning; history has no meaning; there is no answer to the question: "what shall we ever do?" The only thing that has meaning is the abstract game which they are to play, a game in which the meaning is assigned and arbitrary, meaning by convention only—in short, a game of chess.

This interpretation will account in part for the pointed reference to Cleopatra in the first lines of the section. But there is, I believe, a further reason for the poet's having compared the lady to Cleopatra. The queen in Shakespeare's drama—"Age cannot wither her, nor custom stale / Her infinite variety"—is perhaps the extreme exponent of love for love's sake—the feminine member of the pair of lovers who threw away an empire for love. But the infinite variety of the life of the woman in "A Game of Chess" *has* been staled. There is indeed no variety at all, and love simply does not exist. The function of the sudden change in the description of the carvings and paintings in the room from the heroic and magnificent to the characterization of the rest of them as "other withered stumps of time" is obvious. But the reference

2. First published in 1927.

to Philomela is particularly important, for Philomela, it seems to me, is one of the major symbols of the poem.

Miss Weston points out (in *The Quest of the Holy Grail*) that a section of one of the Grail manuscripts, which is apparently intended as a gloss of the Grail story, tells how the court of the rich Fisher King was withdrawn from the knowledge of men when certain of the maidens who frequented the shrine were raped and had their golden cups taken from them. The curse on the land follows from this act. Miss Weston conjectures that this may be a statement, in the form of parable, of the violation of the older mysteries which were probably once celebrated openly, but were later forced underground into secrecy. Whether or not Mr. Eliot noticed this passage or intends a reference, the violation of a woman makes a very good symbol of the process of secularization. John Crowe Ransom makes the point very neatly for us in his *God Without Thunder*. Love is the aesthetic of sex; lust is the science. Love implies a deferring of the satisfaction of the desire; it implies even a certain asceticism and a ritual. Lust drives forward urgently and scientifically to the immediate extirpation of the desire. Our contemporary waste land is in a large part the result of our scientific attitude—of our complete secularization. Needless to say, lust defeats its own ends. The portrayal of "The change of Philomel, by the barbarous king" is a fitting commentary on the scene which it ornaments. The waste land of the legend came in this way—the modern waste land has come in this way.

That this view is not mere fine-spun ingenuity is borne out somewhat by the change of tense which Eliot employs here and which Mr. Edmund Wilson has commented upon: "And still she cried, and still the world pursues." Apparently the "world" partakes in the barbarous king's action, and still partakes in that action.

To "dirty ears" the nightingale's song is not that which filled all the desert with inviolable voice—it is "jug, jug." Edmund Wilson has pointed out that the rendition of the bird's song here represents not merely the Elizabethans' neutral notation of the bird's song, but carries associations of the ugly and coarse. The passage is one therefore of many instances of Eliot's device of using something which in one context is innocent but in another context becomes loaded with a special meaning.

The Philomela passage has another importance, however. If it is a commentary on how the waste land became waste, it also repeats the theme of the death which is the door to life—the theme of the dying god. The raped woman becomes transformed through suffering into the nightingale; through the violation comes the "inviolable voice." The thesis that suffering is action, and that out of suffering comes poetry is a favorite one of Eliot's. For example, "Shakespeare, too, was occupied with the struggle—which alone constitutes life for a poet—to transmute his personal and private agonies into something rich and strange, something universal and impersonal."[3] Consider also his statement with reference to Baudelaire: "Indeed, in his way of suffering is already a kind of presence of the supernatural and of the superhuman. He rejects always the purely natural and the purely human; in other words, he is neither 'naturalist' nor 'humanist.' " The theme of the life which is death is stated specifically in the conversation between the man and the woman. She asks the question "Are you alive, or not?" and this time we are sufficiently prepared by the Dante references in "The Burial of the Dead" for the statement here to bear a special meaning. (She also asks "Is there nothing in your head?" He is one of the Hollow Men—"headpiece stuffed with straw.") These people, as people in the waste land, know nothing, see nothing, do not even live.

But the protagonist, after this reflection that in the waste land of modern life even death is sterile—"I think we are in rats' alley / Where the dead men lost their bones"—remembers a death which was not sterile, remembers a death that was transformed into something rich and strange, the death described in the song from *The Tempest*—"Those are pearls that were his eyes."

The reference to this section of *The Tempest* is, like the Philomela reference, one of Eliot's major symbols. We are to meet it twice more, in later sections of the poem. Some more general comment on it is therefore appropriate here. The song, one remembers, was sung by Ariel in luring Ferdinand, Prince of Naples, on to meet Miranda, and thus to find love, and through this love, to effect the regeneration and deliverance of all the people on the island. Ferdinand says of the song:

> The ditty doth remember my drowned father.
> This is no mortal business, nor no sound
> That the earth owes . . .

The allusion is an extremely interesting example of the device of Eliot's already commented upon, that of taking an item from one context and shifting it into another in which it assumes a new and powerful meaning. This description of a death which is a portal into a realm of the rich and strange—a death which becomes a sort of birth—assumes in the mind of the protagonist an association with that of the drowned god whose effigy was thrown into the water as a symbol of the death of the fruitful powers of nature but which was taken out of the water as a symbol of the revivified god. (See *From Ritual to Romance*.) The passage therefore represents the perfect antithesis to the passage in "The Burial of the Dead": "That corpse you planted last year in your garden," etc. It also, as we have already pointed out, finds its antithesis in the sterile and unfruitful death "in rats' alley" just commented upon. (We

3. From "Shakespeare and the Stoicism of Seneca" (1927). The following quotation is from "Baudelaire."

shall find that this contrast between the death in rats' alley and the death in *The Tempest* is made again in "The Fire Sermon.")

We have yet to treat the relation of the title of the section, "A Game of Chess," to Middleton's play, *Women beware Women*, from which the game of chess is taken. In the play, the game is used as a device to keep the widow occupied while her daughter-in-law is being seduced. The seduction amounts almost to a rape, and in a *double entendre*, the rape is actually described in terms of the game. We have one more connection with the Philomela symbol therefore. The abstract game is being used in the contemporary waste land, as in the play, to cover up a rape and is a description of the rape itself.

In the second part of "A Game of Chess" we are given a picture of spiritual emptiness, but this time, at the other end of the social scale, as reflected in the talk between two cockney women in a London pub. The account here is straightforward enough and the only matter which calls for comment is the line spoken by Ophelia in *Hamlet* which ends the passage. Ophelia, too, was very much concerned about love, the theme of conversation of the two ladies. As a matter of fact, she was in very much the same position as that of the woman who has been the topic of conversation between the two good ladies we have just heard. She had remarked too once that

> Young men will do 't, if they come to 't;
> By cock, they are to blame.

And her poetry (including the line quoted from her here), like Philomela's, had come out of suffering. I think that we are probably to look for the relevance of the allusion to her in some such matter as this rather than in an easy satiric contrast between Elizabethan glories and modern sordidness. After all (in spite of the Marxists) Eliot's objection to the present world is not merely the sentimental one that this happens to be the twentieth century after Christ and not the seventeenth.

III

"The Fire Sermon" makes much use of several of the symbols already developed. The fire is the sterile burning of lust, and the section is a sermon, although a sermon by example only. This section of the poem also contains some of the most easily apprehended uses of literary allusion. The poem opens on a vision of the modern river. In Spenser's "Prothalamion" the scene described is also a river scene at London, and it is dominated by nymphs and their paramours, and the nymphs are preparing for a bridal. The contrast between Spenser's scene and its twentieth century equivalent is jarring. The paramours are now "the loitering heirs of city directors," and, as for the bridals of Spenser's Elizabethan maidens, in the stanzas which follow we learn a great deal about those. At the end of the section the speech of the third of the Thames-nymphs summarizes the whole matter for us.

The waters of the Thames are also associated with those of Leman —the poet in the contemporary waste land is in a sort of Babylonian Captivity.

The castle of the Fisher King was always located on the banks of a river or on the sea shore. The title "Fisher King," Miss Weston shows, originates from the use of the fish as a fertility or life symbol. This meaning, however, was often forgotten, and so the title in many of the later Grail romances is accounted for by describing the king as fishing. Eliot uses the reference to fishing for reverse effect. The reference to fishing is part of the realistic detail of the scene—"While I was fishing in the dull canal." But to the reader who knows the Weston references, the reference is to that of the Fisher King of the Grail legends. The protagonist is the maimed and impotent king of the legends.

Eliot proceeds now to tie the waste-land symbol to that of *The Tempest*, by quoting one of the lines spoken by Ferdinand, Prince of Naples, which occurs just before Ariel's song, "Full Fathom Five," is heard. But he alters *The Tempest* passage somewhat, writing not, "Weeping again the king my father's wreck," but

> Musing upon the king my brother's wreck
> And on the king my father's death before him.

It is possible that the alteration has been made to bring the account taken from *The Tempest* into accord with the situation in the Percival stories. In Wolfram von Eschenbach's *Parzival*, for instance, Trevrezent, the hermit, is the brother of the Fisher King, Anfortas. He tells Parzival, "His name all men know as Anfortas, and I weep for him evermore." Their father, Frimutel, is of course dead.

The protagonist in the poem, then, imagines himself not only in the situation of Ferdinand in *The Tempest* but also in that of one of the characters in the Grail legend; and the wreck, to be applied literally in the first instance, applies metaphorically in the second.

After the lines from *The Tempest*, appears again the image of a sterile death from which no life comes, the bones, "rattled by the rat's foot only, year to year." (The collocation of this figure with the vision of the death by water in Ariel's song has already been commented on. The lines quoted from *The Tempest* come just before the song.)

The allusion to Marvell's "To His Coy Mistress" is of course one of the easiest allusions in the poem. Instead of "Time's winged chariot" the poet hears "the sound of horns and motors" of contemporary London. But the passage has been further complicated. The reference has been combined with an allusion to Day's "Parliament of Bees." "Time's winged chariot" of Marvell has not only been changed to the modern automobile; Day's "sound of horns and hunting" has changed to the horns of the motors. And Actaeon will not be brought face to face with Diana, goddess of chastity; Sweeney, type of the vulgar bourgeois, is to be brought to Mrs. Porter, hardly a type of chastity. The reference in the ballad to the feet "washed in soda water" reminds the poet ironically of another sort of foot-washing, the sound of the children singing in the dome heard at the ceremony of the foot-washing which precedes the restoration of the wounded Anfortas (the Fisher King) by Parzival and the taking away of the curse from the waste land. The quotation thus completes the allusion to the Fisher King commenced in line 189—"While I was fishing in the dull canal."

The pure song of the children also reminds the poet of the song of the nightingale which we have heard in "The Game of Chess." The recapitulation of symbols is continued with a repetition of "Unreal city" and with the reference to the one-eyed merchant.

Mr. Eugenides, the Smyrna merchant, is the one-eyed merchant mentioned by Madame Sosostris. The fact that the merchant is one-eyed apparently means in Madame Sosostris' speech no more than that the merchant's face on the card is shown in profile. But Eliot applies the term to Mr. Eugenides for a totally different effect. The defect corresponds somewhat to Madame Sosostris' bad cold. The Syrian merchants, we learn from Miss Weston's book, were, with slaves and soldiers, the principal carriers of the mysteries which lie at the core of the Grail legends. But in the modern world we find both the representatives of the Tarot divining and the mystery cults in decay. What he carries on his back and what the fortune-teller was forbidden to see is evidently the knowledge of the mysteries (although Mr. Eugenides himself is hardly likely to be more aware of it than Madame Sosostris is aware of the importance of her function). Mr. Eugenides, in terms of his former function ought to be inviting the protagonist to an initiation into the esoteric cult which holds the secret of life, but on the realistic surface of the poem, in his invitation to "a week end at the Metropole" he is really inviting him to a homosexual debauch. The homosexuality is "secret" and now a "cult" but a very different cult from that which Mr. Eugenides ought to represent. The end of the new cult is not life but, ironically, sterility.

In the modern waste land, however, even the relation between man and woman is also sterile. The incident between the typist and the carbuncular young man is a picture of "love" so exclusively and practically pursued that it is not love at all. The scene, as Allen Tate puts it, is one of our most terrible insights into Western civilization. The tragic chorus to the scene is Tiresias, into whom perhaps Mr. Eugenides may be said to modulate, Tiresias, the historical "expert" on the relation between the sexes.

The allusions to Sappho's lines and to Goldsmith's made in this passage need little comment. The hour of evening, which in Sappho's poem brings rest to all and brings the sailor home, brings the typist to her travesty of home—"On the divan . . . at night her bed"—and brings the carbuncular young man, the meeting with whom ends not in peace but in sterile burning.

The reminiscence of the lines from Goldsmith's song in the description of the young woman's actions after the departure of her lover gives concretely and ironically the utter break-down of traditional standards.

It is the music of her gramophone which the protagonist hears "creep by" him "on the waters." Far from the music which Ferdinand heard bringing him to Miranda and love, it is, one is tempted to think, the music of "O O O O that Shakespeherian Rag" of "A Game of Chess."

But the protagonist says that he can *sometimes* hear "The pleasant whining of a mandoline." Significantly enough, it is the music of the fishmen (the fish again as a life symbol) and it comes from beside a church (though—if this is not to rely too much on Eliot's note—the church has been marked for destruction). Life on Lower Thames Street, if not on the Strand, still has meaning as it cannot have meaning for either the typist or the rich woman of "A Game of Chess."

The song of the Thames-daughters brings us back to the opening section of "The Fire Sermon" again, and once more we have to do with the river and the river-nymphs. Indeed, the typist incident is framed by the two river-nymph scenes.

The connection of the river-nymphs with the Rhine-daughters of Wagner's *Götterdämerung* is easily made. In the passage in Wagner's opera to which Eliot refers in his note, the opening of Act III, the Rhine-daughters bewail the loss of the beauty of the Rhine occasioned by the theft of the gold and then beg Siegfried to give them back the Ring made from this gold, finally threatening him with death if he does not give it up. Like the Thames-daughters they too have been violated; and like the maidens mentioned in the Grail legend, the violation has brought a curse on gods and men. The first of the songs depicts the modern river, soiled with oil and tar. (Compare also with the description of the river in the first part of "The Fire Sermon.") The second song depicts the Elizabethan river, also evoked in the first part of "The Fire Sermon." (Leicester and Elizabeth ride upon it in a barge of state. Incidentally, Spenser's "Prothalamion" from which quotation is made in the first part of "The Fire Sermon" mentions Leicester as having formerly lived in the house which forms the setting of the poem.)

In this second song there is also a definite allusion to the passage in *Antony and Cleopatra* already referred to in the opening line of "A Game of Chess."

> Beating oars
> The stern was formed
> A gilded shell

And if we still have any doubt of the allusion, Eliot's note on the passage with its reference to the *barge* and *poop* should settle the matter. We have already commented on the earlier allusion to Cleopatra as the prime example of love for love's sake. The symbol bears something of the same meaning here, and the note which Eliot supplies does something to reinforce the "Cleopatra" aspect of Elizabeth. Elizabeth in the presence of the Spaniard De Quadra, though negotiations were going on for a Spanish marriage, "went so far that Lord Robert at last said, as I [De Quadra was a bishop] was on the spot there was no reason why they should not be married if the queen pleased." The passage has a sort of double function. It reinforces the general contrast between Elizabethan magnificence and modern sordidness: in the Elizabethan age love for love's sake has some meaning and therefore some magnificence. But the passage gives something of an opposed effect too: the same sterile love, emptiness of love, obtained in this period too: Elizabeth and the typist are alike as well as different. (One of the reasons for the frequent allusion to Elizabethan poetry in this and the preceding section of the poem may be the fact that with the English Renaissance the old set of supernatural sanctions had begun to break up. See Eliot's various essays on Shakespeare and the Elizabethan dramatists.)

The third Thames-daughter's song depicts another sordid "love" affair, and unites the themes of the first two songs. It begins "Trams and *dusty* trees." With it we are definitely in the waste land again. Pia, whose words she echoes in saying "Highbury bore me. Richmond and Kew / Undid me" was in Purgatory and had hope. The woman speaking here has no hope—she too is in the Inferno: "I can connect / Nothing with nothing." She has just completed, floating down the river in the canoe, what Eliot has described in *Murder in the Cathedral* as

. . . the effortless journey, to the empty land
. . . .
Where the soul is no longer deceived, for there are no objects, no
    tones,
Where those who were men can no longer turn the mind
To distraction, delusion, escape into dream, pretence,
No colours, no forms to distract, to divert the soul
From seeing itself, foully united forever, nothing with nothing,
Not what we call death, but what beyond death is not death . . .

Now, "on Margate sands," like the Hollow Men, she stands "on this beach of the tumid river."

The songs of the three Thames-daughters, as a matter of fact, epitomize this whole section of the poem. With reference to the quotations from St. Augustine and Buddha at the end of "The Fire Sermon" Eliot states that "The collocation of these two representatives of eastern and western asceticism, as the culmination of this part of the poem, is not an accident."

It is certainly not an accident. The moral of all the incidents which we have been witnessing is that there must be an asceticism—something to check the drive of desire. The wisdom of the East and the West comes to the same thing on this point. Moreover, the imagery which both St. Augustine and Buddha use for lust is fire. What we have witnessed in the various scenes of "The Fire Sermon" is the sterile burning of lust. Modern man, freed from all restraints, in his cultivation of experience for experience's sake burns, but not with a "hard and gemlike flame."[4] One ought not to pound the point home in this fashion, but to see that the imagery of this section of the poem furnishes illustrations leading up to the Fire Sermon is the necessary requirement for feeling the force of the brief allusions here at the end to Buddha and St. Augustine.

IV

Whatever the specific meaning of the symbols, the general function of the section, "Death by Water," is readily apparent. The section forms a contrast with "The Fire Sermon" which precedes it—a contrast between the symbolism of fire and that of water. Also readily apparent is its force as symbol of surrender and relief through surrender.

Some specific connections can be made, however. The drowned Phoenician Sailor recalls the drowned god of the fertility cults. Miss Weston tells that each year at Alexandria an effigy of the head of the god was thrown into the water as a symbol of the death of the powers of nature, and that this head was carried by the current to Byblos where it was taken out of the water and exhibited as a symbol of the reborn god.

Moreover, the Phoenician Sailor is a merchant—"Forgot . . . the profit and loss." The vision of the drowned sailor gives a statement of the message which the Syrian merchants originally brought to Britain and which the Smyrna merchant, unconsciously and by ironical negatives, has brought. One of Eliot's notes states that the "merchant . . . melts into the Phoenician Sailor, and the latter is not wholly distinct from Ferdinand Prince of Naples." The death by water would seem to be equated with the death described in Ariel's song in *The Tempest*. There is a definite difference in the tone of the description of this death—"A current under sea / Picked his bones in whispers," as compared with the "other" death—"bones cast in a little low dry garret / Rattled by the rat's foot only, year to year."

4. A reference to the Conclusion of Walter Pater's *The Renaissance* (1893), which rather scandalously recommended, "To burn always with this hard, gem-like flame, to maintain this ecstasy, is success in life."

Farther than this it would not be safe to go, but one may point out that whirling (the whirlpool here, the Wheel of Madame Sosostris' palaver) is one of Eliot's symbols frequently used in other poems (*Ash Wednesday*, "Gerontion," *Murder in the Cathedral*, and "Burnt Norton") to denote the temporal world. And one may point out, supplying the italics oneself, the following passage from *Ash Wednesday*:

> Although I do not hope to *turn* again
> . . . .
> Wavering between the *profit and the loss*
> In this brief transit where the dreams cross
> The dream crossed twilight *between birth and dying*.

At least, with a kind of hindsight, one may suggest that "Section IV" gives an instance of the conquest of death and time, the "perpetual recurrence of determined seasons," the "world of spring and autumn, birth and dying" through death itself.

V

The reference to the "torchlight red on sweaty faces" and to the "frosty silence in the gardens" obviously associates, as we have already pointed out, Christ in Gethsemane with the other hanged gods. The god has now died, and in referring to this, the basic theme finds another strong restatement:

> He who was living is now dead
> We who were living are now dying
> With a little patience

The poet does not say "We who *are* living." It is "We who *were* living." It is the death-in-life of Dante's Limbo. Life in the full sense has been lost.

The passage on the sterility of the waste land and the lack of water which follows, provides for the introduction later of two highly important passages:

> There is not even silence in the mountains
> But dry sterile thunder without rain—

lines which look forward to the introduction later of "what the thunder said" when the thunder, no longer sterile, but bringing rain speaks.

The second of these passages is, "There is not even solitude in the mountains," which looks forward to the reference to the Journey to Emmaus theme a few lines later: "Who is the third who walks always beside you?" The god has returned, has risen, but the travelers cannot tell whether it is really he, or mere illusion induced by their delirium.

The parallelism between the "hooded figure" who "walks always beside you," and the "hooded hordes" is another instance of the sort of parallelism that is really a contrast, one of the type of which Eliot is fond. In the first case, the figure is indistinct because spiritual; in the second, the hooded hordes are indistinct because completely *unspiritual*—they are the people of the waste land—

> Shape without form, shade without colour,
> Paralysed force, gesture without motion—

to take two lines from "The Hollow Men," where the people of the waste land once more appear. Or to take another line from the same poem, perhaps their hoods are the "deliberate disguises" which the Hollow Men, the people of the waste land, wear.

Eliot, as his notes tell us, has particularly connected the description here with the "decay of eastern Europe." The hordes represent then the general waste land of the modern world with a special application to the breakup of Eastern Europe, the region with which the fertility cults were especially connected and in which today the traditional values are thoroughly discredited. The cities, Jerusalem, Athens, Alexandria, Vienna, like the London of the first section of the poem are "unreal," and for the same reason.

The passage which immediately follows develops the unreality into nightmare, but it is a nightmare vision which is not only an extension of the passage beginning, "What is the city over the mountains"—in it appear other figures from earlier in the poem: the lady of "A Game of Chess" who, surrounded by the glory of history and art sees no meaning in either and threatens to rush out into the street "With my hair down, so," has here let down her hair and fiddles "whisper music on those strings." One remembers in "A Game of Chess" that it was the woman's hair that spoke:

> . . . her hair
> Spread out in fiery points
> Glowed into words, then would be savagely still.

The hair has been immemorially a symbol of fertility, and Miss Weston and Frazer mention sacrifices of hair in order to aid the fertility god.

As we have pointed out earlier in dealing with "The Burial of the Dead," this whole passage is to be connected with the twelfth chapter of *Ecclesiastes*. The doors "of mudcracked houses," and the cisterns in this passage are to be found in *Ecclesiastes*, and the woman fiddling music from her hair is one of "the daughters of music" brought low. The towers and bells from the Elizabeth and Leicester passage of "The Fire Sermon" also appear here, but the towers are upside down, and the bells, far from pealing for an actual occasion or ringing the hours, are "reminiscent." The civilization is breaking up.

The "violet light" also deserves comment. In "The Fire Sermon" it is twice mentioned as the "violet hour," and there it has little more than a physical meaning. It is a description of the hour of twilight. Here it indicates the twilight of the civilization, but it is perhaps something more. Violet is one of the liturgical colors of the Church. It symbolizes repentance and it is the color of baptism. The visit to the Perilous Chapel, according to Miss Weston, was an initiation—that is, a baptism. In the nightmare vision, the bats wear baby faces.

The horror built up in this passage is a proper preparation for the passage on the Perilous Chapel which follows it. The journey has not been merely an agonized walk in the desert, though it is that, or merely the journey after the god has died and hope has been lost; it is also the journey to the Perilous Chapel of the Grail story. In Miss Weston's account, the Chapel was part of the ritual, and was filled with horrors to test the candidate's courage. In some stories the perilous cemetery is also mentioned. Eliot has used both: "Over the tumbled graves, about the chapel." In many of the Grail stories the Chapel was haunted by demons.

The cock in the folk-lore of many peoples is regarded as the bird whose voice chases away the powers of evil. It is significant that it is after his crow that the flash of lightning comes and the "damp gust / Bringing rain." It is just possible that the cock has a connection also with *The Tempest* symbols. The first song which Ariel sings to Ferdinand as he sits "Weeping again the king my father's wreck" ends

> The strain of strutting chanticleer,
> Cry, cock-a-doodle-doo.

The next stanza is the "Full Fathom Five" song which Eliot has used as a vision of life gained through death. If this relation holds, here we have an extreme instance of an allusion, in itself innocent, forced into serious meaning through transference to a new context.

As Miss Weston has shown, the fertility cults go back to a very early period and are recorded in Sanscrit legends. Eliot has been continually in the poem linking up the Christian doctrine with the beliefs of as many peoples as he can. Here he goes back to the very beginnings of Aryan culture, and tells the rest of the story of the rain's coming, not in terms of the setting already developed but in its earliest form. The passage is thus a perfect parallel in method to the passage in "The Burial of the Dead":

> You who were with me in the ships *at Mylae!*
> That corpse you planted *last year* in your garden . . .

The use of Sanscrit in what the thunder says is thus accounted for. In addition, there is of course a more obvious reason for casting what the thunder said into Sanscrit here: onomatopoeia.

The comments on the three statements of the thunder imply an acceptance of them. The protagonist answers the first question, "what have we given?" with the statement:

> The awful daring of a moment's surrender
> Which an age of prudence can never retract
> By this, and this only, we have existed.

Here the larger meaning is stated in terms which imply the sexual meaning. Man cannot be absolutely self-regarding. Even the propagation of the race—even mere "existence"—calls for such a surrender. Living calls for—see the passage already quoted from Eliot's essay on Baudelaire—belief in something more than "life."

The comment on *dayadhvam* (sympathize) is obviously connected with the foregoing passage. The surrender to something outside the self is an attempt (whether on the sexual level or some other) to transcend one's essential isolation. The passage gathers up the symbols previously developed in the poem just as the foregoing passage reflects, though with a different implication, the numerous references to sex made earlier in the poem. For example, the woman in the first part of "A Game of Chess" has also heard the key turn in the door, and confirms her prison by thinking of the key:

> Speak to me. Why do you never speak. Speak.
> What are you thinking of? What thinking? What?
> I never know what you are thinking. Think.

The third statement made by the thunder, *damyata* (control) follows the logical condition for control, sympathy. The figure of the boat catches up the figure of control already given in "Death by Water"— "O you who turn the wheel and look to windward"—and from "The Burial of the Dead" the figure of happy love in which the ship rushes on with a fair wind behind it: "*Frisch weht der wind . . .*"

I cannot accept Mr. Leavis' interpretation of the passage, "I sat upon the shore / Fishing, with the arid plain behind me," as meaning that the poem "exhibits no progression." The comment upon what the thunder says would indicate, if other passages did not, that the poem does "not end where it began." It is true that the protagonist does not witness a revival of the waste land; but there are two important relationships involved in his case: a personal one as well as a general one. If secularization has destroyed, or is likely to destroy, modern civilization, the protagonist still has a private obligation to fulfill. Even if the civilization is breaking up—"London Bridge is falling down falling down falling down"—there remains the personal obligation: "Shall I at least set my lands in order?" Consider in this connection the last sentences of Eliot's "Thoughts After Lambeth": "The World is trying the experiment of attempting to form a non-Christian mentality. The experiment will fail;

but we must be very patient awaiting its collapse; meanwhile redeeming the time: so that the Faith may be preserved alive through the dark ages before us; to renew and rebuild civilization, and save the World from suicide."[5]

The bundle of quotations with which the poem ends has a very definite relation to the general theme of the poem and to several of the major symbols used in the poem. Before Arnaut leaps back into the refining fire of Purgatory with joy he says: "I am Arnaut who weep and go singing; contrite I see my past folly, and joyful I see before me the day I hope for. Now I pray you by that virtue which guides you to the summit of the stair, at times be mindful of my pain." This note is carried forward by the quotation from *Pervigilium Veneris*: "When shall I be like the swallow." The allusion also connects with the Philomela symbol. (Eliot's note on the passage indicates this clearly.) The sister of Philomela was changed into a swallow as Philomela was changed into a nightingale. The protagonist is asking therefore when shall the spring, the time of love return, but also when will he be reborn out of his sufferings, and—with the special meaning which the symbol takes on from the preceding Dante quotation and from the earlier contexts already discussed—he is asking what is asked at the end of one of the minor poems: "When will Time flow away."

The quotation from "El Desdichado," as Edmund Wilson has pointed out, indicates that the protagonist of the poem has been disinherited, robbed of his tradition. The ruined tower is perhaps also the Perilous Chapel, "only the wind's home," and it is also the whole tradition in decay. The protagonist resolves to claim his tradition and rehabilitate it.

The quotation from *The Spanish Tragedy*—"Why then Ile fit you. Hieronymo's mad againe"—is perhaps the most puzzling of all these quotations. It means, I believe, this: the protagonist's acceptance of what is in reality the deepest truth will seem to the present world mere madness. ("And still she cried, and still the world pursues / 'Jug Jug' to dirty ears.") Hieronymo in the play, like Hamlet, was "mad" for a purpose. The protagonist is conscious of the interpretation which will be placed on the words which follow—words which will seem to many apparently meaningless babble, but which contain the oldest and most permanent truth of the race:

Datta.   Dayadhvam.   Damyata.

After this statement comes the benediction:

Shantih   Shantih   Shantih

5. An essay published in 1931 after one of the Lambeth Conferences of the Church of England.

The foregoing account of *The Waste Land* is, of course, not to be substituted for the poem itself. Moreover, it certainly is not to be considered as representing *the method by which the poem was composed.* Much which the prose expositor must represent as though it had been consciously contrived obviously was arrived at unconsciously and concretely.

The account given above is a statement merely of the "prose meaning," and bears the same relation to the poem as does the "prose meaning" of any other poem. But one need not perhaps apologize for setting forth such a statement explicitly, for *The Waste Land* has been almost consistently misinterpreted since its first publication. Even a critic so acute as Edmund Wilson has seen the poem as essentially a statement of despair and disillusionment, and this account sums up the stock interpretation of the poem. Indeed, the phrase, "the poetry of drouth," has become a *cliché* of left-wing criticism. It is such a misrepresentation of *The Waste Land* as this which allows Eda Lou Walton to entitle an essay on contemporary poetry, "Death in the Desert"; or which causes Waldo Frank to misconceive of Eliot's whole position and personality.[6] But more than the meaning of one poem is at stake. If *The Waste Land* is not a world-weary cry of despair or a sighing after the vanished glories of the past, then not only the popular interpretation of the poem will have to be altered but also the general interpretations of post-War poetry which begin with such a misinterpretation as a premise.

Such misinterpretations involve also misconceptions of Eliot's technique. Eliot's basic method may be said to have passed relatively unnoticed. The popular view of the method used in *The Waste Land* may be described as follows: Eliot makes use of ironic contrasts between the glorious past and the sordid present—the crashing irony of

> But at my back from time to time I hear
> The sound of horns and motors, which shall bring
> Sweeney to Mrs. Porter in the spring.

But this is to take the irony of the poem at the most superficial level, and to neglect the other dimensions in which it operates. And it is to neglect what are essentially more important aspects of his method. Moreover, it is to overemphasize the difference between the method employed by Eliot in this poem and that employed by him in later poems.

The basic method used in *The Waste Land* may be described as the application of the principle of complexity. The poet works in terms of

---

6. Eda Lou Walton's "Death in the Desert" first appeared in *Saturday Review* (August 26, 1933), pp. 61–63. The offending Waldo Frank essay is perhaps "The 'Universe' of T. S. Eliot," *New Republic* (October 26, 1932), pp. 294–95.

surface parallelisms which in reality make ironical contrasts, and in terms of surface contrasts which in reality constitute parallelisms. (The second group set up effects which may be described as the obverse of irony.) The two aspects taken together give the effect of chaotic experience ordered into a new whole though the realistic surface of experience is faithfully retained. The complexity of the experience is not violated by the apparent forcing upon it of a predetermined scheme.

The fortune-telling of "The Burial of the Dead" will illustrate the general method very satisfactorily. On the surface of the poem the poet reproduces the patter of the charlatan, Madame Sosostris, and there is the surface irony: the contrast between the original use of the Tarot cards and the use made here. But each of the details (justified realistically in the palaver of the fortune-teller) assumes a new meaning in the general context of the poem. There is then in addition to the surface irony something of a Sophoclean irony too, and the "fortune-telling" which is taken ironically by a twentieth-century audience becomes *true* as the poem develops—true in a sense in which Madame Sosostris herself does not think it true. The surface irony is thus reversed and becomes an irony on a deeper level. The items of her speech have only one reference in terms of the context of her speech: the "man with three staves," the "one-eyed merchant," the "crowds of people, walking round in a ring," etc. But transferred to other contexts they become loaded with special meanings. To sum up, all the central symbols of the poem head up here, but here, in the only section in which they are explicitly bound together, the binding is slight and accidental. The deeper lines of association only emerge in terms of the total context as the poem develops—and this is, of course, exactly the effect which the poet intends.

This transference of items from an "innocent" context into a context in which they become charged and transformed in meaning will account for many of the literary allusions in the poem. For example, the "change of Philomel" is merely one of the items in the decorative detail in the room in the opening of "A Game of Chess." But the violent change of tense—"And still she cried, and still the world pursues"—makes it a comment upon, and a symbol of, the modern world. And further allusions to it through the course of the poem gradually equate it with the general theme of the poem. The allusions to *The Tempest* display the same method. The parallelism between Dante's Hell and the waste land of the Grail legends is fairly close; even the equation of Baudelaire's Paris to the waste land is fairly obvious. But the parallelism between the death by drowning in *The Tempest* and the death of the fertility god is, on the surface, merely accidental, and the first allusion to Ariel's song is merely an irrelevant and random association of the stream-of-consciousness:

Is your card, the drowned Phoenician Sailor,
(Those are pearls that were his eyes. Look!)

And on its second appearance in "A Game of Chess" it is still only an
item in the protagonist's abstracted reverie. Even the association of *The
Tempest* symbol with the Grail legends in the lines

While I was fishing in the dull canal
. . . .
Musing upon the king my brother's wreck

and in the passage which follows, is ironical merely. But the associations
have been established, even though they may seem to be made in ironic
mockery, and when we come to the passage, "Death by Water," with its
change of tone, they assert themselves positively. We have a sense of revelation out of material apparently accidentally thrown together. I have
called the effect the obverse of irony, for the method, like that of irony, is
indirect, though the effect is positive rather than negative.

The "melting" of the characters into each other is, of course, an
aspect of this general process. Elizabeth and the girl born at Highbury
both ride on the Thames, one in the barge of state, the other supine
in a narrow canoe, and they are both Thames-nymphs, who are violated
and thus are like the Rhine-nymphs who have also been violated, etc.
With the characters as with the other symbols, the surface relationships
may be accidental and apparently trivial and they may be made either
ironically or through random association or in hallucination, but in the
total context of the poem the deeper relationships are revealed. The
effect is a sense of the oneness of experience, and of the unity of all
periods, and with this, a sense that the general theme of the poem is
true. But the theme has not been imposed—it has been revealed.

This complication of parallelisms and contrasts makes, of course, for
ambiguity, but the ambiguity, in part, resides in the poet's fidelity to
the complexity of experience. The symbols resist complete equation
with a simple meaning. To take an example, "rock" throughout the
poem seems to be one of the "desert" symbols. For example, the "dry
stone" gives "no sound of water"; woman in the waste land is "the Lady
of the Rocks," and most pointed of all, there is the long delirium passage in "What the Thunder Said": "Here is no water but only rock,"
etc. So much for its general meaning, but in "The Burial of the Dead"
occur the lines

Only
There is shadow under this red rock,
(Come in under the shadow of this red rock).

Rock here is a place of refuge. (Moreover, there may also be a reference
to the Grail symbolism. In *Parzival*, the Grail is a stone: "And this

stone all men call the grail. . . . As children the Grail doth call them, 'neath its shadow they wax and grow.") The paradox, life through death, penetrates the symbol itself.

To take an even clearer case of this paradoxical use of symbols, consider the lines which occur in the hyacinth girl passage. The vision gives obviously a sense of the richness and beauty of life. It is a moment of ecstasy (the basic imagery is obviously sexual); but the moment in its intensity is like death. The protagonist looks in that moment into the "heart of light, the silence," and so looks into—not richness—but blankness: he is neither "living nor dead." The symbol of life stands also for a kind of death. This duality of function may, of course, extend to a whole passage. For example, consider:

> Where fishmen lounge at noon: where the walls
> Of Magnus Martyr hold
> Inexplicable splendour of Ionian white and gold.

The function of the passage is to indicate the poverty into which religion has fallen: the splendid church now surrounded by the poorer districts. But the passage has an opposed effect also: the fishmen in the "public bar in Lower Thames Street" next to the church have a meaningful life which has been largely lost to the secularized upper and middle classes.

The poem would undoubtedly be "clearer" if every symbol had one, unequivocal meaning; but the poem would be thinner, and less honest. For the poet has not been content to develop a didactic allegory in which the symbols are two-dimensional items adding up directly to the sum of the general scheme. They represent dramatized instances of the theme, embodying in their own nature the fundamental paradox of the theme.

We shall better understand why the form of the poem is right and inevitable if we compare Eliot's theme to Dante's and to Spenser's. Eliot's theme is not the statement of a faith held and agreed upon (Dante's *Divine Comedy*) nor is it the projection of a "new" system of beliefs (Spenser's *Faerie Queene*). Eliot's theme is the rehabilitation of a system of beliefs, known but now discredited. Dante did not have to "prove" his statement; he could assume it and move within it about a poet's business. Eliot does not care, like Spenser, to force the didacticism. He prefers to stick to the poet's business. But, unlike Dante, he can not assume acceptance of the statement. A direct approach is calculated to elicit powerful "stock responses" which will prevent the poem's being *read* at all. Consequently, the only method is to work by indirection. The "Christian" material is at the center, but the poet never deals with it directly. The theme of resurrection is made on the surface in terms of the fertility rites; the words which the thunder speaks are Sanscrit words.

We have been speaking as if the poet were a strategist trying to win acceptance from a hostile audience. But of course this is true only in a sense. The poet himself is audience as well as speaker; we state the problem more exactly if we state it in terms of the poet's integrity rather than in terms of his strategy. He is so much a man of his own age that he can indicate his attitude toward the Christian tradition without falsity only in terms of the difficulties of a rehabilitation; and he is so much a poet and so little a propagandist that he can be sincere only as he presents his theme concretely and dramatically.

To put the matter in still other terms: the Christian terminology is for the poet here a mass of *clichés*. However "true" he may feel the terms to be, he is still sensitive to the fact that they operate superficially as *clichés*, and his method of necessity must be a process of bringing them to life again. The method adopted in *The Waste Land* is thus violent and radical, but thoroughly necessary. For the renewing and vitalizing of symbols which have been crusted over with a distorting familiarity demands the type of organization which we have already commented on in discussing particular passages: the statement of surface similarities which are ironically revealed to be dissimilarities, and the association of apparently obvious dissimilarities which culminates in a later realization that the dissimilarities are only superficial—that the chains of likeness are in reality fundamental. In this way the statement of beliefs emerges *through* confusion and cynicism—not in spite of them.

DELMORE SCHWARTZ

T. S. Eliot as the International Hero†

A culture hero is one who brings new arts and skills to mankind. Prometheus was a culture hero and the inventors of the radio may also be said to be culture heroes, although this is hardly to be confounded with the culture made available by the radio.

The inventors of the radio made possible a new range of experience. This is true of certain authors; for example, it is true of Wordsworth in regard to nature, and Proust in regard to time. It is not true of Shakespeare, but by contrast it is true of Surrey and the early Elizabethan playwrights who invented blank verse. Thus the most important authors are not always culture heroes, and thus no rank, stature, or scope is of necessity implicit in speaking of the author as a culture hero.

† From *Partisan Review* 12 (Spring 1945): 199–206. Reprinted by permission of Robert Phillips, Executor for the Literary Estate of Delmore Schwartz. All notes are by the editor of this Norton Critical Edition.

When we speak of nature and of a new range of experience, we may think of a mountain range: some may make the vehicles by means of which a mountain is climbed, some may climb the mountain, and some may apprehend the new view of the surrounding countryside which becomes possible from the heights of the mountain. T. S. Eliot is a culture hero in each of these three ways. This becomes clear when we study the relationship of his work to the possible experiences of modern life. The term, possible, should be kept in mind, for many human beings obviously disregard and turn their backs upon much of modern life, although modern life does not in the least cease to circumscribe and penetrate their existence.

The reader of T. S. Eliot by turning the dials of his radio can hear the capitals of the world, London, Vienna, Athens, Alexandria, Jerusalem. What he hears will be news of the agony of war. Both the agony and the width of this experience are vivid examples of how the poetry of T. S. Eliot has a direct relationship to modern life. The width and the height and the depth of modern life are exhibited in his poetry; the agony and the horror of modern life are represented as inevitable to any human being who does not wish to deceive himself with systematic lies. Thus it is truly significant that E. M. Forster, in writing of Eliot, should recall August 1914 and the beginning of the First World War; it is just as significant that he should speak of first reading Eliot's poems in Alexandria, Egypt, during that war, and that he should conclude by saying that Eliot was one who had looked into the abyss and refused henceforward to deny or forget the fact.[1]

We are given an early view of the international hero in the quasi-autobiographical poem which Eliot entitles: "Mélange Adultère Du Tout."[2] The title, borrowed from a poem by Corbière, is ironic, but the adulterous mixture of practically everything, every time and every place, is not ironic in the least: a teacher in America, the poem goes, a journalist in England, a lecturer in Yorkshire, a literary nihilist in Paris, overexcited by philosophy in Germany, a wanderer from Omaha to Damascus, he has celebrated, he says, his birthday at an African oasis, dressed in a giraffe's skin. Let us place next to this array another list of names and events as heterogeneous as a circus or America itself: St. Louis, New England, Boston, Harvard, England, Paris, the First World War, Oxford, London, the Russian Revolution, the Church of England, the post-war period, the world crisis and depression, the Munich Pact, and the Second World War. If this list seems far-fetched or forced, if it seems that such a list might be made for any author, the

1. See Forster's essay "T. S. Eliot," originally published in 1928 and later included in *Abinger Harvest* (New York: Harcourt, Brace, 1936).
2. A poem originally written in French after the example of Tristan Corbière (1845–1875), French Symbolist poet. The description that follows is essentially a prose translation of the poem.

answer is that these names and events are *presences* in Eliot's work in a way which is not true of many authors, good and bad, who have lived through the same years.

Philip Rahv has shown how the heroine of Henry James is best understood as the heiress of all the ages. So, in a further sense, the true protagonist of Eliot's poems is the heir of all the ages. He is the descendant of the essential characters of James in that he is the American who visits Europe with a Baedeker[3] in his hand, just like Isabel Archer. But the further sense in which he is the heir of all the ages is illustrated when Eliot describes the seduction of a typist in a London flat from the point of view of Tiresias, a character in a play by Sophocles. To suppose that this is the mere exhibition of learning or reading is a banal misunderstanding. The important point is that the presence of Tiresias illuminates the seduction of the typist just as much as a description of her room. Hence Eliot writes in his notes to *The Waste Land* that "what Tiresias *sees* is the substance of the poem." The illumination of the ages is available at any moment, and when the typist's indifference and boredom in the act of love must be represented, it is possible for Eliot to invoke and paraphrase a lyric from a play by Oliver Goldsmith. Literary allusion has become not merely a Miltonic reference to Greek gods and Old Testament geography, not merely the citation of parallels, but a powerful and inevitable habit of mind, a habit which issues in judgment and the representation of different levels of experience, past and present.

James supposed that his theme was the international theme: would it not be more precise to speak of it as the transatlantic theme? This effort at a greater exactness defines what is involved in Eliot's work. Henry James was concerned with the American in Europe. Eliot cannot help but be concerned with the whole world and all history. Tiresias sees the nature of love in all times and all places and when Sweeney outwits a scheming whore, the fate of Agamemnon becomes relevant. So too, in the same way exactly, Eliot must recognize and use a correspondence between St. Augustine and Buddha in speaking of sensuality. And thus, as he writes again in his notes to *The Waste Land*, "The collocation of these two representatives of eastern and western asceticism as the culmination of this part of the poem is not an accident." And it is not an accident that the international hero should have come from St. Louis, Missouri, or at any rate from America. Only an American with a mind and sensibility which is cosmopolitan and expatriated could have seen Europe as it is seen in *The Waste Land*.

A literary work may be important in many ways, but surely one of the ways in which it is important is in its relationship to some important human interest or need, or in its relationship to some new aspect of

3. A popular guide book.

human existence. Eliot's work is important in relationship to the fact that experience has become international. We have become an international people, and hence an international hero is possible. Just as the war is international, so the true causes of many of the things in our lives are world-wide, and we are able to understand the character of our lives only when we are aware of all history, of the philosophy of history, of primitive peoples and the Russian Revolution, of ancient Egypt and the unconscious mind. Thus again it is no accident that in *The Waste Land* use is made of *The Golden Bough*, and a book on the quest of the Grail; and the way in which images and associations appear in the poem illustrates a new view of consciousness, the depths of consciousness and the unconscious mind.

The protagonist of *The Waste Land* stands on the banks of the Thames and quotes the Upanishads, and this very quotation, the command to "give, sympathize, and control," makes possible a comprehensive insight into the difficulty of his life in the present. But this emphasis upon one poem of Eliot's may be misleading. What is true of much of his poetry is also true of his criticism. When the critic writes of tradition and the individual talent, when he declares the necessity for the author of a consciousness of the past as far back as Homer, when he brings the reader back to Dante, the Elizabethans and Andrew Marvell, he is also speaking as the heir of all the ages.

The emphasis on a consciousness of literature may also be misleading, for nowhere better than in Eliot can we see the difference between being merely literary and making the knowledge of literature an element in vision, that is to say, an essential part of the process of seeing anything and everything. Thus, to cite the advent of Tiresias again, the literary character of his appearance is matched by the unliterary actuality by means of which he refers to himself as being "like a taxi throbbing waiting." In one way, the subject of *The Waste Land* is the sensibility of the protagonist, a sensibility which is literary, philosophical, cosmopolitan and expatriated. But this sensibility is concerned not with itself as such, but with the common things of modern life, with two such important aspects of existence as religious belief and making love. To summon to mind such profound witnesses as Freud and D. H. Lawrence is to remember how often, in modern life, love has been the worst sickness of human beings.

The extent to which Eliot's poetry is directly concerned with love is matched only by the extent to which it is concerned with religious belief and the crisis of moral values. J. Alfred Prufrock is unable to make love to women of his own class and kind because of shyness, self-consciousness, and fear of rejection. The protagonists of other poems in Eliot's first book are men or women laughed at or rejected in love, and a girl deserted by her lover seems like a body deserted by the soul.

In Eliot's second volume of poems, an old man's despair issues in part from his inability to make love,[4] while Sweeney, an antithetical character, is able to make love, but is unable to satisfy the woman with whom he copulates. In *The Waste Land*, the theme of love as a failure is again uppermost. Two lovers return from a garden after a moment of love, and the woman is overcome by despair or pathological despondency. A lady, perhaps the same woman who has returned from the garden in despair, becomes hysterical in her boudoir because her lover or her husband has nothing to say to her and cannot give her life any meaning or interest: "What shall I do now?" she says, "what shall I ever do?" The neurasthenic lady is succeeded in the poem by cockney women who gossip about another cockney woman who has been made ill by contraceptive pills taken to avoid the consequences of love; which is to say that the sickness of love has struck down every class in society: "What you get married for, if you don't want children?" And then we witness the seduction of the typist; and then other aspects of the sickness of love appear when, on the Thames bank, three girls ruined by love rehearse the sins of the young men with whom they have been having affairs. In the last part of the poem, the impossibility of love, the gulf between one human being and another, is the answer to the command to give, that is to say, to give oneself or surrender oneself to another human being in the act of making love.

*   *   *

*   *   * But we ought to remember that the difficulty of making love, that is to say, of entering into the most intimate of relationships, is not the beginning but the consequence of the whole character of modern life. That is why the apparatus of reference which the poet brings to bear upon failure in love involves all history ("And I Tiresias have foresuffered all") and is international. So too the old man who is the protagonist of "Gerontion" must refer to human beings of many nationalities, to Mr. Silvero at Limoges, Hakagawa, Madame de Tornquist, Fräulein von Kulp and Christ [the tiger] and he finds it necessary to speak of all history as well as his failure in love. History is made to illuminate love and love is made to illuminate history. In modern life, human beings are whirled beyond the circuit of the constellations: their intimate plight is seen in connection or relation with the anguish of the Apostles after Calvary, the murder of Agamemnon, the insanity of Ophelia and children who chant that London bridge is falling down. In the same way, the plight of Prufrock is illuminated by means of a rich, passing reference to Michelangelo, the sculptor of the strong and heroic man. Only when the poet is the heir of all the ages can he make significant use of so many different and distant kinds of experience. But

---

4. A reference to "Gerontion."

conversely, only when experience becomes international, only when many different and distant kinds of experience are encountered by the poet, does he find it necessary to become the heir of all the ages.

Difficulty in love is inseparable from the deracination and the alienation from which the international man suffers. When the traditional beliefs, sanctions and bonds of the community and of the family decay or disappear in the distance like a receding harbor, then love ceases to be an act which is in relation to the life of the community, and in immediate relation to the family and other human beings. Love becomes purely personal. It is isolated from the past and the future, and since it is isolated from all other relationships, since it is no longer celebrated, evaluated and given a status by the community, love does become merely copulation. The protagonist of "Gerontion" uses one of the most significant phrases in Eliot's work when he speaks of himself as living in a *rented* house; which is to say, not in the house where his forbears lived. He lives in a rented house, he is unable to make love, and he knows that history has many cunning, deceptive, and empty corridors. The nature of the house, of love and of history are interdependent aspects of modern life.

＊   ＊   ＊

To be international is to be a citizen of the world and thus a citizen of no particular city. The world as such is not a community and it has no constitution or government: it is the turning world in which the human being, surrounded by the consequences of all times and all places, must live his life as a human being and not as the citizen of any nation. Hence, to be the heir of all the ages is to inherit nothing but a consciousness of how all heirlooms are rooted in the past. Dominated by the historical consciousness, the international hero finds that all beliefs affect the holding of any belief (he cannot think of Christianity without remembering Adonis); he finds that many languages affect each use of speech (*The Waste Land* concludes with a passage in four languages).

＊   ＊   ＊

Modern life may be compared to a foreign country in which a foreign language is spoken. Eliot is the international hero because he has made the journey to the foreign country and described the nature of the new life in the foreign country. Since the future is bound to be international, if it is anything at all, we are all the bankrupt heirs of the ages, and the moments of the crisis expressed in Eliot's work are a prophecy of the crises of our own future in regard to love, religious belief, good and evil, the good life and the nature of the just society. *The Waste Land* will soon be as good as new.

Reconsiderations and New Readings

DENIS DONOGHUE

The Word within a Word†

The publication of the first drafts of *The Waste Land*[1] has not greatly eased the difficulty of reading the poem. We now know that the poem issued, however circuitously, from the unhappiness of Eliot's first marriage—though certain lines and passages in the first drafts were written before 1915—but we hardly know what to make of that fact, unless it prompts us to say that the dominant feeling in the poem is not universal despair but particular guilt, and that the specific movement of feeling through the words corresponds, however obscurely, to the act of penance. Some readers of *The Waste Land* feel that Eliot is saying: 'God, I thank thee that I am not as the rest of men, extortioners, unjust, adulterers, or even as this small house-agent's clerk.' But this sense of the poem is unworthy, false to its spirit as a whole, though there are a few passages which support it. The area of feeling which the poem inhabits is the general provenance of guilt, fear, dread; the presence of disgust, including self-disgust, is not surprising. The first drafts show, and this is more to the point, that the poet's original sense of his poem made it, even more than the final version, a medley. Pound's criticism tightened the poem, but did not otherwise alter its movement. One characteristic of the poetry remains. Eliot's poems often try to escape from the emotional condition which incited them, not by willing its opposite but by working through a wide range of alternative conditions. The poems find safety and relief in numbers. One mood is answered not by another, equal and opposite, but by a diversity of moods. It is the diversity that saves. The medley of poems which eventually became *The Waste Land* was designed, it appears, with this diversity in view.

† From *"The Waste Land" in Different Voices*, ed. A. D. Moody (London: Edward Arnold, 1974), pp. 185–201. Copyright © 1974 by A. D. Moody. Reprinted by permission of the publisher. The author's notes have been edited.
1. In *The Waste Land: A Facsimile of the Original Drafts Including the Annotations of Ezra Pound*, ed. Valerie Eliot (New York: Harcourt Brace Jovanovich, 1971).

To the charge that Eliot's poem is the work of a Pharisee, therefore, I would not reply that on the contrary it is the work of a publican, but rather that it effects a movement of feeling to make penance possible. Diversity, number and allusion are the auspices under which the poem moves.

I want to suggest now that this sense of the poem is related to our recognition of its character as a distinctively American work. Specifically, the poem is, in Hawthorne's terminology, a romance. In the Preface to *The House of the Seven Gables*, Hawthorne distinguished between romance and novel. The novel aims at minute fidelity to the probable, but the romance, claiming 'a certain latitude', proposes to present 'the truth of the human heart' under circumstances 'to a great extent of the writer's own choosing or creation.'[2] There has always been an implication, in later comments on the romance, that it is the form of fiction most congenial to those feelings for which social correlatives are not available; or, if available, seriously inadequate. It is a commonplace that the romance, in Hawthorne's sense, holds a special position in American literature and that it is particularly serviceable to the writer who feels his imagination driven back upon its own resources. One of the tenable generalizations we continue to make about English literature is that its position is not desperate in this regard. The English writer generally thinks himself ready to establish his feeling in a particular setting and to let it develop and take its chance there. He declares a certain confidence in representing the life of feeling in terms of man, Nature, and society. Nearly everything is allowed to depend upon the relation of man to the society in which he lives, the relation of person to person and to place. We say that English literature is personal, meaning that it is social, historical, and political. We do not say this of American literature. The question of locality is important to American writers, not least to Hawthorne in *The House of the Seven Gables*, but in American literature generally, and especially in the literature of the nineteenth-century a shadow falls between person and place. The feelings in the case are rarely entrusted to that relation, or indeed to any other: there is an impression that such feelings cannot hope to be fulfilled in such relations. There is a remainder of feeling which cries for release in dream, nightmare and fantasy. I want to pursue the notion that *The Waste Land* is best understood as an American romance.

It may be useful to recall Eliot's sense of American literature. He rejected the assertion that there is an American language distinct from English: in his view, both languages use the same notes, even if the fingering is sometimes different. He was not of Mencken's party in that argument. As for the literature, he registered New England as a moral

2. Nathaniel Hawthorne, *The House of the Seven Gables* (Centenary edition, Ohio State University Press, 1965), vol. II, 1.

presence, a regiment in the army of unalterable law, but he was not intimidated by it. He reflected upon the complex fate of being an American when he read Hawthorne and, still more, Henry James, who embodied one of the great possibilities consistent with that fate. In an essay on James he wrote that 'it is the final perfection, the consummation of an American to become, not an Englishman, but a European—something which no born European, no person of any European nationality, can become.'[3] Of the relation between Eliot and Whitman it is enough to say that Whitman is audible, for some good but more ill, in the third section of 'The Dry Salvages', providing Eliot with a somewhat insecure tone. Of Mark Twain Eliot is on record as saying in praise that he was one of those writers who discover 'a new way of writing, valid not only for themselves but for others',[4] but I cannot recall any occasion on which Eliot moved in Twain's direction, despite 'the river with its cargo of dead negroes' in 'The Dry Salvages'. The question of his relation to Poe is far more interesting, because it is strange that he should have had any interest in such a writer. In fact, he did not admire Poe's poems, he thought them adolescent things; Poe had never grown up. But there were two aspects of the matter which he could not ignore. The first concerned Poe's style of incantation which, Eliot said, 'because of its very crudity, stirs the feelings at a deep and almost primitive level'.[5] Eliot had his own style of incantation, and he was greatly taken by Poe as a master in the singing style. The second consideration was that Poe's work, fruitless in the English and American traditions, had entered the sensibilities of the great French poets and especially of Baudelaire, Mallarmé and Valéry. Eliot was interested in this event, and he pondered it. There is almost a suggestion that Poe had somehow achieved the final perfection of an American by becoming a European, reincarnated in Baudelaire, Mallarmé and Valéry. Eliot was strongly engaged by Poe, as by Swinburne, for a similar reason, the call of one verbalist to another.

The great interest of American literature arises, it is commonly agreed, from the sense of American feeling as making a new start, every day, with little or nothing regarded as capital saved from yesterday. The world is all before the American writers. So these writers naturally think of making everything new, they do not feel overwhelmed by the weight of previous achievement. American writers burn their bridges behind them, relegating the previous, as James said of his compatriots generally in *The American Scene*, to the category of wan misery. If *The Waste Land* is written by an American who has set out to make himself a European, its chief labour toward that perfection is the assumption of

3. 'Henry James', reprinted in *The Shock of Recognition*, ed. Edmund Wilson (New York, 1955), vol. II, 855.
4. 'American Literature and the American Language', reprinted in *To Criticize the Critic*.
5. 'From Poe to Valéry', reprinted in *To Criticize the Critic*.

the burden of history. The allusions in Eliot's poem show not the extent of his learning but the gravity of the whole enterprise, the range of those responsibilities he is ready to accept in such a cause. What most of the allusions say is: 'there have been other times, not utterly lost or forgotten; we ourselves were not born this morning.'

We may press the argument a little further. If English literature is devoted to the relation between person, place, and time, it acts by a corresponding syntax of prescribed relations. The first result is that the chief function of one word is to lead the mind to the next. No detail in *Middlemarch* is as important as the entire network of relations, word by word, sentence by sentence: the reader's mind is not encouraged to sink into the recesses of a word, but to move forward until the pre-scribed affiliations are complete. The modesty with which a word sends the reader's mind running to the next is the verbal equivalent of de-pendency in a given society, as one person accepts his enabling relation to another. But the modern revolution in such American poems as *The Waste Land* and *Hugh Selwyn Mauberley* depends upon a different sense of life and therefore upon a different syntax. One's first reading of these poems leaves an impression of their poetic quality as residing in their diction: the animation of the verse arises from the incalculable force of certain individual words or phrases which stay in the mind without necessarily attracting to their orbit the words before or after. The memorable quality of those phrases seems to require a clear space on all sides, and it has little need of before and after. I take this to mean that the relations to which the words of an American poem refer are not prescribed or predictive but experimental. Around each word there is a space or a void in which nothing is anticipated, nothing enforced. Every relation must be invented, as if the world had just begun. Harold Rosenberg has argued that this is the chief characteristic of modern French poetry, though he offers a different explanation. 'Lift-ing up a word and putting a space around it has been the conscious enterprise of serious French poetry since Baudelaire and Rimbaud'; and a little later he speaks of 'the space around words necessary for con-sciousness'.[6] In Eliot's early poems an American is trying to make him-self a Frenchman, perfecting himself in the creation of Jules Laforgue; an enterprise capable of producing, in the longer run, the magisterial achievement of making himself a European. The space around the words is necessary for consciousness, and it puts at risk the continuity of relations, as between one person and another. In Eliot, consciousness is the most available form of virtue, to be conscious is to be holy: an equation which causes great difficulty in the later plays, and especially in *The Cocktail Party*. But the words thus surrounded by empty space receive a corresponding halo of significance, they compel the imagi-

6. Harold Rosenberg, *The Tradition of the New* (London, 1970 reprint), 86, 89.

nation not by their relation but by their isolation. Such words take unto themselves a force of radiance, an exceptional power which Eliot in the later plays ascribes to saints and martyrs. Martyrdom is Eliot's favourite version of the Sublime.

There is a passage in *Writing Degree Zero* where Roland Barthes offers virtually the same distinction between what he calls classical language and modern language. In classical language the meaning is continuous, linear, it is always deferred until the end. So the mind, like the eye, runs along beside the words, and the movement is gratifying. But in modern poetry it is the word 'which gratifies and fulfills like the sudden revelation of a truth'. The word has lost its prescribed relations, but for that very reason it has acquired a magical power, it has become complete in itself, a revelation in its own recesses. Giving up its old dependency, the word acquires Sibylline presence; it stands there like Rilke's archaic torso of Apollo.[7] It is a mark of such words that we cannot read them, but they read us, they affront us by presenting their significance in relation to themselves. Barthes says of such words that they 'initiate a discourse full of gaps and full of lights, filled with absences and over-nourishing signs, without foresight or stability of intention, and thereby so opposed to the social function of language that merely to have recourse to a discontinuous speech is to open the door to all that stands above Nature'. Classical language 'establishes a universe in which men are not alone, where words never have the terrible weight of things, where speech is always a meeting with the others'. Modern language presupposes a discontinuous Nature, 'a fragmented space, made of objects solitary and terrible because the links between them are only potential'. I would say that the links between them must be invented and are then fictive rather than prescribed or agreed: they have the freedom of fiction and, paying the price, the loneliness of being arbitrary. Such words, since they cannot be continuous with Nature, must be above or below it, two conditions about equally lonely. They are exceptions deprived of a rule. These words become names because of their oracular power, but what they name cannot be defined; they are like Stetson in *The Waste Land*, whose chief character is that he does not answer, though he instigates, the questions addressed to him. Stetson is the name for the interrogation, but he is under no obligation to reply. *The Waste Land* is the name of another interrogation, and its words are less answers than hints and guesses. Barthes says of these modern words generally—'words adorned with all the violence of their irruption, the vibration of which, though wholly mechanical, strangely affects the next word, only to die out immediately'—that they

---

7. "Archaic Torso of Apollo," in Rainer Maria Rilke's *Sonnets to Orpheus*, all of which were written in a few months in 1922 [*Editor*].

'exclude men: there is no humanism of modern poetry'.[8] Stetson is not related to his interrogator or to London or even to Mylae, he is an oracle who stirs a nervous quiver of interrogation, and dies out in a line from Baudelaire.

Classical language, then, is a system organized on the assumption that Nature is continuous; hence the primacy of syntax. Classical poems stand in apposition to a seamless web of relations which we agree to call Nature: when the web is domestic we call it Society. The poems testify to those webs by enacting them in miniature. The long poem is valued as an extended ritual, offered to Nature in the grandest terms, a celebration of prescribed relations. The reader may still be surprised, because he does not know at any moment which of the indefinitely large number of relations the writer will enact, but he knows that one of them will be invoked. Each word is faithful to the others. But in modern poems, according to this distinction, the words are independent and therefore lonely. In *The Waste Land* we respond most deeply to the individual words and phrases with a sense of their exposure. The words are not obscure, because we know what the dictionary says of them and, mostly, we know where they come from. But they are Sibylline because of the darkness between them: they challenge us to provide them with a continuous syntax and they mock our efforts to do so; that was not what they meant at all. The whole poem looks like the sub-plot of a lost play; what is lost is the main plot, Nature as a significant action. The attempt to specify the form of *The Waste Land* is doomed because the form is not specific, it is not—to use Blackmur's word—predictive. The poem cries for its form: what it shows forth in itself is not form but the desperate analogy of form, tokens of a virtual form which would be valid if there were such a thing. What holds the several parts of the poem together is the need, which is at once the poet's need and our own, to keep life going, including the life of the poem in the dark spaces between the words. The problem is not that the poem lacks form but that it has a passion for form, largely unfulfilled, and—to make things harder—the memory of lost forms. Those lost forms would not answer the present need, even if they could be recovered: this is what Blackmur meant by saying of Eliot's early poems and *The Waste Land* that 'they measure the present by living standards which most people relegate to the past'.[9] What is present and vivid to us in the poem is the cry for form, the loud lament of that disconsolate chimera, and the cry is so pure that it almost makes up for what is merely lost. If the poem proliferates in little forms, it is because these

---

8. Roland Barthes, *Writing Degree Zero*, translated by Annette Lavers and Colin Smith (London, 1967), 54–5.

9. R. P. Blackmur, *Form and Value in Modern Poetry* (New York, 1957), 143.

are variations on an absent theme, a theme of which only the variations are known. The variations are recited from many different sources, and with increasing urgency toward the end of the poem, the sources being older versions of form, present now as broken images. In their bearing upon the reader, these images tell upon his conscience, forcing him to live up to the exactitude of the poem and to reject false consolations. If the poem is to be read as prologomena to penance, it is also, in its bearing upon the reader, an incitement to scruple.

So Blackmur on another occasion spoke of Eliot's task as a poet: 'he has in his images to remind reason of its material, to remind order of its disorder, in order to create a sane art almost insane in its predicament.' He has 'to make a confrontation of the rational with the irrational: a deliberate reversal of roles.'[1] But in fact Eliot had to make a double confrontation, the violence going both ways. He had to confront the rational with the irrational, with what is below Nature, and the images used for this violence are mostly those he associated with Conrad's hollow men and *Heart of Darkness*. In the passage which Eliot wanted to use as the epigraph to *The Waste Land* before he came upon Petronius' Sibyl, Conrad's Marlow says of Kurtz:

> Did he live his life again in every detail of desire, temptation, and surrender during that supreme moment of complete knowledge? He cried in a whisper at some image, at some vision,—he cried out twice, a cry that was no more than a breath—'The horror! the horror!'

The confrontation of the rational with the irrational is propelled by the assumption that complete knowledge is possible and its horror inescapable. So I have always believed that the reader of *The Waste Land* ought to take Tiresias seriously as the name of such a possibility, and such a horror. But the other confrontation is equally valid: the irrational is confronted with the rational in all those ways for which, in the poem, the rational imagination is represented by Shakespeare, Spenser, St Augustine, and, in the first version, by a passage from Plato's *Republic* which Pound deleted: 'Not here, O Ademantus, but in another world.' The line comes from a famous passage in Book IX where Glaucon says that the city which has been described is merely verbal, it does not exist anywhere on earth; and Socrates answers, 'Well, perhaps there is a pattern of it laid up in heaven for him who wishes to contemplate it and so beholding to constitute himself its citizen.'[2] The contemplation of the City of God is also complete knowledge, above Nature, its sublimity compelling to the citizen, and its finality is asserted in the repeated Sanscrit word with which the poem ends. A Tiresias would see

---

1. R. P. Blackmur, *Anni Mirabiles 1921–1925* (Washington, Library of Congress, 1956), 31.
2. *The Republic*, book IX, 592-A-B, quoted from the Loeb edition in *Facsimile*, 128.

the City of God as clearly as the Unreal City, its malign counterpart.
So the poem moves between *Heart of Darkness* and 'heart of light'.
Words stand between reason and madness, touched by both adversaries.

We need an authoritative example; from Section III of *The Waste
Land*, 'The Fire Sermon':

> But at my back in a cold blast I hear
> The rattle of the bones, and chuckle spread from ear to ear.
>
> A rat crept softly through the vegetation
> Dragging its slimy belly on the bank
> While I was fishing in the dull canal
> On a winter evening round behind the gashouse
> Musing upon the king my brother's wreck
> And on the king my father's death before him.
> White bodies naked on the low damp ground
> And bones cast in a little low dry garret,
> Rattled by the rat's foot only, year to year.
> But at my back from time to time I hear
> The sound of horns and motors, which shall bring
> Sweeney to Mrs. Porter in the spring.
> O the moon shone bright on Mrs. Porter
> And on her daughter
> They wash their feet in soda water
> *Et O ces voix d'enfants, chantant dans la coupole!*

It is useless to ask of that passage such questions as the following: who
is speaking? what is the point of his narrative? whose white bodies lay
naked on the ground? Such questions assume that there is a world-
without-words to which Eliot's words pay tribute; as, in common usage,
the word 'box' acknowledges the existence of a certain object which
does not depend upon a word for its existence. A reader determined to
give some kind of answer might say, to the first question: Tiresias; but
he somehow includes the Buddha, Ferdinand Prince of Naples, Ovid
and Verlaine. And to the second he might say: Well, the narrative is
merely ostensible, we are not meant to think of it as a story, the words
in that order make a kind of landscape in the reader's mind, Marshall
McLuhan calls it psychological landscape, which is at once subject and
object; it has to do with Eliot's theory of the objective correlative or
Santayana's theory of the correlative object. And the answerer might
say to the third question: The king my brother and the king my father,
I suppose, but again the point is verbal and atmospheric rather than
denotative. Questions more in accord with the nature of the passage
would include the following: what is going on, when 'rat's foot' is preceded by the punning rhyme, 'rattled'? What is going on when the
speaker, whoever he is, quotes several fragments from Ovid, Verlaine,
the Grail Legend, Australian popular song, Marvell, *The Tempest*, John

Day, and Middleton? Why does the passage suddenly change its tone at that first insistent rhyme, 'year' with 'hear'? Why are we given 'wreck' instead of 'wrack' in the quotation from *The Tempest*? These questions are not likely to set anyone's heart astir, but they are more in accord with Eliot's poem because they do not call another world in judgement upon the words. The questions keep strictly to language, and in this respect they follow the rhetoric of the poem. Symbolist poetry yearns for a world governed by the laws of Pure Poetry; internal laws, marking purely internal liaisons between one word and another, without any reference to Nature as a court of appeal. In such a world, time would take the form of prosody. In the passage from 'The Fire Sermon' no effect is allowed to escape from the words, to leave the medium of language. The images and figures do not leave the poem, they refuse to leave a setting which is assertively verbal. It is permissible to say that the speaker here and throughout the poem is Tiresias; but that is like saying that something is the speech of God, it merely replaces one problem by another. The words of the Sermon are not completed by our conceiving for their speaker a personal identity. It is more useful to imagine a possible state of feeling which is secreted in the words. The best way to read the lines is not to ask that each phrase give up its meaning, as if that meaning were then to replace the words; but to ask what quality, in each sequence, the phrases share. That quality may be found to attach itself to a state of feeling which cannot be given in other terms. Not a seamless narrative, but a set of lyric moments, each isolated for consciousness.

It is customary to say that the explanation for this use of language is to be found in the works of F. H. Bradley and in Eliot's thesis, *Knowledge and Experience in the Philosophy of F. H. Bradley*. I quote a few sentences in which Eliot summarizes Bradley's argument: kinship between Eliot's prose and Bradley's has been noted. 'It is only in immediate experience that knowledge and its object are one.' 'We have no right, except in the most provisional way, to speak of *my* experience, since the I is a construction out of experience, an abstraction from it; and the *thats*, the browns and hards and flats, are equally ideal constructions from experience, as ideal as atoms.' 'The only independent reality is immediate experience or feeling.' ' "My" feeling is certainly in a sense mine. But this is because and in so far as I am the feeling.' 'Experience is non-relational.'[3] These sentences refer to Bradley's general philosophical position but more especially to certain passages in his *Essays on Truth and Reality*, including this one:

> Now consciousness, to my mind, is not original. What comes first in each of us is rather feeling, a state as yet without either an

3. *Knowledge and Experience in the Philosophy of F. H. Bradley* (London, 1964), 19, 30, 31, 27.

object or subject. . . . Feeling is immediate experience without
distinction or relation in itself. It is a unity, complex but without
relations. And there is here no difference between the state and its
content, since, in a word, the experienced and the experience are
one.[4]

In Eliot's version, 'feeling is more than either object or subject, since
in a way it includes both'. Furthermore,

In describing immediate experience we must use terms which offer
a surreptitious suggestion of subject or object. If we say presentation, we think of a subject to which the presentation is present as
an object. And if we say feeling, we think of it as the feeling of a
subject about an object. . . . It may accordingly be said that the
real situation is an experience which can never be wholly defined
as an object nor wholly enjoyed as a feeling, but in which any of
the observed constituents may take on the one or the other aspect.[5]

Perhaps this is enough to suggest what Eliot means when he speaks of
'the continuous transition by which feeling becomes object and object
becomes feeling'. The language of 'The Fire Sermon' is surreptitious
in the sense that its objectivity is merely ostensible. The rat creeping
through the vegetation has only as much to do with animal life as is
required to incite a certain feeling in the speaker. The rat has crept
into the words and lost itself there; what transpires in the words is a
certain feeling, in this case more subject than object. The meaning of
a phrase, a line, a word, in 'The Fire Sermon' is every impression that
attaches itself to those sounds under the pressure of consciousness; an
assertion which reminds us that the famous Chapter XIV of Bradley's
Essays on Truth and Reality is called 'What is the real Julius Caesar?'
The real *Waste Land* is a sequence of those impressions, incited by the
sequence of words: the impressions are different for each reader.

   There is nothing unorthodox in this, from the standpoint of a philosophical idealist. It would be possible to quote Susanne Langer or
Cassirer just as relevantly as Bradley. It is also orthodox Symbolism, of
the kind which Valéry treats in 'Analecta, Tel Quel II', where he says
that 'the self flees all created things, it withdraws from negation to
negation: one might give the name "Universe" to everything in which
the self refuses to recognize itself'.[6] The self refuses to recognize itself
in any part of the objective world, so called, until the world is transformed into subjective terms, every apprehended object become subject. But the self is always willing to recognize itself in language and

4. F. H. Bradley, *Essays on Truth and Reality* (Oxford, 1914), 194.
5. *Knowledge and Experience*, 22, 25.
6. For Stuart Gilbert's slightly different translation of this passage from *Analecta*, a group of
   personal jottings originally published in 1926, see Paul Valéry, *Analects* (Princeton: Princeton
   University Press, 1970), p. 280 [*Editor*].

symbols. Thinking of Eliot's poem, one might give the name 'language' to that alone in which the self recognizes itself. As for Eliot himself, recognition may be willing or desperate: willing if we emphasize the luxury of the words, the gypsy phrases and cadences, the impression that a man who passes his entire life among such words is the happiest of men; desperate, if we emphasize the allusions, and Eliot's need of them, the accepted weight of responsibility, those fragments shored against his ruin. The allusions are Eliot's insignia, and they have this further point; they give his sensibility other ground than itself, ground in history, literature, religion, revelation, through the words, the ground of our beseeching.

For while the self flees every created thing and refuses to recognize itself anywhere but in words, it needs something besides itself. Perhaps language is enough, but we must leave that question open. In a chapter on solipsism Eliot writes:

> The point of view (or finite centre) has for its object one consistent world, and accordingly no finite centre can be self-sufficient, for the life of a soul does not consist in the contemplation of one consistent world but in the painful task of unifying (to a greater or less extent) jarring and incompatible ones, and passing, when possible, from two or more discordant viewpoints to a higher which shall somehow include and transmute them[7]

In *The Waste Land* Eliot calls this higher perspective Tiresias: 'we are led to the conception of an all-inclusive experience outside of which nothing shall fall', he says in the thesis on Bradley.

A year after the publication of *The Waste Land* Eliot reviewed Joyce's *Ulysses*, and proposed there a distinction which depends upon the idea of greater and lesser perspectives. In this distinction between two methods of fiction, 'narrative method' is based upon the commonly accepted separation of subject and object. The personal equivalent is the notion of a literary character, cut out from his surroundings and endowed with certain qualities. The medium is words, but most of them are common and they are placed in accepted arrangements. Books based upon these arrangements are called novels, so the novel as a form of art came to an end, according to Eliot in 1923, with Flaubert and James. (He later repudiated this obituary, by the way.) The 'mythical method' of fiction, on the other hand, is based upon immediate experience, the primacy of feeling, the idea of subject and object melting into each other beyond positivist redemption, and at last transcended in a quasi-divine perspective, Tiresias in *The Waste Land*, the Homeric archetype in *Ulysses*. But we should not identify Tiresias with the ultimate form of consciousness. It is necessary to think of language (Valéry's 'Saint Langage'

7. *Knowledge and Experience*, 147–8.

in 'La Pythie') as issuing from a perspective grander even than Tiresias', since Tiresias can only see the world as one alienated from it: he does not give or sympathize, he does not participate in the suffering and transformation of 'What the Thunder Said'. It is necessary for the poem, and for poetry, to go beyond the phase of consciousness which Eliot calls Tiresias. The 'going beyond' has no name, it is the action of the poem itself. Instead of common words in common places there is language itself, construed now as a great treasury of images and figures and, increasingly in Eliot, identified with the Word of God. Using language in this way, it seems natural to have Ferdinand Prince of Naples, the Phoenician sailor, the one-eyed seller of currants, and all the women in the world becoming Tiresias. For Eliot, as for Bradley, there is no question of a Wordsworthian liaison between man and Nature. The only part of Bradley's *Appearance and Reality* which Eliot chose to quote in his notes to *The Waste Land* disengages itself from any such hope. In Ch. XXIII Bradley says that 'we behave as if our internal worlds were the same'. But we err:

> Our inner worlds, I may be told, are divided from each other, but the outer world of experience is common to all; and it is by standing on this basis that we are able to communicate. Such a statement would be incorrect. My external sensations are no less private to myself than are my thoughts or my feelings. In either case my experience falls within my own circle, a circle closed on the outside; and, with all its elements alike, every sphere is opaque to the others which surround it. . . . In brief, regarded as an existence which appears in a soul, the whole world for each is peculiar and private to that soul.[8]

Perhaps our first impression here is wonder that such a view of the mind's predicament could ever have secreted, in Bradley's pupil, a major poem. But the second impression is better, that for such a poet language is the only possible home: either language or that metalanguage we call silence. But we are in danger of confounding the pupil with his master. Just as Bradley cleared himself of a charge of solipsism by arguing, in *Appearance and Reality*, that 'we can go to foreign selves by a process no worse than the construction which establishes our own self', so Eliot cleared himself of a charge of philosophy by becoming a poet; that is, by attending to all the affiliations of words, including their old hankering after objects. Against the persuasion of his idealism, there are the deep persuasions of Dante, Shakespeare, Virgil; and there is eventually the persuasion of Christian belief in which time is redeemed and the higher dream is made flesh. Perhaps these are the necessary qualifications to make while returning to the poem. Without them, we

8. F. H. Bradley, *Appearance and Reality* (London, 1902), 346. [The passage quoted below is from p. 258. — *Editor*]

are in danger of turning the poem into a set of more or less interesting ideas; forgetting that to Eliot, as to Bradley, 'a mere idea is but a ruinous abstraction'; forgetting, too, that it was Eliot who praised Henry James for possessing a mind so fine that no idea could violate it. With the passage from 'The Fire Sermon' in front of us again, we see that what came first was not an idea but feeling, 'a state as yet without either an object or subject'. The nearest expressive equivalent is rhythm, at this stage not yet resolved in words. In 'The Music of Poetry' Eliot reported that in his own experience 'a poem, or a passage from a poem, may tend to realize itself first as a particular rhythm before it reaches expression in words, and that this rhythm may bring to birth the idea and the image'.[9] An account of our passage would be a blunt affair if it did not point to the changes of rhythm as among the chief moments; where the echo of Marvell's 'To His Coy Mistress' imposes a new and deeper tone upon the verse; and from there until the line from Verlaine the transitions become more abrupt. Eliot remains true to the original feeling by remaining true to its rhythm. The words, when they are found, maintain a double allegiance: they are required to define the rhythm of the first feeling, and they must also allow for the melting of one experience into another.

The first consequence is that, to a reader sceptical of idealist assumptions, many of these lines appear wilfully arch and secretive: they appear to go through the motions of grammar and syntax without committing themselves to these agencies. They are neither one thing nor the other, neither wholly subject nor wholly object: without proposing themselves as paradoxes, they are paradoxical. A further result is that, in verse of this kind, incidents drawn from whatever source cannot have the status which they would have in a novel or in another poem. In the *Metamorphoses* Ovid tells the story of the rape of Philomela by King Tereus of Thrace. Eliot recalls the story in 'A Game of Chess'. Trico's song in Lyly's *Alexander and Campaspe* has the lines:

> Oh, 'tis the ravished nightingale.
> *Jug, jug, jug, jug, tereu!* she cries.

Matthew Arnold's 'Philomela' is one story, John Crowe Ransom's is another, the story is diversely told. How it appears in the mind of God, there is no knowing; what is the real Philomela is a hard question. How it appears in the inordinate mind of Tiresias is given in *The Waste Land*:

> Twit twit twit
> Jug jug jug jug jug jug
> So rudely forc'd.
> Tereu

9. *On Poetry and Poets*, 38.

—being the twit of the swallow, the Elizabethan nightingale-call and, by curious association, the word for 'slut', a fine phrase of justice from Middleton's A *Game at Chess*, and lastly the simple vocative, 'Tereu'. Ovid's story is given, indeed, but only the gist of it, the story insofar as it survives transposition in the inclusive consciousness of Tiresias. In that strange place, one image melts into another; hence Eliot's idiom of melting, transition, becoming, deliquescence, and so forth.

To resume a long story: it is easy to think of Eliot as he thought of Swinburne: 'only a man of genius could dwell so exclusively and consistently among words.'[1] In Swinburne, as in Poe, words alone are certain good. But it is well to qualify that report by adding another, from 'The Music of Poetry', where Eliot speaks of the poet as occupied with 'frontiers of consciousness beyond which words fail, though meanings still exist'. In the plays this exorbitant work is done by miracle, 'the way of illumination'. Tiresias is the Unidentified Guest, until he too is transcended in Celia.[2] The effort of the plays is to allow people to live by a holy language. Language, the ancient place of wisdom, is guaranteed by conscience and consciousness, as in *Four Quartets*. That is why, at last, 'the poetry does not matter'. The procedures of *The Waste Land*, which were sustained by the force of language itself, are transposed into the idiom of characters acting and suffering: transitions and perspectives, verbal in *The Waste Land*, take more specific forms in the later poems and plays, the forms of personal action, chances and choices. The frontier of consciousness is not the place where words fail but where self dies, in the awful surrender of faith. Bradley is not repudiated, but he is forced to accommodate himself to the Shakespeare of A *Winter's Tale* and *The Tempest*: that is one way of putting it.

I have been arguing that it is characteristic of Eliot's language in *The Waste Land* to effect an 'absence in reality', and to move words into the resultant vacuum. At first, the words seem to denote things, *sensibilia* beyond the lexicon, but it soon appears that their allegiance to reality is deceptive, they are traitors in reality. So far as the relation between word and thing is deceptive, so far also is 'objective' reality undermined. The only certainty is that the absence in reality has been effected by the words, and now the same words are enforcing themselves as the only presences. What we respond to is the presence of the words. In this way the words acquire the kind of aura, or the kind of reverberation, which we feel in proverbs; with this difference, that proverbs appeal to our sense of life, an inherited wisdom in our sense of things; Eliot's words appeal to primordial images and rhythms which can be felt, though they cannot well be called in evidence. I cannot

---

1. From "Swinburne as Poet," originally included in *The Sacred Wood* (1920). "The Music of Poetry" (1942) is included in *On Poetry and Poets* [*Editor*].
2. A reference to Eliot's play *The Cocktail Party* (1949) [*Editor*].

explain this use of language except by suggesting that if the common arrangements of words issue from the common sense of time, Eliot's arrangements issue from the quarrel between time and myth: I assume that myth is a way of breaking the chain of time, the chain of one thing after another. Eliot is using words as if their first obligation were neither to things nor to time. Philip Wheelwright has called this kind of imagination 'archetypal', the imagination 'which sees the particular object in the light of a larger conception or of a higher concern'. Nearly everything in Eliot's language can be explained by his feeling that the truth of things resides in an indeterminate area: neither subject nor object, but a state compounded of both; neither time nor eternity, but a state in which the double obligation is registered; neither man nor God, but a being, conceivable in words but not in fact, who is vouched for not in identifiable speech but in language itself, eventually to be invoked as Logos. I am not indeed maintaining that the word 'rat', in 'The Fire Sermon', has ceased to observe all relation to a certain rodent, but rather that the word is a double agent, it accepts the friction between reality and language, but it does not give total allegiance to either party. On one side stands the world of things; on the other, a rival world of dissociated forms, Platonic cities. Between these worlds stands the individual word, maintaining a secret life, double allegiance or double treachery.

It is characteristically American of Eliot to place these inordinate burdens upon language and the poetic imagination. The imagination must do nearly everything because reality cannot be relied on to do much. In the relation between reality and the imagination, he has established conditions extremely favourable to the imagination. This is only another way of saying that language commands the otherwise empty space between consciousness and experience, consciousness and action, consciousness and the earth.

ROBERT LANGBAUM

The Walking Dead†

* * *

In *The Waste Land*, the buried life manifests itself through the unconscious memory of figures from the past. There is already some reaching toward this method in "Prufrock," where Prufrock *consciously* thinks he might have been John the Baptist, Lazarus, Hamlet. But the

† From *The Mysteries of Identity: A Theme in Modern Literature* (New York: Oxford University Press, 1977), pp. 91–97. Copyright © 1977 by Robert Langbaum. Reprinted by permission of Oxford University Press.

emphasis is on the ironical disparity between these legendary figures and Prufrock's actual character or lack of character. Prufrock does not in fact fulfill the destinies of these legendary figures. In *The Waste Land*, however, the speakers do in spite of themselves unconsciously fulfill destinies laid out in myth; and their unconscious identification with the legendary figures who have already walked through these destinies gives them the only identity they have.

Compared to the characters in *The Waste Land*, Prufrock, for all his lack of vitality, has the sharp external delineation of a character in, say, Henry James. He has a name (a characterizing one), a social milieu to which he genuinely belongs, a face (we all have our idea of what he looks like, probably like Eliot). Prufrock has—his deliberate trying on of masks is a sign of this—a clear idea of himself. The characters in *The Waste Land*, however, are nameless, faceless, isolated, and have no clear idea of themselves. All they have is a sense of loss and a neural itch, a restless, inchoate desire to recover what has been lost. But in this very minimum of restless aliveness, they repeat the pattern of the Quest. And it is the archetypal Quest pattern, exemplified in the Grail legend, that gives whatever form there is to the protagonist's movement through the poem.

We would not know what to make of the characters were it not for the intrusion of a narrating consciousness that assimilates them to figures of the past. This is done through the double language of the Stetson passage. The same purpose is accomplished in Part II through shifting references. Part II opens with an opulently old-fashioned blank-verse-style description, not so much of a lady as of her luxurious surroundings. The chair she sits in reminds us of Cleopatra's "burnished throne" and the stately room of Dido's palace, while a picture recalls the rape of Philomela. The shifting references—showing how Eliot mythologizes his unhappy marriage—suggest that the lady is seductive, but that she is also, like Cleopatra with Anthony and Dido with Aeneas, one of those who is in the end violated and abandoned by a man. The theme of violation takes over; for the picture shows Philomela's change, after her rape, into a nightingale whose wordless cry rings down through the ages:

> So rudely forced; yet here the nightingale
> Filled all the desert with inviolable voice
> And still she cried, and still the world pursues,
> "Jug Jug" to dirty ears.   (100–103)

The nightingale's *voice*, the story's meaning, is inviolable; but the violation of innocence in the waste land goes on.

When the lady finally speaks, she utters twentieth-century words that her prototypes of the past would not have understood: " 'My nerves are bad to-night. Yes, bad. Stay with me.' " We gather from the passage that the lady is rich, that her house is filled with mementoes of the past which she understands only as frightening ghosts, that the protagonist to whom she speaks is her lover or husband, and that he has in some special modern sense violated her. The violation would seem to lie in his inability to communicate with her:

> "Speak to me. Why do you never speak. Speak.
>   What are you thinking of? what thinking? What?
> I never know what you are thinking. Think."
>   (112–14)

The modern situation is unprecedented and meaningless; therein lies the poem's negative impulse. But deep down these people are repeating an ancient drama with ancient meanings; therein lies the poem's positive impulse. The shifting references to various ladies of the past evoke the archetype that subsumes them—the archetype already revealed in Part I, where the protagonist has his fortune told by Madame Sosostris. "Here," she says, pulling a card from the ancient Tarot deck, "is Belladonna, the Lady of the Rocks, / The lady of situations" (49–50). Because all the ladies referred to are Belladonnas, we understand the character of our modern rich lady and the character—in the abrupt shift to a London pub—of the working-class Belladonna who tells a friend of her efforts to steal away the husband of another friend, another Belladonna, who has ruined her health and looks with abortion pills. Beneath the meaningless surface, the underlying tale tells again of violation in the desert—violation of innocence, sex, fertility.

The protagonist's card is "the drowned Phoenician Sailor." This explains not only the Stetson passage, but also the protagonist's reflection after his card has been drawn: "Those are pearls that were his eyes" (48). The line is from Ariel's song in *The Tempest*, addressed to Prince Ferdinand, who thinks his father, the King of Naples, has been drowned. Lines from *The Tempest* keep running through the protagonist's head, because *The Tempest* is a water poem in which all the human characters are sailors, having sailed to the island. Drowning and metamorphosis, the consolation in Ariel's song, relate to drowning and resurrection in the cult of the Phoenician fertility god Adonis (an effigy of the dead Adonis was cast upon the waves, where resurrection was assumed to take place).[1]

Among the other Tarot cards named is "the one-eyed merchant"; he turns up in Part III as the Smyrna merchant who makes the protagonist a homosexual proposition. Eliot in a note explains his method of characterization:

---

1. Eliot knew Colin Still's interpretation of *The Tempest* as a Mystery ritual of initiation (*Shakespeare's Mystery Play*, London: Cecil Palmer, 1921).

Just as the one-eyed merchant, seller of currants, melts into the Phoenician Sailor, and the latter is not wholly distinct from Ferdinand Prince of Naples, so all the women are one woman, and the two sexes meet in Tiresias. What Tiresias *sees*, in fact, is the substance of the poem.

The figures either on the Tarot cards, or in some cases frankly imagined by Eliot to be on them, provide the archetypes from which the nameless, faceless modern characters derive identity. Tiresias, not a Tarot figure but the blind hermaphroditic prophet of Greek mythology, appears only once—in the Part III episode about another violated Belladonna, the typist whose mechanical fornication with a clerk leaves her neither a sense of sin nor a memory of pleasure.

The central consciousness, which intruded through the double language of the Stetson passage and the cultural memory of Part II's introductory passage, now takes on the name of Tiresias: "I Tiresias, old man with wrinkled dugs / Perceived the scene, and foretold the rest." After the scene has been enacted, Tiresias interjects:

> (And I Tiresias have foresuffered all
> Enacted on this same divan or bed;
> I who have sat by Thebes below the wall
> And walked among the lowest of the dead.)
> (228–29, 243–46)

Again we are enabled to understand the contrast between the passionate auspicious fornications of the past and this modern perfunctory performance. Again we are reminded that this scene is nevertheless a *re*-enactment. Sexual union was used in the fertility ceremonies to promote by sympathetic magic the fertility of the soil. But modern sexuality is sterile.

Through the Tiresias consciousness in him, the protagonist repeatedly finds an underlying ancient pattern but also sees that in the modern situation the pattern does not come to the preordained conclusion. This gives a direction to his Quest—to complete the pattern by restoring fertility. It is a sign of their connection that Tiresias appears as a stand-in for the protagonist in just the scene the protagonist can only have imagined.

To say that all the characters meet in Tiresias is to suggest that archetypal identities emerge from larger archetypes, in the way smaller Chinese boxes emerge from larger. The Smyrna merchant, identified with the Tarot one-eyed merchant, propositions the protagonist, who is identified with the Phoenician Sailor. Yet we are told that the one-eyed merchant melts into the Phoenician Sailor; so that the protagonist really stands on both sides of the proposition. In the same way the protagonist is identified with the Quester of the Grail legend, who sets out to find the Grail and thus cure the ailing Fisher King whose wound, symbolizing a loss of potency, has caused the land to lose fertility. The protagonist is the Quester inasmuch as he moves through the episodes of the poem to arrive at the Perilous Chapel. But in the following lines he is the Fisher King, whose illness is in some Grail romances assigned to the King's brother or father:

> While I was fishing in the dull canal
> On a winter evening round behind the gashouse
> Musing upon the king my brother's wreck
> And on the king my father's death before him.
>
> (189–92)

He is also—according to the method of shifting references—Prince Ferdinand (from whom, in *Tempest* I.ii. 390–91, the last two lines derive), Hamlet, Claudius: all of whom have to do with dead kings who in turn recall the murdered kings of vegetation ritual. All this combines with the modern industrial setting to portray the modern moment with modern voices and collapse them into timeless archetypes. At the end of the poem, the protagonist is both Quester and Fisher King; he is the Fisher King questing for a cure: "I sat upon the shore / Fishing, with the arid plain behind me" (V. 423–24).

Since the protagonist plays at one and the same time both active and passive roles, we must understand all the characters as aspects or projections of his consciousness—that the poem is essentially a monodrama. It is difficult to say just where the various characters melt into the protagonist and where the protagonist melts into the poet. We have to distinguish the scenes in which the protagonist himself plays a part —the recollection of the Hyacinth garden, the visit to Madame Sosostris, the meeting with Stetson, the scene with the rich Belladonna— from the scenes in the pub and at the typist's. We can either consider that the protagonist overhears the first and imagines the second, or that at these points the poet's consciousness takes leave of the protagonist to portray parallel instances. I prefer the first line of interpretation because it yields a more consistent structure on the model of romantic monodrama. In *Faust* and *Manfred*, the other characters do not have the same order of existence as the protagonist because the protagonist's consciousness blends with the poet's. We must understand the other characters, therefore, as ambiguously objective, as only partly themselves and partly the projection of forces within the protagonist and ultimately within the poet. If we take the line that Eliot's poem is what the protagonist *sees*, then Tiresias becomes the figure in which the protagonist's consciousness blends perfectly with the poet's so that the protagonist can *see* imaginatively more than he could physically.

(Tiresias' hermaphroditism characterizes the all-inclusive poetic imagination; Pound in one of his annotations to the manuscript calls Eliot Tiresias.)[2]

But the poet's consciousness is itself an aspect of the age's. We get the overheard scraps of conversation, miscellaneous literary tags, and incoherent cultural recollections that would stock a cultivated mind of 1920—an agitated mind in which the fragments recur compulsively. This is where Western culture has come to, the poem is telling us, as of 1920. The protagonist's consciousness emerges from the collective consciousness of the time as another nameless, faceless modern voice. The protagonist has no character in the old-fashioned sense; for he acquires delineation or identity not through individualization, but through making connection with ancient archetypes.

*   *   *

MARIANNE THORMÄHLEN

[The City in *The Waste Land*]†

In *The Waste Land*, as in most of those Eliot poems which are soaked in urban imagery, a small number of fixed topographical features keep cropping up. Not unexpectedly, the most frequent one is the street motif which, Rudolf Germer argues, stands for the ugliness and repulsiveness of reality.[1] Basically, the street looms as the only alternative to the closed room—"I shall rush out as I am, and walk the street / With my hair down, so"—and yet it constitutes no escape from private agony. Emerging into the street from a person-to-person deadlock in a shuttered room can be no relief, since there is no communication with the passers-by either. At times in Eliot's early poetry the street is not only a scene but an agent, as when it pursues Prufrock or decoys the walker, by means of lamplight patterns, to a spiritual crucifixion ("The Little Passion: From 'An Agony in the Garret' ", p. 52 of the Notebook).[2] In "Preludes", the street is equipped with rational faculties ("You had such a vision of the street / As the street hardly understands"). Usually, how-

2. *The Waste Land: A Facsimile and Transcript of the Original Drafts Including the Annotations of Ezra Pound*, ed. Valerie Eliot (New York: Harcourt Brace Jovanovich, 1971), p. 47.
† From *"The Waste Land": A Fragmentary Wholeness* (Lund: C. W. K. Gleerup, 1978), pp. 133–38, 140. Copyright © 1978 by Marianne Thormählen. Reprinted by permission of the author. The author's notes have been edited.
1. Rudolf Germer, "T. S. Eliots Anfänge als Lyriker (1909–1965)," *Jahrbuch für Amerikastudien*, Beiheft 17 (1966): 70.
2. See T. S. Eliot, *Inventions of the March Hare: Poems 1909–1917*, ed. Christopher Ricks (New York: Harcourt Brace, 1996), p. 57 [*Editor*].

ever, it is a natural stage on which the dreary drama of modern urban
existence is enacted. The street is where people move, meet and observe
other people, vanish into buildings and emerge from them, all in accordance with the traditional idea of streets as the veins of a city. In
The Waste Land, several references to London streets are made, and
the MSS show that Eliot took pains to get them right—Queen Victoria
Street is substituted for Cannon Street in l. 258 (actually, neither connects directly with the Strand); Lower Thames Street is changed to
Upper Thames Street in the *Criterion* issue of 1922 and then altered
back to the original reading (it might be added that Oxford Street was
obviously not, in Eliot's view, an appropriate place for acquiring classy
apparel). The buildings lining the street, and the district through which
it runs, are implied in the street name (if Eliot had placed the "public bar" of l. 260 in Cheyne Walk—or made the Burial of the Dead
speaker bump into Stetson in Park Lane—the whole situation would
obviously have had a different accent). Lower Thames Street means
wharves, warehouses, barges, fish vendors and menial labour; and by
staging the Stetson encounter among white-collar workers surging into
the City Eliot suggests an aspect of timelessness in the movement of
the masses, an aspect also hinted at in the *Inferno* allusions and the
reference to the Punic wars. This is as good a place as any to mention
Eliot's use of London landmarks throughout his works. Under the spell
of the city which claimed him as a young man and retained him until
his death,[3] he made poetry out of London's streets, squares, buildings,
and districts (cf. the compelling ll. 27–28 of "A Cooking Egg"). The
unpublished poems supply further examples. In *The Waste Land* as
published Eliot restricts himself to exploiting the ring of City street
names and churches (excepting the riverside localities mentioned in
the Thames daughters passage).

   The London of *The Waste Land* is not exclusively that of the City
and the Thames, though. One instance of North London suburbia
crops up in the lines on the first Thames daughter, whose Highbury
background was originally sketched in some detail—Pound felt doubtful
about the passage ("Type out this anyhow") and Eliot cancelled it himself. The picture given by the lines on the girl's social setting is less
genteel than that which is presented in "The Death of the Duchess",
enacted in Hampstead and Marylebone[4] complete with silk hats and
aspidistras, but the difference between the depressing existence of

---

3. See Hubert Howarth, *Notes on Some Figures behind T. S. Eliot* (London: Chatto & Windus,
   1965), p. 222.
4. Anyone who chooses to do so may see a biographical connexion here; Hampstead and Marylebone were areas where the first years of Eliot's married life were spent. ["The Death of
   the Duchess" is one of the unfinished pieces Eliot once considered for parts of *The Waste
   Land.*—Editor]

the Highbury family and the time-killing activities of Hampstedians is slight: city denizens and suburbanites alike are "bound upon the wheel".

No fierce lights beat on Eliot's fog-ridden, dusky city. The gloom is only briefly broken by the pale winter sunrays which skirt the typist's bulky underwear.[5] Any other bright spots are provided by artificial devices, and they are few and far between. The street-lamps which were so frequent in Eliot's earliest poems have disappeared, leaving the violet air to spread undisturbed throughout the city, until the night allows Mrs. Porter to bask in the moonlight. Like the capital Perle of Alfred Kubin's dream kingdom[6] and Baudelaire's hibernal Paris, Eliot's London admits no brilliant colours. He hardly ever allows his readers to enter his metropolis in the summer months;[7] even when a geranium is allowed to signal the warm season, it is "sunless" and "dry" ("Rhapsody on a Windy Night"). Prufrock ventures forth on an October night, and the "Preludes", like *The Waste Land*, are set in a winter city. A reader familiar with the foggy boulevards of the French inheritance has no difficulty in recognising the atmosphere, and the darkness of *Inferno*—"Oscura e profond'era e nebulosa" (iv, 1. 10)[8]—is surely relevant, too.

By way of recapitulation, the city in *The Waste Land* is not merely a stage subordinated to the action upon it; it helps direct the action and the action reflects on it, too. It is an urban counterpart to the desert depicted in What the Thunder Said; in Elizabeth Drew's words, "The city was a maternal symbol to the ancients, but it is now utterly barren".[9] It is neither a Biblical harlot nor a City of God. In Eliot's poetry, and particularly in *The Waste Land*, the metropolis is a huge, decaying receptacle which holds millions of people unable to reach across to one another. This conception of the modern city distinguishes the urban images in Eliot's youth poems from the widening visions of *The Waste Land*.[1] The cancelled MS material, and especially the London lines in The Fire Sermon, accentuate that vague awareness of impending doom. Among the great number of supposed sources and influences on Eliot listed in critical works, one name connected with this pessimistic view of the modern city is conspicuous in its absence. Mentioned

---

5. In the MSS, there is a slightly brighter outlook in places. The last line in the cancelled Burial of the Dead opening provides a sobering sunrise; and the sun is the instrument of Fresca's awakening.
6. Alfred Kubin's *Die andere Seite* (1908; translated into English as *The Other Side*) is situated in a "dream kingdom" made out of buildings resituated from all over Europe [*Editor*].
7. One exception is found among the unpublished poems. The "First Debate between the Body and Soul" opens with a city scene which takes place towards the end of summer. [See *Inventions of the March Hare*, p. 64.—*Editor*]
8. "So dark and deep and misty" (Italian) [*Editor*].
9. Elizabeth Drew, *T. S. Eliot: The Design of His Poetry* (New York: Scribners, 1949), p. 73.
1. See Stephen Spender, *The Destructive Element* (London: Cape, 1935), p. 140.

in passing by a few critics,[2] Oswald Spengler, whose *Untergang des Abendlandes* was so widely read all over the Western world, published his *magnum opus* in the very years (1919–1922) which saw Eliot coming to grips with his "long poem". Only C. R. Jury[3] seems to have given some thought to the possibility of a connexion between Spengler and Eliot. Spengler's "colour is undoubtedly there", as is Freud's, says this critic (p. 11), later adding some pertinent observations regarding Spengler's view of intelligence as the destroyer of culture (p. 18). Actually, I think it is possible to add to these observations. Before doing so, though, one must ask oneself what the chances were that Eliot had seen *Der Untergang des Abendlandes* and been directly affected by it.

On this point, as on so many others, certainty is hard to come by. Spengler's work had matured for a period of years, part of it existing in manuscript at the outbreak of the War (the title was fixed as early as 1912, according to the author), but a first version—disparagingly referred to as a fragment in the preface to the 1922 edition—had gone to press early in 1918. It is unlikely to have roused any interest in England, particularly since Spengler professed his loyalty to the German war effort, but when the War was over and the complete work appeared in the course of the immediate post-war years, Spengler's views spread fast. Eliot, whose *Criterion* bears witness to his impatience with British cultural insularity,[4] may never have studied *Der Untergang des Abendlandes*, but it is highly unlikely that its basic ideas could have failed to reach him one way or another. I do not think Spengler influenced Eliot in the sense that the latter definitely drew on the German's work when writing his poem. To begin with, most of it will have been on paper before Eliot could have heard much about Spengler's discussion of the modern metropolis. In any case, many of the "Spenglerian" motifs in *The Waste Land* are also present in earlier poems, belonging securely in the continuity of Eliot's work. * * *

* * *

By way of summing up Spengler's significance where *The Waste Land* is concerned, it might be said that the apocalyptic dimension in the poem—implicit but potent—reflects an atmosphere which prevailed in the post-war years, an atmosphere to which Spengler's theories con-

2. See Spender, *The Destructive Element*, p. 140; Alec Brown, "The Lyric Impulse in the Poetry of T. S. Eliot", *Scrutinies* II, London 1931, 19–20; Haydn Moore Williams, p. 69 (to see *The Waste Land* as "a sort of poetic equivalent of Oswald Spengler's *Decline of the West*" is "a misconception", says Williams). Johannes Fabricius' *The Unconscious and Mr. Eliot: A Study in Expressionism* (Copenhagen, 1967) draws attention to some points which Eliot and Spengler had in common (pp. 72 and 74)—such as views on art and history—but does not go into details and makes no attempt to assess the possibility of influence.
3. C. R. Jury, "T. S. Eliot's *The Waste Land*: Some Annotations," Pamphlet No. 1 of the English Association, Adelaide, Australia, 1932.
4. Hermann Hesse's article on recent German poetry was among the first contributions to the review.

tributed to some degree. It is important to remember, though, that the roots of this international cultural pessimism went deep. Spengler had several precursors in the nineteenth century, and others before him had denounced modern urban existence.

There is a German inspirational source whose significance is indisputable: Hermann Hesse's *Blick ins Chaos*, published in 1919. The book presents a view of the decline of Europe which corresponds to Spengler's in several ways. Deeply impressed by Hesse's essays, Eliot went to see him in May, 1922,[5] a couple of months before *The Waste Land* was published. The importance of the writer of *Demian* and *Siddhartha* to Eliot remains to be analysed in detail; there can be little doubt that it is worth doing. Their interests corresponded to a high degree, as the works mentioned show, and it is reasonable to assume that their personalities must have matched fairly well. *Siddhartha* appeared in the same year as *The Waste Land*, and it is highly probable that Eliot and Hesse found other things to talk about besides the decline of the West—an important component in *Demian*—during the former's visit to Montagnola. Hesse may in fact have transmitted much of the literary climate in Germany to Eliot throughout the years of their acquaintance; the fact that he admired Heym and Kubin is a slight indication of what such a transmission may have meant.

* * *

It would be futile to insist on any direct influence of the Germans on Eliot. The obtrusive similarities between Eliot's themes and images on one hand and those of Georg Heym, Trakl,[6] etc. on the other are perhaps merely a result of their mutual apprenticeship to French poets, especially Baudelaire and Rimbaud. Nevertheless, the resemblances are often so striking, not least on points where the French heritage is of secondary importance, that it is difficult to dismiss them as entirely coincidental. For instance, while Baudelaire and Rimbaud saw and wrote of urban squalor and splendour in varying forms, doubtless influencing Eliot's city imagery, the apocalyptic element apprehensible in *The Waste Land* is less easy to relate to them. By contrast, Expressionist Berlin was, in the eyes of its poets, indeed teetering on the verge of an abyss which would swallow the whole of Western civilisation. The metrical point of view is also interesting. Incidentally, they frequently used the trivial in order to set off the terrible—a device often employed by Eliot, too. As for Kubin's novel, the dream kingdom described there, its capital—characterised, San Simeon-like, by churches, houses, and

5. See Bernhard Zeller, *Hermann Hesse in Selbstzeugnissen und Bilddokumenten*, Rowohlt Monographien (Hamburg, 1963), p. 93.
6. Georg Heym (1887–1912) and Georg Trakl (1887–1914), German Expressionist poets. Thormählen suggests an especial affinity between *The Waste Land* and Heym's "Der Gott der Stadt" and Trakl's "Trübsinn" [*Editor*].

palaces removed from their original European setting and rebuilt in the *Traumreich*—and its destruction also fit into the pattern. In fact, Eliot's "Song (for the Opherion)"[7] in the miscellaneous leaves reads in part like a lyrical digest of this terrifying book.

Few poets could be farther removed than Eliot from the strain of nature poetry which had set the pattern for poetry in England throughout the nineteenth century.[8] Even when he uses natural imagery, it bears the stamp of human hands; his roses and hyacinths are decorously rooted in garden beds and bowls, and his woods are not English forests but sacrificial groves. * * * The modern city, as the concentrated pool of barren humanity, is where he prefers to lay his scene; it was left to him finally and decisively to reverse the ecstatic picture of London which Wordsworth impressed on generations of English schoolchildren. In achieving this feat, he takes his place in the Symbolist tradition which had already bred outstanding city poets in France, Belgium, and Germany, to name but a few nations that witnessed poetry's retreat from Nature and its subsequent entrance on the urban scene, and which attained one of its high-water marks with the publication of *The Waste Land*. In this poem the city is, in a sense, "the most important personage . . . uniting all the rest". The early poetry can (much simplified) be said to describe the human condition in the modern city; in *The Waste Land* the human condition and the modern city are one. The later poems distance themselves from this vision, leaving the urban setting as the sombre background to man's struggle to attain the Eternal.

A. D. MOODY

A Cure for a Crisis of Civilisation?†

'Shantih' thrice repeated is a strange ending to a poem so ambitious to reform the mind in its own language. Whatever might be 'our equivalent', those words to most of us must be quite meaningless. If we recall that Hieronymo used strange tongues to mask his true intent, we may suspect that the Sanskrit is meant not to be readily understood. Its plain meaning may be just that it does pass beyond what we are likely to

---

7. Another of the unfinished, fragmentary pieces Eliot once thought of as potential parts of *The Waste Land* [*Editor*].
8. See Spender, *The Destructive Element*, p. 144. Cf. J. W. Beach, *The Concept of Nature in Nineteenth Century English Poetry* (New York, 1956), pp. 554 ff., where Eliot is upbraided for being "insensible" to natural beauty, and James G. Southworth in *Sowing the Spring* (New York, 1940), p. 91. Rather unexpectedly, John Senior argues—on the basis of his study on the sense of time in various literary works—that "the poet Eliot most resembles . . . is Wordsworth" (p. 173).
† From *Thomas Stearns Eliot: Poet* (Cambridge: Cambridge University Press, 1979), pp. 106–11. Copyright © 1979 by A. D. Moody. Reprinted by permission of Cambridge University Press. All notes are by the editor of this Norton Critical Edition.

think and say. Its deeper meaning may be set dead against our likely turn of mind. In fact the ready way so many readers have taken to the poem makes me wonder if it has been seen for what it is. To most of us, in our customary minds and ways of life, it must be radically subversive. If it appears to confirm some of our ideas and emotions, it probably does so in a way we never meant.

This may become clear if we consider how *The Waste Land* is at once the fulfilment and the contradiction of the romantic tradition in English poetry. The wanting to cease to suffer, and to be at peace, pensive peace, is a main characteristic of the line of poetry which descends from Milton down to Arnold, to go no further. *Il Penseroso* and *Lycidas* are the obvious beginnings, but it is as much a motive in the major poems. Milton's paradise is on the verge of eighteenth-century pastoral, and shades as easily towards the tranquil evening scene. The closing departure from Eden, resolving loss into sad harmony, completes the transposition of the epic 'tale of the tribe' into terms and feelings near to those of Gray's *Elegy*. At the end of *Samson Agonistes* we find the key terms for an age of poetry:

> His servants he with new acquist
> Of true experience from this great event
> With peace and consolation hath dismist,
> And calm of mind all passion spent.

The endings of *Hamlet* and *Lear* leave us lucidly facing what is beyond ordinary endurance. But in this later form of catharsis there is not that gathering up of agonising reality into an intelligible whole, nor the deepening of our capacity for experience. Rather there is a dissolving of the burden of existence in the comfort of ceasing to suffer. Submission, consolation, calm, and above all freedom from troubling passion, these are the states cultivated by all but the greatest poetry in the eighteenth century.

Gray's melancholy musings upon mortality are a way of reconciling his sensitive soul to its failure to cope with the world; and his attitude in death—'Here rests his head upon the lap of earth'—is the one he had taken up in life. Even Johnson, who mocked the illusions of pastoral paradises, and for whom melancholy was a black dog to be fought off, could end *The Vanity of Human Wishes* with a prayer in the manner of the minor verse of the time

> for a healthful mind,
> Obedient passions, and a will resign'd;
> For love, which scarce collective man can fill;
> For patience sov'reign o'er transmuted ill . . .

The last line can be connected with 'What the Thunder Said'; yet the quality of feeling is nearer to Cowper, 'a stricken deer that left the herd

. . . To seek a tranquil death in distant shades'. That this form of mind
was not abnormal, but was the dominant one, is demonstrated by Richardson's *Clarissa*. Surely the most representative literary work of its age,
and the one with the best claim to be regarded as its epic, it is at once
the complete expression of the Christian-romantic sensibility founded
upon Milton, and itself the determining form for the emotional and
moral structure of the English novel down to James' *The Wings of the
Dove* and Conrad's *Victory*.

Wordsworth gave a new strength and substance to the sensibility in
poetry which he inherited, by developing the interest in the self and
world which were to be harmonised. He did not want simply to escape
the world that is too much with us, but to recompose a universe of
being within the imagination. His tranquil mood is one

> In which the burthen of the mystery,
> In which the heavy and the weary weight
> Of all this unintelligible world,
> Is lightened;—that serene and blessed mood,
> In which the affections gently lead us on,—
> Until, the breath of this corporeal frame
> And even the motion of our human blood
> Almost suspended, we are laid asleep
> In body, and become a living soul:
> While with an eye made quiet by the power
> Of harmony, and the deep power of joy,
> We see into the life of things.[1]

'For it is ultimately the function of art, in imposing a credible order
upon ordinary reality, and thereby eliciting some perception of an order
in reality, to bring us to a condition of serenity, stillness and reconciliation . . .' .[2] That is Eliot, of course, and it suggests the profound correspondence, which goes with the profound difference, between his use
of poetry and Wordsworth's.

Arnold, at the moment when English romanticism was about to fall
into decadence, has the special interest of being both an example of its
weakness, and its diagnostician. His poetry, saturated with unresolved
longing to be at peace within himself and with his world, resumes
much of the elegiac verse of the preceding two hundred years. His
Scholar Gipsy is in a direct line of descent from Milton through Gray
and Keats. But Arnold felt how near the consolations of 'Sad Patience'
could be to despair. He accepted with Wordsworth that the poet's work
was to master his oppressive world in vision; and he saw that the melancholy which haunted his own and so much romantic poetry came

1. "Lines Written a Few Miles Above Tintern Abbey" (1798), ll. 39–49.
2. From "Poetry and Drama" (1951), included in *On Poetry and Poets* (1957), p. 87.

from a failure to see modern life clearly and to see it whole. When Eliot called Tennyson the great master of melancholia, and associated him with Virgil as Dante saw him, 'among the Great in Limbo', he could have been applying 'On the Modern Element in Literature' to the representative poet of Arnold's own time. Tennyson's doubt and despair made him 'the most instinctive rebel against [his] society', in Eliot's view; but he 'turned aside from the journey through the dark night', and became 'the most perfect conformist'—'Tennyson seems to have reached the end of his spiritual development with *In Memoriam*; there followed no reconciliation, no resolution.'[3] That, I should think, places him with Gerontion.

The romantic poets did not know enough, according to Arnold. To Eliot the graver defect was that they did not feel enough. Tennyson should have felt the anguish of spirit in his busy world 'as immediately as the odour of a rose'. Arnold, thinking it 'an advantage to a poet to deal with a beautiful world', did not penetrate beneath both beauty and ugliness to 'the vision of the horror and the glory'. He did not comprehend that the new conditions of life required 'a new discipline of suffering'.[4] Eliot might have thought the same of Wordsworth's always connecting wisdom with gentleness, serenity, tranquillity. It was because he had 'no ghastly shadows at his back, no Eumenides to pursue him, that he went droning on the still sad music of infirmity'. In general, from his point of view, the romantic poets had consoled themselves with melancholy ruminations, when only keen and intense suffering could have saved them. They were at once weary of the world and resigned to it; if they could not master it spiritually, they would have been better broken or ruined. They should have suffered more, instead of wishing not to suffer.

The Waste Land put an end to English romanticism by taking absolutely seriously the feelings it had soothed. Poets had listened to nightingales and been sad, or 'half in love with easeful death': Eliot meant to live the reality behind the myth. Arnold had found in Dante's *la sua volontade è nostra pace*[5] a touchstone of peace and consolation: Eliot set himself to practise the stern discipline of feeling which might bring him to that condition. What he found in the *Vita Nuova* was a *practical* sense of realities; and his anti-romanticism consisted in putting romantic feelings into practice. The oppression of the alien world, the withdrawal into the wilderness, the ecstasy of love sharpening the grief of loss: these were afflictions to be cultivated, once they were perceived

3. From *"In Memoriam"* (1936), included in *Essays Ancient and Modern* (1936).
4. From the chapter on Matthew Arnold in *The Use of Poetry and the Use of Criticism* (1933). The next quotation is from the chapter on Wordsworth and Coleridge.
5. "And in His will is our peace" (Italian), *Paradiso*, Canto 3. The *Vita Nuova* (literally "The New Life") is an autobiographical prose piece by Dante with inset poems.

to be not the opposites of perfect peace, but the very way to attain it. This was to fulfill the romantic tradition, but critically, as Christ's death fulfilled the hopes of the Old Testament.

Yet its readers received the poem as if it were expressing the old weariness with the world and the old hopes for its renewal. Civilisation was breaking down but might be restored to its former glory; the sterile would become fertile; the sexually exhausted might be mystically revitalised. Eliot reflected in wry understatement: 'I may have expressed for them their own illusion of being disillusioned, but that did not form part of my intention.'[6] What had happened appears to have struck him as oddly like the reception of *In Memoriam*—whatever the prevailing beliefs and illusions there is always the same wish to have them confirmed:

> Apparently Tennyson's contemporaries, once they had accepted *In Memoriam*, regarded it as a message of hope and reassurance to their rather fading Christian faith. It happens now and then that a poet by some strange accident expresses the mood of his generation, at the same time that he is expressing a mood of his own which is quite remote from that of his generation.[7]

Beyond question he had his own similar experience in mind. The rest of that essay expresses his conviction that the poet must not submit to the mood or mind of his generation. When his poetry and criticism after *The Waste Land* made explicit how remote in feeling he was from most of his readers, there was a defensive tendency to find that he had betrayed his own real convictions as well as theirs. It is hard to accept that the poet who is using our language greatly is using it for purposes alien to us. Yet the simple truth of the matter is that Eliot had been working from the start for another world than the one men and women make up together.

The cause of the general misapprehension could be that modern readers, like romantic poets, do not *feel* enough. Certainly we hear the music of feeling—it is what most of us first respond to. But when we come to think and talk about the poem we put the music in the background, and ask 'what does the poem mean?' When we would be serious we grow rational, and regard feelings as less real than ideas and opinions. Yet the profound and original life of the poetry, which is the life of feeling, is all in its music. To neglect that is to miss the essential action, the patient dying in order to pass beyond death.

> He was so conscious of what, for him, poetry was *for*, that he could not altogether see it for what it is. And I am not sure that he was

6. From "Thoughts after Lambeth" (1931). See "[The Disillusionment of a Generation]," p. 112.
7. From "*In Memoriam*."

highly sensitive to the musical qualities of verse. His own occasional bad lapses arouse the suspicion; and so far as I can recollect he never emphasises this virtue of poetic style, this fundamental, in his criticism. What I call the 'auditory imagination' is the feeling for syllable and rhythm, penetrating far below the conscious levels of thought and feeling, invigorating every word; sinking to the most primitive and forgotten, returning to the origin and bringing something back, seeking the beginning and the end. It works through meanings, certainly, or not without meanings in the ordinary sense, and fuses the old and the obliterated and the trite, the current and the new and surprising, the most ancient and the most civilised mentality. Arnold's notion of 'life', in his account of poetry, does not perhaps go deep enough.[8]

The last remark should make us realise, if we had not already been aware, that throughout the passage Eliot is talking of poetry and life as one thing. What he would remind us of is what Aristotle noted about the rites at Eleusis, that 'the initiated do not learn anything, so much as feel certain emotions, and are put into a certain frame of mind'. In spite of that, if published criticism is fair evidence of our more advanced reading habits, we mainly strive to be dull heads and dry brains. A superfetation of commentary and interpretation prevents the direct experience of the word in the ear. The critiques of the myth and the studies of the sources have perhaps seen as far as Tiresias, but no further. All our information and interpretation is vain unless it is caught up into the immediate, musical experience which carries us quite beyond it.

Eliot's interest in myth, old story and ancient ritual, was not for the sake of pure learning. It was intelligently practical: he wanted a *rite de passage* that would work. The ancient forms, as dug up and pieced together by scholarship, could not be revived. For the modern world a new form had to be found; and Eliot, in his poetry, did what he could. If *From Ritual to Romance* does elucidate the poem, it is less by glossing allusions, than by reminding us what kind of a poem it would be: a way of passing through death to a new life.

But is it a valid rite, will it work, for the civilisation of Europe in our time? It is a rite, I think, for the dying and the dead. There are other rites for the living, as that of Eleusis,[9] which enacted the love that sustains the vital universe. The discerning reader of Lévi-Strauss and of Ezra Pound will know that that is neither 'primitive' nor superseded. The rite of *The Waste Land* is one to save the self alone from an alien

---

8. From the Arnold chapter in *Use of Poetry*.
9. The rites at Eleusis, in ancient Greece, were mysterious initiation rituals. Pound believed that "a light from Eleusis persisted throughout the middle ages and set beauty in the song of Provence and of Italy" ("Credo," 1930).

world. The poet's negative relations, with his fellows and with his beloved, are improved only by being made nearly absolute, so that whatever is other (and therefore unreal) may be annihilated in the supreme
I AM. There is no impulse towards a renewal of human love, and no
energy is generated for that. Even less is there a movement toward a
human city or civilisation. In short, this is the rite of Eliot's Saint Narcissus.[1] Thus to act out love's negatives may be indeed a necessary and
inescapable phase, especially in a world that does not live by love. In
such a world as ours to save even oneself takes courage, even heroism,
and Eliot's poetry shows him to have had enough for that. But the
heroism of *The Waste Land* is of the kind which would end the human
world, not give new life to it.

RONALD BUSH

Unknown Terror and Mystery†

* * *

On the evidence of the manuscripts collected by Valerie Eliot, "The
Fire Sermon" was the first full movement of *The Waste Land* Eliot
attempted.[1] Out of the fragments he had been collecting since 1914,
at Margate Eliot chose a passage already several years old as a starting
point:

> London, the swarming life you kill and breed,
> Huddled between the concrete and the sky,
> Responsive to the momentary need,
> Vibrates unconscious to its formal destiny,
>
> Knowing neither how to think, nor how to feel,
> But lives in the awareness of the observing eye.
> Phantasmal gnomes, burrowing in brick and stone and steel!
> Some minds, aberrant from the normal equipoise
> (London, your people is bound upon the wheel!)
> Record the motions of these pavement toys
> And trace the cryptograms that may be curled

1. See "The Death of Saint Narcissus," an early poem once considered for a place in *The Waste
Land*, now in *The Waste Land: A Facsimile and Transcript of the Original Drafts Including
the Annotations of Ezra Pound*, ed. Valerie Eliot (New York: Harcourt Brace Jovanovich,
1971).

† From *T. S. Eliot: A Study in Character and Style* (New York: Oxford University Press, 1984),
pp. 56–67. Copyright © 1984 by Ronald Bush. Reprinted by permission of Oxford University
Press.

1. See Grover Smith, "The Meaning of *The Waste Land*," *Mosaic* 6.1 (1972): 127–141; and
Hugh Kenner, "The Urban Apocalypse," in A. Walton Litz, ed., *Eliot in His Time* (Princeton:
Princeton University Press, 1973), pp. 23–49.

Within these faint perceptions of the noise
Of the movement, and the lights![2]

This is a programmatic statement, an announcement that at least "The Fire Sermon" would consist of a hypersensitive record of two things—London's teeming crowds and the "cryptogram" of significance curled around them.[3] Eliot's portraits would be the stuff of journalism, his method spiritual analysis, his manner nightmare-gothic, and his emotional subject the emptiness of lives bound upon the wheel of passion and misdirected by the values of the modern city.

That was the program, but the way Eliot phrased it would not do. (Pound later dismissed it with a slash of red ink and a disgusted "B—ll—S.")[4] To conform to the standards Eliot and Pound had been enunciating for several years, Eliot's theme would have to be embodied in comment-free dramatic vignettes. And when Eliot finally conjured these vignettes out of the air, his program fell away and his writing was in the power of his demon. Heeding advice he had recently given others ("the bad poet is usually unconscious where ought to be conscious, and conscious where he ought to be unconscious. Both errors tend to make him 'personal' "),[5] Eliot seized on images and impressions that had struck his imagination and did not belabor their moral significance.[6] Beginning with "The Fire Sermon," he drew on memories of London formed during the preceding summer, when his attention was sharpened to visionary intensity by the presence of his mother;[7] on scenes

2. I cite from Eliot's typed version of a holograph manuscript. See *The Waste Land: A Facsimile of the Original Drafts Including the Annotations of Ezra Pound*, ed. Valerie Eliot (New York: Harcourt Brace Jovanovich, 1971), pp. 42–43 and 36–37. Lyndall Gordon dates the holograph 1917 or 1918 in *Eliot's Early Years* (Oxford: Oxford University Press, 1977), p. 95.
3. This corresponds to the way Anthony Cronin remembers Eliot explaining the origins of the poem. As far back as 1918, Eliot told Cronin, he had been meditating "a certain sort of poem about the contemporary world." See "A Conversation with T. S. Eliot about the Connection Between *Ulysses* and *The Waste Land*," in *The Irish Times* for 16 June 1972, p. 10.
4. See *Facsimile*, p. 31.
5. See "Tradition and the Individual Talent," p. 119 [*Editor*].
6. Conrad Aiken goes further and suggests that Eliot, though he believed his work was "pure calculation of effect," was actually indulging himself in "selfdeception." See Joseph Killorin, ed., *Selected Letters of Conrad Aiken* (New Haven: Yale University Press, 1978), pp. 185–186.
7. Eliot first recorded many of these impressions (including his visit to Magnus Martyr on a dreary lunch hour, his living through a "hot rainless spring" and his witnessing an outbreak of the flu that "leaves extreme dryness and a bitter taste in the mouth") in 1921 "London Letters" for the *Dial* and the *Nouvelle Revue Française*. A. Walton Litz discusses these letters and their provenance in "*The Waste Land* Fifty Years After" (see *Eliot in His Time*, pp. 13–17), but concludes that they are finally less important for the poem than the reading which shaped Eliot's imagination: Pound, Bradley, James, Conrad, Frazer and Joyce. I would agree that, in themselves, these impressions are only "raw materials," but hesitate to go further. From his first awareness of them to the time they assumed their place in his completed poem, Eliot's privileged moments were shaped as much by the sea-world of his non-literary sensibility as by any of his literary models. [For excerpts from these London Letters, see "The True Church and the Nineteen Churches" and "[*The Rite of Spring* and *The Golden Bough*]," pp. 131–33.—*Editor*]

from his own life, particularly from his life with Vivien;[8] and on the
horrible noises and the disagreeable neighbors he complained of to
John Quinn.[9] Through all of these, like wine through water, ran the
nightmarish emotional charge of Eliot's vague but intensely acute horror and apprehension of the "unknown terror and mystery in which
our life is passed."[1] As Eliot said about Jonson's plays, that was enough
to give the fragments a "dominant tone," a "unity of inspiration that
radiates into plot and personages alike." What he had sensed at the very
bottom of Johnson's constructions became the primary—almost the
only—unity of his own poem. To appropriate Richard Poirier on a
famous collection of popular songs, the fragments "emanated from
some inwardly felt coherence that awaited a merely explicit design, and
they would ask to be heard together even without the design."[2]

Some of Eliot's *images trouvailles* were drawn from actual nightmares. When Bertrand Russell, for example, told him about a hallucination Russell had that London Bridge would collapse and sink and
the whole great city would "vanish like a morning mist,"[3] Eliot suffused
it with the energy of a nursery rhyme gone mad and made it the keynote
of his finale. Other images drew on literary nightmares, or combinations of literature and fact, but were no less imaginatively transformed.
Out of his recollections of the murdered young women in Dostoyevsky's
Crime and Punishment and *The Idiot* (and of an actual incident of a
man murdering his mistress),[4] Eliot created yet another poetic sequence
about the mangling of "La Figlia Che Piange." Participating in the
sense of emotional strangulation that suffuses that early poem, the betrayed women in *The Waste Land* also absorb the complex ambivalence
associated in Eliot's mind with Vivien. These women anticipate Harry's
murdered wife in *The Family Reunion* and Sweeney's murdered neigh-
bor in *Sweeney Agonistes*. They are also the immediate successors of
the girl in Eliot's abandoned long poem of the mid-teens, "The Love
Song of St. Sebastian," who was strangled by her neophyte-lover be-

8. As we know from Valerie Eliot's notes to the *Facsimile*, Eliot sketched "Marie" in "The Burial of the Dead" from a woman he had met and shaped some of "The Game of Chess" from his own conversations with Vivien. See *Facsimile*, p. 126.
9. Another note in the *Facsimile* explains that the last dialogue of "A Game of Chess" was modeled after the words of Eliot's maid, Ellen Kellond (p. 127).
1. T. S. Eliot, "London Letter," *The Dial* 73 (September 1922): 330. Eliot comments on Jonson's plays in "Ben Jonson," originally included in *The Sacred Wood* (1920) [*Editor*].
2. From "Learning from the Beatles," in *The Performing Self: Compositions and Decompositions in the Language of Contemporary Life* (New York: Oxford University Press, 1971), p. 137.
3. *The Autobiography of Bertrand Russell: 1914–1944* (Boston: Little, Brown, 1968), p. 7. The full passage is worth quoting: "After seeing troop trains departing from Waterloo, I used to have strange visions of London as a place of unreality. I used in imagination to see the bridges collapse and sink, and the whole great city vanish like a morning mist. Its inhabitants began to seem like hallucinations, and I would wonder whether the world in which I thought I had lived was a mere product of my own febrile nightmares. . . . I spoke of this to T. S. Eliot, who put it into *The Waste Land*."
4. See "Eeldrop and Appleplex I," originally in the May 1917 *Little Review*, reprinted in Mar-garet Anderson, ed., *The Little Review Anthology* (New York: Horizon, 1953), p. 104: "In Gopsum Street a man murders his mistress."

tween his bleeding knees.[5] Unlike "St. Sebastian," which was to have one strangling episode as centerpiece, *The Waste Land* has many, all brief (some, like "Philomela," nearly invisible). Together they provide an undercurrent to the poem, dominating it the way a buried incident that is too terrifying to confront dominates a nightmare and occasionally breaks its surface. As Hugh Kenner observed many years ago, this buried sequence ties together a number of guilty protagonists and a long list of potential or real corpses: the hyacinth girl, Ophelia, "that corpse you planted last year in your garden," "bones cast in a little low dry garret," and so on.[6]

The subject of *The Waste Land*'s literary borrowings, now that it has been raised, commands a moment's reflection. It should be clear by now that contrary to the assumptions of generations of readers, for Eliot literary borrowings were more appropriations of other people's feelings than tools for ironic comment. He once put it this way: "Immature poets imitate; mature poets steal; bad poets deface what they take, and good poets make it into something better, or at least something different. The good poet welds his theft into a whole of feeling which is unique, utterly different from that from which it was torn."[7] In *The Waste Land* as elsewhere in his writings, images borrowed from other writers serve the same purpose as images found in everyday life—they provide nuggets of the objective world charged with feelings and untarnished by the deadening, conventional rhetoric of Eliot's personal will. They are thus uncontaminated by the acquired self, rooted in what lies below it and good fodder for a new "whole of feeling." Hence the presence in *The Waste Land* of Ovid's sweet-singing nightingale or Shakespeare's intensely mourned Ophelia.

But there is another way that the literature of the past makes itself felt in *The Waste Land*, a way that also has nothing to do with allusion as we normally think of it. We have seen that in poems like "Burbank with a Baedeker," the resonant poetry of the past is likely to become simply the rhetoric of the present. In *The Waste Land* Eliot's pervasive speaker—if one may use the word "speaker" to describe a vehicle for the "dominant tone" of subconscious feeling—is intensely aware of the literaryness, the rhetorical quality, of his utterance. Much of the poem's poetic sophistication comes from this self-consciousness, which is the enormously subtle dramatization of Eliot reacting against his own inherited disposition to rhetoric. As in not only Eliot's own experience but the fictional lives of Prufrock and Gerontion, one of the terrors of the speaker of *The Waste Land* is that he has forfeited life to books,

---

5. Now available in *Inventions of the March Hare: Poems 1909–1917*, ed. Christopher Ricks (New York: Harcourt Brace, 1996) [*Editor*].
6. See Hugh Kenner, *T. S. Eliot: The Invisible Poet* (New York: Citadel, 1959), pp. 161 ff.
7. From "Philip Massinger," originally published in *The Sacred Wood* (1920) [*Editor*].

and is trapped in ways of thinking and feeling acquired through convention. To use Eliot's bitter phrases, his emotional life is a terminal victim of "the pathology of rhetoric" and the "pastness of the past." And so in a sequence like the opening of "The Fire Sermon"—one of the finest and most terrifying passages of the poem—the other horrors of Eliot's nightmare are compounded by a self-consciousness that shadows every attempted escape from an isolated emptiness into the imaginative richness of poetry. In a passage like the following, every allusion has implied quotation marks around it and so renders a self-consciousness on the part of the speaker as much as it alludes to something outside the poem. (Where else in our poetry can a poem like Verlaine's "Parsifal" be sounded—a wondrously passionate poem considered by itself—and yet be charged with the coldness of irony simply by the context of its new surroundings? In *"Et O ces voix d'enfants"* Verlaine expressed indescribable aspiration; here the short line expresses that and also an ironic awareness that poetry is only literature, and to quote poetry is less to relieve genuine feeling than to succumb to monkish temptation.)

> The river's tent is broken; the last fingers of leaf
> Clutch and sink into the wet bank. The wind
> Crosses the brown land, unheard. The nymphs are departed.
> Sweet Thames, run softly, till I end my song.
> The river bears no empty bottles, sandwich papers,
> Silk handkerchiefs, cardboard boxes, cigarette ends
> Or other testimony of summer nights. The nymphs are departed.
> And their friends, the loitering heirs of city directors;
> Departed, have left no addresses.
> By the waters of Leman I sat down and wept . . .
> Sweet Thames, run softly till I end my song,
> Sweet Thames, run softly, for I speak not loud or long.
> But at my back in a cold blast I hear
> The rattle of the bones, and chuckle spread from ear to ear.
> A rat crept softly through the vegetation
> Dragging its slimy belly on the bank
> While I was fishing in the dull canal
> On a winter evening round behind the gashouse
> Musing upon the king my brother's wreck
> And on the king my father's death before him.
> White bodies naked on the low damp ground
> And bones cast in a little low dry garret,
> Rattled by the rat's foot only, year to year.
> But at my back from time to time I hear
> The sound of horns and motors, which shall bring
> Sweeney to Mrs. Porter in the spring.
> O the moon shone bright on Mrs. Porter
> And on her daughter

They wash their feet in soda water
Et O ces voix d'enfants, chantant dans la coupole!

Below the level of allusion, the passage presents the characteristic emotions of *The Waste Land*. Melancholy, loss, isolation and fear of a meaningless death adhere to "impersonal" objects in a "world" of awareness. The elements of this world arise from observation and memory (sometimes literary), and they strike us as complex sensations that have not been homogenized into a univalent pattern—a nameable feeling. But behind the pieces we sense an emotional logic that is "constantly amalgamating"[8] fragments into a single vision, and we are drawn into the poem's "point of view." Once we have given ourselves over to the emotional pressure of the poem we accept its coherence as we would accept the sequence of events in a dream, where objects quite often have an order, an emotional charge and a significance very different from the ones they have in waking consciousness. (Think of how often, for example, familiar people or objects terrify us in a nightmare when the same images in our sight or in our daydreams would not make us think twice.)

The opening movement of "The Fire Sermon" is "Hell" as Edward describes it in *The Cocktail Party*:

> What is hell? Hell is oneself,
> Hell is alone, the other figures in it
> *Merely projections.*[9]

It takes its dominant tone from a series of surrealistic images in which subconscious anxiety, as in a bad dream or a psychotic delusion, is projected onto human and non-human objects. Harry, in *The Family Reunion*, describes it this way:

> I could not fit myself together:
> When I was inside the old dream, I felt all the same emotion
> Or lack of emotion, as before: the same loathing
> Diffused, I not a person, in a world not of persons
> But only of contaminating presences.
>
> (CPP, 272)

But what Harry describes, the opening of "The Fire Sermon" presents. In it, emotional fantasies, sometimes of self-loathing, extend through a series of unconnected images in a medium where ego-integration seems to be non-existent. In synechdochic progression, a river, falling leaves, the brown land, bones, a rat, Ferdinand, his brother and his father, Mrs. Porter and her daughter all become extensions of

---

8. From "The Metaphysical Poets." See p. 125 [*Editor*].
9. T. S. Eliot, *Complete Poems and Plays* (New York: Harcourt Brace, 1971), p. 342. Hereafter CPP. Emphasis is the author's [*Editor*].

a whole (but not continuous) state of anxiety. Eliot's speaker (if—
again—one can use that noun in a case where utterance seems to come
from below the level of ordinary speech), projects his feelings of isolation, vanished protection and loss first onto the river, whose tent of
leaves is "broken" (the inappropriately violent adjective emphasizes the
feeling of grief behind the loss), and then onto the falling leaves, which
animistically have fingers that "clutch" for support as they sink into
decomposition and oblivion. Then defenselessness becomes a shrinking
from attack as the leaves fade into the brown land, "crossed" by the
wind. (Ten lines later the crossing wind will become a "cold blast"
rattling sensitive bones and, metamorphosed, the insubstantial malev-
olence of a "chuckle spread from ear to ear.") Still later, after an in-
terlude of deep-seated loss, isolation turns into self-disgust as the
"speaker" projects himself into a rat with a human belly creeping softly
and loathsomely through the vegetation. (Both rat and vegetation are
extensions of the decomposing leaves.) And as this horrified fascination
with the process of decomposition increases, the rat's living body merges
with a corpse's and the "speaker" apprehends himself first as rotting
and sodden flesh, feeling "naked on the low damp ground," and then
as dry bones, rattled by the rat's foot as he was rattled before by the
cold wind. (In a nightmare one can be both rat and bones.)

In the conclusion of the passage, the threatening vital force which
had been apprehended as the wind's blast reasserts itself as raucous
sound and the impinging moon, and the poem reacts once again with
revulsion, now animating the behavior of Mrs. Porter and her daughter,
who insulate themselves in a vivid but ineffective gesture. (According
to the bawdier versions of a popular ballad, their "feet" are a euphe-
mism and the soda water is a prophylactic douche; one does not need
to know that to feel the compulsive defensiveness in their unexplained
washing.)

There is more. The opening of "The Fire Sermon" is not simply an
English version of the kind of French poetry that uses symbols to express the ambivalence of the subconscious mind. Eliot's poetry is self-
dramatizing. In the way it echoes literature of the past and in its
self-conscious use of elevated or colloquial language, it dramatizes a
Prufrockian sensibility with a subtlety unavailable to the Eliot of 1911.
In the passage we are considering, this sensibility is caught between
two double binds: a yearning for the vitality of common life combined
with a revulsion from its vulgarity; and an inclination toward poetry
combined with a horror of literature. This vacillation, superimposed
over the poetry's *progression d'effets*, brings the world of unconscious
impulse into contact with the humanized world of language. In "The
Fire Sermon" *this* drama begins as the literary word "nymphs" emerges
from a series of more or less pure images. As it unfolds, the phrase "the
nymphs are departed" suggests Eliot's desire to recuperate his lost sense

of fullness in a world of pastoral poetry, and for a moment Eliot appropriates Spenser's voice. "Sweet Thames, run softly, till I end my song." The immediate result is a disgust with modern life worthy of Burbank. Hence the following three lines, where that disgust can be heard in a series of jolting colloquialisms. But both Eliot's poetic nostalgia and his disgust with the quotidian soften in the ninth line: there is a real sorrow in the speaker's statement that the "nymphs" and their vulgar friends have deserted him, a sorrow sounded in the repetition of "departed" twice in two lines. When the speaker reassumes the linguistic personae of the past in the *glissando* of the next three lines, therefore, it strikes us as a gesture taken *faute de mieux*. That is, we sense by this point that Eliot's speaker already has some awareness that the great phrases of the past are as unreal as they are beautiful. As his reminiscence (shall we call it memory?) of Spenser's "Prothalamion" sounds, we detect a note of self-consciousness in the nostalgia, as if the voice inhabiting the lines were feeling its own inauthenticity. When yet a third quotation is added to the Psalms and to Spenser, this discomfort, which stems from an awareness of the inadequacy of rhetoric to sustain true feeling or ward off grief, explodes in mid-flight. "But at my back," the speaker begins, and we expect to hear the rest of Marvell's immortal lines: "But at my back I always hear / Time's winged chariot hurrying near." Instead, the feeling of desolation which had called up the line swells out into bitterness: even the cherished texts of the past cannot charm away the bleak realities of life. To pretend that they can is a fraud. In Keats's "Ode to a Nightingale," this chilling realization generates yet two more sublime verses: "Adieu! the fancy cannot cheat so well / As she is famed to do, deceiving elf." In *The Waste Land*, the same realization shatters Eliot's poetic continuity, and causes him to interrupt Marvell's lines with a sardonic assertion of the primacy of the here and now:

> But at my back in a cold blast I hear
> The rattle of the bones, and chuckle spread from ear to ear.

Unlike Burbank then, this speaker is aware of the pathology of his rhetoric; all his literary utterances remind him of it. No sooner does he begin to transfigure the death of his father with it in the language of *The Tempest*, than he rebukes himself with an unidealized image of death. The image is close to pure terror; it is his own death as well as his father's that obsesses him:

> While I was fishing in the dull canal
> On a winter evening round behind the gashouse
> Musing upon the king my brother's wreck
> And on the king my father's death before him.
> White bodies on the low damp ground. . . .

The same pattern repeats itself three lines later, only this time the sequence has become more agitated:

> But at my back from time to time I hear
> The sound of horns and motors, which shall bring
> Sweeney to Mrs. Porter in the spring.

This tune is not Spenserian, and its leering swell mocks the legendary powers of music itself. Finally, the last line combines the highest reaches of expressive eloquence with an icy rejection of eloquence itself: *"Et O ces voix d'enfants, chantant dans la coupole!"* Oh those voices. Oh those children's voices.

In passages like this one, then, the anxiety we feel has two sources: a sequence of anxiety-charged images and the increasingly agitated self-laceration of a speaker conscious of his own rhetorical bent. Fueling both is a terrified awareness of death and a near-desperate sense that there is no escape from it. The pattern, moreover, resembles a certain kind of nightmare: a situation both desired and feared arises. Then, fueled by underlying desire, the situation develops. Meanwhile a dream censor is trying to suppress the clarity of the situation and terminates the sequence before the significance of a briefly glimpsed climax can be elaborated.

This configuration describes a great many of the separate vignettes that make up the first three movements of *The Waste Land*. What connects them is precisely what connects the disparate segments of our most distressing dreams. When we do not wake up after our first approach to a piece of heavily charged psychic material, we quite often play out the same pattern in situations that have different manifest elements but draw on the same body of latent content. That is, when the dream censor is able to agitate and then shatter a fantasy that gets too close to some forbidden truth, the forces that initiated the fantasy start the whole struggle again. In each segment, the same impulses reappear veiled in different objects or personae, unifying them from below. A dramatic situation emerges, intensifies mysteriously, reverberates with frightening tension and then, just before the situation is clarified, disperses; then a new situation arises that seems comfortingly different but is in fact the same anew.

I use the analogy of nightmare here with premeditation, but also with some diffidence. There are, of course, other, more subtle, ways of making sense of the tensions, the dramatic unity and the emotional progression of the first three movements of *The Waste Land*, and the best of them use a vocabulary generated to describe related examples of post-romantic poetry. Yet, dealing with a poem whose emotional immediacy has been slighted for so many years, I think it is of real use to apply an analogy drawn from common experience. And I would point out that the analogy is sanctioned by Eliot's own prose.

"The Burial of the Dead" begins as a voice remarks on the cruelty of "Memory and desire." Then, transformed, these feelings are absorbed in a dramatization. But the woman in the dramatization seems unconscious of the desire that conjured her up. We know of it by inference, from the particulars of her vision. She is oblivious to it, and she is just as oblivious to her own anxieties. We read them from the defensive stance of her protestations: why, we must guess, is she so eager not to be identified as Russian? Her interjection, apparently meaningless, is, in Eliot's words, a "tremendous statement, like statements made in our dreams."[1]

Her appearance in the dream, however, comes to an abrupt end. There is something, apparently, she is afraid to face: "In the mountains, *there* you feel free." Apparently, *here* you do not. Why? Her non sequitur in the next line does not tell us, although it speaks of her uneasiness. But before her uneasiness is allowed to grow the scene is over. It is Marie's evasion that leads to the next verse paragraph, which vibrates with a terror of what cannot be evaded even as we ask ourselves what it has to do with the story we have just heard. The paragraph ends, moreover, with a line (Eliot stole it from "Meditation IV" in Donne's *Devotions*) that represents a threshold over which the poem's voice cannot step: "I will show you fear in a handful of dust."

The next three scenes repeat a sequence the first verse paragraph began: the desolation latent in *Oed' und leer das Meer* is profound enough to foreclose further examination, and the latent content of the thing "One must be so careful [of] these days" is too threatening to name. Finally, in a conclusion that resembles the end of a nightmare sequence, the narrative becomes so agitated it cannot continue, and is shattered by an unexpected incident and a feverish inquisition. Without warning an unexplained encounter verges on some kind of recognition ("There I saw one I knew, and stopped him, crying, 'Stetson!' "), then explodes. There follow three hysterical questions, two lines of reverberating prophesy and then, from out of nowhere, Baudelaire's "You! hypocrite lecteur!"—a fragment which, in context, confronts us like the menacing ravings of a lunatic. Whatever charges Eliot's memory and desire from below has come so close to the surface that the sequence can no longer contain it, and so disintegrates.

At the center of "The Burial of the Dead," and at the center of the nightmare of *The Waste Land* lies the episode of the Hyacinth garden. Like Marie's summer memory, the episode begins on the note of romantic desire, this time with full-throated song, slightly melancholy, but rising to an unqualified yearning to have the romance of the past restored. Wagner's lyric acts as an epigraph to the drama that follows. As the German suggests a love lost and remembered, the girl who now

1. From "Swinburne as Poet," originally published in *The Sacred Wood* (1920) [*Editor*].

appears before the speaker recalls a luminous moment when love *re-named* her, and made her part of the spring: "They called me the hyacinth girl." As in "La Figlia,"[2] the girl's condition mirrors the speaker's own emotional life, caught for a second in one of its infrequent blossomings. But his moment of self-transcendence—transcending himself through love and transcending his always hollow-sounding voice through images—fades. His qualification "Yet" suggests he is again conscious of himself, and places us at the center of one of Eliot's recurrent obsessions. If his speaker can sustain his love into eternity, if this moment can be made the foundation of a set of permanent values, then his emotional self will have been validated and the warnings of his acquired self will be proved worthless. If, however, the moment cannot be sustained, if the promise of love turns out to be illusory and "the awful separation between potential passion and any actualization possible in life"[3] is as real as he suspected, then the worst of his fears will have been realized, and he will be trapped forever in an emotional waste land where "eyes fix you in a formulated phrase."

What then transpires can only be suggested by a reading alive to the way Eliot's poetry renders small movements of the heart. Eliot's speaker tries to prolong his memory and the feelings attached to it, and we hear his feeling swell in two pronounced spondees: "Your arms full, and your hair wet." But a second caesura introduces the plaintive words "I could not":

> I could not
> Speak and my eyes failed, I was neither
> Living nor dead, and I knew nothing,
> Looking into the heart of light, the silence.
> *Oed' und leer das Meer.*

Could he not speak because speech had been transcended or because the limitation of speech prevented him from fulfilling the moment? Did his eyes fail because he experienced what was beyond vision or because sight prevented him from the vision that he sought? Did he know nothing because worldly knowledge had fallen away or because he understood the nothing that is the ultimate truth? We would need to answer all of these questions if the speaker's statements were not given in the past tense. Since they are, it is clear that the questions they imply are his as much as ours. Looking back at his moment in the garden, the speaker ponders the issues on which his life turns. He has reached a moment like the one Celia describes in *The Cocktail Party*:

2. "La Figlia che Piange," originally published in *Prufrock and Other Observations* (1917) [*Editor*].
3. T. S. Eliot, "Beyle and Balzac," *Athenaeum* 4648 (May 30, 1919): 393.

I have thought at moments that the ecstasy is real
Although those who experience it may have no reality.
For what happened is remembered like a dream
In which one is exalted by intensity of loving
In the spirit, a vibration of delight
Without desire, for desire is fulfilled
In the delight of loving. A state one does not know
When awake. But what, or whom I loved,
Or what in me was loving, I do not know.
And if that is all meaningless, I want to be cured
Of a craving for something I cannot find
And of the shame of never finding it.

                                        (CPP, 363)

In the Hyacinth garden episode, Eliot dramatizes both Celia's "dream" and her wondering afterwards "if that is all meaningless." Reliving his failure to speak, to see, to know, the voice of *The Waste Land* gives us the agonized speculation of a man asking ultimate questions and being unable—or afraid—to answer. And since the sequence itself not only contains a dream but enacts one, this speculation swells out into another "tremendous statement," cast in a timeless present participle and balanced between the possibilities of nihilism and a mystic vision. Is he "looking into the heart of light" or the "silence"? As Celia puts it,

            Can we only love
      Something created by our own imagination?
      Are we all in fact unloving and unlovable?
      Then one *is* alone, and if one is alone
      Then lover and beloved are equally unreal
      And the dreamer is no more real than his dreams.
                                        (CPP, 362)

These questions, wrung out of Eliot by the most rigorous discipline of honesty, hang over the first three sections of *The Waste Land.* * * * They appear to represent Eliot's deepest fears: that we are alone, that what seems our most authentic emotional life is an illusion, that we are consequently worthless, and that reality itself is meaningless.

The Waste Land itself returns continually to that moment and those questions, as if to some feared truth which its speakers would do anything to avoid and yet are doomed to confront. As with a criminal returning to the scene of his crime (a murdered girl, a buried life), all things lead to that. And along the way of this compulsive, nightmarish vacillation, every instrument of answering the doubts, of testing the truth, is itself questioned. Nothing, not the authority of history or of

literature or of language itself is allowed to go unsuspected in this horrified interrogation of the moment in the garden. History may be lies,
literature may be rhetoric, memory may be illusion, the rambling self
may be but an artificial construct, sensation may be hallucination, even
language may be a "natural sin."[4] And—uncannily—at the center of
this nightmarish questioning stands the figure of Tiresias. How many
of Eliot's readers have noticed that the figure he affixed to his disembodied narrator, the figure who unites all the dream's men and all the
dream's women, is also at the center of Freud's archetypal myth of the
tormented human psyche turned back against itself—the Oedipus
myth?[5]

MAUD ELLMANN

A Sphinx without a Secret†

In a fable of Oscar Wilde's, Gerald, the narrator, finds his old companion Lord Murchison so puzzled and anxious that he urges him to
unburden his mind. Murchison confides that he fell in love some time
ago with the mysterious Lady Alroy, whose life was so entrenched in
secrecy that every move she made was surreptitious, every word she
spoke conspiratorial. Fascinated, he resolved to marry her. But on the
day he planned for his proposal, he caught sight of her on the street,
"deeply veiled", and walking swiftly towards a lodging house, where she
let herself in with her own key. Suspecting a secret lover, he abandoned
her in rage and stormed off to the Continent to forget her. Soon afterwards, however, he learnt that she was dead, having caught pneumonia
in the theatre. Still tormented by her mystery, he returned to London
to continue his investigations. He cross-examined the landlady of the
lodging house, but she insisted that Lady Alroy always visited her rooms
alone, took tea, and left as blamelessly as she had come. " 'Now, what
do you think it all meant?' " Murchison demands. For Gerald, the
answer is quite simple: the lady was " 'a sphinx without a secret.' "[1]

Now, *The Waste Land* is a sphinx without a secret, too, and to force
it to confession may also be a way of killing it. This poem, which has
been so thoroughly *explained*, is rarely *read* at all, and one can scarcely

---

4. T. S. Eliot, "The Post-Georgians," *Athenaeum* 4641 (April 11, 1919): 171.
5. But see Cleanth Brooks, *Modern Poetry and the Tradition* (Chapel Hill: North Carolina
   University Press, 1939; rpt., New York: Oxford University Press, 1965), p. 154; and A. D.
   Moody, *Thomas Stearns Eliot: Poet* (Cambridge: Cambridge University Press, 1979), p. 292.
† From *The Poetics of Impersonality: T. S. Eliot and Ezra Pound* (Cambridge: Harvard University Press, 1987), pp. 91–109. Copyright © 1987 by Maud Ellmann. Reprinted by permission
   of Harvard University Press. The author's notes have been edited.
1. Oscar Wilde, "A Sphinx without a Secret," *Complete Writings*, 10 vols. (New York: Notting-
   ham Society, 1905–1909), Vol. 8, pp. 121–132.

see the "waste" beneath the redevelopments. Most commentators have been so busy tracking its allusions down and patching up its tattered memories that they have overlooked its broken images in search of the totality it might have been. Whether they envisage the poem as a pilgrimage, a quest for the Holy Grail, an elegy to Europe or to Jean Verdenal, these readings treat the text as if it were a photographic negative, tracing the shadows of a lost or forbidden body.[2]

This is how Freud first undertook interpretation, too, but his patients forced him to revise his method, and his experience may shed a different kind of light upon *The Waste Land*. In *Studies on Hysteria*, Freud and Breuer argue that "hysterics suffer mainly from reminiscences" (and by this definition, *The Waste Land* is the most hysterical of texts).[3] Since the hysteric somatises her desire, enciphering her memories upon her flesh, Freud imagined that he could alleviate her suffering by salvaging the painful recollections. However, these archaeologies would leave her cold. For this reason, he shifted his attention from the past to the present, from reminiscence to resistance, from the secrets to the silences themselves.

Now, *The Waste Land*, like any good sphinx, lures the reader into hermeneutics, too: but there is no secret underneath its huggermuggery. Indeed, Hegel saw the Sphinx as the symbol of the symbolic itself, because it did not know the answer to its own question: and *The Waste Land*, too, is a riddle to *itself*.[4] Here it is more instructive to be scrupulously superficial than to dig beneath the surface for the poem's buried skeletons or sources. For it is in the silences *between* the words that meaning flickers, local, evanescent—in the very "wastes" that stretch across the page. These silences curtail the powers of the author, for they invite the *hypocrite lecteur* to reconstruct their broken sense. Moreover, the speaker cannot be identified with his creator, not because he has a *different* personality, like Prufrock, but because he has no stable identity at all. The disembodied "I" glides in and out of stolen texts, as if the speaking subject were merely the quotation of its ante-

2. In fact the criticism reads more like a quest for the Holy Grail than the poem does. For the Holy Grail interpretation, see Grover Smith, *T. S. Eliot's Poetry and Plays: A Study in Sources and Meaning* (Chicago: University of Chicago Press, 1956), pp. 69–70, 74–7; and Edmund Wilson, *Axel's Castle: A Study in the Imaginative Literature of 1870–1930* (New York and London: Scribner's, 1931), pp. 104–5. Helen Gardner subscribes to this position with some qualifications in *The Art of T. S. Eliot* (London: Cresset Press, 1949), p. 87. George Williamson reconstructs *The Waste Land* ingeniously in *A Reader's Guide to T. S. Eliot* (New York: H. Woolf, 1953), esp. pp. 129–130. For Jean Verdenal see John Peter, "A New Interpretation of *The Waste Land*," in *Essays in Criticism*, 2 (1952), esp. p. 245; and James E. Miller, *T. S. Eliot's Personal Waste Land: Exorcism of the Demons* (University Park, Pennsylvania: Pennsylvania State University Press, 1977), *passim*.
3. Freud revises this formula, however, in *The Interpretation of Dreams*, where he states that "Hysterical symptoms are not attached to actual memories, but to phantasies erected on the basis of memories." *Complete Psychological Works of Sigmund Freud*, tr. James Strachey (London: Hogarth, 1953–1974), Vol. 5, p. 491.
4. See *Hegel's Aesthetics: Lectures on Fine Art*, trans. T. M. Knox (Oxford: Clarendon, 1975), pp. 360–1.

cedents. Indeed, this subject is the victim of a general collapse of boundaries. This chapter examines *The Waste Land* in the light of Freud—and ultimately in the darkness of *Beyond the Pleasure Principle*—to trace the poem's suicidal logic.

Throbbing between Two Lives

Let us assume, first of all, that *The Waste Land* is about what it declares—waste. A ceremonial purgation, it inventories all the "stony rubbish" that it strives to exorcise (20).[5] The "waste *land*" could be seen as the thunderous desert where the hooded hordes are swarming towards apocalypse. But it also means "waste ground", bomb sites or vacant lots, like those in "Rhapsody on a Windy Night", where ancient women gather the wreckage of Europe.[6] It means Jerusalem or Alexandria or London—any ravaged centre of a dying world—and it foreshadows the dilapidation of centricity itself. The poem teems with urban waste, butt-ends of the city's days and ways: "empty bottles, sandwich papers, / Silk handkerchiefs, cardboard boxes, cigarette ends" (177–8). However, it is difficult to draw taxonomies of waste, because the text conflates the city with the body and, by analogy, the social with the personal. Abortions, broken fingernails, carious teeth, and "female smells" signify the culture's decadence, as well as bodily decrepitude. The self is implicated in the degradation of the race, because the filth without insinuates defilement within.[7]

It is waste *paper*, however, which appals and fascinates the poem, the written detritus which drifts into the text as randomly as picnics sink into the Thames (177–8). Many modernist writers comb the past in order to recycle its remains, and Joyce is the master of the scavengers: "Nothing but old fags and cabbage-stumps of quotations", in D. H. Lawrence's words.[8] Joyce treats the rubbish heap of literature as a fund of creativity ("The letter! The litter!"), disseminating writings as Eliot strews bones.[9] A funeral rather than a wake, *The Waste Land* is a lugubrious version of Joyce's jubilant "recirculation" of the past, in which all waste becomes unbiodegradable: "Men and bits of paper, whirled

5. Just as "Ash-Wednesday" strives to be a prayer, *The Waste Land* aspires to the condition of ritual. This fascination with cathartic rites drew Eliot towards the theatre in his later work, but his poems also crave performance, incantation. [The numbers given in parentheses in the text are line numbers to *The Waste Land.*—*Editor*]
6. Suggested by Peter Middleton, "The Academic Development of *The Waste Land*," in *Demarcating the Disciplines: Philosophy, Literature, Art*, ed. Samuel Weber (Minneapolis: University of Minnesota Press, 1986), pp. 153–80.
7. Paul Ricoeur has pointed out that "impurity was never literally filthiness" and "defilement was never literally a stain", for the notion of impurity is "primordially symbolic". See Ricoeur, *The Symbolism of Evil*, trans. Emerson Buchanan (Boston: Beacon Press, 1967), pp. 35, 39.
8. Quoted by Jennifer Schiffer Levine in "Originality and Repetition in *Finnegans Wake* and *Ulysses*", *PMLA*, 94 (1979), 108.
9. James Joyce, *Finnegans Wake* (New York: Viking, 1967), p. 93, line 24.

by the cold wind . . ."[1] Indeed, *The Waste Land* is one of the most abject texts in English literature, in every sense: for abjection, according to Bataille, "is merely the inability to assume with sufficient strength the imperative act of excluding abject things", an act that "establishes the foundations of collective existence."[2] Waste is what a culture casts away in order to determine what is not itself, and thus to establish its own limits. In the same way, the subject defines the limits of his body through the violent expulsion of its own excess: and ironically, this catharsis *institutes* the excremental. Similarly, Paul Ricoeur has pointed out that social rituals of "burning, removing, chasing, throwing, spitting out, covering up, burying" continuously *reinvent* the waste they exorcise.[3]

The word "abject" literally means "cast out", though commonly it means downcast in spirits: but "abjection" may refer to the waste itself, together with the violence of casting it abroad. It is the ambiguity of the "abject" that distinguishes it from the "object", which the subject rigorously jettisons (ob-jects). According to Julia Kristeva, the abject emerges when exclusions fail, in the sickening collapse of limits. Rather than disease or filth or putrefaction, the abject is that which "disturbs identity, system, order": it is the "inbetween, the ambiguous, the composite."[4] In the "brown fog" of *The Waste Land*, for example, or the yellow fog of "Prufrock", the in-between grows animate: and Madame Sosostris warns us to fear death by water, for sinking banks betoken glutinous distinctions. In fact, the "horror" of *The Waste Land* lurks in the osmoses, exhalations and porosities, in the dread of *epidemic* rather than the filth itself, for it is this miasma that bespeaks dissolving limits.[5] The corpses signify the "utmost of abjection", in Kristeva's phrase, because they represent "a border that has encroached upon everything": an outside that irrupts into the inside, and erodes the parameters of life.[6] It is impossible to keep them underground: Stetson's garden is an ossuary, and the dull canals, the garrets, and the alleys are littered with unburied bones. "Tumbled graves" (387) have overrun the city, for the living have changed places with the dead: "A crowd flowed over London Bridge, so many, / I had not thought death had undone so many" (62–3). *The Waste Land* does not fear the dead themselves so much as their invasion of the living; for it is the collapse of boundaries that

1. The quotation is from Eliot's poem "Burnt Norton," section 3, line 15. The term "recirculation" is taken from *Finnegans Wake*, p. 3 [*Editor*].
2. Quoted in Julia Kristeva, *Powers of Horror: An Essay on Abjection*, trans. Leon S. Roudiez (New York: Columbia University Press, 1982), p. 56.
3. Ricoeur, *Symbolism of Evil*, p. 35.
4. Kristeva, *Powers of Horror*, p. 4; see also p. 9.
5. Eliot originally quoted Kurtz's last words "The horror! the horror!" from Conrad's *Heart of Darkness* as the epigraph to *The Waste Land*: see *The Waste Land: A Facsimile and Transcript of the Original Drafts Including the Annotations of Ezra Pound*, ed. Valerie Eliot (London: Faber, 1971), p. 3.
6. Kristeva, *Powers of Horror*, pp. 4, 3.

centrally disturbs the text, be they sexual, national, linguistic, or authorial.

Kristeva derives her notion of abjection from Freud's *Totem and Taboo*, which was written ten years before the publication of *The Waste Land* and anticipates its itch for anthropology.[7] Like Eliot, Freud draws analogies between the psychic and the cultural, linking "civilised" obsessionality to "savage" rites. In both cases the ritual "is ostensibly a protection against the prohibited act; but *actually* . . . a repetition of it."[8] *The Waste Land* resembles this obsessive rite, because it surreptitiously repeats the horror that it tries to expiate. In particular, it desecrates tradition. The poem may be seen as an extended "blasphemy", in Eliot's conception of the term, an affirmation masked as a denial. For the text dismantles Western culture as if destruction were the final mode of veneration. As Terry Eagleton argues:

> behind the back of this ruptured, radically decentred poem runs an alternative text which is nothing less than the closed, coherent, authoritative discourse of the mythologies which frame it. The phenomenal text, to use one of Eliot's own metaphors, is merely the meat with which the burglar distracts the guard-dog while he proceeds with his stealthy business.[9]

However, Eagleton omits a further ruse: for the poem uses its nostalgia to conceal its vandalism, its pastiche of the tradition that it mourns. Indeed, a double consciousness pervades the text, as if it had been written by a vicar and an infidel. The speaker is divided from himself, unable to resist the imp within who cynically subverts his pieties. Thus, Cleopatra's burnished throne becomes a dressing table, time's winged chariot a grinning skull (77, 186): but there are many subtler deformations.

Take, for instance, the opening words. The line "April is the cruellest month" blasphemes (in Eliot's sense) against the first lines of *The Canterbury Tales*, which presented April's showers as so sweet. At once a nod to origins and a flagrant declaration of beginninglessness, this allusion grafts the poem to another text, vaunting its parasitic inbetweenness. Only the misquotation marks the change of ownership, but the author's personality dissolves in the citational abyss. This is why Conrad Aiken once complained that Eliot had created " 'a literature of literature' . . . a kind of parasitic growth on literature, a sort of mistletoe . . .".[1] As blasphemy, *The Waste Land* is obliged to poach upon the

7. For contemporary interest in anthropology, see Stephen Kern, *The Culture of Time and Space* (Cambridge: Harvard University Press, 1983), pp. 19–20, 32, 34.
8. Freud, *Complete Works*, Vol. 12, p. 50.
9. Terry Eagleton, *Criticism and Ideology: A Study in Marxist Literary Theory* (London: Verso, 1978), pp. 149–150.
1. See Conrad Aiken, "An Anatomy of Melancholy," p. 148 [*Editor*].

past, caught in a perpetual allusion to the texts that it denies.[2] For it is only by corrupting Chaucer's language that Eliot can grieve the passing of his world:

> April is the cruellest month, breeding
> Lilacs out of the dead land, mixing
> Memory and desire, stirring
> Dull roots with spring rain.
> Winter kept us warm, covering
> Earth in forgetful snow, feeding
> A little life with dried tubers.

(1–7)

Because these lines allude to Chaucer, they invoke the origin of the tradition as well as the juvescence of the year.[3] But words like "stirring", "mixing", and "feeding" profane beginnings, be they literary or organic, provoking us to ask what "cruelty" has exchanged them for uniting, engendering, or nourishing. Thus the passage whispers of the words *its* words deny, and sorrows for the things it cannot say. Most of the lines stretch beyond the comma where the cadence falls, as if the words themselves had overflown their bounds, straining towards a future state of being like the dull roots that they describe. They typify the way *The Waste Land* differs from itself, forever trembling towards another poem which has already been written, or else has yet to be composed.

This betweenness also overtakes the speaking subject, for the first-person pronoun roams from voice to voice.[4] The "us" in "Winter kept us warm" glides into the "us" of "Summer surprised us," without alerting "us", the readers, of any change of name or locus. At last, the "us" contracts into the couple in the Hofgarten, after having spoken for the human, animal and vegetable worlds. What begins as an editorial "we" becomes the mark of a migration, which restlessly displaces voice and origin. Throughout the poem, the "I" slips from persona to persona, weaves in and out of quoted speech, and creeps like a contagion through the *Prothalamion* or Pope or the debased grammar of a London pub, sweeping history into a heap of broken images.

However, Eliot insisted in the Notes to *The Waste Land* that Tiresias should stabilise this drifting subject, and rally the nomadic voices of the text:[5]

---

2. Thus it could be said that writing *engenders* blasphemy, just as law is the prerequisite to crime.
3. See Chaucer, General Prologue to *The Canterbury Tales*, lines 1–4.
4. Alick West pointed this out long ago: see *Crisis and Criticism* (London: Lawrence and Wishart, 1937), pp. 5–6, 28.
5. For critics who see Tiresias as an omniscient narrator, see *inter alia* Grover Smith, *Eliot's Poetry and Plays*, pp. 72–6; F. O. Matthiessen, *The Achievement of T. S. Eliot* (Boston: Houghton-Mifflin, 1935), p. 60. For critics more sceptical of Tiresias's role, see Graham Hough, *Image and Experience: Studies in a Literary Revolution* (London: Duckworth, 1960), p. 25; Juliet McLaughlin, "Allusion in *The Waste Land*", *Essays in Criticism*, 19 (1969), 456; Paul LaChance, "The Function of Voice in *The Waste Land*", *Style*, 5, no. 2 (1971), 107ff.

218. Tiresias, although a mere spectator and not indeed a "character", is yet the most important personage in the poem, uniting
all the rest. Just as the one-eyed merchant, seller of currants, *melts
into* the Phoenician Sailor, and the latter is *not wholly distinct* from
Ferdinand Prince of Naples, so all the women are one woman,
and the *two sexes meet* in Tiresias. What Tiresias *sees*, in fact, is
the substance of the poem.[6]

But what *does* Tiresias see? Blind as he is, the prophet has a single
walk-on part, when he spies on the typist and her lover indulging in
carbuncular caresses.[7] In this Note, moreover, Eliot emphasises the *os-
mosis* of identities more than their reunion in a central consciousness.
For Tiresias's role within the poem is to "melt" distinctions and confuse
personae:

> I Tiresias, though blind, throbbing between two lives,
> Old man with wrinkled female breasts, can see
> At the violet hour, the evening hour that strives
> Homeward, and brings the sailor home from sea,
> The typist home at teatime, clears her breakfast, lights
> Her stove, and lays out food in tins.
> Out of the window perilously spread
> Her drying combinations touched by the sun's last rays,
> On the divan are piled (at night her bed)
> Stockings, slippers, camisoles, and stays.
> I Tiresias, old man with wrinkled dugs
> Perceived the scene, and foretold the rest—
> I too awaited the expected guest.
> He, the young man carbuncular, arrives. . . .
>
> (218–31)

Here the seer turns into a peeping Tom, the most ambiguous of spec-
tators. "Throbbing between two lives", Tiresias could be seen as the
very prophet of abjection, personifying all the poem's porous mem-
branes. A revisionary, he foresees what he has already foresuffered, mixing memory and desire, self and other, man and woman, pollution and
catharsis. The Notes which exalt him are "abject" themselves, for they
represent a kind of supplement or discharge of the text that Eliot could
never get "unstuck", though he later wished the poem might stand
alone.[8] Now that the manuscript has been released (1971), the poem
throbs between two authors and three texts—the Notes, the published
poem, and the drafts that Pound pruned so cunningly. The text's integrity dissolves under the invasion of its own disjecta. Just as its quo-

---

6. Emphasis added, except for "sees."
7. Genevieve W. Forster takes the extraordinary view that the scene with the typist is therefore
   the "substance of the poem": in "The Archetypal Imagery of T. S. Eliot", *PMLA*, 60 (1945),
   573.
8. See Eliot's comments on the notes, p. 113. See also p. 21, n. 1[*Editor*].

tations confuse the past and present, parasite and poet, the poem leaks in supplements and prolegomena.

The typist symptomises this betweenness, too. Her profession parodies the poet's, demoted as he is to the typist or amanuensis of the dead. Too untidy to acknowledge boundaries, she strews her bed with stockings, slippers, camisoles, and stays, and even the bed is a divan by day, in a petit bourgeois disrespect for definition. She resembles the neurotic woman in "A Game of Chess", who cannot decide to go out or to stay in, as if she were at enmity with their distinction. Eliot himself declares that all the women in *The Waste Land* are one woman, and this is because they represent the very principle of unguency. "Pneumatic bliss" entails emulsive demarcations.[9] Yet the misogyny is so ferocious, particularly in the manuscript, that it begins to turn into a blasphemy against itself. For the poem is enthralled by the femininity that it reviles, bewitched by this odorous and shoreless flesh. In fact, woman is the spirit of its own construction, the phantom of its own betweennesses. In "The Fire Sermon", Eliot personifies his broken images in a woman's bruised, defiled flesh; and it is as if the damsel Donne once greeted as his new found land had reverted to the old world and an urban wilderness:

> "Trams and dusty trees.
> Highbury bore me. Richmond and Kew
> Undid me. By Richmond I raised my knees
> Supine on the floor of a narrow canoe."

> "My feet are at Moorgate, and my heart
> Under my feet. After the event
> He wept. He promised 'a new start'.
> I made no comment. What should I resent?"

> "On Margate Sands.
> I can connect
> Nothing with nothing.
> The broken fingernails of dirty hands.
> My people humble people who expect
> Nothing."
>   la la

> To Carthage then I came

> Burning burning burning burning
> O Lord Thou pluckest me out
> O Lord Thou pluckest

> burning

(292–311)

9. A quotation from Eliot's "Whispers of Immortality," originally published in *Poems* (1920) [*Editor*].

The body and the city melt together, no longer themselves but not yet
other. It is as if the metaphor were stuck between the tenor and the
vehicle, transfixed in an eternal hesitation. Both the woman and the
city have been raped, but the "he" seems passive in his violence, weeping at his own barbarity. The victim, too, consents to degradation as if
it were foredoomed: "I raised my knees / Supine. . . . What should I
resent?" (As Ian Hamilton observes, "no one in *The Waste Land* raises
her knees in any other spirit than that of dumb complaisance."[1] "Undone", the woman's body crumbles in a synecdochic heap of knees,
heart, feet, weirdly disorganised: "My feet are at Moorgate, and my
heart / Under my feet." But the city which undid her decomposes, too,
in a random concatenation of its parts—Highbury, Richmond, Kew,
Moorgate—and ends in broken fingernails on Margate Sands.

Itinerant and indeterminate, the "I" slips from the woman to the city,
and then assumes the voice of Conrad's Harlequin in *Heart of Darkness*, who apologises for a humble and exploited race. At last it merges
with the "I" who came to Carthage in St Augustine's *Confessions*. As
the last faltering words suggest, it is impossible to "pluck" the speaking
subject out of the conflagration of the poem's idioms. The I cannot
preserve its own identity intact against the shrieking voices which assail
it, "Scolding, mocking, or merely chattering" according to their whim.[2]
In *The Waste Land*, the only voice which *is* "inviolable" is the voice
that does not speak, but only sings that phatic, faint "la la."

These notes allude to the warblings of the nightingale, who fills the
desert "with inviolable voice" (101). In Ovid, however, the nightingale
was born in violation. Tereus, "the barbarous king" (99) raped his wife's
sister Philomela, and cut out her tongue so that she could not even
name her own defiler ("Tereu . . ." [206]). But Philomela weaves a
picture of his crime into her loom so that her sister, Procne, can decode
her wrongs.[3] In this way, her web becomes a kind of writing, a dossier
to defend her speechless flesh. After reading it, Procne avenges Philomela by feeding Tereus the flesh of his own son. In *The Waste Land*,
Eliot omits the web, and he ignores this violent retaliation, too. He
alludes only to the ending of the myth, when the gods give both the
sisters wings to flee from Tereus's wrath. They change Philomela into
a nightingale to compensate her loss of speech with wordless song.[4] By
invoking this story, Eliot suggests that woman is excluded from language

1. Ian Hamilton, *"The Waste Land"*, in *Eliot in Perspective: A Symposium*, ed. Graham Martin
   (London: Macmillan, 1960), p. 109.
2. Quoted from "Burnt Norton," section 5, line 18 [*Editor*].
3. While Freud once said that weaving was woman's only contribution to civilisation, and that
   it originates in the "concealment of genital deficiency" (*Complete Works*, Vol. 22, p. 132),
   Ovid makes women's weaving into the invention of the *text*.
4. Ovid juxtaposes her story to Arachne's, another weaving tattle-tale, who fraught her web with
   "heavenly crimes", depicting Zeus in all the shapes he took to ravish nymphs and mortal
   women: *Metamorphoses*, VI, 103–33. [For the story of Philomela, see the selection from Ovid's
   Metamorphoses, pp. 46–50.—*Editor*]

through the sexual violence of a man. As Peter Middleton has pointed out, she is awarded for her pains with a pure art which is powerless and desolate—"la, la."

In *The Waste Land* as in Ovid, writing provides the only refuge from aphasia, but it is a weapon that turns against its own possessor. Rather than the record of the victim's wrongs, writing has become the very instrument of violation: and it invades the male narrator's speech as irresistably as the "female stench" with which it comes to be associated.[5] Although Eliot quotes Bradley to the effect that "my experience falls within my own circle, a circle closed on the outside", this circle has been broken in *The Waste Land* (411n.). Here no experience is proper or exclusive to the subject. Moreover, the speaker is possessed by the writings of the dead, and seized in a cacophony beyond control.

Prince of Morticians

> Curious, is it not, that Mr. Eliot
> Has not given more time to Mr. Beddoes
> (T. L.) prince of morticians
> Pound, Canto LXXX

In "Tradition and the Individual Talent" Eliot celebrates the voices of the dead, but he comes to dread their verbal ambush in *The Waste Land*.[6] In the essay, he claimed that "not only the best, but the most individual poetry" is that which is most haunted by its own precursors. Only thieves can truly be original. For any new creation gains its meaning in relation to the poems of the past, and writing is a voyage to the underworld, to commune with the phantasmal voices of the dead. Eliot published this essay immediately after World War I, in 1919, the same year that Freud was writing *Beyond the Pleasure Principle*. As Middleton has pointed out, they both confront the same material: the unprecedented death toll of the First World War. Like Freud's theory of repetition, Eliot's account of influence attempts to salvage something of a past that had never been so ruthlessly annihilated—however fearsome its reanimation from the grave. Whereas Freud discovers the death drive in the compulsion to repeat, *The Waste Land* stages it in the compulsion to citation.

In 1919 Freud also wrote his famous essay on the "uncanny", which he defines as "whatever reminds us of this inner compulsion to repeat."[7] *The Waste Land* is uncanny in a double sense, for it is haunted by the

---

5. *Facsimile*, p. 39.
6. Helen Gardner argues that *The Waste Land* is an "exercise in ventriloquism", but she makes the dead the dummies, Eliot the ventriloquist. I suggest that the poem works the other way around. [See Gardner, "*The Waste Land*: Paris 1922," p. 79.—*Editor*]
7. "The Uncanny," in *Complete Works*, Vol. 17, p. 238. The reference below to the *unheimlich* is from the same essay, pp. 222–6.

repetition of the dead—in the form of mimicry, quotation and pastiche—but also by a kind of Hammer horror: bats with baby faces, whisper music, violet light, hooded hordes, witches, death's heads, bones, and zombies (378–81). According to Freud, "heimlich" literally means "homely" or familiar, but it develops in the direction of ambivalence until it converges with its opposite, *unheimlich* or uncanny. Thus the very word has grown unhomely and improper to itself. The passage Eliot misquotes from *The White Devil* provides a good example of the double meaning of uncanniness:

> O keep the Dog far hence, that's friend to men,
> Or with his nails he'll dig it up again!
>
> (74–5)

Since the passage is purloined from Webster, the very words are ghostly revenants, returning as extravagant and erring spirits. This kind of verbal kleptomania subverts the myth that literary texts are private property, or that the author can enjoy the sole possession of his words. But Eliot writes Dog where Webster wrote Wolf, and friend where Webster wrote foe. Thus he tames the hellhound in the same misprision that domesticates the discourse of the past. Friendly pet and wild beast, the Dog becomes the emblem of the poem's literary necrophilia, and the familiar strangeness of the past that Eliot himself has disinterred.

Quotation means that words cannot be anchored to their authors, and the fortune-tellers in the text personify this loss of origin. For prophecy means that we hear about a thing before it happens. The report precedes the event. The bell echoes before it rings. Tiresias, for instance, has not only foreseen but actually "foresuffered all", as if he were a living misquotation. A fake herself, Madame Sosostris lives in fear of imitators ("Tell her I bring the horoscope myself"), nervous that her words may go astray ("One must be so careful these days"). This anxiety about originality and theft resurges in the form of Mr Eugenides. A Turkish merchant in London, he also speaks demotic French: and the word "demotic", Greek in etymology, alludes to Egyptian hieroglyphics. Being a merchant, he is not only the product but the sinister conductor of miscegenation, intermingling verbal, sexual and monetary currencies. Even his pocketful of currants could be heard as "currents", which dissolve identities and definitions, like the "current under sea" that picks the bones of Phlebas, his Phoenician alter ego.[8] His reappearances suggest that repetition has become an virus, unwholesome as the personages who recur. Indeed, the poem hints that literature is nothing but a plague of echoes: that writing necessarily deserts its author, spreading like an epidemic into other texts. Any set

---

8. I owe this pun and some of the preceding formulations to my student John Reid at Amherst College, 1986.

of written signs can fall into bad company, into contexts which pervert their meaning and their genealogy.

The worst company in *The Waste Land*, both socially and rhetorically, is the London pub where Lil is tortured by her crony for her bad teeth and her abortion. Here, the publican's cry, "HURRY UP PLEASE ITS TIME", becomes as vagrant as a written sign, orphaned from its author. Any British drinker knows its origin, of course, so Eliot does not identify the speaker, but sets the phrase adrift on a semantic odyssey. When it interrupts the dialogue, the two discursive sites contaminate each other.

> You ought to be ashamed, I said, to look so antique.
> (And her only thirty-one.)
> I can't help it, she said, pulling a long face,
> It's them pills I took, to bring it off, she said.
> (She's had five already, and nearly died of young George.)
> The chemist said it would be all right, but I've never been the same.
> You *are* a proper fool, I said.
> Well, if Albert won't leave you alone, there it is, I said,
> What you get married for if you don't want children?
> HURRY UP PLEASE ITS TIME
> Well, that Sunday Albert was home, they had a hot gammon,
> And they asked me in to dinner, to get the beauty of it hot—
> HURRY UP PLEASE ITS TIME
> HURRY UP PLEASE ITS TIME
> Goonight Bill. Goonight Lou. Goonight May. Goonight.
> Ta ta. Goonight. Goonight.
> Good night, ladies, good night, sweet ladies, good night, good night.
>   (156–72)

This is the same technique that Flaubert uses in the fair in *Madame Bovary*, where Emma and Rodolph wallow in romance, while the voice of the Minister of Agriculture splices their sentiment with swine. In *The Waste Land*, the more the publican repeats his cry, the more its meaning strays from his intentions. Instead of closing time, it now connotes perfunctory and brutal sexuality: it means that time is catching up with Lil, in the form of dentures and decay, and rushing her culture to apocalypse. There is no omniscient speaker here to monitor these meanings, no "pill" to control their pullulation. It is as if the words themselves had been demobbed and grown adulterous. When Ophelia's good-byes creep in, just as the dialogue is closing, the allusion dignifies Lil's slower suicide: "Good night, ladies, good night, sweet ladies, good night, good night." Yet at the same time, the text degrades Ophelia by suturing her words to Lil's, reducing Shakespeare to graffiti.[9]

9. Andrew Parker pointed out to me in conversation that "degradation" in the poem always occurs through the association with the lower classes.

In general, the poem's attitude towards Shakespeare and the canon resembles taboos against the dead, with their mixture of veneration and horror. As Freud says, "they are expressions of mourning; but on the other hand they clearly betray—what they seek to conceal—hostility against the dead . . .".[1] But he stresses that it is not the dead themselves so much as their "infection" which is feared, for they are charged with a kind of "electricity." The taboo arises to defend the living subject from their sly invasions. But strangely enough, the taboo eventually becomes prohibited itself, as if the ban were as infectious as the horrors it forbids. Prohibition spreads like a disease, tainting everything that touches it, "till at last the whole world lies under an embargo." A similar reversal takes place in *The Waste Land* where the rituals of purity are perverted into *ersatz* desecrations of themselves. When Mrs. Porter and her daughter wash their feet in soda water, the ceremony of innocence is drowned, and the baptismal rite becomes its own defilement.

According to Freud, there are two ways in which taboo can spread, through contact and through mimesis. To touch a sacred object is to fall under its interdict. But the offender must also be tabooed because of "the risk of imitation", for others may follow his example.[2] These two forms of "transference" work like tropes, since the first, like metonymy, depends on contiguity, the second on similitude like metaphor. Freud adds that taboo usages resemble obsessional symptoms in that "the prohibitions lack any assignable motive", and they are "easily displaceable". It is as if the spread of the taboo depended on the power of rhetorical displacement: and underneath the fear of the contagion is the fear of tropes, the death-dealing power of figuration.

Displacement is indeed the malady the poem strives to cure, but its own figures are the source of the disorder. Though Eliot condemns Milton for dividing sound from sense, it is precisely this dissociation which produces the semantic epidemic of *The Waste Land*. It is the rats, appropriately, who carry the infection. They make their first appearance in "rats' alley"; but here a note refers us mischievously to Part III, where another rat peeks out again, like a further outbreak of the verbal plague:

> White bodies naked on the low damp ground
> And bones cast in a little low dry garret,
> Rattled by the rat's foot only, year to year.

However, Eliot seems to have forgotten one rodential apparition in between:

1. Freud, *Complete Works*, Vol. 13, p. 61. For the other quotations in this paragraph, see pp. 20–22, 41, and 27 in the same volume.
2. Freud, *Complete Works*, Vol. 13, p. 33. For the other quotations in this paragraph, see pp. 27 and 28.

But at my back in a cold blast I hear
The *rattle* of the bones, and chuckle spread from ear to ear.

A *rat* crept softly through the vegetation
Dragging its slimy belly on the bank
While I was fishing in the dull canal
On a winter evening round behind the gashouse
Musing upon the king my brother's wreck
And on the king my father's death before him.
White bodies naked on the low damp ground
And bones cast in a little low dry garret,
Rattled by the *rat's* foot only, year to year.
                    (185–95: my emphases)

It is the sound, here, which connects the rattle to the rat, as opposed to a semantic link between them. And it is the rattle of the words, rather than their meaning, that propels the poem forward. Indeed, the sound preempts the sense and spreads like an infection.

Notice that the text associates the rattle of the rats with "the king my brother's wreck" and "the king my father's death before him." For the contiguity suggests that it is these calamities that taint these signs, causing them to fester and grow verminous. Wrenched from their context in *The Tempest*, these deaths suggest the downfall of the father, as do the oblique allusions to the Fisher King, a figure Eliot derives from Jessie Weston's study of the Grail romance.[3] According to this legend, the King has lost his manhood, and his impotence has brought a blight over his lands. Eliot connects the Fisher King to "the man with three staves" in the Tarot pack, as if to hint that both have failed to fecundate the waste land, to fish the sense out of its floating signifiers. Their emasculation corresponds to other injuries, particularly to the mutilation of the voice: as if the phallus were complicit with the Logos. Lacking both, language has become a "waste of breath", a barren dissemination: "Sighs, short and infrequent, were exhaled . . .".

In the *Waste Land* manuscript, this anxiety about the Logos remains explicit. For here the pilgrim is searching for the "one essential word that frees", entrammelled in his own "concatenated words from which the sense seemed gone."[4] In the finished poem, all that remains of the lightning of the Word is the belated *rattle* of the sign, the "dry sterile thunder" of the desert (342). And this is why the poem is for ever grieving its belatedness: for not only does it come too late to establish an originary voice, but after the nymphs, after the messiah, after the tradition:

---

3. See Jessie Weston, *From Ritual to Romance* (1920; rpt. Garden City, New York: Doubleday, 1957), Ch. 9, pp. 113–36. [For a selection from this chapter, see "The Fisher King," p. 38.—Editor]

4. *Facsimile*, pp. 109, 113. The following quotation from the *Waste Land* manuscript is also from p. 109.

> After the torchlight red on sweaty faces
> After the frosty silence in the gardens
> After the agony in stony places. . . .
>
> (322–4)

The manuscript goes on at this point to lament the lateness of its own inditing: "After the ending of this inspiration." For writing, in the waste land, is the "wake" of voice—at once the after-image of the author and his obsequies.

If writing is in league with death, however, it is also in cahoots with femininity. In *The Waste Land*, the "hearty female stench" converges with the odour of mortality—and both exude from *writing*, from the violated and putrescent corpse of speech. To use the text's sexology, writing and the stink of femininity have overpowered the priapic realm of voice. Eliot to some extent repressed this hearty female stench when he excised it from the manuscript: but it survives in the strange synthetic perfumes of the lady in "A Game of Chess", which "troubled, confused / And drowned the sense in odours". ("Sense", here, may be understood as both semantic and olfactory: as if, under the power of the feminine, the sense of words becomes as "unguent . . . or liquid" as her scents.) Now, the strange thing about smell, as opposed to vision for example, is that the subject smelling actually imbibes the object smelt, endangering their separation and integrity. And it is the fear of such *displacements* that Eliot's misogyny reveals, a terror deeper even than the dread of incest, which is merely the most scandalous offence to place. In *The Waste Land*, the fall of the father unleashes infinite displacements, be they sexual, linguistic or territorial. Even personal identity dissolves into the babble of miscegenated tongues.[5] As effluvia, the feminine dissolves the limits of the private body, and the boundaries of the self subside into pneumatic anarchy. It is as if the father's impotence entailed the dissolution of identity, imaged as asphyxiation in the body of the feminine.

At the end of the poem, Eliot demolishes the discourse of the West, petitioning the East for solace and recovery.

> London Bridge is falling down falling down falling down
> *Poi s'ascose nel foco che gli affina*
> *Quando fiam uti chelidon*—O swallow swallow
> *Le Prince d' Aquitaine à la tour abolie*
> These fragments I have shored against my ruins

5. Lacan claims that the paternal law is "identical to an order of Language. For without kinship nominations, no power is capable of instituting the order of preferences and taboos which bind and weave the yarn of lineage down through succeeding generations." ("The Function of Language in Psychoanalysis", in *The Language of the Self*, ed. Anthony Wilden [New York: Dell, 1968], p. 40). In *The Waste Land*, the phallus stands for these discriminations, but all three staves have detumesced, and the father has been shipwrecked on the ruins of his own distinctions.

Why then Ile fit you. Hieronymo's mad againe.
Datta. Dayadhvam. Damyata.
Shantih shantih shantih

(426–33)

Here at last the poem silences its Western noise with Eastern blessings. But ironically, the effort to defeat its own "concatenated words" has only made the text more polyglot, stammering its orisons in Babel. It is as if the speaking subject had been "ruined" by the very fragments he had shored. " 'Words, words, words' might be his motto", one of Eliot's earliest reviewers once exclaimed, " 'for in his verse he seems to hate them and to be always expressing his hatred of them, in words.' "[6] Because the poem can only abject writing with more writing, it catches the infection that it tries to purge, and implodes like an obsessive ceremonial under the pressure of its own contradictions.

The Violet Hour

It is in another ceremonial that Freud discovers the compulsion to repeat, in the child's game he analyses in *Beyond the Pleasure Principle*. Here, his grandchild flings a cotton-reel into the abyss beyond his cot, and retrieves it with an "aaaa" of satisfaction, only to cast it out again, uttering a forlorn "oooo." Freud interprets these two syllables as primitive versions of the German words "fort" (gone) and "da" (here), and he argues that the child is mastering his mother's absences by "staging" them in the manipulation of a sign.[7] Indeed, Freud compares this theatre of abjection to the catharses of Greek tragedy, and he sees the child's pantomime renunciation as his first "great cultural achievement."

It is important, however, that the *drama* fascinates the child rather than the toy itself, for the bobbin belongs to a series of objects which he substitutes indifferently for one another.[8] While the cotton-reel stands for the mother, rehearsing her intermittencies, it also represents the child himself, who sends it forth like an ambassador. As if to emphasise this point, he tops his first act by staging his own disappearance. Crouching underneath a mirror, he lisps, "Baby o-o-o-o!" [Baby gone!], in a kind of abject inversion of Narcissus. By casting *himself* out, the child founds his subjectivity in a game that can only end in death. As Kristeva writes: "I expel *myself*, I spit *myself* out, I *abject* myself within

6. Anon., review of *Ara Vos Prec*, *TLS*, no. 948 (1920), 184. See also Graham Pearson, "Eliot: An American Use of Symbolism", in Martin, ed., *Eliot in Perspective*, pp. 83–7, for an illuminating discussion of "the social as well as verbal logic" of "the conversion of words into the Word."
7. Freud, *Complete Works*, Vol. 18, p. 28.
8. In the same way, Ricoeur argues that defilement is acted out through "partial, substitutive and abbreviated signs" which "mutually symbolise one another": *Symbolism of Evil*, p. 35.

the same motion through which 'I' claim to establish *myself*."[9] By attempting to control his world with signs, the subject has himself become a function of the sign, *subjected to* its own demonic repetition.

In this scenario, Freud intervenes between the mother and the child, bearing the law of language. For it is he who transforms the oscillation of the child's vowels into intelligible speech. But he neglects the vengeful pleasure that the infant takes in their vibratory suspense and in the *rattle* of their sounds. It is significant, moreover, that the little boy never changed his "o-o-o-o" into the neutral "fort" when he acquired the command of language. Instead, he sent his bobbin to the trenches. "A year later", Freud writes:

> the same boy whom I had observed at his first game used to take a toy, if he was angry with it, and throw it on the floor, exclaiming: "Go to the fwont!" He had heard at that time that his absent father was "at the front," and was far from regretting his absence. . . .[1]

Like this child, *The Waste Land* is confronting the specific absence that succeeded World War I, and it evinces both the dread and the desire to hear the voices at the "fwont" again. In fact, the poem can be read as a seance, and its speaker as the medium who tries to raise the dead by quoting them. Its ruling logic is "prosopopeia", as Paul De Man defines the trope:

> the fiction of an apostrophe to an absent, deceased, or voiceless entity, which posits the possibility of the latter's reply and confers upon it the power of speech. Voice assumes mouth, eye and finally face, a chain that is manifest in the etymology of the trope's name, *prosopon poien*, to confer a mask or face (*prosopon*).[2]

With the dead souls flowing over London Bridge, the corpses in the garden and the hooded hordes, *The Waste Land* strives to give a face to death. But it is significant that these figures have no faces, or else that they are hidden and unrecognisable:

> Who is the third who walks always beside you?
> When I count, there are only you and I together
> But when I look ahead up the white road
> There is always another one walking beside you
> Gliding wrapt in a brown mantle, hooded
> I do not know whether a man or a woman
> —But who is that on the other side of you?
>
>   (359–65)

9. Kristeva, *Powers of Horror*, p. 3.
1. Freud, *Complete Works*, Vol. 18, p. 16.
2. Paul De Man, "Autobiography as De-facement", *Modern Language Notes*, 94 (1979), 926; repr. as Ch. 4 in *The Rhetoric of Romanticism* (New York: Columbia University Press, 1984).

Here, these nervous efforts to reconstitute the face only drive it to its disappearance. Neither absent nor present, this nameless third bodies forth a rhetoric of disembodiment, and figures the "continual extinction" of the self. For the speaker rehearses his own death as he conjures up the writings of the dead, sacrificing voice and personality to their ventriloquy. Freud compares his grandchild to victims of shell-shock, who hallucinate their traumas in their dreams, repeating death as if it were desire. This is the game *The Waste Land* plays, and the nightmare that it cannot lay to rest, for it stages the ritual of its own destruction.

TIM ARMSTRONG

Eliot's Waste Paper†

* * *

In *The Waste Land*, the discourses of economic and bodily waste * * * merge. It is a Veblenian[1] poem in the broad sense of describing a place in which social waste is apparent both in the sterility and luxury of the rich and the indigence and eugenic incontinence of the poor. But it is also a poem which takes pleasure in the production of waste; as Maud Ellmann comments, 'one of the most abject texts in English literature'.[2] The materials of abjection include bodily parts (dirty ears, hands, feet; teeth, parted knees, bones, hair), clothing (underwear), places (dead land, desert), animals (scorpions, bats), acts (rape, abortion, copulation), and actors. The draft is particularly productive of dirt, though Pound and Eliot's editing intrudes here: in 'The Fire Sermon' the 'dirty camisoles' of the draft lose their adjective; the young man's hair, 'thick with grease, and thick with scurf' is excised; his urination and spitting are cut.[3]

Recent criticism has linked the recurrent reference to the body in *The Waste Land* to the hystericization of poet, poem, and of Vivien Eliot.[4] The hysteria here is nominally associated with femininity, as in Eliot's 1921 comments on H. D.'s wasteful copiousness: 'many words should be expunged and many phrases amended . . . I find a neurotic

---

† From *Modernism, Technology, and the Body: A Cultural Study* (Cambridge: Cambridge University Press, 1998), pp. 69–74. Copyright © 1998 by Tim Armstrong. Reprinted by permission of Cambridge University Press. The author's notes have been edited.
1. Reference to Thorstein Veblen's *Theory of the Leisure Class* (1899), in which he argues that "conspicuous consumption" and "conspicuous waste" are necessary by-products of capitalism [*Editor*].
2. Maud Ellmann, *The Poetics of Impersonality: Eliot and Pound* (Brighton: Harvester, 1987), p. 93. [See also this volume, p. 261.—*Editor*]
3. *The Waste Land: A Facsimile and Transcript of the Original Drafts Including the Annotations of Ezra Pound*, ed. Valerie Eliot (London: Faber & Faber, 1971), pp. 45–47.
4. See Ellmann and Wayne Koestenbaum, *Double Talk: The Erotics of Male Literary Collaboration* (New York: Routledge, 1989).

carnality which I dislike.'[5] But F. L. Lucas's comment on *The Waste Land* places Eliot in the same camp: 'we have the spectacle of Mr Lawrence, Miss May Sinclair, and Mr Eliot . . . all trying to get children on mandrake roots instead of bearing their natural offspring'.[6] Eliot's 'cure' at Lausanne in late 1921 was designed to alleviate his own distractedness. From there he wrote to his brother on the lack of 'hygiene' endemic to the family: 'The great thing I am trying to learn is how to use all my energy without waste'; adding 'I realize that our family never was taught mental, any more than physical hygiene, and so we are a seedy lot.'[7]

The hygiene which Eliot seeks is visible in Pound's 'surgical' intervention as editor, which excluded much waste material from a poem which Pound saw as fascinatingly excremental ('It also, to yr. horror probably, reads aloud very well. Mouthing out his o o o o o o z e'). Pound tended, as Forrest Read comments, to see poetry as 'phallic' and prose as 'excremental', related to elimination; a distinction which is part of his assessment of Henry James, and which he put to work in editing the more cloachal passages in Joyce's *Ulysses*.[8] Eliot himself figured Pound's editing as purification: 'It will have been three times through the sieve by Pound as well as myself' (sieving is a process applied to sewage).[9] Pound's advice also applied to the bodies of Eliot and his wife. His recuperation at Lausanne was the culmination of years of worry about the health of both. His letters in the late 1910s and early 1920s weave reports on his progress as a man of letters with comments on Vivien's bodily states: teeth, abscesses, neuralgia, nerves, and menstrual problems. In June 1922, Eliot reported to Ottoline Morrell that Vivien had been finally diagnosed as having a dual source for her illnesses: 'glands', and 'poisoning from colitis'. She was to be treated with animal glands (hormones—Eliot adds 'this at present is purely experimental'), and by 'very strong internal disinfection' (fasting).[1] The diagnosis prompted a series of letters to Pound on glands. In July, Eliot replied to Pound on three occasions that he would be glad to meet Louis Berman, twice mentioning the English endocrinologist Thomas Hogben. Both these letters end with a different glandular transaction, however: with invocations of Pound's own virility, one an ideogram-

5. Eliot to Richard Aldington, 17 November 1921, *The Letters of T. S. Eliot*, vol. 1, 1898–1922, ed. Valerie Eliot (New York: Harcourt Brace Jovanovich, 1988), p. 488. [H. D. is the American poet Hilda Doolittle (1886–1961), to whom Aldington was married at this time. —*Editor*]
6. F. L. Lucas, *New Statesman*, 22 (3 November 1923), 116–118; rep. in *T. S. Eliot: Critical Assessments*, ed. Graham Clarke, 4 vols. (London: Christopher Helm, 1990), 2:118. [The reference is to John Donne's "Song": "Go and catch a falling star, / Get with child a mandrake root. . . ."—*Editor*]
7. Eliot to Henry Eliot, 13 December 1921, *Letters*, p. 493.
8. Pound to Eliot, 24 December 1921, *Letters*, p. 497; Forrest Read, ed. *Pound/Joyce: The Letters of Ezra Pound to James Joyce* (New York: New Directions, 1967), p. 146.
9. Eliot to Scofield Thayer, 20 January 1922, *Letters*, p. 502.
1. Eliot to Ottoline Morrell, 15 June 1922, *Letters*, p. 529.

like transcription of the Nagali *Kama-Sutra*, 'grow fat and libidinous' appended; the other a more direct 'good fucking, brother'.[2] Here, as Wayne Koestenbaum suggests, is a circulation of masculine energy conducted around Vivien's body, with the injection of glandular matter from Pound paralleling the treatment Vivien was undergoing.

Yet, for all that the Pound-Eliot team might be seen as acting to 'disinfect' waste coded as 'feminine', *The Waste Land* remains a text with a troubling relation to the waste it describes. Notably, there is an absence of any redeeming vision of social order, or of an internal aesthetic of efficiency. As Cecelia Tichi argues, if 'Ezra Pound cut the "waste" from *The Waste Land* in editorial excision'—a task at best partially achieved—'the poem itself offers no alternative world'.[3] Instead it accumulates detritus. Jean Verdenal—the 'occasion' in part of *The Waste Land*—wrote, on another Christmas day, 1912, that cramming for an examination made his head 'like a department store stocked with anything and everything to hood wink the public'.[4] This is, in fact, the way the poem was seen by many reviewers, particularly in America: as an undergraduate parade of citations. Louis Untermeyer criticized 'a pompous parade of erudition . . . a kaleidoscopic movement in which the bright-coloured pieces fail to atone for the absence of an integrated design'; the poem as window-dressing.[5]

As well as this overproduction of the material of previous culture, reconceived as waste, the poem responds to what it sees as the cheapening of mass culture, towards which it is simultaneously fascinated and repelled. The 'human engine' which waits 'like a taxi throbbing' at the violet hour is a machine not for work, but for leisure—in the seduction scene which follows, and even more clearly in the draft section from which the lines were incorporated.[6] The materials of mass culture are crammed in: gramophones, songs, pubs, convenience foods. The borders of the text are a particularly rich source of such products —a fact reflected in the list of drinks, dinners, cigarettes, prostitutes, cabs in the original opening; or the negative catalogue in 'The Fire Sermon': tonight, 'The river bears no empty bottles, sandwich papers, / Silk handkerchiefs, cardboard boxes, cigarette ends.' The excised 'London' section deals with mass society: 'swarming creatures' driven by social tropisms, 'responsive to the momentary need', puppet-like in their 'jerky motions'. The presence of these objects in the text's margins suggests the way in which Eliot cannot fully incorporate all his mate-

---

2. Eliot to Pound, 9 and 19 July 1922, *Letters*, pp. 539, 550.
3. Cecelia Tichi, *Shifting Gears: Technology, Literature and Culture in Modernist America* (Chapel Hill: University of North Carolina Press, 1987), p. 71.
4. Verdenal to Eliot, 26 December 1912, *Letters*, p. 36. [For the notion that Verdenal might be the "occasion" of *The Waste Land*, see Christine Froula in this volume, pp. 280–81.—*Editor*]
5. Louis Untermeyer, "Disillusion vs. Dogma," *Freeman*, 7 January 1923, 453; rep. in *Critical Assessments*, 2:81.
6. *Facsimile*, p. 31, 43. The quotations following are from p. 37.

rials; his fragments remain undigested. *The Waste Land* thus bespeaks a simultaneous fascination with, and revulsion from, waste. The poem seems to revel in excess, consuming conspicuously in its gratuitous piling of allusions and eclectic cultural borrowings. Like a potlatch, it participates in a paradoxical order, destroying culture in order to reinforce it. The process of waste-production is knitted into its cultural moment: it cannot (and Pound cannot) 'edit out' all the waste, because it *is* waste material; both the abject and a valuable surplus which enables culture to continue, creating its own moment as it orders its abjection.[7] There can be no production without waste.

A more extended illustration of this process is provided by one issue: waste paper.[8] Here Eliot does comment on the 'waste' intrinsic in American capitalism. Late in the war, in April 1918, he wrote to his mother of the limits of frugality across the Atlantic: 'while America is very conscientiously "conserving foodstuffs" etc. she is as wasteful of paper as ever. I fear it would take very serious privation indeed to make Americans realize the wastefulness of such huge papers filled with nonsense and personalities.'[9] He contrasts European carefulness and adds that 'if less pulp were wasted on newspapers, good books could perhaps be printed more cheaply'. Eliot repeatedly links waste paper with the press, from the inhabitants of Hampstead in the drafts of *The Waste Land*—'They know what they are to feel and what to think, / They know it with the morning printer's ink'—to the press in section v of 'The Dry Salvages'.[1] Pound agreed: if 'The greatest waste in ang-sax letters at the moment is the waste of Eliot's talent', what threatens him is *journalism*.[2]

The Waste Land is caught up in this debate. At least one reviewer called the poem 'a waste of paper'.[3] It incorporates a great deal of 'pulp', the stuff of scandal-sheets and the popular press: 'personalities' like Madame Sosostris and Mr Eugenides, occultism, royal processions, popular songs, scandal, references to polar explorers. In bodily terms, waste paper is also toilet-paper. The abandoned 'Fresca' section equates faeces with the sexually ambiguous literature disparaged by Modernism as Fresca, 'baptised in a soapy sea / of Symonds—Walter Pater—Vernon Lee', shits while reading Samuel Richardson (more direct, Joyce's Bloom wipes himself on the popular press after reading it—in a passage which Pound cut from the *The Little Review*). We might see the same

7. "I expel *myself*, I spit *myself* out, I abject *myself* within the same motion through which 'I' claim to establish *myself*." Julia Kristeva, *Powers of Horror: An Essay on Abjection*, trans. Leon S. Roudiez (New York: Columbia University Press, 1982), p. 3.
8. Ellmann comments on waste paper in *Poetics of Impersonality*; my reading pursues a more literal line.
9. Eliot to Charlotte Eliot, 28 April 1918, *Letters*, pp. 229–230.
1. *Facsimile*, p. 105.
2. Pound to Eliot, 14 March 1922, *Letters*, pp. 511, 514.
3. Humbert Wolfe, "Waste Land and Waste Paper," *Weekly Westminster*, 1 (November 1923), 94; rept. in *Critical Assessments*, 2:120–122. [See also Charles Powell, "(So Much Waste Paper)," p. 156.—*Editor*]

excremental preoccupations in the fears of a chaos of paper which accompanied the poem's creation. In a letter to Mary Hutchinson written in July 1919, in which Eliot expounds a number of the ideas of order which appear the same year in 'Tradition and the Individual Talent', he writes 'I have a good deal to say which would simply appear as an illegible mass of blottings and scratchings and revisions, on paper.'[4] He distinguishes between 'civilized' and 'cultivated', adding 'I certainly do not mean a mass of chaotic erudition which simply issues in giggling.' *The Waste Land* has its own chaotic erudition in a conscious evocation—'on paper'—of the decadence described above, so hopelessly clotted that Eliot had to hand it to Pound in order that it might find a shape.

At the same time as it mocks pulp, the poem in its publication as a book also involved Veblenian waste in the sense of the gratuitous consumption of paper. Famously, Eliot claimed to have provided the footnotes in order to flesh out the pages at the end which the printers had to put in to get the sections right, an action which we might see as attempting to cover the 'luxury' of blank pages, producing a text which balances modesty and value, yet which at the same time reverses Pound's hygienic editing, reinflating the text because of the demands of commerce (Horace Liveright, the publisher, was worried about length, and suggested to Pound that Eliot add more).[5] Compare Pound lecturing Margaret Anderson in 1917 on the possibility of expanding *The Little Review*: 'Lady C[unard] says "DONT make it bigger. DONT make it any bigger, or I won't have time to read it." C'est une egoisme.' He adds, however, that 'ON the other hand "the public" likes a lot of paper for its money. One has to think of it both ways.'[6] Pound was, admittedly, more boosting to Quinn a few months earlier, writing that he wanted to publish Joyce and Ford 'after I have succeeded in enlarging the paper. (That may be nerve, but still one may as well expect to "enlarge")'.[7] Swelling phallically and creatively for Quinn, Pound stresses exclusivity when dealing with an aristocrat. In negotiating to set up the *Criterion* in 1922—a project which became involved with arrangements over *The Waste Land*—Eliot was deeply concerned with economy and not allowing contributors to overrun; he reported to Pound that he had decided on 'quite a good small format and paper, neat but no extravagance and not arty'.[8]

4. Eliot to Hutchinson, 11 July 1919, *Letters*, p. 317.
5. Lawrence Rainey, "The Price of Modernism: Reconsidering the Publication of *The Waste Land*," *Critical Quarterly*, 31.4 (1989):21–47. [See also this volume, p. 96.—*Editor*]
6. Pound to Anderson, 12 November 1917. *Pound/The Little Review: The Letters of Ezra Pound to Margaret Anderson*, ed. Thomas L. Scott and Melvin J. Friedman (London: Faber & Faber, 1989), p. 151.
7. Pound to Quinn, 17 May 1917, *Selected Letters of Ezra Pound to John Quinn 1915–1920*, ed. Timothy Materer (Durham: Duke University Press, 1991), p. 117.
8. Eliot to Pound, 12 March 1922, *Letters*, p. 507.

Eliot thus thinks of waste in deeply antithetical ways: as that to be eliminated from the poem; and—less explicitly—as that which is central to its production. The poem is uncertain of its status; producing waste, yet also curtailing it via Pound's editing, with the notes figuring explication as a necessarily wasteful supplement. There is a comparable double-economy in the negotiations over selling the poem. Lawrence Rainey points out that, on the one hand, Eliot discussed a 'fair' price with Scofield Thayer at *The Dial*, noting that George Moore had been paid £100 for a short story; on the other hand negotiations, under Pound's guidance, ballooned to take in book publication and the *Dial* prize, producing an unprecedented total of $2,800 for the package, as if anticipating the hectic financial expansion of the 1920s.[9]

 * * * If *The Waste Land* embodies an overproduction which is a necessary part of its richness, Eliot's late poetry, in contrast, seeks solitude, concentration, and pattern, just as it seeks to curb the hysterical voices of the popular press. The abject body is excluded. The 'indigestible portions' of the speaker which 'the leopards reject' in *Ash Wednesday*, particularly the strings of the eyes, suggest something beyond the body and luxury. There is a point of resolution beyond the inside—outside dialectics of the human engine in the evocation of the dance in the heavens and the earth, and in the search for the still or balanced point in the second section of 'Burnt Norton'. The 'trilling wire in the blood' and the 'dance along the artery' are in the body, yet Eliot's still point is 'Neither flesh nor fleshless':

> The release from action and suffering, release from the inner
> And the outer compulsion, yet surrounded
> By a grace of sense, a white light still and moving,
> *Erhebung* without motion, concentration
> Without elimination . . .

'Elimination' here also means waste; we might even, excrementally, see a pun in 'motion'. Eliot's late poetry, with its fascination with systems, the circulation of messages, feedback, seeks to eliminate the wasteful flows of the early poetry, so that 'dung and death' are subsumed to their proper time. Even where it describes the blood (for example in 'East Coker' IV), it is to evoke the 'wounded surgeon' Christ and his saving sacrifice.[1] Where James had disciplined his textual body, Eliot frees himself from the flesh, from the pain-economy, and seeks an aesthetics of purification, as if the problems of production and consumption and their troubling relation to the body had melted away.

9. Rainey, "The Price of Modernism."
1. John Gordon has recently argued that *"The Waste Land* and *Four Quartets* enact a classic opposition between head and heart" or between nerves and blood. Certainly nerves dominate the earlier poem, but the blood of *"Quartets"* seems to me much more sublimated. "T. S. Eliot's Head and Heart," *ELH*, 62.4 (1995): 979–1000.

T. S. Eliot: A Chronology

1888 Born on September 26 in St. Louis, Missouri.
1898 Attends Smith Academy, St. Louis.
1904 Attends St. Louis World's Fair.
1905 Graduates from Smith. Spends the academic year 1905–06 at Milton Academy, Milton, Massachusetts.
1906 Matriculates at Harvard.
1907 Publishes several poems in the *Harvard Advocate*. Meets Conrad Aiken.
1909 Joins the editorial board of the *Advocate*, having published several more poems there. Receives his B.A. and begins graduate work in literature and philosophy.
1910 Delivers Class Ode at graduation. Receives his M.A., having studied with Irving Babbitt and George Santayana. Travels to Paris to attend Sorbonne. Attends lectures of Henri Bergson at the Collège de France. Meets Alain-Fournier and Jean Verdenal.
1911 Visits London for the first time. Returns to the United States and to Harvard Graduate School to pursue a Ph.D. in philosophy. Completes "Prufrock," "Portrait of a Lady," and "Preludes."
1913 Reads F. H. Bradley's *Appearance and Reality*. Studies with Josiah Royce.
1914 Meets Bertrand Russell, visiting at Harvard. Receives a Sheldon Travelling Fellowship to study philosophy at Merton College, Oxford. In London, meets Ezra Pound, who sends "Prufrock" to *Poetry*. Earliest fragments of *The Waste Land* (later incorporated into the poem as ll. 377–84) composed.
1915 Marries Vivien Haigh-Wood on June 26. "Prufrock," "Preludes," and "Portrait of a Lady" published. After a visit to his parents in the United States, decides to return to England and make his permanent home there. Teaches at High Wycombe Grammar School.
1916 Teaches at Highgate Junior School. Thesis accepted at Harvard. Through Russell, gains acquaintance with Bloomsbury Group, including Virginia Woolf.

1917 Takes a job in the Colonial and Foreign department of Lloyds Bank. *Prufrock and Other Observations* published.

1919 "Tradition and the Individual Talent" published in *The Egoist*. *Poems* published by Leonard and Virginia Woolf at Hogarth Press.

1920 *Ara Vos Prec* published in England, *Poems* by Knopf in the United States. Meets James Joyce in Paris. *The Sacred Wood*, Eliot's first collection of essays, published. First explicit mention of *The Waste Land* in letter to his mother, September 20.

1921 After mental and physical collapse, given three months leave from Lloyds. Spends time at Margate in October, then goes to Lausanne for treatment in November, during which time the *Waste Land* drafts are completed.

1922 Pound and Eliot revise *The Waste Land*, which appears in the first issue of *The Criterion*, a new magazine edited by Eliot, and then in *The Dial*. Published in book form in December by Boni and Liveright.

1923 *The Waste Land* published in England by Leonard and Virginia Woolf at Hogarth Press.

1924 *Homage to John Dryden*, a second collection of essays, published.

1925 Leaves Lloyds to join Faber & Gwyer (later Faber & Faber) as editor and publisher. *Poems 1909–1925* (including "The Hollow Men") published by Faber.

1926 Delivers the Clark Lectures at Cambridge. *Sweeney Agonistes* published in *The Criterion*.

1927 Joins the Church of England and becomes a British citizen.

1928 Publishes *For Lancelot Andrewes: Essays on Style and Order* and in the preface delivers his famous self-description: "classicist in literature, royalist in politics, and anglo-catholic in religion."

1930 *Ash-Wednesday* published.

1932 Begins academic term as Charles Eliot Norton Professor of Poetry at Harvard.

1933 Harvard lectures published as *The Use of Poetry and the Use of Criticism*. Delivers lectures at University of Virginia later published as *After Strange Gods*. Separates from Vivien Eliot.

1935 *Murder in the Cathedral* first performed.

1936 *Burnt Norton* published in *Collected Poems 1909–1935*.

1938 Vivien Eliot certified insane and committed to an asylum for the rest of her life.

1939 *The Criterion* ceases publication. *The Family Reunion* first performed. *Old Possum's Book of Practical Cats* published.

1943 Complete version of *Four Quartets* published.

1947 Vivien Eliot dies.

1948   Awarded the Order of Merit and the Nobel Prize for Literature. *Notes towards the Definition of Culture* published.
1949   *The Cocktail Party* first performed.
1953   *The Confidential Clerk* first performed.
1957   Marries Valerie Fletcher on January 10. *On Poetry and Poets* published.
1958   *The Elder Statesman* first performed.
1964   Awarded U.S. Medal of Freedom.
1965   Dies on January 4. Ashes deposited at East Coker.

Selected Bibliography

BIBLIOGRAPHIES

Blalock, Susan E. *Guide to the Secular Poetry of T. S. Eliot*. New York: G. K. Hall, 1996.
Frank, Mechthild, Armin Paul Frank, and J. P. S. Jochum. *T. S. Eliot Criticism in English, 1916–1965: A Supplementary Bibliography*. Edmonton: Yeats Eliot Review, 1978.
Gallup, Donald. *T. S. Eliot: A Bibliography*. New York: Harcourt, Brace & World, 1969.
Knowles, Sebastian D. G. and Scott A. Leonard. *An Annotated Bibliography of a Decade of T. S. Eliot Criticism: 1977–1986*. Orono, Me.: National Poetry Foundation, 1992.
Martin, Mildred. *A Half-Century of Eliot Criticism: An Annotated Bibliography of Books and Articles in English, 1916–1965*. Lewisburg: Bucknell University Press, 1972.
Ricks, Beatrice. *T. S. Eliot: A Bibliography of Secondary Works*. Metuchen, N.J., and London: Scarecrow Press, 1980.

BIOGRAPHIES

Ackroyd, Peter. *T. S. Eliot: A Life*. New York. Simon and Schuster, 1984.
Behr, Caroline. *T. S. Eliot: A Chronology of His Life and Works*. London: Macmillan, 1983.
Gordon, Lyndall. *T. S. Eliot: An Imperfect Life*. New York: Norton, 1998.
Kirk, Russell. *T. S. Eliot and His Age*. New York: Random House, 1971.

WORKS AND EDITIONS

Prufrock and Other Observations. London: Egoist Press, 1917.
Poems. London: Hogarth Press, 1919.
Ara Vos Prec. London: Ovid Press, 1920.
Poems. New York: Knopf, 1920.
The Sacred Wood. London: Methuen, 1920.
The Waste Land. New York: Boni & Liveright, 1922.
Homage to John Dryden. London: Hogarth Press, 1924.
Poems 1909–1925. London: Faber & Gwyer, 1925.
For Lancelot Andrewes: Essays on Style and Order. London: Faber & Gwyer, 1928.
Ash-Wednesday. London: Faber & Faber; New York: Putnam's, 1930.
Selected Essays, 1917–1932. London: Faber & Faber; New York: Harcourt, Brace, 1932.
Sweeney Agonistes. London: Faber & Faber, 1932.
The Use of Poetry and the Use of Criticism. London: Faber & Faber; Cambridge, Mass.: Harvard University Press, 1933.
After Strange Gods. London: Faber & Faber; New York: Harcourt, Brace, 1934.
Murder in the Cathedral. London: Faber & Faber; New York: Harcourt, Brace, 1935.
Collected Poems: 1909–1935. London: Faber & Faber; New York: Harcourt, Brace, 1936.
Essays Ancient and Modern. London: Faber & Faber; New York: Harcourt, Brace, 1936.
The Family Reunion. London: Faber & Faber; New York: Harcourt, Brace, 1939.
The Idea of a Christian Society. London: Faber & Faber, 1939.
Old Possum's Book of Practical Cats. London: Faber & Faber; New York: Harcourt, Brace, 1939.
Four Quartets. London: Faber & Faber; New York: Harcourt, Brace, 1943.
Notes towards a Definition of Culture. London: Faber & Faber, 1948.

The Cocktail Party. London: Faber & Faber; New York: Harcourt, Brace, 1950.
The Confidential Clerk. London: Faber & Faber; New York: Harcourt, Brace, 1954.
On Poetry and Poets. London: Faber & Faber; New York: Farrar, Straus, 1957.
The Elder Statesman. London: Faber & Faber; New York: Farrar, Straus, 1959.
Collected Poems 1909–1962. London: Faber & Faber; New York: Harcourt, Brace & World, 1963.
Knowledge and Experience in the Philosophy of F. H. Bradley. London: Faber & Faber; New York: Farrar, Straus, 1964.
To Criticize the Critic. London: Faber & Faber; New York: Farrar, Straus, 1965.
Complete Plays. New York: Harcourt, Brace, 1967.
Poems Written in Early Youth. London: Faber & Faber; New York: Farrar, Straus, 1967.
Complete Poems and Plays. London: Faber & Faber, 1969.
The Waste Land: A Facsimile and Transcript of the Original Drafts Including the Annotations of Ezra Pound. Ed. Valerie Eliot. London: Faber & Faber; New York: Harcourt Brace Jovanovich, 1971.
The Letters of T. S. Eliot. Ed. Valerie Eliot. London: Faber & Faber; San Diego: Harcourt Brace Jovanovich, 1988.
The Varieties of Metaphysical Poetry: The Clark Lectures at Trinity College, Cambridge, 1926, and the Turnbull Lectures at the Johns Hopkins University, 1933. Ed. Ronald Schuchard. London: Faber & Faber, 1993.
Inventions of the March Hare: Poems 1909–1917. Ed. Christopher Ricks. London: Faber & Faber; New York: Harcourt Brace, 1996.

CRITICISM

• indicates works included or excerpted in this Norton Critical Edition.

•Aiken, Conrad. "An Anatomy of Melancholy." *New Republic*, 7 February 1922, 294–95.
Albright, Daniel. *Quantum Poetics: Yeats, Pound, Eliot, and the Science of Modernism.* Cambridge: Cambridge University Press, 1997.
•Armstrong, Tim. *Modernism, Technology, and the Body.* Cambridge: Cambridge UP, 1998.
Bedient, Calvin. *He Do the Police in Different Voices: "The Waste Land" and Its Protagonist.* Chicago: University of Chicago Press, 1986.
Bergonzi, Bernard. *T. S. Eliot.* New York: Macmillan, 1972.
Bishop, Jonathan. "A Handful of Words: The Credibility of Language in *The Waste Land*." *Texas Studies in Language and Literature* 27.1 (spring 1985): 154–77.
Blackmur, R. P. "T. S. Eliot." *Hound and Horn* 1 (1928): 187–210.
———. *Anni Mirabiles, 1921–1925.* Washington: Library of Congress, 1956.
Bolgan, Anne C. *What the Thunder Really Said: A Retrospective Essay on the Making of "The Waste Land."* Montreal: McGill-Queen's University Press, 1973.
Brooker, Jewel Spears. *Mastery and Escape: T. S. Eliot and the Dialectic of Modernism.* Amherst: University of Massachusetts Press, 1994.
Brooker, Jewel Spears and Joseph Bentley. *Reading "The Waste Land": Modernism and the Limits of Interpretation.* Amherst: University of Massachusetts Press, 1990.
•Brooks, Jr., Cleanth. *Modern Poetry and the Tradition.* Chapel Hill: University of North Carolina Press, 1939.
•Bush, Ronald. *T. S. Eliot: A Study in Character and Style.* New York: Oxford University Press, 1983.
———, ed. *T. S. Eliot: The Modernist in History.* Cambridge: Cambridge University Press, 1991.
Calder, Angus. *T. S. Eliot.* Brighton: Harvester Press, 1987.
Clarke, Graham, ed. *T. S. Eliot: Critical Assessments.* London: Christopher Helm, 1990.
Craig, David. "The Defeatism of *The Waste Land*." *Critical Quarterly* 2 (1960): 241–52.
Crawford, Robert. *The Savage and the City in the Work of T. S. Eliot.* Oxford: Clarendon Press, 1987.
Cuddy, Lois A. and David Hirsch, eds. *Critical Essays on T. S. Eliot's "The Waste Land."* Boston: G. K. Hall, 1991.
Davidson, Harriet. *T. S. Eliot and Hermeneutics: Absence and Interpretation in "The Waste Land."* Baton Rouge: Louisiana State University Press, 1985.

Drew, Elizabeth. *T. S. Eliot: The Design of His Poetry*. New York: Scribners, 1949.

•Ellmann, Maud. *The Poetics of Impersonality: T. S. Eliot and Ezra Pound*. Brighton: Harvester, 1987.

Froula, Christine. "Eliot's Grail Quest: Or, the Lover, the Police, and *The Waste Land*." *Yale Review* 78.2 (winter 1989): 235–53.

———. "Corpse, Monument, *Hypocrite Lecteur*." *Text* 9 (1996): 297–314.

Frye, Northrop. *T. S. Eliot*. Chicago: University of Chicago Press, 1963.

Gardner, Helen. *The Art of T. S. Eliot*. New York: Dutton, 1959.

Grant, Michael, ed. *T. S. Eliot: The Critical Heritage*. London: Routledge and Kegan Paul, 1982.

Gray, Piers. *T. S. Eliot's Intellectual and Poetic Development 1909–1922*. Sussex: Harvester Press, 1982.

Hay, Eloise Knapp. *T. S. Eliot's Negative Way*. Cambridge: Harvard University Press, 1982.

Jay, Gregory. *T. S. Eliot and the Poetics of Literary History*. Baton Rouge: Louisiana State University Press, 1983.

Kearns, Cleo McNelly. *T. S. Eliot and Indic Traditions: A Study in Poetry and Belief*. Cambridge: Cambridge University Press, 1987.

Kenner, Hugh. *The Invisible Poet: T. S. Eliot*. New York: Harcourt, Brace & World, 1959.

Koestenbaum, Wayne. *Double Talk: The Erotics of Male Literary Collaboration*. New York: Routledge, 1989.

•Langbaum, Robert. *The Mysteries of Identity: A Theme in Modern Literature*. New York: Oxford University Press, 1977.

•Leavis, F. R. *New Bearings in English Poetry*. London: Chatto and Windus, 1932.

Lentricchia, Frank. *Modernist Quartet*. Cambridge: Cambridge University Press, 1994.

Levenson, Michael. *A Genealogy of Modernism: A Study of English Literary Doctrine, 1908–1922*. Cambridge: Cambridge University Press, 1984.

Litz, A. Walton, ed. *Eliot in His Time*. Princeton: Princeton University Press, 1973.

Longenbach, James. *Modernist Poetics of History: Pound, Eliot, and the Sense of the Past*. Princeton: Princeton University Press, 1987.

Manganaro, Marc. "Dissociation in 'Dead Land': The Primitive Mind in the Early Poetry of T. S. Eliot." *Journal of Modern Literature* 13.1 (1986): 97–110.

Martin, Graham, ed. *Eliot in Perspective*. London: Macmillan, 1970.

Materer, Timothy. *Vortex: Pound, Eliot, and Lewis*. Ithaca: Cornell University Press, 1979.

Matthiessen, F. O. *The Achievement of T. S. Eliot*. Boston: Houghton Mifflin, 1935.

Menand, Louis. *Discovering Modernism: T. S. Eliot and His Context*. New York: Oxford University Press, 1987.

•Moody, A. D., ed. *"The Waste Land" in Different Voices*. London: Edward Arnold, 1974.

•———. *Thomas Stearns Eliot: Poet*. Cambridge: Cambridge University Press, 1979.

———, ed. *The Cambridge Companion to T. S. Eliot*. Cambridge: Cambridge University Press, 1994.

Moretti, Franco. *Signs Taken for Wonders: Essays in the Sociology of Literary Forms*. Tr. Susan Fischer, David Forgacs, and David Miller. London: Verso, 1983.

•Munson, Gorham. "The Esotericism of T. S. Eliot." *1924*, 1 July 1924, 3–10.

North, Michael. *The Political Aesthetic of Yeats, Eliot, and Pound*. Cambridge: Cambridge University Press, 1991.

———. *The Dialect of Modernism: Race, Language, and Twentieth Century Literature*. Oxford: Oxford University Press, 1994.

———. *Reading 1922: A Return to the Scene of the Modern*. Oxford: Oxford University Press, 1999.

Pearce, Roy Harvey. *The Continuity of American Poetry*. Princeton: Princeton University Press, 1961.

Perl, Jeffery M. *Skepticism and Modern Enmity: Before and After Eliot*. Baltimore: Johns Hopkins University Press, 1989.

•Rainey, Lawrence. *Institutions of Modernism: Literary Elites and Public Culture*. New Haven: Yale University Press, 1998.

•Ransom, John Crowe. "Waste Lands." *New York Evening Post Literary Review*, 14 July 1923, 825–26.

•Richards, I. A. *Principles of Literary Criticism*. New York: Harcourt, Brace, 1926.

Ricks, Christopher. *T. S. Eliot and Prejudice*. Berkeley: University of California Press, 1988.

Riquelme, John Paul. " 'Withered Stumps of Time': Allusion, Reading and Writing in *The Waste Land*." *Denver Quarterly* 15 (1981): 90–110.

Rosenthal, M. L. *Sailing into the Unknown: Yeats, Pound, and Eliot.* New York: Oxford University Press, 1978.

Ross, Andrew. *The Failure of Modernism: Symptoms of American Poetry.* New York: Columbia University Press, 1986.

•Schwartz, Delmore. "T. S. Eliot as International Hero." *Partisan Review* 12 (spring 1995): 199–206.

Schwartz, Sanford. *The Matrix of Modernism: Pound, Eliot, and Early Twentieth Century Thought.* Princeton: Princeton University Press, 1985.

Scofield, Martin. *T. S. Eliot: The Poems.* Cambridge: Cambridge University Press, 1988.

•Seldes, Gilbert. "T. S. Eliot." *The Nation,* 6 December 1922, 614–16.

Shusterman, Richard. *T. S. Eliot and the Philosophy of Criticism.* New York: Columbia University Press, 1988.

Smith, Grover. *T. S. Eliot's Poetry and Plays.* Chicago: University of Chicago Press, 1974.

——. *The Waste Land.* London: Allen and Unwin, 1983.

Spanos, William. "Repetition in *The Waste Land*: A Phenomenological De-Struction." *Boundary* 2 7 (1979): 225–85.

Spender, Stephen. *T. S. Eliot.* New York: Viking, 1975.

Spurr, David. *Conflicts in Consciousness: T. S. Eliot's Poetry and Criticism.* Urbana: University of Illinois Press, 1984.

Stead, C. K. *Pound, Yeats, Eliot and the Modernist Movement.* Basingstoke: Macmillan, 1986.

Tate, Allen, ed. *T. S. Eliot: The Man and His Work.* New York: Delacorte, 1966.

•Thormählen, Marianne. *"The Waste Land": A Fragmentary Wholeness.* Lund: Gleerup, 1978.

Trotter, David. "Modernism and Empire: Reading *The Waste Land*." *Critical Quarterly* 28.1–2 (1986): 143–53.

•Wilson, Edmund. "The Poetry of Drouth." *The Dial* 73 (December 1922): 611–16.

——. *Axel's Castle.* New York: Charles Scribner's Sons, 1931.

•Wylie, Elinor. "Mr. Eliot's Slug-Horn." *New York Evening Post Literary Review,* 20 January 1923, 396.